Iran

CSIS Middle East Dynamic Net Assessment

Iran

Dilemmas of Dual Containment

Anthony H. Cordesman
and Ahmed S. Hashim

WestviewPress
A Division of HarperCollins*Publishers*

Copyright © 1997 by Anthony H. Cordesman

Published in 1997 in the United States of America by Westview Press, 5500 Central Avenue, Boulder, Colorado 80301-2877, and in the United Kingdom by Westview Press, 12 Hid's Copse Road, Cumnor Hill, Oxford OX2 9JJ

A CIP catalog record for this book is available from the Library of Congress.
ISBN 0-8133-3237-0.—ISBN 0-8133-3238-9 (pbk.)

This book was typeset by Letra Libre, 1705 Fourteenth Street, Suite 391, Boulder, Colorado 80302.

The paper used in this publication meets the requirements of the American National Standard for Permanence of Paper for Printed Library Materials Z39.48-1984.

10   9   8   7   6   5   4   3   2

Contents

Tables and Illustrations

Maps

Preface

This volume is part of an ongoing dynamic net assessment of the Gulf. The project was conceived by David Abshire and Richard Fairbanks of the Center for Strategic and International Studies, and focuses on the foreign policy, military forces, politics, economics, energy sector, and internal security of each Gulf state, and US strategy and power projection capabilities in the Gulf. Separate volumes are available on Kuwait, Iran, Iraq, Saudi Arabia, and US forces. Bahrain, Oman, Qatar, and the UAE are combined into a single volume.

Each of these volumes is interlinked to provide comparable data on the current situation and trends in each country and to portray the overall trends in key areas like energy and the military balance. The volume on Iran provides a detailed graphic overview of the military trends in the region, but each volume shows how the key energy and military developments in each country relate to the developments in other Gulf countries.

At the same time, this series deliberately emphasizes nation-by-nation analysis. Iran and Iraq clearly deserve separate treatment. The Southern Gulf states are largely independent actors and are driven by separate strategic, political, economic, and military interests. In spite of the creation of the Arab Gulf Cooperation Council (GCC), there is little practical progress in strategic, economic, or military cooperation, and there are serious rivalries and differences of strategic interest between Bahrain, Kuwait, Oman, Qatar, Saudi Arabia, and the UAE. The Southern Gulf cannot be understood in terms of the rhetoric of the Arab Gulf Cooperation Council, or by assuming that developments in Bahrain, Kuwait, Oman, Qatar, Saudi Arabia, and the UAE are similar and these states have an identity of interest.

These Gulf studies are also part of a broader dynamic net assessment of the Middle East, and a separate study is available of the trends in the Arab-Israeli military balance and the peace process. See Anthony H. Cordesman, *Perilous Prospects*, Boulder, Westview, 1996.

Anthony H. Cordesman
Ahmed S. Hashim

Acknowledgments

The authors would like to thank Kimberly Goddes and Kiyalan Batman-glidj for their research and editing help in writing this series, and Thomas Seidenstein and David Hayward for helping to edit each volume.

Many US and international analysts and agencies played a role in commenting on drafts of the manuscript, so did experts in each Southern Gulf country. The authors cannot acknowledge these contributions by name or agency but they are deeply grateful. The authors would also like to thank their colleagues at the CSIS who reviewed various manuscripts and commented on the analysis. These colleagues include Richard Fairbanks and Arnaud de Borchgrave, and the Co-Director of the Middle East Program, Judith Kipper.

A.H.C.
A.S.H.

1

Introduction

Any analysis of current security trends in Iran must attempt to answer two key questions. The first is just how serious a threat Iran poses to its neighbors and the West. The second is how best to deal with these threats. These are not easy questions to answer. Iran's military capabilities can be viewed in very different ways, as can the nature of Iran's regime. There is little consensus over the political changes taking place within Iran and no consensus over the political and economic policies that should be pursued in dealing with Iran.

There are also important limits to analysis. No analysis can resolve all the uncertainties surrounding Iran's relations with its neighbors, support of terrorism and extremism, its political structure and internal stability, and its military build-up. No analysis based on unclassified information can describe all of the data on Iran's conventional military forces, efforts to acquire weapons of mass destruction, and war fighting capabilities.

Analysis can, however, provide many important insights into Iran's strategic future. It can look beyond political rhetoric and examine the details of Iran's present and possible military capabilities and the role Iran can and cannot play in the Gulf. Analysis may not be able to resolve the uncertainties regarding Iran's future intentions, but it can provide a picture of the possible paths different types of regimes might follow and indicate the extent to which the West and the Gulf states may be able to influence Iranian behavior.

"Backlash States" and "Dual Containment"

Such analysis is particularly important at a time when the US and many of its allies have very different views of the kind of threats Iran poses to the region, especially when these differences are matched by differences between regional experts and military analysts. The irony is that it is the US that is virtually isolated in its policy of trying to isolate Iran, and it is particularly important to understand how the Clinton Administration has defined its policy towards Iran, exactly what senior US policy makers have said, and how these developments affect the issues to be addressed.

Like the Reagan and Bush Administrations, the Clinton Administration treats Iran as one of several "backlash states" that are dealt with using a common strategy. Anthony Lake, President Clinton's Assistant for National Security Affairs, defined this strategy as:[1]

- Establishing a favorable balance of power;
- Maintaining alliances and deploying military capabilities sufficient to deter or respond to any aggressive act;
- Containing the influence of these states, sometimes by isolation, sometimes through pressure, sometimes by diplomatic and economic measures;
- Engaging in unilateral and multilateral efforts to restrict their military and technological capabilities;
- Employing intelligence, counterterrorism, and multilateral export control policies, especially of weapons of mass destruction and their delivery systems; and
- Encouraging the rest of the international community to join in a concerted effort.

The US has also adopted a strategy of "dual containment" that rejects any effort to use either Iran or Iraq as a means of establishing the favorable balance of power the US is seeking in the Gulf. As Anthony Lake has stated:[2]

> The Clinton Administration's strategy towards these two backlash states begins from the premise that today both regimes pursue policies hostile to our interests. Building up one to counter the other is therefore rejected in favor of a policy of 'dual containment.' In adopting this approach, we are not oblivious to the need for a balance of power in this vital region. Rather, we work with our regional allies to maintain a favorable balance without depending on either Iran or Iraq.

US policy has been careful to differentiate Iran from Iraq. In defining the US strategy of "dual containment," Anthony Lake describes Iran as follows:[3]

> 'Dual containment' does not mean duplicate containment. The basic purpose is to counter the hostility of both Baghdad and Tehran, but the challenges posed by the two regimes are distinct and therefore require tailored approaches. Although neighbors, the two states are quite different in culture and historical experience. In Saddam Hussein's regime, Washington faces an

aggressive, modernist, secular avarice. In Iran, it is challenged by a theocratic regime with a sense of cultural and political destiny and an abiding antagonism toward the United States. . . .

Iran is both a lesser and a greater challenge. On the one hand, the Clinton administration is not confronting a blatantly aggressive state that invaded and occupied a weaker neighbor. More normal relations with the government in Tehran are conceivable, once it demonstrates its willingness to abide by international norms and abandon policies and actions inimical to regional peace and security. On the other hand, political differences with Iran will not be easily resolved. Iran is a revolutionary state whose leaders harbor a deep sense of grievance over the close ties between the United States and the Shah. Its revolutionary and militant messages are openly hostile to the United States and its core interests. This basic political reality will shape relations for the foreseeable future. Reconciliation will be difficult, but the choice is Iran's to make.

The American quarrel with Iran should not be constructed as a 'clash of civilizations' or opposition to Iran as a theocratic state. Washington does not take issue with the 'Islamic' dimension of the Islamic Republic of Iran. As President Clinton has said, America has a deep respect for the religion and culture of Islam. It is extremism, whether religious or secular, that we oppose. The United States is concerned with the actions and policies of the Tehran government. Iran is actively engaged in clandestine efforts to acquire nuclear and other unconventional weapons and long-range missile delivery systems. It is the foremost sponsor of terrorism and assassination worldwide. It is violently and vitriolically opposed to the Arab-Israeli peace process. It seeks to subvert friendly governments across the Middle East and in parts of Africa. It is attempting to acquire offensive conventional capabilities to threaten its smaller gulf neighbors. Its record on treatment of its own citizens—especially women and religious minorities—is deeply disturbing.

President Clinton has also made it clear that the US is willing to conduct a dialogue with Iran, and will resume diplomatic ties if Iran changes its conduct:[4]

We are ready to enter into dialogue with representatives of the Iranian government at any time. . . . It must be clear to the Iranians (however) that resumption of ties is impossible before Tehran stops its unacceptable activities. . . . (Iran provides) direct and indirect support for terrorist organizations, involvement in propaganda against the US, and military threats against neighboring countries. . . . We do not have any problem with the Iranian people. But we are against the behavior of the Iranian government.

At the same time, the US has steadily strengthened its efforts to block any trade between the US and Iran, and limit all foreign investment in Iran. The Clinton Administration and the Congress have sought to deny Iran advanced arms and technology that can be used for weapons of mass destruction, and have funded a $20 million covert action program directed at halting Iran's ability to support hostile action outside its borders and pushing Iran towards a more "democratic" government.[5] The Congress also passed new legislation in 1995 and 1996 that called for a total ban on all trade between Iran and the US (5.277), and which imposed sanctions on all US and foreign companies and persons investing $40 million a year in the development of petroleum resources in Iran (5.630).

Differences of View Regarding Iran's Character and Intentions

This official US strategy and view of Iran raise raises significant questions as to whether the US is correctly characterizing Iran's regime, intentions, and capabilities. Most Western and Southern Gulf governments agree that Iran has a radical regime and continues to promote its version of an Islamic revolution. They agree that Iran has significant forces, and there is little disagreement over the broad nature of the military balance shown in Chart One and Table One. At the same time, most Western and Southern Gulf governments feel that that the Reagan, Bush, and Clinton Administrations have progressively exaggerated the hostility of the Iranian regime and the nature and intent of the Iranian military build-up.

Experts outside governments have different views of the changing character of Iran's politics, of the extent to which the Iranian regime is committed to acting upon its revolutionary ideology, and of the extent to which Iran is seeking regional hegemony through military means.

There are a number of experts who favor political dialogue and trade with Iran. Some experts support such policies because they believe that Iran has become more pragmatic since the death of the Ayatollah Ruhollah Khomeini. They assert that Iran's revolutionary rhetoric is becoming a hollow shell, and that the current government cannot be treated as a monolithic or hostile regime in the way that may be appropriate to Iraq. These experts also note that Iran's recent history has been less aggressive and violent than Iraq's. To justify their position they point to Iran's growing economic ties with the West,what they perceive as its attempts to improve diplomatic relations with the southern Gulf states, to an Iranian ruling elite that no longer seems to retain the revolutionary fervor that existed during the time of the Ayatollah Khomeini, and to an apparent aversion to direct military encounters in the current revolutionary and Islamic ideology emanating from Tehran.

Other experts advocate trade and political dialogue with Iran for very different reasons. They feel that the pragmatists and modernists in the Iranian regime are weak and losing popular support. They contend, however, that most Iranians oppose strict religious rule and the present level of religious interference in the economy, and that attempts to isolate Iran will simply strengthen the extremists and allow them to claim that Iran

Main Battle Tanks in Persian Gulf Forces

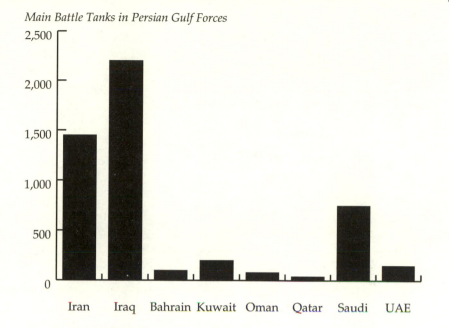

Total Combat Aircraft in Persian Gulf Forces

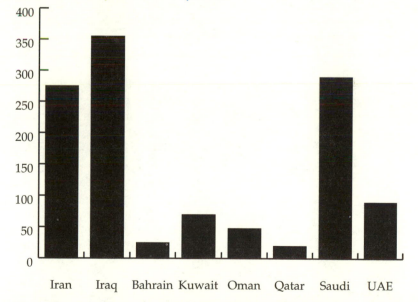

CHART ONE   The Military Balance in the Gulf. *Source:* Adapted by Anthony H. Cordesman from the IISS, *Military Balance, 1995–1996.*

TABLE ONE   Gulf Military Forces in 1996

	Iran	Iraq	Bahrain	Kuwait	Oman	Qatar	Saudi Arabia*	UAE	Yemen
Manpower									
Total Active	320,000	382,500	10,700	16,600	43,500	11,100	161,500	70,000	39,500
Regular	220,000	382,500	10,700	16,600	37,000	11,100	105,500	70,000	39,500
National Guard & Other	100,000	0	0	0	6,500	0	57,000	0	0
Reserve	350,000	650,000	0	23,700	0	0	0	0	40,000
Paramilitary	135,000	24,800	9,250	5,200	4,400	0	15,500	2,700	30,000
Army and Guard									
Manpower	260,000	350,000	8,500	10,000	31,500	8,500	127,000	65,000	37,000
Regular Army Manpower	180,000	350,000	8,500	10,000	25,000	8,500	70,000	65,000	37,000
Reserve	350,000	450,000	0	0	0	0	20,000	0	40,000
Tanks	1,350	2,700	81	220	85	24	910	133	1,125
AIFV/Recce, Lt. Tanks	515	1,600	46	130	136	50	1,467	515	580
APCs	550	2,200	235	199	7	172	3,670	380	560
Self Propelled Artillery	294	150	13	38	6	28	200	90	30
Towed Artillery	2,000	1,500	36	0	96	12	270	82	483
MRLs	890	120	9	0	0	4	60	48	220
Mortars	3,500	2,000+	18	24	74	39	400	101	800
SSM Launchers	46	12	0	0	0	0	10	6	30
Light SAM Launchers	700	3,000	65	48	62	58	650	36	700
AA Guns	1,700	5,500	0	0	18	12	10	62	372
Air Force Manpower	20,000	15,000	1,500	2,500	4,100	800	18,000	3,500	1,000
Air Defense Manpower	15,000	15,000	0	0	0	0	4,000	0	0

(continues)

TABLE ONE (continued)

	Iran	Iraq	Bahrain	Kuwait	Oman	Qatar	Saudi Arabia*	UAE	Yemen
Total Combat Aircraft	295	353	24	76	46	12	295	97	69
Bombers	0	6	0	0	0	0	0	0	0
Fighter/Attack	150	130	12	40	19	11	112	41	27
Fighter/Interceptor	115	180	12	8	0	1	122	22	30
Recce/FGA Recce	8	0	0	0	12	0	10	8	0
AEW C4I/BM	1	0	0	0	0	5	0	0	0
MR/MPA**	6	0	0	0	7	0	0	0	0
OCU/COIN	0	18	0	11	13	0	36	15	0
Combat Trainers	92	200	0	11	22	0	66	35	12
Transport Aircraft**	68	34	3	4	14	5	49	20	19
Tanker Aircraft	4	2	0	0	0	0	16	0	0
Armed Helicoptors**	100	120	10	16	0	20	12	42	8
Other Helicoptors**	509	350	8	36	37	7	138	42	21
Major SAM Launchers	204	340	12	24	0	0	128	18	87
Light SAM Launchers	60	200	0	12	28	9	249	34	0
AA Guns	0	0	0	12	0	0	420	0	0
Navy Manpower	38,000	2,500	1,000	1,500	4,200	1,800	17,000	1,500	1,500
Major Surface Combatants									
Missile	5	0	3	0	0	0	8	0	0
Other	2	1	0	0	0	0	0	0	0
Patrol Craft									
Missile	10	1	4	2	4	3	9	10	7

(continues)

TABLE ONE   *(continued)*

	Iran	Iraq	Bahrain	Kuwait	Oman	Qatar	Saudi Arabia*	UAE	Yemen
Other	26	7	5	12	8	6	20	18	3
Submarines	2	0	0	0	0	0	0	0	0
Mine Vessels	3	4	0	0	0	0	5	0	3
Amphibious Ships	8	0	0	0	2	0	0	0	2
Landing Craft	17	3	4	6	4	1	7	4	2

Note: Does not include equipment in storage. Air Force totals include all helicopters, and all heavy surface to air missile launchers.

*60,000 reserves are National Guard Tribal Levies. The total for land forces includes active National Guard equipment. These additions total 262 AIFVs, 1,165 APCs, and 70 towed artillery weapons.

**Includes navy, army, national guard, and royal flights, but not paramilitary.

Source: Adapted by Anthony H. Cordesman from International Institute for Strategic Studies, *Military Balance* (IISS, London), in this case, the 1995–1996 edition; *Military Technology, World Defense Almanac, 1994–1995*; and Jaffee Center for Strategic Studies, *The Military Balance in the Middle East, 1993–1994* (JCSS, Tel Aviv, 1994).

TABLE TWO   US Sanctions Against Iran

Sanction and Date	Nature	Status
Suspension of Military Aid, November 8, 1979	US halts shipment of all military spare parts	Expired
Prohibition of Oil Imports, November 12, 1979	US halts imports of oil	Lifted
Foreign Assets Control, November 14, 1979	Carter freezes all Iranian assets in the US dispute over assets	Active
Prohibition of Direct Aid, November 20, 1979	US prohibits granting of direct foreign aid	Expired
Export Embargo, April 7, 1980	US imposes embarge on all US exports except medicine, food, and clothing	Lifted
Import Embargo, April 17, 1980	US bans all financial transactions with Iran, prohibits travel to Iran, imposes embargo on Iranian goods	Lifted
Prohibition on sales of Munitions List Items, May, 1982	In accordance with policy of neutrality in Iran-Iraq War, US will not sell or allow third party transfer items on controlled Munitions List	Modified
Sanctions on Trade, Aid, and Arms, January, 1984	Iranian involvement in terrorism leads to more stringent bans on arms, aid, and trade	Modified
Sanctions on Chemical Substances, March 30, 1984	Commerce Dept. bans five chemicals that could be used to make chemical weapons	Modified
Ban on dual-use exports, October 29, 1987	Ban on 14 militarily useful goods previously exported to Iran: motors, communications equipment, generators, hydrofoil vessels	Modified
Prohibition on direct aid, Munitions List Items, Controlled Exports, Nuclear Exports,	Bans weapons exports, controlled technologies, nuclear equipment and materials, US	Active

(*continues*)

TABLE TWO   (*continued*)

Sanction and Date	Nature	Status
Commodity Credit Corporation, October 23, 1992	assistance from international financial institutions	
Prohibition of Goods and Technology Relating to Advanced Conventional Weaponry, October 23, 1992	The Iran-Iraq Non-Proliferation Act bans transfer of goods and technologies contributing to Iran or Iraq's acquisition of advanced conventional weaponry	Modified
Embargo on Exports of Nuclear Equipment and Materials, March 9, 1993	Nuclear Regulatory Commission adds Iran, Iraq, Libya to list of countries embargoed from nuclear materials and equipment	Active
Prohibited Transactions Related to Petroleum Resources, March 15, 1995	President Clinton finds Iran to constitute an unusual and extraordinary threat to national security and prohibits US individuals and companies from engaging in activities relating to the development of Iranian petroleum resources, including a ban on financing, management, or supervision of contracts	Modified
Prohibition of Imports, Exports, Reexports, new investments, May 6, 1995	Steps taken on March 15, 1995, were expanded to prohibit imports to, exports, and reexports from Iran. Also prohibits most financial arrangements including purchases, sales, transportation, swaps, brokered transactions, financing relating to any goods or services of Iranian origin	Active
Prohibition of Transfers of Goods and Technology Related to Chemical, Biological, and Nuclear Weapons, February 10, 1996	The National Defense Authorization Act for 1996 amended the Iran-Iraq Non-Proliferation Act of 1992, expanding its applicability from advanced conventional weaponry to include chemical, biological, and nuclear	Active

(*continues*)

TABLE TWO   (*continued*)

Sanction and Date	Nature	Status
The Iran and Libya Sanctions Act of 1996, August, 1996	The President must impose two out of six sanctions on any company that invests more than $40 million or more (including any combination of investments of at least $10 million, which in total equal or exceed $40 million) in any one year in Libya or Iran. The list of six sanctions includes: No US Export-Import Bank Assistance, no US export licenses to receive goods, not eligible for loans of more than $10 million in any one year from US financial institutions, not eligible to be a primary dealer in US government bonds, not eligible to bid on US contracts, not allowed to export any goods to the US. The President may waive sanctions if the country where the company is based "has agreed to undertake substantial measures, including economic sanctions," to prevent Iran or Libya from acquiring weapons of mass destruction or supporting terrorism or encourages Libya to hand over two men indicted in the 1988 bombing of Pan Am 103. The President must impose two out of six sanctions on any company that violates UN embargoes on Libya, including bans of sales of weapons, aviation, and oil refining equipment.	Active

has no alternative to hostility towards its neighbors and the West. They argue that even if moderates do not have a significant role in ruling Iran today, that outside encouragement can help them become the force that emerges from a "failed revolution."

There are also experts that support the view that Iran represents a major threat to its neighbors and the West. These experts argue that Iran remains under the control of a regime that professes a radical Islamic ideology and that the seeming improvements in Iran's conduct have been forced upon Iran by its internal weakness and lack of offensive military capabilities, rather than any evolution towards moderation. They do not feel Iran is becoming more secular or moderate, and they feel that Iran will only be as pragmatic as it is forced to be.

Many of these experts make the same arguments as the US government. They feel that even when Iran has appeared to seek better relations with its southern Gulf neighbors and the West, it has committed actions and acts of terrorism which indicate that the Iranian regime is divided and still has strong hard-line elements. They cite Iran's seizure of Abu Musa (Jazireh-ye Abu Musa) and the Tunbs (Jazireh-e-Tonb-e Kuchek and Jazireh-ye Tonb e-Bozorg), the military build-up in the Gulf, the seeming victory of hard-line political elements in the Majlis elections of 1996, Iran's opposition to the Arab-Israeli peace process, and Iran's support of the Hezbollah and other radical movements. They assert that Iran continues to engage in acts of international terrorism, and that it may be helping to stimulate internal unrest in Bahrain.

Furthermore, such experts feel that Iran's current trend towards "pragmatism" may be temporary. They see Iran's support of the Hezbollah in Lebanon during 1996 as strong evidence that Iran continues to be an enemy of the peace process. They see the arrests and crackdowns following the elections to the Majlis in 1996 as a warning that hard-liners are becoming stronger, and feel that a hard-line or radical leader will replace President Rafsanjani when he leaves office in 1997.

Differences Between US and Allied Policy Toward Iran

These differences over how to treat Iran's capabilities to threaten the region, and the current and probable future character of Iran, have led to serious differences between the US and most of its allies over how to conduct political, military, and economic relations with Iran.

The US view of the proper policy is clear. Anthony Lake has defined the implementation of the Administration's policy of "dual containment" towards Iran as follows:[6]

In confronting these manifold challenges, the Clinton Administration faces an easier task than in the case of Iraq because Iran's weapons of mass destruction are at a relatively early stage of development. In that sense, it has an opportunity . . . to prevent Iran from becoming in five years what Iraq was five years ago. . . .

But containment is also more difficult because the administration is not backed up by an international consensus reflected in UN Security Council resolutions, as in Iraq's case. . . . It does not have broad sanctions in place to effect changes in Iran's unacceptable behavior. Previous administrations have tried their hand at building up 'moderates' in Iran. What we have learned from that experience is that these same 'moderates' are responsible for the very policies we find so objectionable. However, Iran's economic mismanagement has combined with the downturn in the oil market to produce a near desperate economic situation for the Iranian government. With inflation and debt arrears in short-term payments . . . Iran no longer looks like a good commercial proposition. This makes it easier to argue with US allies against improving ties with Iran for purely commercial motives.

To counter Iran's quest for domination of the Persian Gulf, Washington works closely with friendly governments to prevent Iran from obtaining needed imports for its nuclear and chemical programs, and is vigilant about the transfer of missiles and missile related systems from Iran's current suppliers, including North Korea and China. This does not mean Washington intends to quarantine Iran or deny it all military-related goods. This administration tries to distinguish between defense items that do not affect the regional security environment and those items that have an offensive use and could destabilize the area.

The Clinton Administration has hardened its policy over time, partly as a result of Iran's actions and partly as a result of US domestic politics. Secretary of State Warren Christopher began to refer to Iran as an "outlaw state" during a December 1, 1993, meeting with European Union officials over controls on the transfer of technology to Iran. The US began to refer to Iran as the "most dangerous state sponsor of terrorism," on April 1, 1994, when it issued its annual report on "Patterns of Global Terrorism." The US steadily increased its opposition to all transfers of nuclear reactors and nuclear technology to Iran, regardless of whether these were in technical compliance with the Nuclear Non-Proliferation Treaty.[7] The end result is the list of sanctions shown in Table Two.

In his March 2, 1995, testimony to Congress, Assistant Secretary of State Robert H. Pelletreau summed up US attitudes towards Iran by stating that, "Our policy towards Iran is to pressure Tehran to abandon specific policies we find abhorrent and a threat to vital American interests, including its pursuit of weapons of mass destruction, its sponsorship of terrorism and violence designed to undermine the Middle East peace process, its attempts to destabilize countries of the region, and its record of human rights abuses. It is apparent that Iran will not be convinced to change its behavior until the world community exacts a sufficiently high economic and political price."[8]

Secretary of Defense William Perry announced that the US has adopted the collective security strategy set forth in his speech to the Council on Foreign Relations on May 18, 1995:[9]

> This strategy has three elements to it. . . . The first is to bolster the individual defense capability of the gulf states. . . . The second part of our strategy is working to bolster the collective capability of the gulf nations to defend themselves through the Gulf Cooperation Council. . . . The third component of our regional capability is a series of agreements on access, and we have this with all six of our Gulf partners.

These hardening views of Iran have interacted with Congressional efforts to make Iran a political issue. These efforts have been led by Republican Senator Alfonse D'Amato and Congressman Newt Gingrich. Senator D'Amato's efforts to pass legislation calling for the total boycott of all US trade with Iran and trade sanctions on nations who continue to trade with Iran—helped push the Clinton Administration to bring a halt to US economic contact with Iran. On April 30, 1995, the US embargoed all US trade with Iran—including any investment in Iranian oil and gas facilities. Speaking at the World Jewish Conference in New York, President Clinton stated that, "I am convinced that instituting a trade embargo with Iran is the most effective way our nation can help to curb that nation's drive to acquire devastating weapons and its continued support for terrorism."[10]

The Clinton Administration further hardened its line in 1995 and 1996, again as a result of pressure from the Congress. The Administration accepted a revised version of the D'Amato legislation that put sanctions on foreign firms investing in Iran's energy sector. Senator D'Amato and his co-sponsor Senator Inouye, advanced the new legislation with the argument that, "We view any business deal that provides Iran with hard currency to develop its energy sector as a direct threat to US national security."[11]

This legislation was passed with minor modifications in August 1996, and provided the President with significant waiver authority on national security grounds and the ability to delay sanctions while persuading foreign governments to pressure their own companies, but also gave the President authority to impose sanctions on any US or foreign firm that made an investment of $40 million or more that "significantly and materially contributed to the development of petroleum resources in Iran." The proposed sanctions included denying export licenses for any related equipment to such firms, barring any US financial institution from making any loan over $10 million to such a foreign concern, barring a banking concern from designation by the Federal Reserve as a "primary dealer" in US debt, and precluding any lending bank from serving as a repository for US government funds.[12]

The Clinton Administration also initiated a covert action program against Iran after it came under strong pressure from the Republican Speaker of the House, Newt Gingrich. Gingrich described Iran as, "the most dangerous country in the world," and held the House bill approving funding for the US intelligence community hostage until the Administration approved the authorization of up to $20 million for efforts to block Iranian action overseas and encourage Iranian political moderation and democratization. The bill did not authorize any use of lethal force or efforts to directly overthrow the Iranian government, but it did provoke Iran's foreign minister to charge the US with "outright terrorism," with violating international law, and with promoting, "anarchy . . . in international relations." It also provoked Iran to threaten the US with a suit against this action in the World Court, and the Iranian Majlis to allocate IR 25 billion ($8 million) in Iran's 1996/1997 budget to countering US plots.[13]

The US-Iran confrontation and the quest for allies for their respective positions gathered momentum in the course of the summer of 1996. On August 5, 1996 President Bill Clinton signed into law the D'Amato bill which then became the Iran-Libya Sanctions Act. This act sanctioned foreign companies if they invested $40 million or more in the energy sectors of either Libya or Iran, and was received with anger by both Iran and its trade partners.

Iranian Foreign Minister spokesman, Mohammad Mohammadi, declared that the Act was part of "Clinton's intentions to gain a monopoly over the world's energy sources and fertile economic markets."[14] The nations of western Europe, which import just over 20% of their crude oil from Libya and Iran, also took a strong negative stance.[15] Barely two days after the Act came into force, the European Commission, which coordinates the trade and economic policies of the 15 nations which make up the European Community, issued a statement that it viewed the Act with "considerable concern." It also warned the US that the European Community would "show solidarity" and retaliate fully if the US sought to "punish" any European firm.[16]

Iran's major trading partners in the European Community, namely Germany, Britain, Italy and France, issued individual statements calling the extra-territorial legislation illegal. They indicated that they were exploring a community-wide system of "blocking legislation" to include the redefinition of contracts to exclude "investment," breaking up projects into units worth less than $40 million, and a retaliatory blacklist of American companies.[17]

Many of the Europeans, however, felt the Clinton Administration had accepted the bill as a pre-electioneering gambit in order to avoid being outmaneuvered by the Republicans. Not surprisingly, many European companies decided to wait until after the US presidential elections before they test the extra-territoriality of the Libya-Iran Sanctions Act. As one observer put it: "If companies have any sense they will wait until after the pre-election period in the US. Once the pressure is off, Clinton can tell D'Amato to jump in a lake."[18]

Most Southern Gulf states indicated that they opposed the act, and Turkey made it clear that it would not let the act block its expanding trade with Iran. Barely a week after Bill Clinton signed the Act, Turkey's Islamist Prime Minister, Necmettin Erbakan, visited Tehran in order to improve bilateral ties. These ties had deteriorated significantly during the previous months because of Iran's suspicions over Turkish-Israeli ties, Turkish anger over alleged Iranian support for the Turkish Kurdish PKK organization, Turco-Iranian border clashes coupled with over-flights of Iranian territory by Turkish planes, and mutual suspicion over each others' intentions in northern Iraq.[19]

Erbakan used his visit to improve the already extensive commercial and economic relations between Turkey and Iran. About 100 business-men accompanied Erbakan to Tehran, and the Turkish Prime Minister signed a long-term deal to import $23 billion worth of Iranian gas over the next 20 years.[20] Turkey sought to deflect US opposition to the gas deal by arguing that the deal did not represent Turkish investment in Iran, but merely a trade agreement between the two countries. How-ever, the US responded by arguing that Turkey might not have violated the letter of the legislation, but it had violated its spirit. Pakistan and Malaysia also signed new economic deals with Iran at the end of August. Pakistan's $1.2 billion deal including the construction of a joint refinery and a pipeline that would extend to India. Malaysia's oil company Petronas bought a $300 million share in the development of offshore oil fields.[21]

Russian, French, German, Japanese, and Other Views Toward Sanctions

The US has had some support for its policies from nations like Britain, Abu Dhabi, Israel, and Bahrain. However, many European states, Japan, China, and Russia have taken a different path. These states see Iran's cur-rent regime in far less stark terms than the US. They favor political dia-logue, and are willing to search for Iranian "moderates." They see trade and investment as having a moderating effect on Iran's conduct. Most such states feel the US is pursuing a policy that is more likely to drive Iran towards extremism and violence than contain it. Some states—such as China, North Korea, Pakistan, and Russia—have also refused to support the US in its efforts to limit Iran's military build-up and acquisition of weapons of mass destruction.

The rest of the Southern Gulf states have been divided in their strategies for dealing with Iran, although all see Iran as a potential threat. Saudi Arabia has been very cautious in dealing with Iran, although it has maintained a dialogue with Iran's leaders and has quietly attempted to negotiate over the issues of the Haj and Iranian contacts with Saudi Arabia's Shi'ites. Gulf states like Dubai, Kuwait, Qatar, and Oman have actively sought better relations with Iran. Oman has exchanged naval visits with Iran, and is the first Gulf state to seek better military relations since the Iran-Iraq War.

Russian Views of Sanctions and Dual Containment

Russia has pursued a policy of dialogue with Iran over issues relating to policy towards the Balkans, Caspian Sea, Central Asia, and other areas. It has had considerable success since Yevgeny Primakov became Russian Foreign Minister, in spite of some friction over Russian military actions in Chechnya and Tajikistan. Russia is one of the few nations to sign an agreement with Iran protecting the respective rights of each country's citizens and their property.[22]

Russia and the US have been at odds over the past two years because of growing bilateral Russo-Iranian relations. Specifically, the US has expressed its displeasure over Russo-Iranian civilian nuclear deals and over arms supplies from Russia to Iran. The US is deeply concerned with Iran's nuclear weapons efforts. On September 26, 1994, then CIA Director, James Woolsey warned that Iran was only 8–10 years away from building nuclear weapons and was actively engaged in covert attempts to acquire nuclear materials from Russia. US Secretary of Defense William Perry has stated that Iran was somewhere between 7–15 years away from attaining nuclear status.

The sale of nuclear reactors has been a key issue. In early 1995, Russia and Iran signed a contract worth nearly $1 billion for Russia to build up to four nuclear power reactors in Iran. The US Congress strongly denounced these Russo-Iranian nuclear accords, and Republicans in the Congress threatened to withhold aid to Russia unless Moscow reneged on its agreement. Speaker of the House Newt Gingrich declared, "We cannot tolerate Iran getting weapons of mass destruction."[23]

The Clinton Administration agreed that the Russian sale of reactors to Iran was ill-advised, but faced conflicting policy goals. On the one had, officials like Ashton Carter, Assistant Secretary for International Security, declared that the US should not cut aid to Russia since such aid provided funds to dismantle former Soviet nuclear arms.[24] On the other hand, the Clinton Administration launched an intensive campaign to persuade Russia to cancel the deal.

US Secretary of State Warren Christopher told then Russian Foreign Minister Andrei Kozyrev that the US would give Russia $100 million towards the construction of modern reactors and help in the clean-up of nuclear waste sites.[25] The US also offered to include Russia in the international consortium that was building two light-water reactors for another "rogue" state, North Korea. In March 1995, Secretary of Defense William Perry showed the Russians intelligence which "proved" that Russian nuclear aid to Iran would greatly help the Iranian nuclear weapons program.

Moscow did not accept the US position and offered many reasons for continuing the reactors deal with Iran. As early as September 1994, it dismissed Woolsey's claims and stated that the Russian Foreign Intelligence Service had no evidence that Russia was the center for Iranian covert activities for the procurement of nuclear weapons-related materials.[26] The Russians pointed out that according to the Nuclear Non-Proliferation Treaty (NPT), a country like Iran was entitled to acquire nuclear technology for peaceful purposes.

The Russians tried to strengthen their case in early 1995 with the release of a 73 page report on the nuclear ambitions of over a dozen countries, including Iran. Written by Yvgeni Primakov, now Foreign Minister, the report declared that "convincing signs" of a coordinated nuclear weapons program "have so far not been uncovered," and went on to argue:[27] "The current state of its industrial potential is such that, without help from outside, Iran is not capable of organizing the production of weapons-grade nuclear materials."

The Russians also criticized what they perceived to be US "double-standards" in providing the DPRK with similar light-water reactors but pressuring Russia to deny them to Iran. US double standards have another angle, as put by one Russian Foreign Ministry official: "Washington has double standards, it turns a blind eye to nuclear developments by its strategic allies—Israel and Pakistan, but criticizes Iran."[28]

At the same time, Russian officials like Sergei Tretyakov, the Russian ambassador to Iran, make it clear that economic and strategic factors are involved:[29]

> Cooperation with Iran is very important economically and politically for us. It is a huge country with a wealth of natural resources—one of the leaders of the Muslim world with which we must establish lasting good-neighborly relations. Whereas the West is only interested in our raw material resources, in this world we can sell our high technologies and maintain our scientific and technological potential.

Similarly, Russian Nuclear Energy Minister, Vyascheslav Sychev, argued that the Russo-Iranian deal will help prevent Russian from having to layoff of thousands of workers and contribute to furthering the level of Russian production technologies in the nuclear arena. Sychev concluded that it was the fear of Russian competition in providing cheap reliable reactors rather than the "mythical" threat of Iranian nuclear weapons that has contributed to making an issue of the Russo-Iranian nuclear deal.[30]

The Clinton Administration responded by warning in April 1994, that it would not renew a long-standing treaty of nuclear cooperation between Russia and the US which provided for collaboration on fusion, improvements in nuclear safety, and the study of the effects of radiation on the environment.[31] Washington also claimed that Russia was going to supply Iran with gas centrifuge technology in order to enrich uranium to weapons-grade level. Moscow hastily denied that it had any intention of selling such technology to Iran, and Russian President Boris Yeltsin reiterated this position in a meeting with President Clinton in May 1994.

The US also exerted considerable effort to prevent Russia and other former Warsaw Pact states from selling conventional arms. In early May 1994, Assistant Secretary of State For Near Eastern Affairs, Robert Pelletreau, stated, "We don't feel that they (Iran) have adopted policies that make them a good neighbor in the region."[32] Beginning early 1995, American officials revealed that Iran had begun a military buildup on the islands of Abu Musa and the two Tunbs over which it is involved in a dispute with the United Arab Emirates. The US was clearly disturbed by the possibility that Russian arms sales to Iran might actually accelerate in the coming years.[33] In separate meetings in September 1994 and in May 1995, the Russians pledged that they would sign no new arms contracts with Iran after existing contracts were satisfied.[34]

Unlike the Americans who have had a limited and usually adversarial interaction with Iran since the revolution of 1979, the countries of the European Union have full diplomatic relations with the Islamic Republic. Moreover, European Union diplomatic officials from the Troika Council (which is made up of officials from the foreign ministries of the previous, current, and upcoming country of the European Union presidency) also hold regular meetings twice a year with Iranian Foreign Ministry representatives to discuss matters of mutual concern and interest.[35] These talks—known as "critical dialogue"—have generally had the full support of the European Union's two largest economies, France and Germany.

French Views of Sanctions

France has become one of Iran's major trading partners. Following the imposition of the US economic embargo on Iran in mid-1995, the French

Foreign Minister Alain Juppé cast doubts on the effectiveness of "unilateral decisions," and added that he "does not believe that there is an emergency to justify the US decision."[36] In November 1995, the French ambassador to Iran, Jean-Pierre Masset, expressed France's view of the strategic importance of Iran in the region, a position which had been enhanced by the emergence of the Central Asian states.[37]

France has a strong commercial stake in good relations with Iran. France has recently imported roughly 8 billion French francs worth of oil and agricultural products from Iran and France has exported about 4.5 billion French francs worth of goods to Iran. France also extended $2.2 billion worth of official credits to Iran during 1989–1993, at preferential interest rates of 7–9%. It rescheduled Iran's debt owed to France in 1994, when the arrears rose to $419 million, and made new credits available to Iran in 1995.[38]

Major French industrial enterprises and engineering companies including Saint-Gobain, Legrand, Rhone-Poulenc, Telemecanique, and Soletanche have invested in Iran. The French petroleum engineering company Technip has signed two contracts to build petrochemical plants in Arak and Tabriz.

The withdrawal of the American firm Conoco from an oil deal with Iran's National Iranian Oil Company (NIOC) also allowed Total, a French company, to take over the same deal. Total had operated in Iran between 1954 and 1970.[39] It signed a contract with the NIOC to develop the Sirri fields and to provide the necessary financing in July, 1995. The Sirri fields will eventually attain a production level of 120,000 barrels per day in three years, of which Total is entitled to a third in order to cover its costs and profits.[40] The second part of the contract calls for Total to construct a pipeline to connect Sirri to the Fateh fields in Dubai.

Total officials also indicated that their interest in Iran does not begin and end with the Sirri projects. Total's chairman, Thierry Demarest, stated in July, "We have a long-term interest in Iran. We think that there are lots of things to do in Iran, it is a country with a lot of (oil) fields and there are many possibilities to improve the renewal of reserves."[41] Furthermore, despite the fact that Iran is a relatively poor credit risk the French government authorized Gaz de France to create a joint stock company with NIOC in order to export Iranian natural gas to Europe. The French company Alcatel Radio Telephone is installing a mobile telecommunications system in Tehran. The French automotive company Peugeot has licensed the Iranian company Iran Khodro to build the Peugeot 405.

German Views of Sanctions

Germany is also one of Iran's biggest trading partners. Germany emerged as largest exporter to Iran in 1993 with $6 billion worth of goods to that country, making it Germany's third-largest non-European trading partner.[42] While this trade dropped considerably between 1994–1995 because of Iranian economic difficulties, Germany still remained Iran's leading Western economic partner. Germany extended $5.5 billion in official credits to Iran at below market interest rates between 1990–1993, and allowed Iran to build-up a debt arrears of about $3.4 billion before the rescheduling of Iran's debts in 1994–1995. Germany also extended new credits of over $1 billion in 1995.[43]

The Germans claim they are aware of illicit Iranian efforts to acquire dual-use technology and of the activities of Iranian intelligence activities in their country which they say are carefully monitored by the Bundes Nachrichtendienst (BND). Bonn has insisted that it shares a desire with the US not to see Iran acquire weapons of mass destruction and critical technologies. Bonn would also like to see Iran halt support for terrorism and spying on Iranian expatriates living in Germany. The German Federal Prosecutor's office has issued a warrant for the arrest of Ali Fallahiyan, the director of Iranian intelligence, for his involvement in the murder of three Kurds and their translator in 1992, and German intelligence and the German Office for the Protection of the Constitution have prepared detailed reports criticizing Iranian terrorist activity.[44]

Nonetheless, Bonn is very reluctant to sanction Iran diplomatically and politically for the behavior and activities which the US finds objectionable. Germany argues that economic and political engagement is the best way to moderate Iranian behavior and the best way to strengthen moderates and technocrats.[45]

In the first quarter of 1996 the EU's "critical dialogue" with Iran was faced with significant uncertainties. First, Germany's issuance of an arrest warrant for Iranian Intelligence Minister, Ali Fallahian, came as a blow from Iran's biggest trading partner in the West. Furthermore, some German politicians backed by calls from segments of the German press have called for a curtailment of Iranian-German relations. However, in the absence of any egregious Iranian "terrorist" action, and while Bonn officials recognize that Iranian-German relations have entered a sensitive stage as Foreign Minister Klaus Kinkel put it, the Auswartiges Amt, or Foreign Ministry, is unlikely to listen to calls for a downgrading of relations.

Second, and clearly more damaging to EU-Iran relations was the latter's approval of the series of suicide bombings in Israel in February-March 1996 by Islamists which killed 60 persons. Iran's reaction outraged the European Union whose member countries demanded an explanation from the Iranians. The French, with whom Iran's relations were developing smoothly, were particularly vehement in their reaction to Iran's callous statements. The Germans declared that any evidence of Iranian involvement in or support for the bombing campaign in Israel would force Germany to reconsider its relations with Iran.[46] Taken aback the Iranians changed their tone and on March 12 Iranian President Rafsanjani denounced terrorism, saying that "terrorism will lead nowhere."[47]

Fortuitously for Iran, the Israeli action in Lebanon called "Operation Grapes of Wrath" against the Iranian-supported Hezbollah organization caused the world's attention to be focused on the Lebanese civilians caught in the crossfire. Iran managed to get some sympathy for its view that the Lebanese were fighting against Israeli occupation of south Lebanon, conveniently ignoring the fact that southern Lebanon was the staging ground for Katyusha rocket attacks against northern Israel. In contrast to the Americans and Israelis, the Europeans who sought to play a role in negotiating a cease-fire, believed that Iran played a constructive, rather than a spoiler role.

Japanese Views of Sanctions

Japan is another important trading partner of Iran and imports 600,000 barrels a day of Iranian oil. Japan extended $3.7 billion worth of credit to Iran during 1989–1993, at interest rates of 7–9%. It allowed Iran to build-up at debt arrears of about $2.5 billion before the rescheduling of Iran's debts in 1994.[48]

Japan's overall policy approach to Iran is similar to Germany's. Japan has ignored a US request to suspend its purchases of Iranian oil.[49] It has also argued that engaging Iran economically and politically will help promote the internal stability of Iran and of the Gulf region at large.[50] At the same time, Japan is cautious in its dealing with Iran because of its trading interests with the US, and pays close attention to US sanctions.

Other Views of Sanctions

Iran is expanding its economic ties to a number of smaller Western countries. Two Scandinavian companies, Ericsson of Sweden and Nokia of Finland are helping in the modernization of Iran's telecommunications systems. The Dutch subsidiary of the British firm John Brown Engineering has signed a contract with Iran to restore the Abouzar oil platform which is close to Kharg island. The petrochemical complex at Mah-Shahr, whose construction was abandoned after having been damaged during the Iran-Iraq War, was rebuilt by the Japanese firm Mitsui in cooperation with German, Dutch, and Italian companies advising Iranian engineers and technicians. Multilateral cooperation was also evident in the ongoing construction of the Bandar Asaluyeh refinery being built by Iranian engineers aided by the Italian firm of Snamprogetti and the Japanese company Chiyoda Chemical Engineering Corporation. Belgium continues to trade with Iran, although it has been increasingly cautious after it impounded some 600 pounds of explosives and mortar-like weapons which were hidden in the Irania freighter *Kollahdouz* when it docked in Antwerp on March 14, 1996—on the way to Germany.[51]

Iran is rapidly expanding its ties with leading Asian economic powers and other Third World states. Two South Korean companies, Kiya and Daewoo are involved in the Iranian transportation sector. The former has granted the Iranians a license to assemble cars, while the latter is building a railroad between Bandar Abbas and the Turkmen capital of Ashgabat. Part of this line, which will cost $700 million, is already in service. Daewoo has also been asked to build five oil tankers for the Iranians. The South Korean company, Daelin Industrial Company is building a dam at Godar-e-Landar on the Karun river in southern Iran.

The Indian company Kudremukh Iron Ore has offered its technical services in the modernization of the iron and steel complex at Ahwaz. The Egyptian company Sugar Integrated Industries is constructing five sugar refineries as payment for a $150 million debt owed by the Egyptians to Iran. The Iranian oil company NIOC has formed a joint venture with the South African Strategic Fund to store up to 15 million barrels of Iranian oil destined for Europe and Latin America at Saldanha Bay near Cape Town.

This extensive list of countries investing in Iran suggests that many of Iran's (and the US's) trading partners are not responding to US pressure and sanctions. In fact, the most successful obstacles to greater Iranian commercial links and economic trade with the outside world seem to stem more from the uncertainty in the Iranian economy and political climate, particularly Iran's inability to negotiate effectively and on a basis that offers reasonable return on investment.

The Iranian Response

Iranian officials seem to believe that Iran's major trading partners will take only limited steps to accommodate US pressure. Foreign Minister Alik Akbar Velayati has pointed out that each Western country in the international community has its own national interest and that this does not necessarily coincide with the national interest of another Western country.[52] He has also defined Iran's strategy for developing relations with the rest of the international community as one which rests on three pillars: deepening political and economic relations with neighbors, deepening relations with countries outside the Middle East which have common interests with Iran, and deepening relations with what he calls the "supraregional" states: China, Russia, Germany, and France.

Velayati has claimed that Iran has mapped out a well thought out strategy to develop further relations with these latter states in the economic, political, diplomatic, scientific, and cultural domains.[53] He has indicated that Iran is engaging in deliberate attempting to "outflank" US efforts at containment by strengthening its ties to the nations of Central Asia, Turkey, and Pakistan, and by opening a rail link between Mashad in Iran, Sarakhs on the Turkmen border, and Tedzhen on the Central Asian rail net of the former Soviet Union.

Supporting Policy Debates with Analysis

Analysis cannot resolve many of these differences affecting Western and Gulf policy towards Iran. There are too many legitimate uncertainties that cannot be resolved by the evidence currently available. Analysis can, however, provide important insights into several critical aspects of the policy debate:

- The current trends within the Iranian political system, and the extent to which Iran is or is not moving towards moderation;
- The changes taking place within the Iranian economy and the extent to which these affect Iran's political future and ability to sustain a major military build-up;
- The nature of Iran's efforts to sustain and expand its oil and gas production, and how these efforts affect Iran's attitudes towards its neighbors and the West;
- The character of Iran's relations with other states, and the extent to which these relations have or have not been aggressive;
- The role Iran is playing in terrorism and supporting foreign extremist movements;
- The changes taking place in Iran's conventional military forces and warfighting capabilities; and
- The nature of Iran's effort to acquire weapons of mass destruction.

Each of these areas of analysis is necessarily complex. At the same time, each affects an important aspect of policy. Further, Iran cannot be judged by one variable—either as a "terrorist state" or as a commercial oil exporter. It cannot be judged by internal developments in isolation from external actions, or in terms of one aspect of its military build-up. Policy must deal with Iran as a state, and not a single group of issues and must look towards the future, not simply the present.

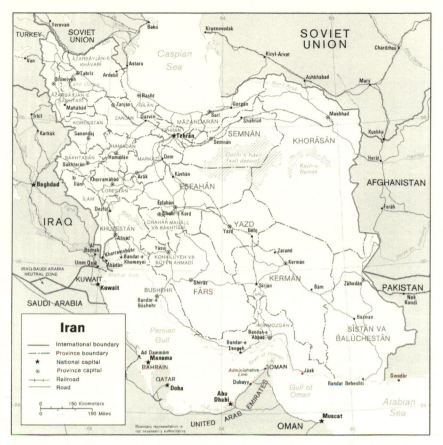

MAP ONE   Iran

2

The Changing Nature of the Iranian Regime

There is no debate over the basic character of Iran's ruling elite. Iran is ruled by a group of religious leaders and their lay associates who share a belief in the legitimacy of a theocratic state, based on Ayatollah Khomeini's interpretation of Shi'ite Islam. Regardless of how the Iranian people may now feel about the Islamic revolution, there is no separation of state and religion.

Clerics continue to dominate all branches of government, and the executive branch and Majlis are dominated by Shi'ite Muslim clergymen and their lay allies. The Ayatollah Ali Khamenei is the Leader of the Islamic Revolution. He functions as the Chief of State, and is also the Commander-in-Chief of the Armed Forces. Ali Akbar Hashemi-Rafsanjani, also a cleric, serves as the Islamic Republic's president. Other government officials, including senior ministers, members of the Council of Guardians, and most members of the Majlis, are all carefully screened to ensure their loyalty to the religious regime.

The Iranian Constitution, which was approved by a popular referendum in 1980 and revised in 1989, declares that the "official religion of Iran is Islam and the sect followed is Ja'fari Shi'ism," although it states that "other Islamic denominations shall enjoy complete respect." The Constitution provides for a Council of Guardians composed of six Islamic clergymen, and six lay members who review all laws for their consistency with Islamic law and the Constitution. The Council plays an important role in ensuring religious rule because it screens political candidates for ideological and religious suitability. It accepts only candidates who support a theocratic state, but clerics who disagree with government policies have also been disqualified. The Council reasserted its right to such powers in July, 1995, although it rejected portions of a new election law that required candidates to be university or Islamic theology school graduates.[54]

There is a debate, however, over the changes taking place within Iran's ruling elite—the extent to which it is growing more pragmatic or moderate or remains radical and extremist. There is a debate over the amount of popular support the regime commands, and a debate over a possible shift towards secularization.

Some experts also feel that Iran's government has important elements of democracy. They cite the fact that Iran has held regularly scheduled elections for the presidency, members of Parliament (the Majlis), and members of the Assembly of Experts, a body responsible for selecting the successor to the Leader of the Revolution. The Constitution provides for a 270-seat unicameral Islamic Consultative Assembly, or Majlis. The Majlis exercises a considerable amount of independence from the executive branch, although its decisions are reviewed by the Council of Guardians. Such experts recognize that most deputies are associated with powerful political and religious officials, but note that they often vote independently and shift from one faction to another. Vigorous parliamentary debates have take place on various issues and in some cases the Majlis has defeated laws proposed by the executive branch. Such experts argue that Iran is one of the few Middle Eastern countries where change can take place without coups or further revolution.

Other experts feel this democracy only extends to those who conform with the basic beliefs of the regime and that the Iranian regime and Majlis have become significantly more hard-line since the Majlis elections of 1996. They note that serious dissidents are suppressed, denied access to the media, suffer political and economic pressure, and/or are imprisoned. They raise questions about what may be a growing hard-line attitude towards peaceful opposition, and the risk of shifts in power which may favor the more extreme and radical elements of the Iranian government.

Political Change After Khomeini

Much of the debate over the current level of pragmatism and moderation in Iran centers around the relative role of Ali Khamenei, the Supreme Leader, the *Faqih or Rahbar*, and the Ayatollah Ali Akbar Hashemi Rafsanjani, Iran's president. This debate has focused on Khamenei's increased power, the Majlis election in 1996, and Rafsanjani's replacement when his term of office expires in 1997. It has also focused on Iran's growing economic problems, the future of the revolution, and Iran's relations with its neighbors and the West.

The Impact of Khomeini's Death

The outcome of the Iran-Iraq War, growing economic problems, and internal struggles for power led to changes within Iran's ruling elite, even before Khomeini's death. A group of pragmatic clerics, like Majlis Speaker Hashemi-Rafsanjani and President Ali Khamenei, spent the year between the acceptance of the cease-fire in July, 1988 and Khomeini's death in June, 1989 implementing a multi-pronged strategy designed to divest more radical clerics of their stranglehold on power by attacking their ideological foundations as irrelevant to Iran's problems and trying to edge them out of positions of power.

The Ayatollah Khomeini's death in June, 1989 accelerated this process. The radicals lost a sympathetic voice and a key protector, allowing clerics led by Rafsanjani to implement constitutional provisions establishing a strong executive under their control. A committee debating the revision of the constitution examined two major options: a parliamentary-style executive with a Prime Minister, or a strong presidential-style executive. The committee opted for the latter alternative. The former, largely ceremonial role of the presidency, which had coexisted uneasily with a powerful Prime Minister, was dropped in favor of a single executive headed by a powerful president with a strong policy-making role.

Rafsanjani then won the July, 1989 presidential elections with an overwhelming majority of the popular vote and used his power to restructure Iran's leadership. Rafsanjani made it clear in 1990 that "economic matters are at the top of the government agenda," and that he did not wish to be sidetracked by ideologues. Despite some pressure from within the Majlis, Rafsanjani refused to include several well-known radical clerics in his first cabinet. He instead chose western-educated technocrats like Mohsen Nourbaksh and Mohammed Adeli who became Minister of Economics and Finance and governor of the central bank, Bank Markazi, respectively. These technocrats asserted that effective economic management could not be based on ideology.[55]

Rafsanjani and Khamenei continued to cooperate in several important instances. This included the selection of candidates for Iran's parliament in 1992, although Rafsanjani played the dominant role. This was the first major election since Khomeini's death and the selection of candidates prior to balloting was critical in determining the outcome. Some 3,240 potential candidates applied to the Council of Guardians to run for the 270 seats in the Majlis, and Rafsanjani was able to use his influence over the Council to weed out some candidates he felt were radical or extremist. The result was a further boost in Rafsanjani's power. The election took place on April 10, 1992, with a second round in early May. Both rounds of voting gave a clear majority in the Majlis to supporters of Rafsanjani and those favoring more pragmatic economic policies. Hard-liners like Mehdi Karrubi, Ali Akbar Mohtashemi, and Mohammed Koiniha lost power, and Rafsanjani was able to replace a large number of hard-line ideologues in the civil service with technocrats.[56] As a result, Iran's relations with its neighbors became less confrontational, the clergy had less political visibility and less direct influence over day-to-day Iranian politics, and Rafsanjani attempted significant economic reforms.

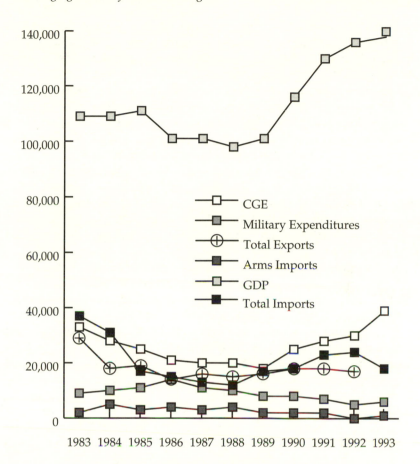

CHART TWO   Iranian Gross Domestic Product, Central Government Expenditures, Military Expenditures, Total Exports, Total Imports, and Arms Import Deliveries: 1983–1993 (Constant $93). *Source:* Adapted by Anthony H. Cordesman from ACDA, *World Military Expenditures and Arms Transfers, 1993– 1994,* ACDA/GPO, Washington, 1995.

The Economic Situation After Khomeini

Rafsanjani had little choice other than to become more pragmatic. A drop in real oil prices, revolution, war, economic mismanagement, population growth, and political instability had led to a major structural crisis in Iran's economy which continues to this day. This crisis affected Iran's economic growth, per capita income, trade, and virtually every other aspect of its economy.

Estimates of the broad trends in Iran's economy differ sharply by source, but there is little controversy over the seriousness of Iran's economic situation. Chart Two shows a US estimate of the trends in Iran's GDP, budgets, military expenditures, and trade since 1983. This chart reflects the negative impact the Iran-Iraq War and the revolution had on Iran's economic growth, and the lack of growth in exports following the Revolution. It is also interesting, however, because it indicates that Iran's military expenditures and arms imports remained a relatively low share of Iran's GDP and central government expenditures.

Chart Three compares the trends in Iran's GDP to its growth in population and per capita income. This chart provides a good picture of the major domestic pressures Iran's leaders faced after the Iran-Iraq War: erratic real economic growth, a steadily rising population, and declining real per capita income which was significantly below the levels reached before the revolution.

Chart Four reflects the near crisis in Iran's trade patterns. It shows the severe drop in the value of oil and total exports that occurred after the revolution, Iran's near total dependence on oil and gas related exports for foreign income, its growing dependence on exports, its growing trade deficit, and problems with its current account. It shows that Iran was moving towards a severe trade crisis by 1991–1992.

These trade problems were compounded by problems in liquidity. Iran had a net liquidity of about $30 billion in 1979, the time of the Shah's fall. Estimates of Iran's liquidity since the fall of the Shah and the beginning of the Iran-Iraq War are extremely uncertain, but they seem to have dropped to about 20–25% of their peak levels at the time Rafsanjani came to power—leaving Iran with constant problems in obtaining hard currency and funding arms purchases.[57]

Attempts at Economic Reform

Having deprived the radicals of much of their power, Rafsanjani and his supporters sought to implement their strategy of reconstruction. This was composed of several integrated elements: economic reconstruction and development, economic reform (*ta'adil eghtesadi*) of a highly distorted economy, and an economic opening to the outside world.

Economic reform implied a clear-cut rejection of the political economy of the radicals. The state would continue to control the commanding heights of the economy, including strategic industries, but the economic liberalism of the technocrats meant abandoning the rigid state-directed economic policies of the past ten years.

In its place, the government preached the virtues of shock-therapy reforms as advocated by the International Monetary Fund and the World

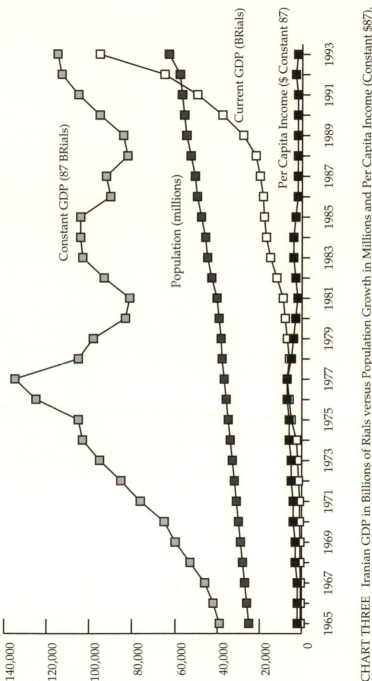

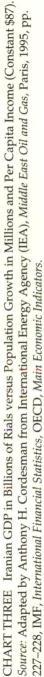

CHART THREE Iranian GDP in Billions of Rials versus Population Growth in Millions and Per Capita Income (Constant $87).
Source: Adapted by Anthony H. Cordesman from International Energy Agency (IEA), *Middle East Oil and Gas*, Paris, 1995, pp. 227–228, IMF, *International Financial Statistics*, OECD, *Main Economic Indicators*.

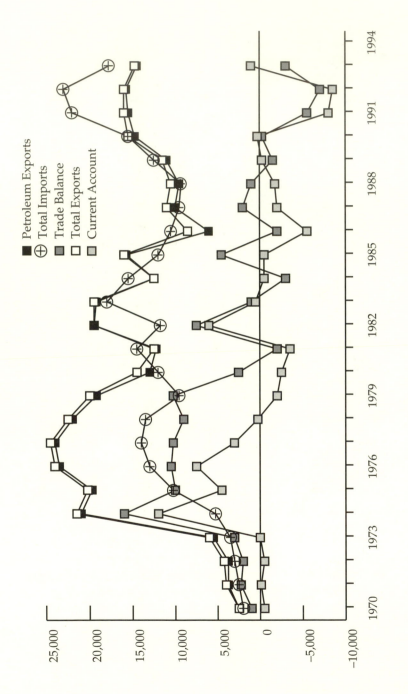

CHART FOUR Iranian Oil and Total Exports versus Total Imports. *Source:* Adapted by Anthony H. Cordesman from
International Energy Agency (IEA), *Middle East Oil and Gas,* Paris, 1995, pp. 227–228.

Bank, with whom the technocrats restored links. The technocrats advocated privatization of inefficient state enterprises, removal of price controls, the elimination of the system of subsidies, and unification of the anarchic system of multiple exchange rates. They wished to strike root and branch at the factors which had caused massive distortion in the economy and contributed to the decline in the standard of living of all socioeconomic strata.

Rafsanjani's reconstruction program was enshrined in the First Five Year Plan of 1990–1994. The pragmatists and technocrats hoped that the implementation of reforms and reversal of the policies of the first decade would ensure not only the survival of the Islamic Republic, but enable it to implement the dream of a model Islamic society, worthy of emulation by other Islamic societies. The reformers had considerable initial success. Between late 1988 and mid-1991, the Iranian economy witnessed a period of dramatic growth—driven in large part by high oil revenues, a post-war boom in domestic consumption, a shift in government spending to the domestic sector and by favorable domestic and international circumstances.[58] This economic recovery gave Rafsanjani both added popular support and power.

The Growing Problem of Debt

There is no way to know what might have happened if Iran's economy had continued to grow. Perhaps that growth would have led Iran to accelerate its military build-up, and a return to revolutionary adventures, or might have led to strengthening the power of Iran's pragmatists and technocrats. After 1993, however, the pace of Iranian economic growth slowed appreciably. Iran's estimated gross domestic product (GDP) growth rate for 1994 was only 1.9 percent, down from 4.5 percent in 1993. Chart Five shows that Iran's liquidity continued to drop and reached near crisis levels.

As Chart Five shows, Iran's total foreign debt rose sharply above the relatively low levels of short and long term debt it owed during the Iran-Iraq War. The OECD data upon which Chart Six is based, however, lag far behind Iran's actual rate of debt obligation.[59] More current sources show that Iran's debt totaled $18.8 billion in 1992, and $28-$32 billion in 1993. By the spring of 1993, Iran was some $3 billion in arrears in making its debt payments. Inflation was not controlled and approached 30% during 1993.[60] By the beginning of 1994, Iran still had $30 billion worth of foreign debt, with $8 billion in arrears. Short-term debt, in the form of letters of credit, comprised about two-thirds of the total.[61]

As Chart Seven shows, Iran's economy had other major problems. Iran developed a growing budget deficit whose effects were compounded by

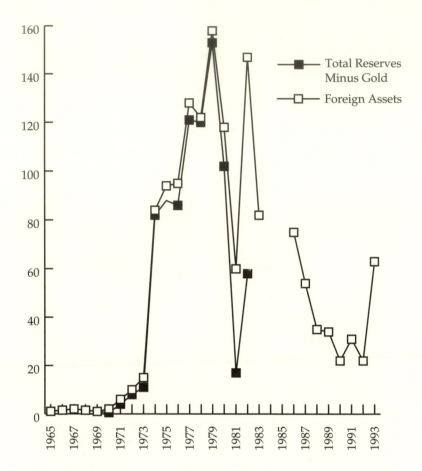

CHART FIVE   Iran: Liquidity: 1960–1993 (In $US Millions). *Note:* No data on foreign assets after 1992. *Source:* Adapted by Anthony H. Cordesman from International Energy Agency (IEA), *Middle East Oil and Gas,* Paris, 1995, pp. 240–241, and based on IMF, *International Financial Statistics.*

the steady inflation of the Iranian Rial (IR), by balance of payment problems, by a drop in world oil prices, and by the problems in oil and gas production described later in this study. In spite of Rafsanjani's efforts at reform, the government was forced to overspend its revenues sharply in order to cope with the virtual collapse of the Rial, and to increase steadily the amount of revenue it took from domestic sources relative to oil revenue. Inflation also made it almost impossible to budget and plan effectively, and efforts to control the level and structure of government spending reached the crisis point by the early 1990s.

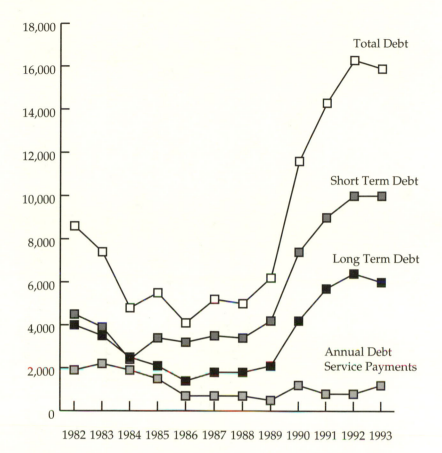

CHART SIX Iranian Short and Long Term Debt Relative to Total Debt Service Payments (In Current $US Millions). *Source:* Adapted by Anthony H. Cordesman from International Energy Agency (IEA), *Middle East Oil and Gas,* Paris, 1995, pp. 241–242, and OECD, *Financing and External Debt of Developing Countries* (debt and debt service data).

The Failure of Economic Reform and Attempts at Recovery

Rafsanjani's reforms failed for a number of interrelated reasons that may produce political and economic instability for some years to come.

- *First, Iran was dependent on oil for most of its capital investment resources and for some 90% of total state revenues, and could not compensate for the impact of major shifts in oil revenues.* Iranian industrial production grew by 16% between 1970 and 1977. Even under the Shah, however,

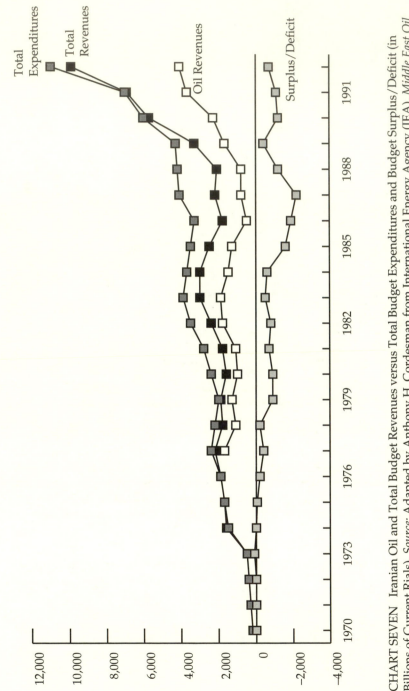

CHART SEVEN Iranian Oil and Total Budget Revenues versus Total Budget Expenditures and Budget Surplus/Deficit (in Billions of Current Rials). *Source:* Adapted by Anthony H. Cordesman from International Energy Agency (IEA), *Middle East Oil and Gas*, Paris, 1995, pp. 227–228.

much of this growth was only made possible by government subsidies, and there were major bottlenecks, such as the lack of skilled managerial and technical personnel. The Revolution, the Iran-Iraq War, and the policies of the post-revolutionary decade made matters far worse. Thousands of skilled personnel fled, and were replaced by incompetent but ideologically correct people who ran industrial concerns into the ground. The revolutionary government nationalized thousands of industrial concerns, and domestic and foreign investment halted.

The post-war situation saw a modest recovery, but many industries only operated at 20%–30% of their post-war capacity a year after the cease-fire. The First Five Year Plan for 1989–1993 allocated $34 billion out of a total of $119 billion in foreign exchange outlays to revive industry. Iran, however, lacked the funds to support a vibrant takeoff in the Iranian industrial sector; could not compensate quickly for the massive destruction resulting from the war; was unable to attract foreign investment; created a wide range of governmental barriers to efficient business operations; and continued to suffer from an acute shortage of skilled personnel.

- *Second, Iran failed to address the need to improve agricultural production.* The revolutionary leadership has blamed the previous regime for neglecting agriculture, but the new regime has made only limited improvements in agricultural policy. Iran has also failed to carry out effective land reform. While the Majlis passed a land reform act in 1982 that was intended to redistribute more land, only 3% of cultivated land was actually redistributed to poor farmers.

  Iran has large amounts of arable land and 45.4 cubic kilometers of internal renewable water resources, which is high for a Middle Eastern country.[62] According to US Department of Agriculture estimates, however, Iran's agricultural production grew by only 1.8% per annum between 1977 and 1989. This rate of growth is only about half the rate of population growth, and agricultural production was 20% lower per capita in the early 1990s than in 1977. Iran has also become heavily dependent on food imports.[63]

- *Third, Iran's continued development and expansion of its oil sector and related infrastructure has consumed much of its domestic and borrowed capital without producing major short-term benefits.* Iran has put greater emphasis on non-oil exports than in the past. Since 1988, Iran has liberalized import controls on inputs and relaxed stringent restrictions on foreign trade. Revenues from non-oil exports which had been almost nonexistent until then, now constitute just under 20% of foreign exchange earnings.[64]

Nevertheless, Iran has concentrated its investment in its oil and gas sectors, and in related areas of production. In 1991 alone, Iran directed $5 billion in investments to rebuild the oil sector in order to maximize production and thus revenues.[65] Although this investment is almost certainly necessary, it leaves Iran heavily dependent on world oil prices.

Iran benefited from the sudden jump in oil prices following the Kuwait crisis, which gave Iran an oil income of almost $20 billion in 1991. As has been discussed earlier, however, Iran's rise in oil income did not last through 1992. Revenues dropped to about $15.9 billion in 1992, and were less than $14.9 billion in 1993—although Iran's oil production rose from 2.4 million barrels a day at the end of the Iran-Iraq War to heights of nearly 4 million barrels in 1993.[66] Iran made barely over $12 billion in 1994, although it may make as much as $16 billion in 1995.[67]

Since 65% of all funds for Iran's five year economic development plan come from oil revenues, this drop in oil prices and revenues had a catastrophic impact on the economic reconstruction programs. This has made it very difficult for Rafsanjani and Iran's technocrats to implement consistent economic reconstruction plans.

- *Fourth, Iran proved unable to manage its foreign borrowing—a factor that has probably done more to discourage foreign loans and investment than the US policy of dual containment.* Iran's radicals opposed any borrowing from Western-dominated international financial markets during the Iran-Iraq War. As a result, Iran emerged from the war with virtually no debt problem. The Islamic Republic's prompt payment of the few debts it did incur and its efficient management of its external finances ensured that the country came out of the Iran-Iraq War with an impressive credit rating.

From 1989 onwards, however, it was clear that Iran's economic reconstruction and recovery program needed access to western capital. The government did not have any significant surplus of capital, and private investors were reluctant to invest in Iran, preferring instead to put their money into dormant savings or property speculation. As a result, the government turned to foreign borrowing, although it avoided long-term debt obligations because of the opposition to such borrowing by Iran's radicals, and because Western lenders were reluctant to lend to Iran on a long-term basis.

Iran's reliance on short-term loans to finance its recovery program resulted in serious problems. The sudden surge in oil prices following Iraq's invasion of Kuwait in August, 1990 tempted the Iranian government into a spending spree, in which Iran's Central Bank (Bank Markazi) lost control over the amounts of letters of credit issued by commercial banks. Iran's foreign debt rose from nearly zero in 1989 to $9 billion in 1991, $18.8 billion in 1992, and $28–$34 billion in 1993.

Low oil revenues then compounded the problem. In 1992, letters of credit payments on short-term debts fell behind schedule for the first time since the revolution, severely damaging Iran's credit reputation. By the spring of 1993 Iran was $2 billion in arrears to Germany, $700 million to Japan, and $150 million to France.[68] Iran was forced to reschedule its debt payments and lost easy access to foreign credit. This helped trigger a new rise in inflation, which approached 30% in 1993 and has been high ever since.[69]

- *Fifth, import reduction contributed further to a recession.* The debt crisis had a ripple effect on the rest of the economy because the government was forced to curtail a post-war import spree that had filled stores. This also resulted in reductions of spare parts and raw materials imported for industry and shortages of consumer goods, basic commodities and spare parts after five years of subsidized abundance. Imports were cut by 50% in 1994, and many state industries were forced to freeze wages and close or lay-off thousands of workers. The Second Five Year Plan had to restrict foreign borrowing heavily— again limiting Iran's economic growth.

- *Sixth, the government did not properly implement three essential elements of its reform program:* The Rafsanjani government either failed to understand the scale of the internal reform that was needed or could not overcome the opposition of religious leaders and the traditional merchant class to rationalization of Iran's convoluted multi-exchange rate system, reduction of Iran's barriers to privatization and foreign investment, the implementation of incentives to encourage the return of skilled expatriates, and the lifting of subsidies.

The government's unification of Iran's three different exchange rates in March, 1993, led to a massive devaluation of the Rial from the highly unrealistic official rate of 70 Iranian Rials to the US dollar, to about 2,700 Rials to the dollar. This led to a steep increase in the price of goods which adversely affected the whole population, irrespective of their income level. As a result, the government was forced to give up on its exchange rate rationalization strategy.

Iran failed to stimulate private investment with a growing economy, stable currency, and receptive social and political institutions.[70] Furthermore, the government failed to reform either a host of contradictory rules and regulations affecting foreign investment or to improve the efficiency of Iran's enormous, red-tape ridden bureaucracy.[71]

The clergy allowed Rafsanjani to liberalize some private economic activity and to invite exiles to return, but not to challenge the clergy's role in the economy. Privatization only occurred in ways that allowed those closest to the regime to profit by buying up state enterprises, when they were put on the market. Private businessmen and industrialists were not allowed to compete with the huge, clerically-dominated corporations, the Bunyods. The ministries in charge of reform also became part of the problem. While the government privatized some 60 companies, the Ministry of Industry retained 200 companies, and the Ministry of Heavy Industry retained over 117.

Expatriates were reluctant to return because of Iran's human rights abuses and its unsettled political and economic climate. Many of those who did return were not able to get their expropriated properties back from the religious foundations, or have found it impossible to deal with Iran's bureaucratic and judicial red-tape. Furthermore, émigrés were often attacked in speeches by leading radicals.[72]

Iran's government reacted to these failures by focusing on Iran's growing debt, trade, and balance of payments problems. It attempted to reduce imports and diversify the country's economy in order to stabilize the country's trade balance. This effort was aided by a March, 1993 devaluation of the Iranian Rial, a subsequent depreciation of the currency during 1994, and government intervention in the foreign exchange market in May, 1995. These efforts cut the Rial's market rate from 2,500 Rials per dollar in February, 1994, to 4,000 Rials per dollar in February 1995.

During the first half of 1994, total Iranian imports fell by about 30 percent to $17.6 billion, while non-oil exports rose 16 percent. These cutbacks in orders continued through the rest of 1994 and all of 1995. Iran limited imports to $12.7 billion in 1995, and made this figure its projected limit for 1996. As a result, Iran's deficit on current account dropped from $1.6 billion in 1994/1995 to around $900 million in 1995/1996. Iran is seeking to cut it to $555 million in 1996/1997, and keep it below $700 million during 1997/1998 through 1998–1999.[73]

At the same time, this cut in imports and severe new restrictions on foreign borrowing made Iran's internal economic situation worse in many ways. Iran entered a recession and Iran's efforts at diversification had little effect. A rise in industrial exports was offset by a decline in carpet exports, and estimated non-oil exports in 1995 totaled $3.8 billion— almost exactly the same level as in 1994 and substantially below the goals set in government balance of payments estimates. There is little chance Iran will meet its goal of increasing non-oil exports from 21–23% of total exports in 1994/1995 to 32% in 1999/2000.[74]

These measures also made it impossible to control inflation. Inflation reached annual levels of at least 30% to 40% during 1992–1994, and reached 60% in 1995. In spite of efforts to bring under control, it was expected to reach at least 25% in 1996 and possibly 40%.

Iran's budget deficit crisis also continued. The new budget for 1996/1997 that the Majlis passed on January 23, 1996, set spending at IR 137.12 million million ($78.7 billion at the official exchange rate)—about $400 million less than the government requested. Revenues were projected at only IR 55.78 million million ($31.9 billion), with oil revenues making up about $16 billion.

There was little improvement in the cost of subsidies. The subsidy for powdered milk dropped $32 million, largely because prices were so low that new controls had to be legislated to prevent the purchase of milk for other purposes. Medicine was subsidized by $388 million, and subsidies for basic food items rose $212 million to a total of $1.46 billion. The Ministry of Defense was allocated IR 2.21 million million ($1.26 billion versus $1.25 billion the previous year), although total defense spending is believed to be closer to IR 5.8 million million ($3.31 billion).[75]

Iran was forced into draconian efforts to reschedule it debt during 1994 and 1995. Iran succeeded in this rescheduling. It rescheduled $14.0 billion worth of debt, and made its first repayment of principal in several years on December 29, 1995. This rescheduling, however, increased Iran's total debt. Iran's central bank (Bank Markazi) reported in October, 1995 that Iran's total principle foreign debt had risen to $23.4 billion, with $20.145 billion in long-term debt and $3.267 billion in short term debt. Iran's total debt stocks, including principal and interest, reached $30.6 billion. Its total annual service of publicly guaranteed medium and long-term debt cost $3.4 billion in 1995/1996. It was scheduled to cost at least $4.3 billion in 1996/1997, $4.4 billion in 1997/1998, $4.7 billion in 1998/1999, and $3.6 billion in 1999/2000—provided that Iran did not increase its debt in the years to come.[76] These trends, and Iran's total debt position, are summarized in Table Three.

To put this debt burden in perspective, oil revenues make up about 90% of the value of Iran's exports. For example, Iran's oil export revenues were just over $14 billion in 1994, and 77 percent of total export earnings. Iran's new annual debt payments totaled $4.3 billion, well over quarter of its annual oil and gas exports. Iran's efforts to reschedule its debt paid off during 1995 to the extent that it avoided a major increase in its debt payments, and limited is total payments to $5.66 billion. Nevertheless, when Iranian planners talked about economic recovery, and about spending some $19 billion in hard currency in Iran's 1996/1997 budget, this still included a debt burden equal to about one-third of all of Iran's hard currency earnings. The proposed Iranian budget assumed some $16 billion in oil export

TABLE THREE   Iran's Total Debt Position ($ Million)

The Build-up of Iran's Debt and Debt Service Problems

| | Total External | Net External | Debt Service Burden | | |
Year	Debt	Financing	Interest	Amortization	Total
1989–1990	—	53	788	373	1,161
1990–1991	—	–182	1,052	495	1,547
1991–1992	—	10,155	1,258	727	1,986
1992–1993	—	7,526	1,319	376	1,695
1993–1994	23,158	715	1,171	2,004	3,175
1994–1995	25,272	–3,430	1,500	4,913	6,412
1995–1996	19,893	–5,339	1,411	3,097	4,508
1996–1997	14,903	–4,783	1,066	4,290	5,357

Key Sources of Iranian Arrears (Countries over $100 million)

| *Industrialized Countries* | | | *Developing Countries* | | |
Country	Peak 1993/1994	Rescheduled 1994/1995	Country	Peak 1993/1994	Rescheduled 1994/1995
Total	9,734	2,518	Total	1,450	764
Germany	3,402	396	South Korea	348	205
Japan	2,157	465	Russia	77	249
Italy	809	512	Turkey	145	57
United			UAE	175	—
Kingdom	823	365	China	95	—
Switzerland	743	449			
France	419	130			
Austria	327	13			
Netherlands	266	78			
Sweden	175	—			
Denmark	160	—			
Belgium	116	50			
Spain	99	33			

Source: Part 1 is adapted from Institute for International Finance, *Islamic Republic of Iran, Country Report,* October 25, 1995, p. 4; Part 2 is adapted from IMF Report SM/95/240, *Islamic Republic of Iran: Country Distribution of External Arrears, 1993/94–1994/1995.*

earnings and $3 billion in non-oil export earnings. Iran had to use $1.6 billion of this total to reduce its debt stock. It also assumed about $5 billion in total short-term debt and medium-term obligations—a figure higher than the cost of publicly guaranteed medium and long-term debt alone.[77]

Iran's probable near term economic growth was projected at only 3% per year, versus the 5% projected by the government, and this growth was less than adequate to deal with the impact of Iran's increases in population. Iran's problems were not growing worse, but the living standards of the ordinary Iranian were still far below the standards reached at the time the Shah fell.[78]

These developments meant that Rafsanjani's attempts at economic reform failed to provide Iran with sustained economic growth, and failed to meet the needs and expectations of the Iranian people. Iran's economy developed at a much lower rate than was needed to recover from war and revolution. Living standards remained low, and Iran continued to have a lower real per capita income than it did it before the oil boom began or during the last half decade under the Shah.[79]

Revolution Versus Technocracy

Iran's economic reforms are only indirectly related to its security policies, but they illustrate the limits to Iran's moderation and pragmatism. Rafsanjani could not push through economic reforms when their effects threatened the power of the clerical regime or the more radical elements of Iranian politics.

Although Rafsanjani's statements sometimes indicated his frustration over the obstacles he faced, he often accommodated the clergy. This was reflected in his approach to subsidies, one of his *bete noires*. In April 1994, Rafsanjani launched a long polemic, in which he stated that many subsidies were extremely costly to the economy and did not benefit the poor. Yet he also emphasized that reform in this area must be carried out slowly so as not to sacrifice social justice—one of the principles of the revolution—and moved very slowly in making actual reforms.[80]

Rafsanjani was cautious for other reasons. He cited the experience of other countries that have undertaken reforms as a reason for caution in Iran. He pointed to the differences in the speed of reforms undertaken by the USSR and the People's Republic of China, stating that the Soviets under Gorbachev moved too fast too soon, leading to their loss of power. He contrasted this experience with the Chinese position (i.e. gradual and cautious) which he asserts was much more logical than the Soviets, adding that "the Soviets (sic) are now facing tremendous problems while the Chinese have maintained their *domestic power and strength.*"[81]

Rafsanjani and his team of technocratic reformers also sometimes worked at cross purposes. The technocrats have found the political leaders in the government and the Majlis are unwilling to pay the short-term domestic political costs of economic reforms. They have found themselves unable to implement long-term strategic planning because of political unpredictability and interference by other government departments in their respective domains. This criticism has been voiced by technocrats like Muhammad Husayn Adeli, the former governor of the Central Bank.[82]

As a result, Iran's technocrats became increasingly demoralized. Not only did they quarrel among themselves, unnecessarily highlighting divisions within their ranks, they also publicly pointed out structural deficiencies within the reform programs.[83] They questioned the President's more gradualist, politically motivated approach, and some have repeatedly threatened to resign their posts.

Further, the lack of a social base of support for the economic reform programs significantly restricted Rafsanjani's and the technocrats' current room for maneuver. The failure of economic reform led to the alienation of those groups most heavily affected by the restructuring programs, namely the lower classes, the state functionaries, and the Bazaaris. At the same time, many members of the Westernized middle class have withdrawn further and further into their villas in the suburban enclaves of northern Tehran. They indulge their taste for things Western behind the walls of their homes, and ignore the increasingly vocal campaign against the Western cultural onslaught.

Rafsanjani and Iran's technocrats did not, however, give up. As has been discussed earlier, they dealt with Iran's debt issues and inflation, and put restrictions on imports. Rafsanjani also organized an "economic reform lobby" in advance of the 1996 elections for the Majlis. On January 18, 1996, sixteen pro-Rafsanjani officials made a public statement in a Tehran newspaper that the main threat to Iran's future did not come from outside forces, but internal economic difficulties, and stated that supporting Rafsanjani, "means continuing the clear ideological line and the high goals of the revolution." These officials included ten cabinet ministers and four vice presidents—including Mohsen Nourbakhsh, the governor of the central bank. They also included Gholamhossein Karabaschi, the mayor of Tehran. The Ata'ollah Mohajerani also began publishing a liberal journal called Bahman in an effort to support both reform and political pluralism.[84]

The Role of the Clergy

Other forces in Iranian politics have proved to be far less progressive. The Iranian clergy has become a "new class" founded on state subsidized wealth in much the same way as did the senior members of the communist party in Russia and Eastern Europe after World War II. This has made the clergy even more disinclined to promote change. In particular, Rafsanjani has not been able to deal with the Bunyods, the main instrument of clerical power in the economy. The Bunyods are large foundations which were formed to manage the property and other assets confiscated from the Shah and his supporters after the Revolution. These foundations have given the clergy considerable wealth and economic leverage. The largest Bunyod, the Bunyod Mustazafan or Foundation for the Oppressed, had a budget of $10 billion in 1992 and $12 billion in 1995, and controlled hundreds of companies. It is run by Khamenei's brother-in-law, Mohsen Rafiqdust—a revolutionary hard-liner and former Minister of the Islamic Revolutionary Guards Corps who has shown himself to be more adept, if more corrupt, as a corporate manager than as a military leader.[85]

There are many similar organizations, and control of such Bunyods has given the clergy a strong reason to block many aspects of reform, inhibit the creation of many private enterprises, and limit or vitiate efforts to liberalize foreign trade and foreign investment. Rafsanjani was forced to recognize this as early as 1991, when he declared that the foundations would not be dismantled, even though they constitute a major source of the distortion within the economy.[86] At the same time, the Bunyods serve as a power base for the clergy in politics and act as another force opposing political reform. Ironically, Persian fundamentalism has proved capable of doing just as much damage to Iran's economy as secular Arab Socialism has done to the economies of nations like Algeria, Egypt, Syria, and Iraq.

Economic Unrest and Internal Violence

The failure of economic reform also did more than undercut Rafsanjani's power and that of Iran's technocrats; it led to a steady rise in popular discontent.[87] This discontent became apparent when riots and demonstrations began in major cities like Arak, Isfahan, Mashhad, and Shiraz between April and June, 1992. The disturbances began with protests by workers in the oil industry in Abadan, Tehran, Isfahan, and Shiraz. The riots then spread to include war veterans and thousands of ordinary people. These disturbances were caused by deteriorating municipal infrastructure, poor social services, inadequate housing, and rampant inflation.

The government's reaction was initially low-key and that of the security forces was sluggish. Nonetheless, the government was forced to set up special anti-riot police forces and Iran's Chief Justice, Mohammad Yazdi, went so far as to threaten swift punishment including the use of firing squads. This did not stop new riots in Tabriz the same year, when some 30,000 protesters reacted violently to the razing of 300 squatter dwellings.

The growing level of discontent was reflected in the fact that Rafsanjani had only moderate support when he was re-elected to the presidency on June 10, 1993. He won 63% of the votes cast, but the election was scarcely a triumph for the regime. The four authorized candidates that the Council of Guardians chose to run against Rafsanjani, out of 128 applicants, were comparative unknowns and several spent more time praising Rafsanjani than campaigning for themselves. Some 13 million people, or half the electorate, abstained. Rafsanjani had to use the security services to suppress hard-line opposition and criticism after the election, resulting in the arrest of key hard-liners. He had only partial success in making hard-line papers like *Salam* and *Kayhan* alter their content and style. Even so, the most right-wing candidate, Ahmad Tavakoli, won 27% of the vote.[88]

Social and economic discontent, together with resentment at the power of the Bunyods and the blatant corruption of the Mullahs, grew steadily after the presidential elections and affected the Majlis as well as the people. This was reflected in the fact that the Majlis refused to give Mohsen Nurbakhsh, Rafsanjani's choice as Finance Minister, a majority on August 17, 1993—after a bitter two day debate about the government's mismanagement of the economy. Iranian public opinion polls also showed a growing popular pessimism regarding the ability of the revolution to offer an improved living standard.[89]

More riots and demonstrations took place in various Iranian cities in 1994. In February, 1994, security forces killed a number of Sunni Muslims who staged a demonstration in the southeastern city of Zahedan to protest the Government's destruction of a local Sunni mosque as well as the government-sponsored propagation of the Shi'ite faith in Sunni regions. Afterwards a hitherto unknown group calling itself the Islamic Movement of the Sunni People in Iran took responsibility for explosions at a Shi'ite mosque in Zahedan.

On June 20, 1994, a powerful bomb exploded in the sanctuary of the Imam Reza Mosque in Mashhad killing over 20 people and wounding some 70 others. This was a sacrilegious act which stunned Iranians. The government used it as an opportunity to pin blame on the opposition *Mujahedin-e-Khalq* organization, even though the culprit was more likely to have been an extremist Sunni organization linked to Sunni groups in Afghanistan and Pakistan. The Islamic Movement of the Sunni People of Iran again took responsibility for this attack.[90]

In August 1994, a large spontaneous demonstration broke out in the northwestern industrial city of Qazvin after the Majlis rejected a proposal to detach the city from Zanjan province and designate it as a separate province. The government dispatched troops to quell the disturbance, which reportedly attracted up to 100,000 demonstrators.

During their efforts to restore order, the troops reportedly killed dozens of demonstrators, wounded hundreds more, and arrested some 3,000 persons. Credible reports indicated that many of the detainees were released only after they had signed a false confession stating that they were members of the Mujahedin-e-Khalq.[91] In late August, 1994, citizens of Tabriz rioted for two days shouting anti-regime slogans and rioting flared up again in September, this time over the scarcity of food.[92]

At the same time, the regular army and the Pasdaran proved less than enthusiastic in suppressing the rioters. Not long after the Qazvin riots, senior officers of the army and the Pasdaran addressed a communiqué to Supreme Leader Ayatollah Ali Khamenei, in which they said that "the role of a country's armed forces is to defend its borders and to repel foreign enemies from its soil, not to control the internal situation or to strengthen one political faction above another."[93]

More disturbances erupted in 1995 due to the continued deterioration of the economy and the government's raising of prices on basic food-stuffs, public transportation, and gas. These price hikes came about in spite of pleas by the Minister of Interior, Ali Mohammad Besharati, not to raise prices during *Nouruz*—the Iranian New Year celebrations—which took place in March 1995. Riots broke out in the poor lower class suburbs of Tehran, like Ribat Karim, Ali Shah Avaz, Islamshahr and Akbarabad, which the regime had previously considered bastions of the Revolution. The population of these areas had included some of the most ardent supporters of the Revolution, and roughly 1% of this population had been killed in the Iran-Iraq War.

There were reports that the Army refused to use force to intervene in this disturbance, just as it refused to fire on the crowd during the August, 1994, protests in Qazvin. Other reports indicated that Major General Ali Shahbazi, the army chief of staff, refused to send in units of the regular army. A retired Iranian general, Rahimi, is reported to have said that the army would not face the people as it had during the revolution in 1979.[94] Some reports indicated the Revolutionary Guards also resisted being used to deal with civil disorders, although other reports indicated the regime used the 27th Division and 66th Special Division, both of the IRGC, to put down the disturbances.

The government had to turn to the Basij for support, a force increasingly associated with Khamenei. Basij units had conducted mass arrests in Qazvin in August, 1994, and some reports indicated they had killed up to 40 people. They played a major role in putting down the riots in Ribat Karim, Ali Shah Avaz, Islamshahr and Akbarabad in April, 1995, and then conducted large scale "security" exercises in each of these cities in June and August.

The regime staged huge, if somewhat poorly organized, military maneuvers involving both Revolutionary Guards and Basij forces near Islamshahr and Arhbarabad and small settlements near the southern reaches of Tehran in mid-June. These maneuvers made extensive use of the Basij battalions, but were supported by infantry units of the Revolutionary Guards and by various law enforcement agencies.

According to Major-General Mohsen Rezaii, these "Ashura" maneuvers were intended to test the capabilities of these forces to conduct "their responsibilities within the national boundaries."[95] According to other reports, the regime was attempting to establish firm control over both the military and training forces to suppress urban riots and uprisings. This may be the explanation behind a series of large scale "urban defense" exercises in Tehran in late September, 1995. Some commentators also believe that the promotion of Hassan Firouzabadi from a command in the Basij to Major General and Chief of Staff of the Iranian forces in April, 1995, was related to the regime's need to strengthen its political control over the armed forces.[96]

The new sanctions the Clinton Administration imposed in May, 1995 almost certainly played a role in this unrest. Iran was having serious problems with inflation and in maintaining the value of the Rial, even before the sanctions. Although the new US measures hardly resulted in a trade embargo, or even a lasting drop in Iranian exports, the Iranian market initially panicked, and the Rial-to-dollar exchange rate suddenly rose from 3,500:1 to 7,000:1. Inflation reached 58% per year by the end of May. Iran's complex three level exchange rate broke down, and Iran's ability to import virtually collapsed. The Bazaari reacted by making profiteering price rises in the goods sold in Iran, and Iran's problems in meeting its debt payments increased.[97] These problems had eased by October, but a new series of banking scandals and reports of corruption in the *Bonyad-e Mostazafin* had made the government's economic reputation even worse. Ironically, the only positive side in Iran's economy was that exchange rate problems led to a sharp fall in Iran's imports from Japan, Germany, France, Italy, and the UK.[98] As a result, Iran's balance of payments deficit turned into a surplus of nearly $1 billion by late 1995.

The Changing Role of Rafsanjani and Khamenei

Rafsanjani's decline also affected the character of Iran's political leadership. Rafsanjani and Khamenei held the two key pillars of the Islamic Republic in the post-1989 period—the offices of the President and of the Supreme Leader, the *Faqih* or *Rahbar*. These two institutions control the Islamic Republic's political-religious and political-administrative apparatus.

As Rafsanjani weakened, Khamenei's role as Supreme Leader became more important, although it is unclear that he can ever properly fill the role that Khomeini intended in creating this position. The institution of the *velayat-e-faqih* ('Guardianship of the Jurisprudent' or 'God's Deputy on Earth') is an innovation in Shi'ite jurisprudence that was formulated by Ayatollah Khomeini to provide the ideological framework for rule by a jurist or *Faqih* who combines in his person the necessary religious and political qualifications to make him supreme leader of the land.

A *marja-e-taqlid* ('source of emulation') or senior legal authority is supposed to be the most senior religious scholar in the Shi'ite world because of his knowledge and writings and the edicts of the *faqih* are declared as binding on the community of believers. His political qualifications should include the administrative competence and political skills necessary to govern the Islamic Republic and to implement divine law, the Shari'a.

The Ayatollah Khomeini had the necessary qualifications to be the *velayat-e-faqih*. Furthermore, his immense charisma as the revolutionary leader who overthrew the Shah strengthened his political credentials. Although many high ranking Shi'ite clerics disagreed with the concept of *velayat-e-faqih* from the outset, most chose not to oppose Khomeini directly and so it remained. None of Khomeini's followers among the political clergy—save possibly Ayatollah Montazeri, who was designated successor to Khomeini until he was abruptly removed—had the requisite religious qualifications to challenge him as a *'marja' or 'marja'iya.'* This is a position which requires many years of hard study, published works and acceptance by others as a source of emulation.[99]

Amendments to the constitution in 1989 also greatly strengthened the formal powers of the *Faqih*. For example, the revised constitution stated that the President is accountable not only to the people but also to the *Faqih*, and can be removed by him. There was no mention of his accountability to the *Faqih* in the 1979 constitution. The range of the Supreme Leader's political powers are enormous and include:

- Determining the general policies of the Islamic Republic;
- Supervision of the implementation of the policies of the Islamic Republic of Iran;
- The post of Supreme commander of the armed forces of the Islamic Republic of Iran;
- Authority to declare war and peace and to order mobilization;
- Impeachment of the President in the national interest pursuant to a verdict by the Supreme Court confirming violation of his duties or following a vote of no confidence by the Majlis.

- Ability to regulate relations among the three branches of government: the executive, legislative and judiciary.
- Power to appoint and dismiss: members of the Council of Guardians, head of the judiciary, director of radio and TV, chief of staff of armed forces, and commander of the Islamic Revolutionary Guards Corps.[100]

The Supreme Leader's array of institutional and state political powers are buttressed by an equally impressive array of parastatal and informal powers. He has a vast network of supporters, both clerical and lay, ensconced in various institutions and organizations throughout the country. He controls the Central Council of Friday Prayer Leaders, which consists of clerics whose Friday sermons throughout the country set the tone of national political and social debate.

The Supreme Leader has ultimate control of the huge economically and politically powerful foundations, such as the Bunyod Mostazafan, which is run by his brother-in-law, Mohsen Rafiqdust. While these foundations represent an enormous source of patronage for the Supreme Leader, they have distorted the economy and played a major role in the setbacks dealt to the economic reform programs. The government has no control over them, because they are exempt from paying taxes and are not required to provide annual reports, undergo audits, or abide by the state's general accounting laws. In short, they can neither be reined in nor dismantled without the authority of the Supreme Leader who, despite the massive scandal roiling the Bonyad Mostazafan, recently reinstated Mohsen Rafiqdust as the head of the foundation.[101] In the final analysis, Ayatollah Khamenei is at the apex of an enormous bureaucracy—a privileged class headed by clerics, and those linked to them by ties of blood or marriage, who have benefited through privileged access to the black market, higher education, and the medical system.

The Ayatollah Seyyed Ali Khamenei had problems in using this power during Rafsanjani's early years in power. He did not have all of the proper religious and spiritual qualifications to be Supreme Leader and was unable to match Khomeini's religious and political qualifications. He came from a religious Azeri family, originally from Tabriz, which was forced to move to Mashhad for political reasons several decades before Khamenei came to power. He undertook a theological education at the holy city of Qom, where he came under the influence of the revolutionary *political* thinking of Ayatollah Khomeini.

In 1980, Khamenei was a mere *hojjatolislam*, or minor cleric, who devoted his life to political activism. During the 1980s, Khamenei's political connection to Khomeini allowed for his rapid ascent to the presidency of the Islamic Republic. Since he was declared an Ayatollah rather than earning the title, however, he could only accede to the supreme leadership after the clerical establishment decided that his political leadership sufficiently compensated for his lack of admitted scholarly and religious qualifications.[102]

The inevitable consequence was a separation of the religious authority—*marja'iyat*—from the political leadership—*rahbariyat*. This bifurcation of the powers of the Supreme Leader left Khamenei in an exposed position because he lacked the authority to settle differences between factions, senior clerics, or institutions of the state with Khomeini's authority. Further, his political authority was challenged by the radical-dominated Majlis in 1989 and 1990.

Due to his lack of spiritual prestige and religious scholarship, Khamenei could not claim the title of *marja'iya* following Ayatollah Khomeini's death. The role first devolved upon the politically quiescent Ayatollah Al-Kho'ei of Najaf, in Iraq. On his death in mid-1992, it devolved upon Ayatollah Mohammed al-Golpeyagani of Qom. When Ayatollah Golpeygani died in December 1993, the title of *marja'iya* passed to the infirm and blind 103-year old Ayatollah Araki. During this time, Khamenei tried to marshal his forces and become '*marja*.' He took to issuing pronouncements of spiritual and religious import. His call for the banning of the infliction of knife wounds on the forehead by worshippers during the religious ceremonies of Ashura is one example of such efforts at leadership. So, too, was his declaration that Islam was a religion of logic and not of primitive innovations which had nothing to do with Islam.

Araki died in November 1994, but Khamenei's efforts to become '*marja*' were met with hostility and sometimes ridicule among clerics in Iran and the rest of the Shi'ite world. These clerics resented this patently political ploy which would have devalued the prestige and position of the senior Shi'ite hierarchy. Khamenei had to back down to avoid an acrimonious split in the ranks of the Shi'ite clergy, leaving the contradictions inherent in his position unresolved.

These problems and weaknesses seem to explain why President Rafsanjani may have underestimated both Khamenei's political aspirations and the impact he could have by taking activist positions in favor of the conservatives, rather than Rafsanjani and the reformers. Rafsanjani seems to have felt that Khamenei not only shared his view on the need to reconstruct the country, but also that he could not challenge Rafsanjani's ability to act as a powerful executive.[103]

This seemed to be the case during the first three years of Rafsanjani's presidency. Khamenei lent his political weight to help Rafsanjani purge radicals from powerful positions in state institutions: the ministries, the revolutionary tribunals, and the IRGC. Khamenei did not interfere in the President's executive prerogatives, ministerial choices, or direction of the economy in ways that contradicted or hindered his partner. He aided Rafsanjani by helping to disqualify hundreds of radicals from running for the Majlis—a tactic of questionable legality but useful in reducing the radicals' obstructionism in the parliament. Khamenei also shared Rafsanjani's aversion to the radicals' defense strategy and conduct of the war with Iraq. Not long after Iran's defeat in the war with Iraq, Khamenei indicated his contempt for what he called the 'Molotov cocktail mentality' of those who believed that wars could be won without weapons, technology, and organization.

As time went on, however, Khamenei began to assert his political authority, while he strengthened both his political and religious credentials. He responded to the growing popular and factional criticism of the adverse impact of Rafsanjani's austerity and restructuring measures by putting the brakes on some parts of Rafsanjani's reform program. Rafsanjani and his supporters were increasingly confronted by Khamenei's ability to become the focus of all the vested interests threatened by the reforms, and Khamenei—either out of ideological conviction or political calculation—began to take high profile public positions on domestic and foreign policy issues close to the radicals and conservatives, which embarrassed Rafsanjani and undermined his strategy.

Rafsanjani proved to have other weaknesses that Khamenei could exploit. He failed to develop a firm hold on the levers of government and was unable either to control the worst excesses of the bloated administrative and bureaucratic apparatus or to streamline them. Corruption in the civil service in Iran grew as a result of the low wages of public sector employees and the situation worsened with the onset of high inflation. Those tasked with enforcing the anti-corruption campaign proved to be corrupt and took payoffs from speculators, businessmen and tax evaders to supplement their meager wages. Rafsanjani and Khamenei also failed to agree on what needed to be done. While Rafsanjani and the technocrats attacked corruption as one of the country's most serious problems, the Supreme Leader maintained that the structure of Iranian society was healthy.[104]

The June 1993 presidential elections provided clear signs of Rafsanjani's decline. Although the president was re-elected for his second term, Rafsanjani faced tougher and more meaningful opposition, particularly from Ahmed Tavakkoli—a noted and vocal member of the conservative right, than he had in 1989 when his opponent had been Abbas Sheybani. While the Iranian people had believed in 1989 that Rafsanjani could do the job, they felt in 1993 that he and the Islamic Republic had not delivered the goods. Popular frustration was reflected in both a low turn-out and Rafsanjani's low vote total. In 1989, President Rafsanjani had received almost 95% of the electorate's vote. In 1993 he received 'only' 63%, and only 57% of the eligible population voted—the lowest popular rate of participation since the establishment of the Islamic Republic in 1979.

Khamenei began to exercise his political prerogatives more forcefully following Rafsanjani's weak showing in the presidential elections. He prevented the president from streamlining the administrative machinery, and from purging inefficient public sector employees, managers and mayors. He ensured that his protégés and those of the conservative right remained in charge of high profile and important ministries, or were appointed ministers to them.[105] Khamenei's growing prominence in economic matters became visible in late 1993 when he made plain in a letter to the President his position that the government must pay greater attention to the social needs of the people through a progressive tax system that favored those on low-incomes, improved public services, and a broadening of the social security net.[106]

Rafsanjani's tirade against the distorting effects of subsidies on the economy in April, 1994 further alarmed both Khamenei and the Majlis, and simultaneously strengthened Khamenei's position. The Majlis feared that the President was planning further drastic cuts in government subsidies, and proposed that the power of the government to set the prices of goods and services be transferred from the Supreme Economic Council headed by Rafsanjani to the Majlis itself. The following month Rafsanjani had to back away from his strictures against subsidies.

Rafsanjani's growing frustration was evident in May, 1994 when he warned that Iran's progress was being obstructed by dogmatism—presumably from both the right and the left. In this speech Rafsanjani merely echoed an impatience with ideological stances that had been very evident in an important speech he had delivered in late July, 1990 in which he said:

> None of these two trends (referring to the rightists/conservatives and leftists/radicals) have been in favor of us. The right-wing trend will be satisfied only when the government is returned to the feudal and one-thousand family situation which existed in the past; while the leftists would like to see the country being run as the most extreme communist country.[107]

Rafsanjani's problems were compounded by a de facto alliance emerging between the radicals and the conservatives, both of whom had a common reason to attack the adverse impact of the reform programs on the population. Both groups felt that the social distress caused by Rafsanjani's reform programs were doing little more than eroding the stability of religious rule and Iran's new political system. They found the call that Rafsanjani had issued to expatriates to return to be abhorrent for material and ideological reasons, and the debt crisis led them to attack Iran's renewed subjugation to international institutions, which they charged were under the control of the hegemonic West.

At the same time, the Iranian people were not happy with either group. A poll carried out by an Iranian newspaper in early 1995 concluded that the vast majority of Iranians were aware that the source of the country's woes were internal (inflation, arbitrary application of law and order, corruption, economic mismanagement, and lack of consensus over the future of Iran's political system). Only 5.8% of those polled believed that the main problem facing Iran was Western cultural aggression or *tahajom-e-farhangi*, and only 6.5% believed that the leading cause of Iran's internal problems was the US embargo on Iran.[108] This public opinion poll was a stark contrast to the charges that that the West must be blamed for Iran's hardships and current state of paralysis. It also showed little support for President Rafsanjani's attempt to blame the West for Iran's problems in his February 1995 speech commemorating the 16th anniversary of the Islamic Revolution.[109]

In fact, the regime faced growing popular alienation and distrust. The economy was stagnant with debt repayments to foreign creditors—a source of extreme humiliation—consuming almost $8 billion annually or over half of the country's annual oil revenue. Even Iran's clerics were increasingly worried. They were less and less given to expressing sentiments such as those uttered by President Rafsanjani in early 1993 when he said "we see the revolution as progressive, successful, strong, and dynamic"[110] and reiterated a year later by the Supreme Leader, Ayatollah Khamenei.

Iran's efforts at economic reform were in a near shambles and its supporters in disarray. Rafsanjani had failed to convince the people and the Majlis that the socioeconomic situation would get better as a result of economic reforms, or to convince the clerical elite that such reforms were essential to the long run survival of the Islamic revolution. Many clerics feared they might end up reforming themselves out of existence. The Islamic Republic had also become more susceptible to the vagaries of the international economic system than at any other time in its history. This became clear when the Clinton Administration froze economic and commercial relations in May, 1995. This action had an unsettling psychological effect on Iran and led to a run on the Rial, whose value fell to IR 7,000: US $1 following the announcement of the US trade embargo.

The 1996 Election for the Majlis

The economic situation improved somewhat in 1995 and 1996, but it also became clear that there were growing divisions between Iran's religious conservatives and radicals and the pragmatists and technocrats in the government. The Militant Clergymen's Association, of which Rafsanjani is a leading member, split openly into "modern" and "traditionalist" groups. The "moderns" backed Rafsanjani and the technocrats around him. The "traditionalists" sided more with Khamenei, and were led by figures like Ali Nateq-Nuri, the conservative speaker of the Majlis and radicals like "Major General" Moshen Rezai, the commander of the Revolutionary Guards.

The radical clerical faction, the *Majmue'e Ruhaniyun-e-Mubarez* (Association of Combatant Clergy) was reduced to a shadow of its former self. It continued to adhere to an ideologically hard-line foreign policy, a state-controlled economy and rigid Islamic controls within the country, but it lacked anything approaching the strength it had early in the revolution.[111] In late February 1996, the *Majmue'e Ruhaniyun-e-Mubarez* stated that it was going to boycott the elections.[112]

The split in the Militant Clergymen's Association did not prevent moderate and opposition candidates from running. Nominations for the 270 member Majlis were screened by the Council of Guardians for their belief in Islam, for their expressions of support for Iran's Islamic system of government, and for adherence to the belief that the state should be headed by the *Faqih*, or Supreme religious leader, Ayatollah Khamenei. This screening was conducted in ways which tended to make the elections a contest *within the ruling elite* between those technocratically-minded officials or groups and the more ideologically and clerically-minded groups.

The Council of Guardians did allow most "moderns" and a number of moderate members of the opposition to run, but it was obvious that these choices were a subject of growing debate within Iran's ruling circles. Rafsanjani was forced to make open appeals for unity and tolerance. On January 17, 1996, he called for free elections that would allow all factions to be represented in the Majlis. He stated, "We should not be concerned about the presence of different schools of thought in Majlis. . . . Elections are good tests for groups with different ideas to realize what degree of public support they have."[113]

These appeals may have had an impact on the conduct of the Council of Guardians, but they had considerably less impact on the conduct of the traditionalists and security forces. Conservatives steadily reduced the freedom opposition elements had to campaign against the government and criticize it. This process began at least four months before the election. Iranian security officials stopped an opposition group from holding a press conference to call for free elections on January 10, 1996. The internal security and police forces blocked the meeting on the grounds that they could not guarantee its security.

While Iranian election law made it illegal for campaigning to start until about a week before the March 8 election date, the traditionalists began to openly attack the Rafsanjani and his supporters in the press and in political debate in 1995. The clerical conservatives grouped in the *Jame'e Ruhaniyat-e-Mubarez* (Assembly of Combatant Clergy) were in a good position to attack Rafsanjani's technocratic bloc.[114] The *Jame'e Ruhaniyat-e-Mubarez* dominated the 270 member Majlis with 150–160 members, while Rafsanjani's technocratic bloc only had about 30 to 50 members. In fact, Ali Nategh Nouri disparagingly referred to the technocratic bloc to as the "liberal faction."

This domination of the Majlis by the conservative right-wing clerics led President Rafsanjani to declare in mid-1995, "Of course, as the president, I would like the Majlis to be more in line with and supportive of the policies and decisions of my government."[115] The *Jame'e Ruhaniyat-e-Mubarez* (Assembly of Combatant Clergy) made it equally clear that it opposed Rafsanjani, and this led the technocratic members of the Majlis to organize a response. In December, 1995 a Majlis deputy from Shiraz, Qasim Sholeh-Sa'adi, announced the formation of the equivalent of a new political party called the Iranian People's Independent Party.

More significantly, a "Group of 16" or "G-16" emerged in early January 1996. The G-16 was named after the 14 ministers of Rafsanjani's cabinet who joined the Mayor of Tehran and governor of the Central Bank of Iran, in founding the group. The Group of 16 was made up of highly educated technocrats with long experience in government, and took the title of *Khedmatgozaran-e-Sazandegi* (Servants of Construction) in order to highlight its emphasis on economic reform and development. Its members indicated their strong support for President Hashemi-Rafsanjani, and the creation of the group was a clear sign that Rafsanjani's technocrats were leaving the four year-old conservative-technocratic coalition that had defeated the religious radicals in the *Majmue'e Ruhaniyun-e-Mubarez* in 1992.

The Ayatollah Khamenei stood aside from some of this debate. He publicly welcomed the emergence of the G-16—whose members went out of their way to show that they believed that clerics had a critical role in Iranian politics. However, Khamenei conspicuously failed to provide Rafsanjani with any support.

The *Jame'e Ruhaniyat-e-Mubarez* clearly saw the *Khedmatgozaran-e-Sazandegi* as a major threat, and move aggressively to weaken its ability to campaign. It ensured that the election laws that prevent officials in executive positions from running for the Majlis were enforced. When it seemed that the G-16 might be successful in forming coalitions with other factions such as the *Khane Kargar* (Workers' Union) which had three deputies in the Majlis, and with the Iranian People's Independent Party of Sholeh Sa'adi, the *Jame'e Ruhaniyat-e-Mubarez* shifted its position to call upon the radical clericals in the *Majmue'e Ruhaniyun-e-Mubarez* to participate in the elections and prevent a "victory by the liberals."[116]

The *Jame'e Ruhaniyat-e-Mubarez* used its influence over Iranian officials and the security services to try to alter the course of the elections. Much of this effort was at the local level, but some signs of such activity were clear during the campaign. In late February, newspapers ran a complaint by teachers' associations accusing local officials of promoting candidates they favored and of hindering those they opposed. At the same time, election officials in the capital ruled in thirty cases of unfair electioneering practices.

The security forces stepped up the harassment of secular nationalists and liberals of the Freedom Movement of Iran and the National Front. On March 5, 1996, security officials broke up a news conference by Dr. Ibrahim Yazdi, leader of the Freedom Movement. The FMI had proposed 15 candidates for the parliamentary elections, but the Guardian Council had disapproved 11 of them. Yazdi's response was to withdraw the remaining four whom he claimed were subject to harassment, denial of access to the media, and the Interior Ministry's refusal to allow them to hold public meetings.[117] The Freedom Movement of Iran was a right-wing moderate party that had been affiliated with Mehdi Bazargan before he died in 1995.[118]

The first round of the parliamentary elections were held on schedule on March 8, 1996. Voter turn-out reached 71% of those eligible. This was the highest percentage since the referendum on April 1, 1979, that followed the fall of the Shah and the victory of the Islamic Revolution.[119] A number of factors accounted for this high turn-out. First, the intense debates between the various political factions over the future direction of the Islamic Republic caught voters attention, even though many were bewildered by the proliferation of candidates and ignorant of the differences between them. Second, the Iranian population was expressing its concern over the socioeconomic ills besetting the country. The majority of the people were more concerned with domestic issues than with Iran's confrontation with the 'Great Satan' or the West's 'cultural assault' on Iran. Third, a large number of middle and upper middle class voters and women participated in the elections. Many women were inspired by Faizeh Hashemi, one of the candidates, and one of President Rafsanjani's daughters.

Few candidates won the required one-third of the total votes cast required to enter the Majlis, and this resulted in many run-off elections. These run-off elections were held on April 19. They were held in 75 constituencies and determined the fate of 123 seats in the 270 seat Majlis. They were vigorously contested in the capital, Tehran, where only two candidates, Majlis Speaker Hojjat ol-Islam 'Ali Akbar Nategh Nouri and Faizeh Hashemi, had secured enough votes to win in the initial elections on March 8.

There were many accusations of fraud and unfair election practices. The Council of Guardians inexplicably annulled the results in some smaller provincial towns, and some of the votes were clearly manipulated by the government. For example, Mohammad Ali Chehrgani was a candidate in Tabriz who received enough votes in the first round to win a seat, but the government announced after the election that he had withdrawn as a candidate just before the election took place. Chehrgani later announced he had been arrested by the security forces after the voting, had been held for several days, and was forced to sign a statement announcing his withdrawal.[120]

The fifth Majlis, which took office at the end of May, 1996, was significantly different from the outgoing fourth Majlis and indicated that many Iranian voters wanted changes of kind that were very different from the politics of either the *Ruhaniyat-e-Mubarez* or *Khedmatgozaran-e-Sazandegi*: More than 70% of those elected are new deputies.[121] One Iranian voter in the town of Rafsanjani commented after the incumbent—a relative of President Rafsanjani—was defeated that, "Even if Pinocchio had run against the former deputy, (the latter) would have been defeated since the votes for the competitor were protest votes against the former deputy."[122]

The protest votes made the outcome of the election confusing. For example, the technocrats and pragmatists in the *Khedmatgozaran-e-Sazandegi* did not do as well as they expected in Tehran, but had a respectable performance in the provinces.[123] The G-16 claimed 51 of the 95 provincial deputies were G-16 candidates, 9 were independents, and only 35 were adherents of the conservative right.[124] The conservatives in the *Ruhaniyat-e-Mubarez* retained the majority of the seats, but these results gave the pragmatists and technocrats enough seats in the new parliament to seriously reduce the previous majority. In fact, these gains led the conservative Speaker of the Majlis, Nateq-Nuri, to warn against the "liberals" for their conciliatory approach to foreign relations.[125]

Further, 23 of the 270 seats were left open after The Council of Guardians annulled the votes in 21 constituencies, almost all of which would otherwise have elected moderate or modernist candidates. The

TABLE FOUR Leading Figures in the Khedmatgozaran-e-Sazandegi (G-16)

Name	Education/Specialization	Government Post	Former Positions
Mohammed A. Najafi	M.A. in Math	Minister of Education	Minister of Higher Education, Deputy Head of Radio/T.V.
Mohsen Nourbaksh	Ph.D in Economics	Governor of Bank Markazi	Minister of Finance
Morteza M. Khan	Ph.D in Economics	Minister of Finance	Iran Customs
Seyed M. Gharazi	M.A. in Electrical Engineering	Minister of Post and Telephone	Minister of Oil
Gholamreza Foruzesh	M.A. in Engineering	Minister of Construction	
Akbar Torkan	M.A. in Management	Minister of Roads and Transportation	Minister of Defense and Logistics
Mohammed E. Shustari	Seminarian	Minister of Justice	
Mohammed Nematzadeh	M.A. in Industrial	Minister of Industries Management	
Isa Kalantari	Ph.D in Agricultural Physiology	Minister of Agriculture	
Bijan Zangeneh	M.A. in Construction Engineering	Minister of Energy	Minister of Construction
Gholamreza Shafei	B.Sc. in Mechanical Engineering	Minister of Cooperatives and Budget Organization	Deputy of Planning
Reza Amrollahi	Ph.D in Nuclear Physics	Vice-President, Head of Atomic Energy Organization	
Mohammed Hashemi	M.A. in Economics	Vice-President	
Seyed M. Hashemi Taba	M.A. in Textiles	Vice-President	
Seyed Atallah Mohajerani	Ph.D in History	Vice-President for Parliamentary Affairs	Diplomat
G. Karbatschi	Theological Studies	Mayor of Tehran	Governor of Isfahan Province

results of two others had still not been determined in June 1996, and the government announced that by elections would to be held in October to fill the empty seats. The context of this announcement made it clear that moderates would experience even more problems in running in the by elections.

At the same time, a large number of independents won who were not openly affiliated with either the G-16 or the conservative right. They were independents who represented constituencies that were more concerned with "local politics" and issues such as reconstruction, building projects, and employment, than ideology. It also soon became clear that the conservatives in the *Ruhaniyat-e-Mubarez* were able to wield considerable influence over such independents—some of it by using revolutionary auxiliaries like the Basij Force to put pressure on local constituencies. Further, the *Ruhaniyat-e-Mubarez* showed that it had the votes to force a number of the ministers in the G-16 to resign.

The Presidential Elections of 1997 and Future Trends

The *Ruhaniyat-e-Mubarez* has become more aggressive in other ways since the election. During April and May, 1996, its members sharply stepped up their efforts to blame the West for Iran's problems and to warn of the risk of a US attack or invasion. At the same time, the *Ruhaniyat-e-Mubarez* deployed massive numbers of the Basij Force into virtually every Iranian city and town to crack down on any signs of liberalization and reform and as a show of strength.

The *Ruhaniyat-e-Mubarez* and religious radicals bypassed the government and used the mosques to conduct a massive popular campaign. Well over 100,000 young men were used to track down and arrest men and women who showed signs of wearing Western clothing or failing to cover their hair and ankles properly. This campaign even led to the harassment of Rafsanjani's daughter for riding a bicycle.

While Rafsanjani and his supporters did nothing to endorse this use of the Basij, Ali Akbar Nategh Nouri strongly supported the campaign and seemed to view it as an initial step in his campaign for president. His support also became even more important when he was reelected as speaker on June 5, 1996, with 146 of the 238 votes cast. Mohsen Rezai also supported the new campaign and hinted at purges in the Revolutionary Guard to remove opponents and restore its "integrity." Further, the Revolutionary Guard reacted ruthlessly to new public protests in Tabriz in May, 1996, and may have carried out several public executions.

Further, Khamenei issued his strongest condemnation of Iran's moderates to date on June 1, 1996. While he did not mention Rafsanjani or any of his supporters, he stated that, "The mirage of development risks alienating us from our fundamental values and driving us down the path to dependence. . . . The general trend of the parliament must conform to Islamic values. . . . The illusion of reconstruction is a source of corruption . . . the corrupt liberal culture of the West. . . . Those who claim that by entering the era of reconstruction we should abandon our slogans are a dangerous phenomenon."[126]

It is far too soon to say that these trends mean that the *Khedmatgozaran-e-Sazandegi* and Iran's other technocrats and moderates cannot gain power or that Iran's current tilt towards extremism is its future. Iranian public opinion shows few signs of polarizing around broad support of its religious conservatives and radicals. One thing is also very clear: the presidential elections of 1997 will be of crucial importance, particularly with respect to the religious nature of the regime.

It is impossible to rule out the possibility that Rafsanjani will run again. However, the issue of whether the constitution could be amended to allow Rafsanjani to run for a third consecutive term was raised by one of the president's protégés and advisors, Ata'ollah Mohajerani as early as November, 1994—when Rafsanjani was far stronger and more popular than he his today.[127] Mohajerani's trial balloon was immediately attacked by both the left and right in the Majlis. Both groups claimed that they were worried by the institutionalization of a 'dictatorial presidency,' although their main wish was to see Rafsanjani leave office. Rafsanjani also said that he would not seek to amend the constitution, although other Third World leaders have made similar statements only to change their minds when it became politically convenient.

It is possible that Khamenei may be able to name one of his associates as a leading candidate, or Rafsanjani may designate a possible successor. It is also possible that the next President may not be a cleric. The Ayatollah Mahdavi-Kani, a senior cleric, has suggested that clerics should not run for the presidency. Such declarations scarcely rule out a clerical candidate, but there are also a number of non-clerics who may run for the presidency:

- Gholam Hossein Karbatschi is the tough, no-nonsense, technocratic mayor of Tehran. He has acquired a growing reputation for "doing the impossible" in improving municipal efficiency. Karbatschi, however, has not yet indicated an interest in running for the presidency. He was also a member of the radical left at one time and is associated with central state planning.
- Ali Mohammed Besharati is the powerful Minister of Interior, and a high profile conservative protégé of Ayatollah Khamenei. His role as chief of the internal security services and his conservative ideologi-

cal outlook has made him adopt a tough approach to combating 'social corruption', urban violence, and narcotics. At the same time, he has shown flexibility by indicating his belief that Iranians have proven to be mature enough to form political parties.

- Ali Akbar Velayati has made the transition from pediatrician to for-eign minister, and is a possible "moderate" candidate. He has said that he "will not voluntarily be a candidate," but many leaders have claimed to have had greatness thrust upon them.
- Ali Akbar Nategh Nouri is the speaker of the Majlis, and was reelected to the post on June 5, 1996 by 146 out of 238 votes cost. He has the same power base that Rafsanjani used to come to power, and has kept a high profile in Iranian politics since the days of Khome-ini. He is a strong conservative and opposed the technocrats in Iran's recent elections for the Majlis.
- Hassan Rouhani is the deputy speaker of the Majlis and the secre-tary of the Supreme Council for National Security. He is one of the leading figures in the present government and has the support of a number of senior Ayatollahs.

Regardless of which—if any—of these candidates wins the election, he will be faced with challenges which may lead to a prolonged period of political, economic, and social instability. Major revolutions like the changes in Iranian politics that began in 1979 can easily take a quarter to half a century to reach a new level of political stability and any new pres-ident will be faced with major challenges in revitalizing the economy, sta-bilizing Iran's relations with the outside world, and implementing polit-ical reforms.

The Ayatollah Khomeini's comments that the Iranian revolution was not made to keep down the price of watermelons, and that economics is for donkeys, cannot shape Iran's immediate future. No government can ignore massive inflation, massive unemployment or underemployment, and a drop in real per capita income that has reduced this income to under 25% of the peak level Iranians received under the Shah. Iran must find some way of reducing unemployment, utilizing its industrial capac-ity, and finding meaningful jobs for its youth. It must address its unhealthy reliance on the oil sector, reduce the heavy hand of the public sector in economic activity, and reduce the obstacles to greater privatiza-tion in the economy.

Iran must dismantle the myriad of bureaucratic rules and excessive regulation of its economy, and develop an effective private system to han-dle banking and investment. It must increase the availability of capital for the private sector. This, at a minimum, means fundamental reforms of the Tehran Stock Exchange and the Central Bank of Iran.

Political xenophobia is not a substitute for foreign investment: It is clear that Iran's economic development cannot be undertaken only with domestic capital, and Iran needs to attract foreign capital. This, however, means far-reaching structural changes before it can attract foreign investment. First, the ideological strictures against foreign investment must be curtailed, and the different political factions must agree to stop their three-year long strife over the foreign investment law. Second, Iran must proceed with reform of its foreign policy. This will not be easy and will be a source of heated domestic political debate. Furthermore, the US strategy of putting economic pressure on Iran works to make the county a less than ideal environment for foreign investment.

Iran must concentrate its limited resources on economic development, rather than arms. As the following chapters show, Iran is not engaged in a massive military build-up, but it is committing far more resources to military efforts than it can afford.

More broadly, Iran must also find some consensus regarding the nature of the political and social makeup of an Islamic state, the relationship between state and civil society and between religion and state, or in Islam *din wa dawla*, the extent of political freedoms permitted within a theocratic state, the necessity for political parties including secular ones, and last but not least, the growing pressures for secularization of the Islamic Republic.[128]

Any such consensus may, however, require major changes in the role of Khamenei or his successor. There is a growing political and intellectual debate within Iran concerning the political and religious validity of the office of *velayat-e-faqih* in the post-Khomeini Islamic Republic. Certain basic questions are being asked about the regime which include: should the jurisdiction of the *velayat-e-faqih* be limited to spiritual and religious concerns? Should the offices of *vali/faqih* and president be combined? Or should the Islamic Republic ultimately do away with the concept and practice of *velayat-e-faqih*?[129]

Moderation, Pragmatism, and Reaction

No government is likely to come to grips with all of these challenges in the immediate aftermath of the 1997 election. Iran's most likely near term political future is one where the Islamic Republic continues to 'muddle through,' lurching from crisis to crisis, while trying to find ad hoc solutions to its political and socioeconomic problems. Even if a new government is committed to reform, it may well face the same problems in implementing such reforms as Rafsanjani did. The result is likely to be an erratic government, marred by contradictory and inconsistent tactics, and subject to the political forces of vested interests.[130]

There are, however, alternatives to this scenario:

- Domestic politics might undergo a gradual transformation after the election. This could take the form of the renewed legalization of political parties, an issue which is being increasingly explored by the elite. For example, Rafsanjani hinted in March, 1995 at the possibility that parties could be formed before the Majlis seats are contested in the 1996 elections.[131] Many in the intelligentsia also support such a change. There is no way, however, to predict the outcome of such steps. These changes might allow more moderate secular parties to emerge by the next election, or end in providing a political platform for new forms of radicalism.
- Creeping secular technocracy might gradually replace most aspects of clerical rule without leading to overt political change. The fact that Rafsanjani has failed does not mean that Iran cannot gradually evolve strong technocratic ministries and focus on step by step efforts at reform. Such a regime could retain clerical leadership at top positions, but would allow Iran to solve many of its economic problems slowly, and to improve relations with the West and Iran's neighbors.
- Radicals or hard-liners might carry out a "corrective revolution." Such a regime would put renewed emphasis on distributive economic policies and social justice. It would retain much of the Khomeini legacy in foreign policy with its pronounced opposition to the forces of 'global arrogance.' However, a 'corrective revolution' now seems unlikely. Unlike the plotters of the August, 1991 coup in the Soviet Union, who suffered from a nostalgia for the normality represented by the communist past, the radicals in Iran do not have any 'idyll' to point to. The radicals are divided and their statist economic policies are dated. Their constituency—the dispossessed—is spiritually exhausted and more impoverished than ever. They want results, not slogans. Furthermore, the people have a profound psychological need for predictability in everyday life, a situation which has been sorely lacking in the sixteen years of the Islamic Republic. Only some radical new affirmation of the Revolution—such as a major Arab state joining Iran in the "Islamic Revolution"—seems likely to give the radicals more political force.
- The conservative Islamic right might move the Islamic Republic toward the other pole of the social equilibrium. The right has steadily increased its power since its Majlis victory in 1992. A further shift in power could give control to Iran's conservative clerics and their allies among the leading Bazaari and commercial families.[132] The resulting regime could take several courses. It could provide a

popular palliative to the lower classes in the shape of subsidies and price controls to avoid greater social distress and mass discontent. At the same time, it might seek an increased confrontation between the government and the Bazaaris over hoarding and profiteering, of which the latter stands accused by the authorities. The socially and culturally conservative agenda of such elements in Iranian politics is evident in their recent efforts to thwart the West's 'cultural assault' on the social and cultural integrity of the Islamic Republic. Nothing illustrates this better than the fierce debates in the Majlis on the practicality of banning the thousands of satellite dishes beaming in Western programs that allegedly undermine the social and cultural fabric of the country.

- The growing mix of political and economic pressures within Iran might destabilize the Islamic Republic to the point where the present political system disintegrates. Iranians, however, are politically cynical after sixteen years of revolutionary mobilization, and it is unclear what ideological pressures could attract a large enough following to produce radical political change. Only a virtual collapse of the economy seems likely to trigger the forces necessary to overthrow clerical rule in a sudden manner.

- Iran could decentralize, as Tehran finds it increasingly difficult to come up with the resources to fund development in the provinces. This seems unlikely, but economic collapse and turmoil in several peripheral regions could overwhelm even Iran's huge internal security forces. It is also at least possible that the armed forces would not intervene to attack separatist or regional movements, if this meant massive attacks on civilians. Iran would then be a state governed by a weak political center, with fragmented and factionalized military forces loyal to the provinces, discontented minorities, porous borders, and increased political and economic pressure from the outside world.

- The military could actively intervene—although such intervention could take place to shore up the clerical regime as well as to remove it. The possibility of the 'man on horseback' cannot be excluded. Iran's history has two examples of military leaders—Nader Shah and Reza Shah in the 18th and 20th centuries respectively—stepping into the political process to reverse Iran's decline. The armed forces—both regular and revolutionary—have been under stringent political and ideological control, but they are increasingly dissatisfied. The clerical regime cannot be too sure that this dissatisfaction will not manifest itself in overt opposition. There have been instances in the past of attempted coups by the armed forces, notably in the early 1980s.[133]

It is possible to draw many parallels between Iran's present situation and the fate of other revolutions, but remembering the past is as danger-ous as forgetting it. Revolutions have differed sharply in character, and have rarely evolved towards moderation or extremism in ways that his-torians or political analysts were able to predict. Post-revolutionary regimes have sometimes been more dangerous than the revolutionary regimes that preceded them. The French revolution was most dangerous under the "pragmatism" of Napoleon. The Russian revolution was far more dangerous under Stalin than Lenin. Nazi Germany became far more dangerous after Hitler made compromises with the army and Germany's industrialists than when it actively pursued national socialism. At the same time, there have been many cases where today's radicals have become tomorrow's moderates.

Given this unpredictability, the best the West may be able to do is to continue to seek dialogue with Iran, and create incentives for pragmatic behavior by whatever regime emerges. No effort at dialogue can ensure that Iran ceases to be aggressive, but economic ties between Iran and its neighbors and the West may lead it to act pragmatically out of intelli-gent self-interest. Conversely, it is hard to see how outside efforts to cause the further deterioration of Iran's economy are likely to lead towards moderation.

3

Internal Security

While much of the analysis of the character of the Iranian government focuses on its economic policies and the politics of its ruling elite, there are other important indications of the government's character. Pragmatic efforts to solve economic problems do not necessarily mean a regime is tolerant, moderate, or has changed its original ambitions. The actions of Iran's internal security forces provide additional insights into the attitudes that shape its intelligence operations overseas.

The Iranian Security Forces

Iran's internal security forces have several major elements. Several government agencies are responsible for internal security, including the Ministry of Intelligence and Security, the Ministry of Interior, and the Revolutionary Guards, a military force established after the revolution which is coequal to the regular military. Paramilitary volunteer forces known as Hizbollahis or Basijis also conduct vigilante actions.

Iranian intelligence plays a major role in the surveillance of hostile movements and potentially hostile ethnic and religious groups. The Revolutionary Guards has a major internal security mission, particularly the Guards infantry forces. There are also some 740 Basij Ashura battalions in the Revolutionary Guards for internal security missions and riot control. According to some reports, the Basij now has up to 230,000 young men who are used at the local level to enforce Islamic values, report on threats to the revolution, and act as a mobilization base for the Revolutionary Guards. These Basij forces are present in virtually every public area and activity in Iran and routinely harass any man or woman that deviates from what the Basij regards as the proper norm.

The Ministry of the Interior has a major internal security mission, and law enforcement agencies like the police and gendarmerie often have senior officers from the Revolutionary Guards. There is also a growing force of local volunteers, or Hezbollah, who monitor popular behavior to ensure that it meets Islamic standards, and who increasingly have replaced the Comiteh in performing local security missions.

Although Iran's internal security forces do not have the centralized "police state" character of Iraq's internal security forces, they permeate every aspect of Iranian life. If anything, their "popular" or "revolutionary" character may make them more effective in the surveillance of ordinary citizens, while the strong central elements of state control help to prevent the rise of any organized opposition.

Iran has also steadily strengthened its internal security forces since 1993. It has conducted a long series of "urban defense" exercises to deal with uprisings and riots, and many have been held in or near towns where riots or protests have occurred. Pro-Khamenei and Revolutionary Guard elements of the regime also stepped up surveillance in advance of the 1996 elections.

The Argument Against Moderation

Experts differ, however, over the extent to which Iran's treatment of internal security is repressive. Many secular Iranians, Western scholars, and journalists who visit Iran argue that the regime has relaxed many of its internal security procedures and tolerates growing criticism from its opposition. They argue that charges about the continued extremism and revolutionary character of Iran's internal security apparatus are exaggerated and that Iran's human rights record is no worse than that of many other developing nations.

Some of these observers include scholars who have studied Iran for decades and who have a long record of concern for human rights. Many, however, are either apologists for the regime or base their impressions on visits to Iran where they have had little ability to judge the overall pattern of activity by Iran's internal security forces. Favorable commentary in the past on Nazi Germany, the Soviet Union, and a host of other cases has shown that scholars and journalists find it difficult to judge the true character of authoritarian regimes.

A number of outside organizations are also deeply critical of Iran's internal security methods and human rights record. Amnesty International, Middle East Watch, and the US State Department have all argued that the Iranian government's treatment of internal security issues and human rights has shown far less "moderation" and "pragmatism" than its treatment of economic issues. They have issued reports indicating that Iran has continued to suppress legitimate political opposition ruthlessly. These reports also note increased arrests of protesters and opposition spokesmen as drug sellers and users in an attempt both to discredit them, and to defuse foreign charges of human rights abuses.[134]

Some of these charges raise serious questions about the recent actions of the Iranian government. For example, the Iranian government reported in 1994 that 52,000 out of 100,000 people in Iranian prisons had been convicted on drug charges, but human rights reports indicate that thousands of these prisoners were arrested for political, religious, and ethnic reasons.[135] There are also reports that the Majlis expanded the role of the VEVAK in suppressing domestic political opposition in November, 1994.[136]

The most gratuitous example of Iranian extremism is the government's treatment of Salman Rushdie. In March 1994, the Iranian government reaffirmed its 1989 religious decree condemning British author Salman Rushdie to death for his book, *The Satanic Verses*, as binding and irrevocable. The government has made no public move to repudiate its promise of a cash award to any person who kills Rushdie. In fact, Iran's Foreign Ministry recalled Iran's Ambassador to Norway in January, 1995, for taking a flexible stand on Iran's call for Rushdie's execution.[137]

In March, 1994, the United Nations Commission on Human Rights (UNCHR) concluded that the Iranian government's "continuing" abuse of human rights justified continued international review. The United Nations extended the mandate of Reynaldo Galindo Pohl, its Special Representative on Human Rights in Iran, for another year. Pohl has cited the Iranian government's "extensive" use of the death penalty. Although the domestic press stopped reporting most executions in 1992, they appear to continue at a rate of several hundred a year. Exiles and human rights monitors report that many of those executed for alleged criminal offenses were actually political dissidents and many executions ordered in such cases amount to summary executions.[138]

Recent Human Rights Problems

The most recent US State Department report on human rights in Iran cites a long series of actions, which raise further questions about the level of "moderation" within the Iranian regime.[139] They include:

- Ali Akbar Saidi-Sirjani, a prominent social critic and historian, died in detention in November, 1994—10 months after his arrest on improbable criminal charges including drug trafficking and espionage. The Iranian government claimed Saidi-Sirjani died of a heart attack, but did not permit an independent autopsy. Members of Saidi-Sirjani's family maintain that he had no history of heart disease or drug problems.
- On February 25, 1994, the Iranian government executed 78-year-old Faizullah Makhubat, a Jew, who had been detained under harsh

conditions for 22 months at Evin Prison in Tehran. Makhubat was a leading member of Iran's Jewish community and was convicted of espionage and sabotage. After taking delivery of the body, Makhubat's family members discovered that his eyes had been gouged out, the teeth broken, and the body was covered with contusions and bruises.

- Saidi-Sirjani, a best selling author and prominent advocate of abolishing censorship was arrested on March 14, 1994—along with a journalist named Niazi Kermani. Saidi-Sirjani emphasized respect for individual rights and opposition to tyranny. The reason for their arrest was reported to be the publication of a work questioning the principles of the 1979 revolution. Iranian newspapers published their alleged confessions to crimes of moral turpitude.

- Five members of the outlawed Kurdish Democratic Party of Iran (KDPI) were reportedly executed at Diselabad Prison in Kermanshah in February, 1994, for engaging in unspecified political activity. The five men, Hossein Sobhani, Rauf Mohammadi, Bahman Kosravi, Ghaderi Moradi, and Adel Abdollahi, were all allegedly tortured prior to execution.

- The Iranian government failed to provide adequate protection for three Evangelical Christian leaders who were murdered in 1994 by unknown assailants. In response to an inquiry from the UN Special Representative, the Iranian government claimed in October, 1994, that the ministers were murdered by operatives of the Mujahideen-e Khalq, an opposition group seeking the government's overthrow. The State Department reports that there is no evidence that the Iranian government was involved in the killings, but believes the government failed to provide adequate protection for the three Evangelical Christian leaders. The Iranian government had accused them of seeking converts among Muslims.

- The Reverend Mehdi Dibaj, a pastor of the Assemblies of God church, was arrested in 1993 and sentenced to death for apostasy. He was released from prison in January after his case received international publicity, but was then abducted and murdered. His body was discovered on a Tehran street in July, 1994.

- The Reverend Haik Hovsepian-Mehr, who served as Chairman of the Council of Protestant Ministers and Secretary General of the Assemblies of God church, was abducted in February and found dead a few days later. Prior to his murder, Reverend Hovsepian-Mehr reportedly refused to sign a declaration from the then Ministry of Islamic Guidance stating that Iranian Christians enjoyed full constitutional rights.

- The Reverend Tateos Michaelian, the pastor of St. John Presbyterian Evangelical Church in Tehran and acting chairman of the Council of Protestant Ministers (a position he assumed after the abduction of Reverend Hovsepian-Mehr), was abducted in June. According to the Iranian government, the Reverend Michaelian's body was discovered in July stuffed into a large freezer with bullet wounds in the throat and the back of the neck. The State Department feels the Iranian government bears responsibility for trying the Reverend Dibaj for apostasy and fostering an atmosphere of religious intolerance.
- A German engineer, Helmut Szimkus, was released from Evin prison in Tehran on July 1, 1994, after serving five and one-half years on charges of spying. Szimkus later told reporters that he was tortured in prison and claimed that he had witnessed guards torture children in the presence of their parents to extract confessions from the adults.
- In 1994, Azizollah Amir Rahimi, a former general, distributed open letters and gave interviews to the foreign media, in which he called on President Rafsanjani to step down and organize free elections. Rahimi and his son were reportedly detained on November 1, 1994 for his comments. No information on the status of their cases was available as of the end of 1994.
- In October, 1994, 134 prominent writers distributed an open letter protesting excessive official censorship. In response, the Ayatollah Ahmad Jannati delivered a sermon on November 11, in which he warned that Muslims might take some unspecified "action" against the writers. The semi-official Tehran Times cautioned against freedom of speech, editorializing that such freedom permits the publication of "unsocial, immoral and seditious articles."
- In February, security forces reportedly killed a number of Sunni Muslims, who staged a demonstration in the city of Zahedan to protest the Iranian government's destruction of a local mosque. In August, a large spontaneous demonstration broke out in the city of Qazvin after the Majlis rejected a proposal to designate the city as a separate province. The Iranian government dispatched troops to quell the disturbance, which reportedly attracted up to 100,000 demonstrators. During their efforts to restore order, the troops reportedly killed dozens of demonstrators and wounded hundreds.

There was no improvement in 1995. Iran continued a systematic process of extrajudicial killings and summary executions. There were reports of widespread use of torture, disappearances; arbitrary arrest and detentions, a lack of fair trials, and harsh prison conditions. Iran continued to repress freedom of speech, press, assembly, association, and religion by peaceful critics and members of the opposition, and stepped up its repressive efforts during the period before the March, 1996 elections for the Majlis.

In March, 1995, the United Nations Human Rights Commission (UNHRC) extended the mandate of its Special Representative on Human Rights in Iran for another year. In August, the UN's Sub-Commission on Prevention of Discrimination and Protection of Minorities approved a resolution condemning the "extensive and continuing human rights abuses" by the Iranian government. Similarly, in a 1995 report, the UN Special Rapporteur on Extrajudicial, Summary, or Arbitrary Executions noted "the persistent allegations of violations of the right to life in the Islamic Republic of Iran." Although the domestic press stopped reporting most executions in 1992, executions appear to have continued at a rate of several hundred a year.

The State Department country report on human rights for 1995 notes the following reports of Iranian abuse of human rights:

- The outlawed Kurdish Democratic Party of Iran (KDP-Iran) reported that the Government executed 10 of its members following their arrest for unspecified political activity. Seven of them were executed at Orumiyeh Prison in September. They were identified as Shahabadin Taheri, Sanar Taheri, Teymour Ibrahimi, Muhammad Amin, Avaz (sic), Rahiam (sic), and Rashid Abubakri. Another victim, Sayed Ibrahim Taheri of the village of Pirdabad, was reportedly tortured to death. His body was returned to his family in August. The last two victims were Khoda Karam Ibrahimi, who reportedly died after 2 years of torture at Kermanshah Prison, and Mohammad Ali Norouzi, who reportedly died after being tortured at Nagadeh Prison.
- According to the KDP-Iran, the Government arrested 26 Kurdish civilians from the regions of Orumiyeh and Salmas in August and September, and charged them with membership in that organization. The men were reportedly tortured and face the death penalty.
- An unidentified member of the Fedayeen, an outlawed Marxist group, was reportedly executed for political activity in the city of Langrud in 1995.
- Security forces reportedly used excessive force in crowd control. In April they opened fire on crowds of demonstrators protesting high fuel and water prices in Islamshahr and Akbarabad, two poor suburbs of Tehran. At least a dozen demonstrators were reportedly killed.

- According to the international human rights group, PEN, the body of Ahmad Miralai, an author and translator, was discovered under suspicious circumstances in an alley in Tehran on October 24. Earlier that day, Miralai had been scheduled to introduce author V. S. Naipaul at a lecture. Government officials initially informed Miralai's family that Miralai had died of a stroke. Following an autopsy, whose results have not been released, the family was informed he had died of a heart attack. Miralai was one of the 134 prominent writers who in 1994 had signed an open letter protesting excessive official censorship.
- Amnesty International reported in 1995 that Haji Mohammad Ziaie, a leader of Iran's Sunni Muslim community, died in July 1994 under suspicious circumstances following his interrogation by security forces in the city of Laar. Five days after receiving a summons to report to the local security forces in Laar for questioning, Ziaie's body was found mutilated some 200 kilometers from the city. Ziaie was a critic of the Government's treatment of Iran's Sunni Muslims.
- On July 10, 1995, three members of the Mojahedin-e Khalq, an Iranian group advocating the overthrow of the Government, were assassinated in Baghdad, Iraq. Investigations of Iranian state-sponsored terrorism abroad continued in 1995. For example, the trial of Kazem Darabi, an Iranian charged with murdering four Iranian Kurdish dissidents in Berlin in 1992 under instructions from the Iranian Government, continued in Germany.
- According to Human Rights Watch, the Government arrested Java Rouhani, the son of the Grand Ayatollah Sadeq Rouhani, along with 24 of the Ayatollah's followers in the city of Qom, in July. The detainees were still being held without charge at an undisclosed location at the end of 1995.
- In January 1996, the government released Abbas Amir Entezam, a former deputy minister in the government of Prime Minister Mehdi Bazargan. Entezam had been arrested in 1979 on charges of espionage and sentenced to life in prison.
- Adherents of the Baha'i faith continued to face arbitrary arrest and detention. The Iranian government appeared to adhere to a practice of detaining a small number of Baha'is at any time. The Ayatollah Mohammed Yazdi, Iran's chief judge, stated in May, 1996 that, "In Iran, all religious minorities are free to practice their religion, but Bahaism is not a religion but an espionage network."[140]
- Iran also imprisons Jews and Christians. Two Jews were believed to be in prison in early 1996 because of their religion, and a Christian leader named Beni Paul was also reported to be in detention.

- In January and in June, 1995, Grand Ayatollah Sadeq Rouhani, a preeminent clerical leader, issued two public letters criticizing the government. His second letter criticized arbitrary detention, torture, and extrajudicial killings. The government reportedly detained 25 of his followers from the city of Qom, including his son, Javad Rouhani, apparently because of Rouhani's criticism. The detainees are being held without charge in an undisclosed location.
- In March, 1995, Ayatollah Ebrahim Haj Amini-Najafabadi was prevented from completing a sermon at a mosque after he made critical remarks about the government. The following week, Ayatollah Ali Akbar Meshkini-Qomi protested: "When a person like Ayatollah Amini . . . who is pious from head to toe and loves Islam . . . says something, gives a word of advice, it is not right to censor his remarks."
- The government banned former Interior Minister Mohtashami from delivering a speech on August 16, 1995, at the Teacher Training University in Tehran.
- Paramilitary vigilante groups known as the Hezbollahi and Basiji have harassed public speakers. In July, 1995, such vigilantes incited a crowd to attack prominent Islamic intellectual Abdol Karim Soroush, who was delivering a speech in a mosque in Tehran on Shi'ite theologian Ali Shariati. After the attack, more than 100 professors signed a letter to President Rafsanjani complaining about the incident. In October a Hezbollahi mob prevented Soroush from delivering a scheduled speech at the University of Tehran. Because of these incidents, Soroush left Iran in December out of fear for his safety. In July a mob disrupted a memorial service held in Tehran for Karim Sanjabi, a former foreign minister in the government of Mehdi Bazargan and a leader in the constitutionalist group, the National Front. These efforts were stepped up sharply in April and May, 1996.
- Iran seems to have sharply stepped up its political assassinations of exiles in 1996. It killed at least three members of the Mujahideen-e Khalq in the first four months of 1996, including the killing of Zahra Rajavi in Istanbul on February 20, 1996. It also killed two members of other opposition groups. There were also growing reports that the security forces were locating the family members of exiles that were still iving in Iran and forcing them to write or call exiles and plead with them to halt political activity.[141]
- There are unconfirmed reports that the Iranian government executed up to five men in Tabriz in May, 1996, after public demonstrations over the government's efforts to force Mohammed Ali

Chehrgani to resign from parliament, and left their bodies hanging on construction cranes.

An Uncertain Rule of Law

The US State Department and Amnesty International claim that there are serious weaknesses in the Iranian criminal justice system, which aid the regime in dealing with political and religious opponents. Like a number of other Gulf states, Iran has two court systems: the traditional court system, which adjudicates civil and criminal offenses; and the Islamic Revolutionary Courts, which were established in 1979 to try "political" offenses, narcotics crimes, and "crimes against God." Many aspects of the pre-Revolutionary judicial system survive in the civil and criminal courts. For example, defendants have the right to a public trial, may choose their own lawyer, and have the right of appeal. However, there is no jury system, rather, trials are adjudicated by panels of judges.[142]

Moreover, in the absence of post-Revolution laws, the Iranian government advises judges in civil courts to base their decisions on Islamic law. Civil courts are not fully independent. The revolutionary courts may also consider cases normally in the jurisdiction of the civil and criminal courts and also may overturn their decisions. Assigning cases to either system of courts appears to be done on a haphazard basis. The Supreme Court has limited authority to review cases.

Defendants tried in the revolutionary courts are given very different kinds of trials. These defendants are often held in prolonged pretrial detention without access to attorneys and their attorneys are rarely afforded sufficient time to prepare their defense. Defendants are often indicted for such vague offenses as "moral corruption," "anti-revolutionary behavior," and "siding with global arrogance." Defendants do not have the right to confront their accusers or the right to appeal. Summary trials of five minutes are common. Some trials are conducted in secret. Others are show trials intended to highlight a coerced public confession. Two highly publicized show trials occurred in 1994: one for a person accused of bombing a religious shrine in Mashhad, the other for a person accused of bombing Ayatollah Khomeini's tomb near Tehran. The Iranian government also accused the charged individuals with membership in the Mujahideen-e Khalq. Rather than conduct a genuine investigation into the bombings, the Iranian government linked them to the murders of the Evangelical Christians and characterized all of these events as a Mujahideen plot.

The Majlis approved a law reorganizing the court system in August, 1994, which made this situation significantly worse. Among its provisions, the law authorizes judges to act as prosecutor and judge in the same case. During 1995, the government began implementation of this law reorganizing the court system. The rights of defendants have been further eroded by the fact that many judges retired after the Revolution, and others were disbarred for ideological reasons. The government has replaced them with judges who are regarded as politically acceptable to the regime.

Treatment of Political Prisoners and Dissidents

Although the Iranian constitution prohibits arbitrary arrest and detention, human rights advocates charge that there is no legal time limit on incommunicado detention, or any judicial means to determine the legality of detention. Suspects may be held for questioning in jails or local Revolutionary Guard offices. The security forces often do not inform family members of a prisoner's welfare or whereabouts. Even if known, the prisoner still may be denied visits by family and legal counsel. In addition, families of executed prisoners do not always receive notification of the prisoner's death.

The US State Department indicates that there is no reliable information available on the number of disappearances of political prisoners in 1994. However, the UNCHR conveyed to the Iranian government in 1994 the names of 506 missing persons and the UN Special Representative issued a report in October which noted that he had requested the Iranian government to provide information on 78 reported political prisoners.

The State Department cites what it asserts are credible reports indicating that many detainees are held incommunicado in the period immediately following arrest and that the security forces continue to torture detainees and prisoners. Common methods of torture include suspension for long periods in contorted positions, burning with cigarettes and, most frequently, severe and repeated beatings with cables or other instruments on the back and the soles of the feet. There are many reports of flogging, stoning, amputations, and public executions are common.

Some prisoners are held in solitary confinement or denied adequate rations or medical care in order to force confessions. Female prisoners have reportedly been raped or otherwise tortured while in detention. In the past, prison guards have intimidated the family members of detainees and have sometimes tortured detainees in their presence. Although the Iranian Constitution states that "reputation, life, property, (and) dwelling(s)" are protected from trespass except as "provided by law," the State Department reports that Iranian security forces enter homes and offices, monitor telephone conversations, and open mail without court authorization.

Freedom of Opinion

Iran's critics charge that it has an equally bad record in dealing with freedom of opinion, academic freedom, and labor rights. The Iranian Constitution provides for freedom of the press, except when published ideas are "contrary to Islamic principles, or are detrimental to public rights." However, the State Department indicates that the Iranian government controls most publications. Newspapers are usually associated with various factions in the Iranian government. They may reflect different views and criticize the Iranian government, but are prohibited from criticizing the concept of the Islamic Republic or promoting the rights of ethnic minorities. The Iranian government sometimes harasses or shuts down independent publishing houses that are overly critical of public policy, although some independent publishers out of favor with the Iranian government continue to survive.[143]

No improvement has taken place in Iran's record in recent years. The Government exercised a heavy hand in censorship throughout 1995. In February the Government banned the daily newspaper, Jahan-e Eslam, after it had published editorials written by Ali Akbar Mohtashemi, a former Minister of Interior and a hard-line radical, which were critical of President Rafsanjani. The Government charged Jahan-e Eslam with violating Article 6 of the Press Law, which asserts the "importance of honoring religious sanctities and of respecting national interests and security."

In March, the Government banned the monthly magazine, Takapu, for printing "vulgar poems." In May, the Government banned the university student weekly, Payam-e Daneshjou, for "habitual defamation." The popular student paper was known for its criticism of government leaders, including President Rafsanjani. In October, the Government banned the daily newspaper, Tus, which is published in Mashhad and known for its criticism of the Government. A court convicted Tus's editor, Mohamed Sadeq Javadi Hessar, of "slander" and "divulging secrets." Hessar was sentenced to six months in prison and 20 lashes, but was later released on bail. The Government also seized an edition of the daily newspaper, Payam, reportedly because the paper published articles about embezzlement at the Bank-e Saderat, a corruption case which involved relatives of senior government officials.

The Government took other action to suppress freedom of the press and freedom of expression. In March the Ministry of Islamic Culture and Guidance introduced new regulations that expanded the Government's supervision of the film making industry. In response, 214 film-makers issued a public letter in June calling on the Government to ease these controls.

In June, the Government introduced a revised press law which would increase government control of the press. For example, it required journalists to obtain licenses from the Ministry of Islamic Culture and Guidance. One reporter for the newspaper Salam said in an interview that if the draft was enacted into law, the result would be "legal and clear censorship." The move was opposed by both journalists and the banned political party, the Freedom Movement. The draft law had not been approved by year's end.

The Ministry of Islamic Culture and Guidance is charged with pre-publication review of books to ensure that they do not contain offensive material. The Ministry inspects foreign printed materials prior to their release on the market. However, some books and pamphlets critical of the Government are published without reprisal. On August 22, 1995, a Hezbollahi group fire-bombed a bookstore in Tehran, because it sold a book titled "And God Laughs Only on Mondays." The author had received permission from the Ministry of Islamic Culture and Guidance for its publication.

Agence France Presse reported that arsonists kidnapped a bookstore employee and severely beat the man before releasing him. Later at a Friday sermon, Ayatollah Ahmad Jannati justified the attack, stating: "Propaganda, articles, speeches and books which are contrary to Islam and to public chastity and to the interests of the country are forbidden." He also said, "If someone acted on the basis of the imam's (Ayatollah Khomeini) guidelines, he should not be reprimanded by anybody."

The Iranian government owns all broadcasting facilities and their programming reflects its political and socio-religious ideology. In June, officials reportedly seized 1,995 satellite receiving dishes and videotapes in the port of Bandar Abbas. The Majlis passed a law in January, 1995 banning the import and distribution of satellite dishes and calling for the removal of existing satellite dishes. The law, however, has been declared unconstitutional by the Council of Guardians and its enforcement is uncertain.

The State Department also reports that academic censorship persists, even though restrictions on academic freedom have eased since the immediate post-revolutionary period. In May, 1995, Supreme Leader Khamenei said in a speech at the Islamic Open University that the university's atmosphere "must be protected from the penetration of poisonous and anti-Islamic thoughts" and that the university's administration "is justified in preventing the expression of any remarks against Islamic and revolutionary values." Iranian government informers are said to be common on university campuses. They also monitor classroom material.

Admission to universities is politicized; all applicants must pass "character tests," in which officials screen out applicants critical of the Iranian government's ideology. To achieve tenure, professors reportedly must cooperate with government authorities over a period of years.[144]

Labor has few rights to organize. Although the Labor Code grants workers the right to establish unions, there are no independent unions. A national organization known as the Worker's House, founded in 1982, is the sole authorized labor organization and serves primarily as a conduit for government control. Its leadership coordinates its activities with the Islamic labor councils that are organized in many enterprises. These councils also function as instruments of government control, although they have frequently been able to block layoffs and dismissals. Moreover, a network of government-backed guilds issues vocational licenses, funds financial cooperatives, and helps workers find jobs. The Iranian government does not tolerate any strike deemed to be at odds with its economic and labor policies. In 1993 the Parliament passed a law prohibiting strikes by government workers. It also prohibits government workers from having contacts with foreigners and stipulates penalties for failure to observe Islamic dress codes and principles at work. Workers do not have the right to organize independently and negotiate collective bargaining agreements.[145]

The Constitution permits assemblies and marches "provided they do not violate the principles of Islam." Numerous unplanned demonstrations occurred throughout Iran in 1994. The Constitution also provides for the establishment of political parties, professional associations, and religious groups provided they do not violate the principles of "freedom, sovereignty, (and) national unity," or question Islam or the Islamic Republic.

In practice, most independent organizations are banned, co-opted by the Iranian government, or moribund. In February, the Ministry of Interior granted licenses to some 80 political and professional organizations out of an estimated 400 applications. No major opposition faction was evident among the licensed groups.

The persecution of members of other religions is another indication of Iran's lack of "moderation." The Iranian Constitution recognizes Christianity, Judaism, and Zoroastrianism. Members of these religions elect representatives to reserved Parliamentary seats. They are supposed to be free to practice their religion and instruct their children, but the Iranian government interferes with the administration of their schools and harassment by government officials is common. Christian, Jewish, Zoroastrian, and Baha'i minorities suffer from varying degrees of officially sanctioned discrimination, particularly in employment, education, and public accommodations.[146]

Non-Muslims may not proselytize Muslims, and Muslims who convert to Christianity suffer discrimination. University applicants are required to pass an examination in Islamic theology. Although all public-school students receive instruction in Islam, it is usually insufficient to provide most religious minorities with the knowledge they need to pass university entrance exams. Applicants for public-sector employment are screened for their adherence to Islam. Religious minorities also suffer discrimination in the legal system, receiving lower awards in injury and death lawsuits and incurring heavier punishments than Muslims. Sunni Muslims encounter religious discrimination at the local level as well.[147]

The Iranian government regards the Baha'i community, the largest non-Muslim minority with 300,000 to 350,000 members, as a "misguided sect." It prohibits Baha'is from teaching their faith and from maintaining links with co-religionists abroad. In 1993, the UN Special Representative reported the existence of a government policy directive on the Baha'is. According to this directive, the Supreme Revolutionary Council instructs government agencies to block the progress and development of the Baha'i community; expel Baha'i students from universities; cut the Baha'is' links with groups outside Iran; restrict the employment of Baha'is; and deny Baha'is "positions of influence," including those in education. The Iranian government has claimed the directive is a forgery. However, it appears to be an accurate reflection of current government practice.[148]

In October 1993, the Iranian Majlis approved legislation that prohibits government workers from membership in groups that deny the "divine religions." The Iranian government used such terminology to describe members of the Baha'i faith, and members of the Baha'i faith continued to face arbitrary arrest and detention. The persecution of Baha'is persisted unevenly in 1994. The government continued to return some property previously confiscated from individual Baha'is, but the amount returned was a fraction of the total seized. Property belonging to the Baha'i community as a whole, such as places of worship, remained confiscated.

Other government restrictions were eased, so that Baha'is could obtain food ration booklets and send their children to public schools. However, the prohibition against the admission of Baha'is to universities still appears to be enforced. Thousands of Baha'is who were dismissed from government jobs in the early 1980s receive no unemployment benefits and are required to repay the Iranian government for salaries or pensions received from the first day of employment. Those unable to do so face prison sentences.[149]

As has been noted earlier, the US State Department reports that the Iranian government has tolerated—if not encouraged—violent action against Christian ministers who attempt to proselytize Muslims. It also seems to have imprisoned several Jews for similar behavior. The government permits Iranian Jews to travel abroad, but often denies them the multiple-exit permits normally issued to other citizens. The Iranian government does not normally permit all members of a Jewish family to travel abroad at the same time.

The Problem of Perspective

It is difficult to put these criticisms of Iran's actions into perspective. Any reporting on Iran's internal security apparatus is necessarily second-hand, since Iran does not allow the UN Special Representative to visit Iran for the purpose of making fact-finding trips relating to human rights, nor does it cooperate with most foreign human rights groups.

Critics of US government and other human rights reporting on Iran feel that many reports ignore a significant relaxation of Iranian internal security activity and focus on worst case incidents. They feel that Iran remains divided between moderates and extremists, but that the overall trend has been positive. They point to the fact that the Iranian government hosted a German-Iranian Human Rights Seminar in Tehran in November 1994. It permitted the German participants to visit a prison in Isfahan, and permitted a second visit by journalists to Evin prison in Tehran. They note that Iran has established a human rights committee in the Majlis and a human rights commission in the judiciary, and some echo the view of Iranian government officials that Iran should be judged by Islamic, rather than Western, human rights principles. Such critics point out that human rights reporting is often over-critical of the regime, accepts exaggerated reports of human rights abuses, and fails to understand legitimate internal security needs or to distinguish violent and extremist opponents of regimes from legitimate and peaceful political opposition.

It is also important to remember that human rights abuses and authoritarian behavior cannot be translated into any conclusions about Iranian aggressiveness in dealing with other states, or its efforts to export revolutionary and extremist behavior. There are many governments in the world that are routinely guilty of such abuses, including secular governments like that of Algeria. The US and its allies have strategic and economic relations with many authoritarian regimes and many regimes that are guilty of human rights abuses—in fact, it is doubtful that a successful global strategy could be based solely on relations with "good" governments or that the global economy could function in any other way.

Nevertheless, the charges currently made about Iranian internal security operations raise very important questions about the true nature of the Iranian regime. They make a powerful case that the government's economic pragmatism has been more a sign of opportunism than moderation, and that Iran's revolutionary ideology continues to shape the operations and attitudes of its government. Such criticisms have also been reinforced by less formal reporting on Iranian crackdowns on peaceful critics and dissidents in preparation for the 1996 elections, new internal security exercises by the Revolutionary Guards and Basij, and the growing harassment of private citizens by the Hezbollah.

4

Demographics and Ethnic Pressures

The current trends in Iran's politics and internal security efforts may provide the most important indications of the current nature of Iran's regime, and of the direction it may take in the future. There are, however, other factors that are likely to play a major role in shaping Iran's stability and its relations with its neighbors. These include population pressures, ethnic divisions, and the longer term trends in Iran's ability to exploit its oil and gas resources.

Population Growth

Regardless of the nature of Iran's ruling elite, Iran's population growth will be a demographic time-bomb. Iran's population has already risen from 37 million people in 1979 to over 64 million in 1995—an increase of nearly 30 million people. This increase in population has been coupled with massive rural migration to the cities, putting a further strain on Iran's deteriorating infrastructure, including housing and educational facilities. Roughly 45% of Iran's population is now 14 years of age or younger, and Iran has 3.2 million men and 3.0 million women between the ages of 18 and 22. To illustrate the rate of growth Iran must deal with, it has 3.8 million male and 3.7 million female students in the age group between 13 and 17.[150]

Iran must deal with a huge population of young job seekers and consumers whose material needs are not being satisfied. This group is steadily entering the job market and adding to the ranks of the unemployed in a stagnant economy. As Charts Eight, Nine, and Ten illustrate, a combination of demographic problems, revolution, war, and economic mismanagement have severely limited Iran's per capita wealth. While these charts show that there are definitional differences in estimates of Iran's population growth and per capita income, there are few differences in the estimate of overall trends. It is painfully clear that Iran's per capita

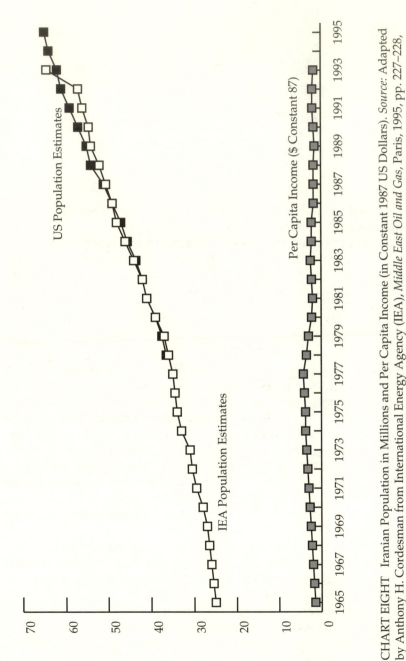

CHART EIGHT Iranian Population in Millions and Per Capita Income (in Constant 1987 US Dollars). *Source:* Adapted by Anthony H. Cordesman from International Energy Agency (IEA), *Middle East Oil and Gas*, Paris, 1995, pp. 227–228, IMF, *International Financial Statistics*, and OECD, *Main Economic Indicators*.

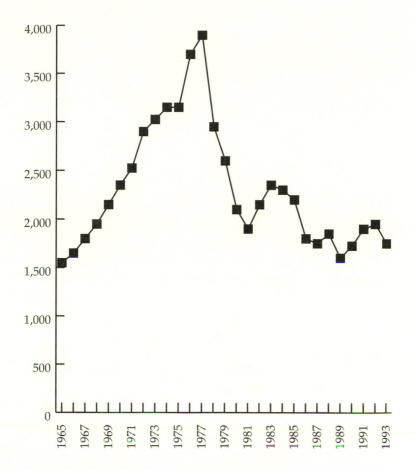

CHART NINE   Iranian Per Capita Income (in Constant 1987 US Dollars). *Source:* Adapted by Anthony H. Cordesman from International Energy Agency (IEA), *Middle East Oil and Gas*, Paris, 1995, pp. 227–228, International Monetary Fund, *International Financial Statistics*, and OECD, *Main Economic Indicators*.

income has not grown since the Iranian revolution, and that a combination of political factors, population growth, war, and economic stability have ensured that Iran's current per capita income is now roughly the same as it was before the oil boom began.

According to OECD and IMF estimates, Iran's population increased from 24.8 million in 1965 to 64.2 million in 1993—an increase of 2.6 times. Iran's per capita income was $1,527 in constant 1987 dollars in 1965. It peaked at $3,882 in 1978—just before the Shah's fall, and then slowly dropped throughout the Iran-Iraq War. It reach a low of $1,583 in 1988—

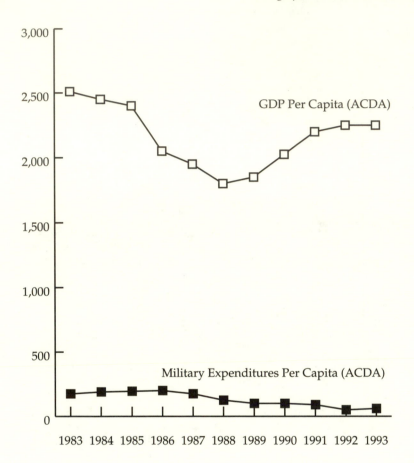

CHART TEN   Real GDP Per Capita in Iran versus Military Expenditures Per Capita: 1983–1993 (in Constant 1993 US$). *Source:* Adapted by Anthony H. Cordesman from ACDA, *World Military Expenditures and Arms Transfers, 1993–1994*, Washington, ACDA, 1995 and material provided by the CIA.

the year of Iran's defeat in the Iran-Iraq War—and then rose slowly to $1,774 dollars in 1993.[151]

US data show similar trends for the period of the Iranian revolution. Iran's real GDP per capita (in constant 1993 dollars) was roughly $1,500 in 1979—the year of the revolution—and dropped to less than $1,200 in 1993. Iran's population grew by around 50% during this period. They also show that Iran has been forced to keep military spending per capita at a relatively constant level, in spite of the drop in total per capita income.[152]

This drop in per capita income is only part of the story. Iran has failed to create new jobs for its youth at anything approaching the necessary rate. While Iran claimed that unemployment was 10–15% in mid-1993, the real figure was probably between 15% and 20%. It may well have reached 20–25% in 1995, including disguised unemployment. Population growth has sharply increased the strain on Iran's educational facilities over the past fifteen years. The number of students in primary schools has almost tripled from 7 million to 19 million since the revolution. As a result, spending on education now takes up more than a quarter of the official national budget.[153] The failure to expand and improve academic institutions has also led to a situation where some 1,000,000 students compete for 60,000 university admission slots annually—40,000 of which have been earmarked for the children of veterans, the IRGC, and members of the Basij militia.[154]

Iran has also done a dismal job of improving the distribution of its wealth. Just as the Shah's "white revolution" stole the wealth of Iran's land-owners and kept it, the Islamic revolution has stolen the wealth of the Shah and kept it. The wealthiest 10% of Iranians now earn about 27 times more than their poor compatriots, and the corruption of Iran's religious and revolutionary leaders and the Bunyods, and the nepotism of the revolution, increasingly discredit its claims to being truly "Islamic."[155]

Charts Eight, Nine, and Ten show that these problems will grow much worse in the future. Iran already has seen its real oil and gas income per capita drop by nearly 50% since 1979, and the prospects for future population growth are frightening. In fact, these population pressures have led the Rafsanjani government to become one of the few Middle Eastern states to actually promote birth control—reversing Khomeini's position on the issue. The Rafsanjani regime doubled population planning funding from $75 million to $150 million between 1991 and 1992.

The Iranian government has since claimed that these efforts have had considerable success and has issued estimates that Iran's population growth rate has dropped from 3.9% in 1985 to 2.7% in late 1991 and 1.75% in 1995. Iran's deputy health minister, Hossain Nalekafzali claimed that 23% of Iran's women were using the birth control pill, 14% had undergone surgical procedures such as tubal ligations, and 7% used intra-uterine devices. Six percent of all couples used condoms and less than 2% of men had undergone vasectomies.[156] These claims seem to be sharply exaggerated. Iran has not legalized abortion, almost always a key tool in producing dramatic drops in population rate. Overall, Iran's combination of legal birth control measures and illegal abortions is unlikely to have cut population growth below 2.3%–2.4%. Other estimates indicate that population growth is much higher than the government claims. The CIA

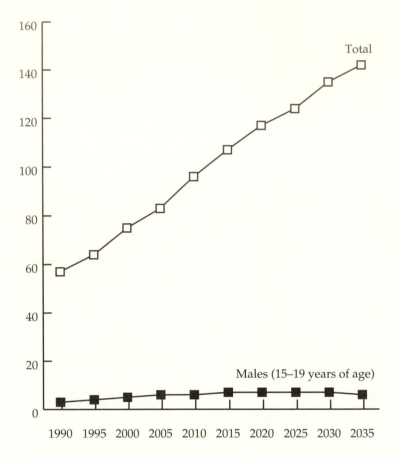

CHART ELEVEN   Estimated Trends in Iranian Population in 1990–2035. *Source:*
Adapted by Anthony H. Cordesman from World Bank, *World Population
Projections, 1994–1995,* Washington, World Bank, 1994 and material provided by
the CIA.

still estimated Iran's population growth rate at 3.46% in 1994, and at 2.3%
in 1995.[157]

This uncertainty about population growth has major strategic implications. Chart Eleven is based on a conservative World Bank estimate that
assumes Iran can limit its future population. The World Bank projects
that Iran's population will grow to 75 million by the year 2000, 96.0 million by 2010, and 117 million by 2020. If Iran's population growth continued at 3.5%, however, it would reach 80.5 million in 2000, 95.4 million in
2005, 113.1 million in 2010, and 158.9 million in 2020. If Iran cuts popula-

tion growth to an average of 2.7%, it will reach 77.0 million in 2000, 88.0 million in 2005, 100.5 million in 2010, and 131.2 million in 2020. Even if Iran's growth dropped consistently to 2%—a figure far lower than that achieved by most developing countries—Iran's population would still reach 73.9 million in 2000, 81.6 million in 2005, 90.1 million in 2010, and 109.8 million in 2020.

Even if Iran does succeed in sharply lowering its birth rate, the large number of children ensure that it will be nearly two decades before any population reduction will ease the growing demand for new jobs and or reduce the strain on Iran's economic, political, and social structure. Iran must deal with a population that already has 20% of its members under the age of five, and 45% under the age of fifteen.

Iran faces a "baby boom" of some 26 million Iranians born since the 1979 revolution who are now approaching the age of marriage. Even if its population reaches the conservative levels projected by the World Bank, it will still face major problems in job creation. The total number of young men reaching job age (14–19 years) will rise from 3.6 million in 1995 to 4.2 million in 2000, 5.1 million in 2005, 5.2 million in 2010, 5.7 million in 2015, and 6.1 million in 2020. In spite of a slight decline caused by improved population control, this age group will remain above 6 million beyond the year 2050.[158]

Ethnic Divisions

Iran's population problems have another dimension. Like Iraq, Iran has deep ethnic divisions. Iran's large population may give it the largest pool of military age manpower of any state in the Persian Gulf, but the ethnic divisions within this population present a number of political problems that may well limit Iran's ability to exploit its manpower base.

Iran is about 51% Persian, 24% Azeri, 8% Gilaki and Mazanderani, 7% Kurd, 2% Lur, 2% Baloch, 2% Turkmen, 1% Arab, and 1% other. Iran has less significant religious divisions than Iraq. It is about 90% Shi'ite Muslim, 8% Sunni Muslim, and 1% Zoroastrian, Christian, Jewish, and Baha'i.[159] Several of Iran's ethnic minorities have sought independence or regional autonomy. Kurds and Azerbaijanis have sometimes clashed with the government.

Iran also has a wide variety of linguistic groups. Only 58% of its population speaks Persian and Persian dialects, 26% speak some form of Turkish or Turkic dialect, 9% speak Kurdish, 2% speak Kuri, 1% speak Baloch, 1% speak Arabic, 1% speak Turkish, and other linguistic groups total about 1% of the population. These linguistic divisions present problems in military training and communications and reinforce the trend towards ethnic separatism.

At present, such ethnic divisions are more a source of political and social friction than a threat to the regime. They are neither a potential source of separatism nor a potential source of a new political elite. They do, however, present another important dimension of the problem Iran faces in regard to its population growth; if Iran cannot meet the economic needs of its people, these ethnic divisions may acquire far more political importance.

Population, Ethnic Divisions, and Dual Containment

The demographic issues may only have a limited near-term impact on Iran's politics and behavior towards other states. They are also scarcely atypical of the kinds of problems that exist in developing states. Nevertheless, they have several important implications for the future. One is that even the best of regimes will have great difficulty in meeting the economic expectations of Iran's youth over the next 10 to 20 years, and this may be a continuing source of political instability. It will be particularly difficult to achieve political popularity in terms of "bread," which may inspire a given regime to try to achieve popularity with "circuses" in the form of ideological movements or foreign adventures.

Iran's demographics also, however, raise serious questions about the economic aspects of dual containment. It is one thing to punish or isolate a regime and another to punish or isolate a people. Iran has now failed to manage growth and economic development for two decades. This failure began with the vaunting ambitions of the Shah, and was then compounded by an inherently unworkable revolutionary ideology, coupled with the impact of the Iran-Iraq War. Policies that deny Iran investment and development can only make thing worse. Furthermore, economic sanctions, embargoes, and measures that weaken Iran's economy and development capability without compelling changes in the behavior of its regime are almost certain to make its demographic problems worse and contribute further to its mid and long-term instability.

5

Economics and Iran's
Future as an Oil Power

Iran's future as an oil power is another major factor that must be considered in shaping policy towards Iran. Iran's oil and gas export revenues shape the health of its economy, and determine its military expenditures and its ability to fund economic development and recovery. They also determine much of Iran's behavior in dealing with other oil and gas exporting states, and the extent to which Iran can or cannot provide the levels of oil and gas necessary to meet rising world demand and keep oil and gas prices moderate.

Oil and gas resources are also the Iranian government's major source of revenues. It owns all of Iran's petroleum and utilities industries and banks, and the revenues that its draws from oil and gas exports fund 90% of the Iranian budget and some 60% of Iran's five year plan. The US Department of Energy indicates that Iran's oil export revenues were estimated at just over $14 billion in 1994, and were 77% percent of total export earnings.

Iran is trying to diversify the country's economy, and to reduce imports in order to stabilize the country's trade balance. It has had some success. Imports fell by about 30 percent in 1994, and dropped to $17.6 billion, while non-oil exports rose 16 percent. This improvement was aided by a March 1993 devaluation of the Iranian Rial as well as a subsequent depreciation of the currency during 1994. In February 1995, the Rial's market rate had dropped to 4,000 Rials per dollar from 2,500 rials per dollar a year earlier.

Iran's Oil Resources

Iran remains a major oil power, but there is considerable debate over how large Iran's oil reserves really are and just how large an oil power Iran will be in the future. A very conservative estimate of Iran's proven, economically recoverable reserves gives it 35.6 billion barrels of oil, or about

4.4% of the world total, and 497 trillion cubic feet (tcf) of gas, or about 12.9% of the world supply. Other estimates of Iran's reserves are much larger. *World Oil* has issued estimates of 61 billion barrels. *Oil and Gas Journal* has estimated 89 billion barrels.

The International Energy Agency (IEA) estimates that Iran has about 89 billion barrels, or about 9% of the world's reserves. The IEA also estimates that Iran has about 21 trillion cubic meters (tcm) of gas or 14% of the worlds total reserves.[160] A recent IEA estimate of how Iran's reserves and production compare to those of other Gulf states is shown in Table Five and Chart Twelve.

Iran has recently claimed reserves of 96 billion barrels and 950 trillion cubic feet of gas—claims of oil reserves which roughly matched those of Iraq and Kuwait during the same period. These claims seem inflated, but many US experts feel that Iran does have at least 93 billion barrels of oil. If these higher estimates are true, they would give Iran about 9–10% of world supply, or near "parity" with Iraq and Kuwait. Still other experts believe that a more demanding set of assumptions reduces Iran's recoverable reserves at current prices to only 65 billion barrels.[161]

The US Department of Energy reports that nearly two-thirds of Iran's oil reserves are located onshore, with most of the rest offshore in the Persian Gulf. More than half of Iran's 40 producing fields contain over 1 billion barrels of oil. The onshore Ahwaz, Marun, Gachsaran, Agha Jari, Bibi Hakimeh, and Pars fields alone account for about half of Iran's oil production. Most of these reserves are light oil, with gravities in the 30–39° API range and low sulfur content.[162]

Oil Production

The National Iranian Oil Company (NIOC) has controlled all aspects of Iranian upstream and downstream operations since the Iranian Revolution in 1979—a role legislated in the Petroleum Act of 1987. The Chairman of the NIOC is the Oil Ministry, and there is little practical difference between the ministry, the NIOC, and the government. The NIOC also controls several key subsidiaries: the National Iranian Drilling Corporation, the Iranian Offshore Oil Corporation, the National Iranian Tanker Corporation, and Naftiran Intertrade Company.

The trends in Iran's oil production are shown in Chart Thirteen, and the trends in Iranian oil revenues are shown in Chart Fourteen. These trends reflect sharp variations over time because of the impact of changes in oil prices, and the drop in Iranian oil production during the Iranian revolution and the Iran-Iraq War. They illustrate both the price Iran has paid for war and political instability, and the severe swings in oil export revenues imposed by the swings in oil prices.

TABLE FIVE   Comparative Oil Reserves and Production Levels of the Gulf States

Comparative Oil Reserves in 1994 in Billions of Barrels

Country	Identified	Undiscovered	Identified and Undiscovered	Proven	% of World Total
Bahrain	—	—	—	.35	
Iran	69.2	19.0	88.2	89.3	8.9
Iraq	90.8	35.0	125.8	100.0	10.0
Kuwait	92.6	3.0	95.6	96.5	9.7
Oman	—	—	—	5.0	NA
Qatar	3.9	0	3.9	3.7	0.4
Saudi Arabia	265.5	51.0	316.5	261.2	26.1
UAE	61.1	4.2	65.3	98.1	9.8
Total	583.0	112.2	695.2	654.1	64.9
Rest of World	—	—	—	345.7	35.1
World	—	—	—	999.8	100.0

(continues)

TABLE FIVE (continued)

Comparative Oil Production in Millions of Barrels per Day

Country	1995 Actual	1995 OPEC Quota	DOE/IEA Estimate of Actual Production 1990	1992	2000	2005	2010	Maximum Sustainable 1995	2000	Announced Capacity in 2000
Bahrain	—	—	—	—	—	—	—	—	—	—
Iran	3,608	3,600	3.2	3.6	4.3	5.0	5.4	3.2	4.5	4.5
Iraq	600	400	2.2	0.4	4.4	5.4	6.6	2.5	5.0	5.0
Kuwait	1,850	2,000	1.7	1.1	2.9	3.6	4.2	2.8	3.3	3.3
Oman	—	—	—	—	—	—	—	—	—	—
Qatar	449	378	0.5	0.4	0.6	0.6	0.6	0.5	0.6	0.6
Saudi Arabia	8,018	8,000	8.5	9.6	11.5	12.8	14.1	10.3	11.1	11.1
UAE	2,193	2,161	2.5	2.6	3.1	3.5	4.3	3.0	3.8	3.2
Total Gulf	—	—	18.6	17.7	26.8	30.9	35.0	23.5	28.2	28.2
World	—	—	69.6	67.4	78.6	84.2	88.8	—	—	—

Source: Adapted by Anthony H. Cordesman from estimates in IEA, *Middle East Oil and Gas*, Paris, OED/IEA, 1995, Annex 2 and DOE/EIA, *International Energy Outlook, 1995*, Washington, DOE/EIA, June, 1995, pp. 26–30, and *Middle East Economic Digest*, February 23, 1996, p. 3. IEA and DOE do not provide country breakouts for Bahrain and Oman. Reserve data estimated by author based on country data.

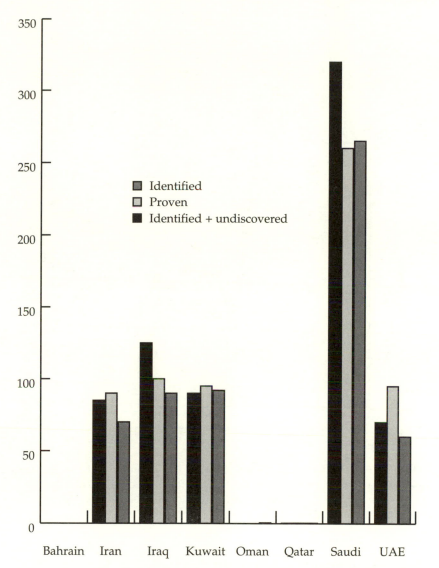

CHART TWELVE   Total Oil Reserves of the Gulf States (in Billions of Barrels).
Source: IEA, *Middle East Oil and Gas,* Paris, OECD, IEA, Annex 2, and data
provided by Bahrain and Oman. Bahrain's reserves are only 350 million barrels
and do not show up on the chart because of scale.

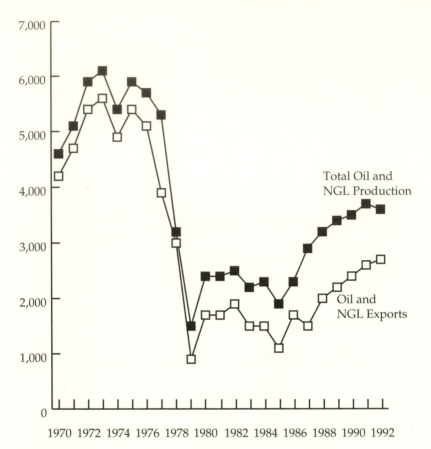

CHART THIRTEEN   Iranian Oil and Natural Gas Liquids Total Production and Exports (in Thousands of Barrels Per Day). *Source:* Adapted by Anthony H. Cordesman from International Energy Agency (IEA), *Middle East Oil and Gas,* Paris, 1995, pp. 232–236.

Trends in Oil Exports and Domestic Demand

Chart Thirteen shows that Iran's oil production and exports have tracked closely over time, but that both have been subject to major swings in volume during the last two decades. Iran's crude oil production peaked in 1974 at around 6.0 MMBD. Oil production then dropped as a result of revolution and war, and crude oil production only averaged 2.23 MMBD in 1988, some 58% lower than before the pre-revolutionary level of 5.26 MMBD (1978). An aggressive drilling and enhanced recovery program then allowed Iranian production to recover partially in the late 1980s and

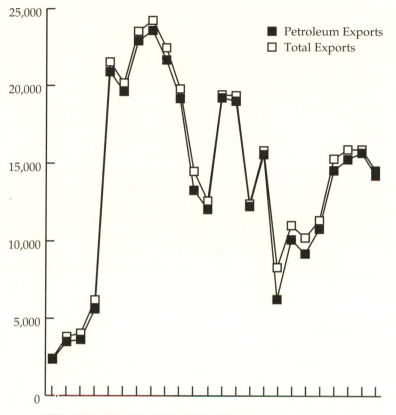

CHART FOURTEEN   Iranian Oil Exports versus Total Imports (in Millions of Current Dollars). *Source:* Adapted by Anthony H. Cordesman from International Energy Agency (IEA), *Middle East Oil and Gas,* Paris, 1995, pp. 227–228, and OPEC, *Annual Statistical Bulletin.*

1990s. Iran produced an average of about 3.1 MMBD of crude oil—and up to 3.6–3.7 MMBD worth of oil, NGL, and refined products—in 1994–1995.[163]

Oil, natural gas liquids (NGL), and refined produce exports—a key indicator of Iran's economic strength—reached a peak of nearly 5.6 million barrels per day (MMBD) between 1974–1979. A combination of revolution and the Iran-Iraq War then drove such exports to a low of 872 MMBD in 1980. Exports built back to nearly 2.0 MMBD during the first part of the Iran-Iraq War, but then dropped to 1.54 MMBD at war's close in 1988. Exports recovered to 2.0 MMBD in 1998, and rose to an average level of 2.7 MMBD in 1993.[164] Iran was able to exceed its OPEC export quota in 1993, and 1994.[165]

Chart Thirteen also shows the growing gap between Iran's exports and its total production of crude oil and NGL. This gap is the function of steadily growing domestic demand, triggered in part by population growth and in part by the sharp underpricing of oil and gas and the stimulation of grossly inefficient use of energy resources.[166] The stimulation of domestic demand has led to a major increase in the domestic use of oil and gas since the revolution, and domestic demand now totals the equivalent of roughly 1.0 MMBD.[167] Until 1995, the Iranian government sold petroleum products at much lower prices that either its Gulf neighbors or OECD countries—about $.025 per liter for gasoline. On March 21, 1995, however, the government doubled the domestic price of all oil products, and announced plans to gradually phase out all subsidies over the next five years. These measures are intended to cut the annual growth in domestic demand for refined products from about 6% per year to 3%, and to reduce domestic demand for crude by up to 300,000 bpd. It is far from clear, however, that the government can obtain popular support for such measures.[168]

Chart Fourteen shows that Iran's oil export revenues are affected as much by oil price as by political instability and war. At the same time, they show that even if oil revenues are measured in current dollars, Iran has never been able to approach the level of oil export earnings ii achieved in the mid to late 1970s. War and revolution cut Iran's oil export earnings sharply in 1980. While revenues recovered during 1981–1983, a drop in oil prices and cuts in exports then cut Iran's export earnings to from one-third to one-half of their pre-revolutionary levels. Although exports then recovered to about 75% of their pre-revolutionary levels in current dollars after the Iran-Iraq War, they had only about 40–50% of these levels in constant dollars. Put differently, Iran's total real oil revenues dropped by around 50% during a period its population increased by roughly 50%.[169]

The Structure of Iran's Oil Production Activity

Iran's total production capacity is controversial. In November 1994, Iranian Oil Minister Gholamreza Aghazadeh stated that the country's production capacity would reach 4.5 million b/d by mid-1995. Iran claimed to have carried out a public test in late 1992 that showed its capacity was 4.02 MMBD—with 3.6 MMBD onshore and 420,000 b/d offshore. The US Department of Energy reports, however, that two key fields were added into Iran's final calculations that were not operational. Industry observers estimate Iran's present sustainable capacity at around 3.6–3.7 MMBD, although a surge capability of 4 MMBD may be possible.[170]

Although Iran's average oil exports met its OPEC quota of 3.604 million barrels in 1994 and 1995, monthly production fluctuated by as much as 200,000 b/d. A confidential report by the National Iranian Oil Company (NIOC) concerning oil field production problems was leaked to the Iranian press in January, 1995, showing that the NIOC had problems in maintaining production levels at its major fields, most of which are mature, fragile structures. Analysts interpreted this "seesaw" effect in production as being the result of a lack of water separation capacity and not simply natural depressurization. According to observers, most NIOC well-heads can handle only 5–10 percent water-cut. In order to solve the water problem, NIOC must rest the fields temporarily to allow water to settle and natural pressure to increase. This means Iran's capacity will not rise above 4 million b/d without an increase in its water separation capacity.[171]

There is broad agreement that Iran must aggressively adopt gas injection and advanced reservoir production control techniques, carry out a major drilling effort with extensive use of horizontal drilling, and develop new offshore fields and wells. This helps explain why Iran's number of new, completed wells expanded from 23 in 1988 to 99 in 1992, and why the NIOC hopes to spend over $1 billion to discover 200–400 million barrels of recoverable oil during 1996–2000. The NIOC is also seeking to increase offshore production by 1 MMBD by the year 2000, and funds and technology to support gas gathering and injection projects, rehabilitate offshore fields, and increase the use of secondary recovery techniques. Iran needs outside capital and technology to carry out such a program, which has been a key factor behind its efforts to obtain foreign investment and support.[172]

Iran has a large domestic network of pipelines, but currently no pipelines for exporting oil. It has, however, signed a protocol with Turkmenistan to create a pipeline to bring in oil from Turkmenistan that Iran could use to meet domestic demand in the north, while exporting more crude in the south. Iran has seven terminals for exporting crude oil and two for exporting refined product. The crude oil terminals at Kharg Island, Lavan Island, and product terminals at Abadan and Bandar Masher were damaged during the Iran-Iraq War and their exact export capability is unknown. Iran claims that reconstruction is complete and that its terminals have a total capacity of 7 MMBD.

All of Iran's crude oil exports from its onshore fields are currently shipped from its Kharg Island terminal located in the northern Gulf. The terminal's original capacity of 7 million barrels per day was nearly eliminated by more than 9,000 Iraqi bombing raids during the

Iran-Iraq War, but Iran has rebuilt its facilities. Some $230 million in repairs to Kharg Island were completed by France's ETPM and South Korea's Daewoo by mid-1994. Kharg's present capacity is at least 5 MMBD, and its piers can handle tankers of 250,000 dead weight tons (dwt), while its Sea Island can handle tankers of 500,000 dwt, and its Darius terminal can handle tankers of 150,000 dwt. Iran can also export smaller amounts of offshore crude oil from terminals on Lavan Island, and has unused terminals at Cyrus and Ras Bah Regan in the southern Gulf. It has transhipment facilities at Larak Island and Sirri Island. It processes refined products at the Abadan refinery and exports them from both Abadan and Bandar Mahshar, which can handle tankers up to 60,000 dwt.[173]

Iran also has large strategic reserves of oil to reduce its vulnerability to attacks on its production and shipping facilities. It is building a total of 15.5 million barrels of storage at Kharg and has storage facilities in Rotterdam, Le Havre, and Greece, and reached an agreement with South Africa in July, 1995, to lease 15 million barrels of capacity at the 45-million barrel storage facility at Saldanha Bay near Cape Town.[174]

Iran has a tanker fleet of at least two ULCCs, ten VLCCs, and ten refined product carriers. It will receive two more VLCCs in 1996 and three more in 1997. It has plans to order 16 more carriers, but has lacked the funds to order more ships. Iran has, however, chartered additional tankers to make up for the loss of the carrying capacity of US oil companies.[175]

Japan has consistently been Iran's largest single market for crude oil sales, although the way Iran markets its oil has changed with time and has been affected by US sanctions. Iran has shifted most of its sales of crude oil exports from the flexible spot arrangements, which were prevalent in the industry in the early 1990s, to the quarterly term contracts. In the process, the NIOC imposed both destination restrictions, eliminating a buyer's ability to resell Iranian crude, and dropped several large Western traders including Glencore and Philbro.

The role of US companies in distributing Iranian oil has also changed with time. US companies bought about 6.8% of Iranian crude in 1991, 19.2% in 1992, 23.2% in 1993, and 23.3% in 1994, although US imports of Iranian oil halted in 1993, and had been well below 100 BPD since 1987.[176] In the first quarter of 1995, Iran shipped an estimated 2.6 MMBD of crude oil exports. These exports were bought by companies or subsidiaries based in Europe (35%), Asia (32%), the United States (23%), South Africa (10%), and Brazil (0.02%).[177] The major US companies which had term contracts to purchase Iranian crude oil included Exxon (250–300,000 barrels per day); Coastal (130,000); Bay Oil (70,000); Caltex (60,000); and Mobil (40–50,000).

The new sanctions the US adopted in March 1995, forced all US-based companies to stop selling Iranian oil to foreign markets. Forcing US companies to terminate their contracts had relatively little impact upon Iran's exports, however, because US sanctions had already prevented the import of Iranian oil into the US and the majority of Iran's crude oil was destined for refineries in Europe and Asia. There were already 44 other buyers of Iranian crude at the time the US imposed sanctions, and European and Asian firms were soon able to replace the US companies. Further, Iran chartered 28 ULCC and VLCC tankers to store any surplus oil production and help distribute its production.[178]

If one looks at typical levels of oil exports before and after sanctions, Iran exported 2.445 MMBD in September 1995, and 2.745 MMBD in October, 1995. It produced a total of 3.7 MMBD in August, 3.495 MMBD in September and 3.795 MMBD in October. Iran had to offer some price incentives to maintain these levels of exports, but it had succeeded in expanding its European markets since the enforcement of new US sanctions, and its exports to Asia in October 1995 totaled 839,000 BPD—slightly higher than its exports of 812,000 barrels per day in 1984 when US-owned oil companies still played a role in oil distribution. Iran has also projected that its average monthly exports will rise from 2.54 MMBD in 1995 to 2.82 MMBD.[179]

There is no evidence that the US policy of containment has had a significant impact on Iran's export revenues relative to the normal fluctuations due to changes in world oil prices. Iranian annual oil and gas exports had a total value of $14.6 billion in 1994/1995, $14.8 billion in 1995/1996. They are projected to drop to $14.5 billion in 1996/1997, but this is due to a weaker oil market, not US sanctions. The IEA and independent experts then project them to rise to $15.0 billion in 1997/1998, $15.2 in 1998/1999, and $15.5 billion in 1999/2000—almost exactly the same level of annual earnings, relative to estimates of world prices, that the IEA made before the US prevented US-based oil companies from distributing Iranian oil.[180]

Iran's trading patterns reflect an increase in exports to several key customers and an effort to reduce imports. US exports to Iran reached only $267 million during the first half of 1995, and halted completely after new US sanctions were imposed. Japan's exports to Iran totaled $496 million during the first three quarters of 1995, a drop of 46% over a similar period a year earlier, although Iranian exports to Japan still totaled $2.1 billion—a drop of only 3%. While it is impossible to make direct comparisons in terms of similar time periods, Italian exports to Iran were down 47% and imports were up 40%, German exports to Iran were down 17% and imports were down 8%, French exports to Iran were down 17% and imports were up 5%, UK exports to Iran were up 5%

because of sales of oil equipment the US would no longer supply but imports from Iran were up 10%. The UAE as a whole did not report on trade with Iran, but Dubai exported $478 million in the first quarter of 1995 and imported $118 million. Dubai's exports had shrunk by 25% over the previous period because of an Iranian crackdown on smuggling and the use of hard currency.[181]

As a result, this aspect of US dual containment policy may prove to be more of an irritant to Iran than anything else. In fact, it may well cost US-based companies more in oil revenues than it costs Iran in oil export income.

Rehabilitating and Expanding Oil Production

Iran is investing heavily in rehabilitating and expanding its oil production. The National Iranian Oil Company has concentrated on frontier exploration efforts, hoping to add 1–2 billion barrels to Iran's reserves by the year 2000 and to increase offshore production capacity from 467,000 barrels a day in 1995 to 1,103,000 barrels a day in 2000. Iran already has had some success. In 1993, it discovered a potential 1.4-billion barrel field near Abadan on the Iraqi border. In March, 1995, Iran discovered an onshore oil field with potentially-recoverable reserves of one billion barrels near the southern port of Ganaveh.[182]

The NIOC is actively exploring Iran's territorial waters in the Caspian Sea and claims to have identified over 40 reservoirs containing as much as 3 billion barrels of oil. In January, 1995, Iran allocated $17 million dollars over the next year for joint drilling efforts with Azerbaijan in the Caspian Sea. It plans to use Azeri and Finnish-built drilling rigs to explore the southeastern regions of the Sea.

The Clinton Administration has had some success in limiting such efforts. In February 1995, Azerbaijan offered Iran a fourth of its 20 percent stake in the $8-billion, multinational Caspian Sea development project. However, Western consortium members subsequently vetoed Azerbaijan's offer to Iran. The five percent Azeri stake was later extended to Exxon in April, 1995. That same month, the US government discouraged the possibility of an Iranian pipeline route for oil exports from Chevron's Tengiz field in Kazakhstan and Azerbaijan's Caspian Sea development.

The possibility of an Iranian swap arrangement is still under consideration for the early phases of the Azeri project. Under the scheme, output is scheduled to begin in mid-1997 with production reaching 80,000 b/d within 18 months. Azeri crude would be supplied to the 112,000 b/d Tabriz refinery for domestic Iranian consumption while Iran would provide the same amount of crude oil to the consortium in the Persian Gulf. Additionally, Azeri crude could be delivered to refineries in

Tehran, Isfahan, and Arak. Iran's total swap capacity is estimated at roughly 250,000 b/d.[183]

Iran's current 5-year oil development plan—which began in 1995—calls for the increased use of enhanced oil recovery (EOR) techniques as well as infill and development drilling. Iran will begin horizontal drilling in the larger fields in southwestern Iran, which account for three-quarters of Iran's total production. Iran hopes that gas injection projects will increase onshore capacity by 200–300,000 b/d by 1999. Most of this increase will come from the 550,000 b/d Marun, 100,000 b/d Karanj, and 80,000 b/d Parsi fields.

Iran's plans to develop its off-shore oil fields have focused on rebuilding damage incurred from Iraqi bombing of platforms and facilities during the Iran-Iraq War. The 140,000 b/d Salman, 110,000 b/d Dorood, 60,000 b/d Forozan, and 40,000 b/d Abuzar fields account for the bulk of Iran's off-shore production and need considerable investment. Iran is also seeking to expand offshore production and develop new fields.[184]

As a result, Iran is seeking foreign investment and has several programs underway which could involve major multinational oil companies. It plans a major gas injection project at the Dorood field near Kharg Island although this $1-billion development program had to be postponed after the loss of World Bank aid in 1993. Darood's associated gas, which presently is flared, was intended to be reinjected with the hope of doubling the field's production to 220,000 b/d.

Iran is seeking to boost its Forozan field which is part of the same structure as the Saudi Arabian Marjan field. Both countries are concerned that measures are taken to ensure optimum reservoir management. In 1994, Saudi Arabia boosted Marjan production from 100,000 b/d to 500,000 b/d with the introduction of two gas-separation plants. The NIOC is currently attempting to raise Forozan production from 60,000 b/d to 100,000 b/d, while recovering associated gas from the field's large gas cap.[185]

The Department of Energy reports that NIOC is actively exploring Iran's territorial waters in the Caspian Sea and that more than 40 reservoirs, containing as much as 3 billion barrels of oil, have been identified. In January 1995, Iran allocated $17 million dollars for joint drilling efforts with Azerbaijan in the Caspian Sea over the next year. Azeri and Finnish-built drilling rigs are being used to explore the southeastern regions of the Sea.

Iran has had serious problems in obtaining the investment it needs. It awarded a $270-million contract to rehabilitate and develop the Abuzar field to McDermott and France's ETPM in 1993. However, the project ran into financing difficulties, and the contract subsequently went to a state-owned Iranian company in November 1994. In February, 1995, NIOC was reported to have sought outside help in the field's development and Australia's Transfield Construction appeared close to winning the contract to boost Abuzar's production to 140,000 b/d.[186]

This need for investment helps explain Iran's effort to make a deal with Conoco. In March, 1995, Conoco announced that it had signed a 20-year, $550-million contract to develop the potential 485-million barrel Sirri A and E structures. These plans would have brought the combined production of the two fields to over 120,000 b/d and would have piped the associated gas 90 miles to Dubai for reinjection into other oil fields. The US government forced Conoco to cancel the deal, which also had not yet received Majlis approval, and President Clinton signed an executive order on March 17, 1995, banning Conoco's deal as well as any "contract for the financing of the development of petroleum resources located in Iran."[187] In addition, the United States placed stricter limitations on the purchases of Iranian oil by US companies and adopted new sanctions which affected other negotiations between US companies and Iran. Arco was discussing the possibility of developing the offshore Balal field, with a production potential of 35,000 b/d. Bechtel, Foster Wheeler, and McDermott were negotiating with Iran for offshore petroleum development projects.[188]

By July, 1995, however, Iran was able to negotiate a replacement deal with Total of France that effectively replaced Conoco.[189] The new contract will cost $600 million over a period of five years, and production from Sirri A (20,000 b/d) and Sirri E (100,000 b/d) is expected to begin in 1997–1998. Tehran radio announced that the French deal would have the same terms and that Iran was negotiating with the Royal Dutch/Shell Group for investments in other fields. This involved a "buyback" arrangement under which Total will finance the project in return for part of the resulting flow of oil.[190] The NIOC also announced in July that it would invite foreign companies to invest in ten other oil projects. These include construction of a gas gathering system, building a second refinery at Bandar Abbas, and expanding the refinery on Lavan Island.[191]

It is too early to say whether US pressures and sanctions will have a major effect in limiting foreign investment in Iran's oil and gas projects. Iran's mismanagement of its economy, its debt burden, its need to expand and improve its oil fields, and its need for foreign capital and technology combine to make Iran vulnerable to the kind of pressure the US is trying to apply. As long as foreign investors see Iran's overall political situation and economic policies as uncertain, it may not take much additional pressure from the US to influence their decisions. At the same time, many European, Asian, and other investors seem unlikely to support US policy for any extended period of time if Iran adopts sounder economic policies, offers more reasonable investment incentives, and a high probability that its politics will protect their investment contracts. Russia and Azerbaijan

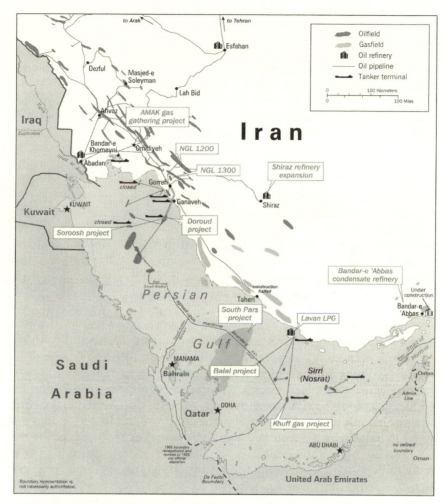

MAP TWO   Iran's Major Energy Projects

have already set up joint drilling companies with Iran, and the previous analysis has shown that many foreign companies are willing to explore investment opportunities in Iran.[192]

Further, this aspect of dual containment is a two-edged sword. It deprives US companies of an export market that is worth billions of dollars, and any US success in limiting outside investment creates the risk that Iran may not be able to produce enough oil to meet the goals called for in the projections of organizations like the International Energy Agency (IEA) and Energy Information Agency (EIA). Virtually all energy models that project moderate increases in world oil prices through 2010 are partially dependent on expanded Iranian oil production. The EIA, for example, projects Iranian oil production at 4.3 MMBD in 2000, with a possible range of 4.2–4.7 MMBD. It projects Iranian oil production at 5.0 MMBD in 2005, with a possible range of 4.4–5.4 MMBD, and at 5.4 MMBD in 2010, with a possible range of 4.9–5.7 MMBD. These projections make Iran the third largest oil producer in the Gulf, with about 20% of all Gulf production.[193]

Domestic Energy Consumption and Energy Exports

Iran has growing problems in allocating its oil and gas resources to exports. As Chart Thirteen shows, Iran's rising domestic energy consumption is reducing the amount of crude oil it can export. In December, 1994, President Rafsanjani announced that increased domestic oil demand would reduce 1995 Iranian oil exports by 130,000 b/d. Much of the rise in domestic demand is the result of Iran's failure to reduce its population growth, coupled with poor economic and investment policies.[194]

Like most Gulf countries, Iran grossly underprices oil and gas relative to world market prices. This artificially stimulates demand and makes the nation structurally dependent on the misuse of energy, as well as depriving it of export earnings. Iran was also slow to distribute gas and develop efficient gas-fired electric generating plants. As a result, domestic demand for oil rose far more quickly than should have been the case, wasting Iran's critical resources. Further, the rise in domestic demand seems to have helped encourage Iran to buy nuclear reactors despite the fact that the higher life-cycle cost of electricity from nuclear plants is likely to be much greater than any additional export revenues Iran can earn from exporting oil and gas.[195]

The Iranian government did double domestic oil product prices in March, 1995, and announced plans to raise prices by 20% per year until 2000. Oil remains badly underpriced, however, and Iran has not made similar adjustments in the real price of gas; this risks trading one form of subsidy for another.[196]

Refineries and Refined Product

Domestic production of refined products grew at an annual rate of about 3.2% between 1971 and 1993, despite the revolution and war. Production totaled 1.07 MMBD in 1993, with 15% gasoline, 27% oil and diesel fuel, 30% residual fuel oil, 12% aviation fuel and kerosene, 10% LPG, and 6% other.

Iran presently has eight refineries with a throughput of 1.184 MMBD. This includes refineries with a capacity of 320,000 bpd in Abadan, 150,000 bpd in Arak, 281,000 bpd in Isfahan, 35,000 bpd in Kermanshah, 23,000 bpd in Lavan, 38,000 bpd in Shiraz, 112,000 in Tabriz, and 224,700 in Tehran.[197] Nevertheless, Iran has had to import refined products since 1982 because of Iraqi attacks on Iran's refineries. This has led to further demands on its foreign exchange resources, already strained by subsidized prices which have raised domestic demand. Iran's imports of refined products rose 115,000 b/d in 1993 to about 150,000 b/d in early 1994.

To deal with this problem, the NIOC is attempting a massive refinery expansion program that might allow Iran to begin exporting products by 2000. The Department of Energy reports that these expansion plans call for an increase in oil refining capacity from just under 1.2 million b/d at present to almost 1.7 million b/d by 1998. Iran has already made one important addition to its refinery profile by beginning operations at the 150,000 b/d Arak refinery in June, 1994. This $1.1-billion refinery has a 25,000 b/d hydrocracker and will be Iran's first producer of high-octane, unleaded gasoline.[198]

Iran is also constructing a 232,000 bpd plant at Bandar Abbas and a 70,000 bpd plant at Bandar Asaluyeh. Work on the Bandar Abbas plant has been delayed by financing problems, but it is planned to be completed in 1996. Work is over two-thirds complete on the $1.3-million Bandar Abbas refinery. This project was started by Italy's Snamprogetti and Japan's Chiyoda, but financing problems led local Iranian contractors to take over construction in mid-1994.

Another 70,000 b/d refinery is under construction at Bandar Asaluyeh. This refinery would process condensate from the Nar-Kangan gas fields. Contractors would be paid in "buy-back" financing with refined products after production start-up.[199] Iran would like to double the capacity of the Arak refinery, and expedite completion of the plant at Bandar Asaluyeh—which is scheduled to run condensate. Its goal is to raise throughput at Abadan to 370,000 bpd. These plans would raise total production capacity to 1,685,000 bpd by 1998–1999.[200]

The NIOC has tentative plans to build a 120,000 b/d refinery at Bin Qasim near Karachi, Pakistan. The proposed plant would cost $717 million and would be designed to process Iranian heavy crude oil. A feasibility study is underway in Vietnam for a possible 100,000 b/d refinery. Other plans for a proposed $3-billion, 225,000 b/d refinery at Chah Bahar on Iran's southeastern coast were postponed indefinitely in July, 1994 due to financing difficulties. In January, 1995, the NIOC announced a 5-year plan to install advanced computer control systems in its refineries to increase product quality and quantity.

Petrochemicals

Iran has invested heavily in petrochemical production, and has done so with some success. The Department of Energy and IEA estimate that Iranian petrochemical production of plastics, chemicals, and fertilizers has risen from 800,000 tons per year in 1989 to 5.5 million tons a year in 1993, and 8 million tons per year in 1995. This production level ranks second only to Saudi Arabia. It may also give Iran the capability it needs to produce feedstocks for chemical weapons.

Iran's current 5-year plan calls for Iran to expand its production capacity to 12–13 million tons per year by 2000—with a 300,000 ton petrochemical complex at Tabriz, a 490,000 ton fertilizer complex at Khorasan, and a 730,000 ton plant at Qeshem Island. The 1995 Iranian Budget calls for $3.8 billion in petrochemical investments over the next 5 years. This figure is slightly lower than the $5 billion invested under the previous 5-year plan.[201] Iran's state-owned National Petrochemical Company hopes to get much of this capital by introducing incentives which would allow 100 percent foreign ownership of ventures and for the creation of free zones, possibly at the petrochemical facilities in Bandar Imam.

Construction of a major new petrochemical plant at Kharg Island began in December 1994. When completed, the plant will produce 660,000-tons per year of methanol and 50,000-tons per year of acetic acid. Financing arrangements are underway for three similar plants at Bandar Imam and for a polymers complex at Isfahan. Once again, however, Iran lacks the required financing, and has not yet offered effective incentives for outside investment. Like its oil and gas projects, many of Iran's petrochemical projects are areas where Iran may be vulnerable to US pressure to limit or halt foreign investment.[202]

Natural Gas

The US Department of Energy and EIA estimates that Iran has natural gas reserves of roughly 21 million cubic meters or 742 trillion cubic feet (Tcf). This would make Iran's reserves the world's second largest after Russia, and equal to 14–14.9% of the world's supply.[203] A recent IEA estimate of the size and relative importance of Iran's gas reserves in shown in Table Six and Chart Fifteen. The trends in Iranian gas production and exports are shown in Chart Sixteen. They are complex, but close attention to the variations in production levels and use over given periods reveal the impact of the Iran-Iraq War, the unsettled import market in the FSU, the growing need for gas reinjection for oil production, and the growth in domestic demand resulting from both population growth and underpricing.

TABLE SIX Gulf and World Gas Reserves and Production

Nation	Reserves in 1995		Percent of World Supply	Production in 1993 (BCM)
	TCF	*BCM*		
Bahrain	—	—	—	—
Iran	741.6	21,000	14.9	60.0
Iraq	109.5	3,100	2.2	2.75
Kuwait	52.9	1,498	1.1	5.17
Oman	—	600–640	—	—
Qatar	250.0	7,070	5.0	18.4
Saudi Arabia	185.9	5,134	4.2	67.3
UAE	208.7	5,779*	4.2	31.63
Gulf	1,548.6	—	31.1	185.25
Rest of World	3,431.7	104,642	68.9	—
World Total	4,980.3	148,223	100.0	—

Note: *Other sources estimate 6,320–7,280 BCM for Abu Dhabi only.

Source: The reserve and production data are adapted by Anthony H. Cordesman from IEA, *Middle East Oil and Gas,* Paris, OECD, IEA, 1995, Annex 2.

Iran has made three large discoveries of over 200 Tcf of reserves since 1992. The largest of these new discoveries is the 100 Tcf South Pars gas field, which is an extension of Qatar's 241 Tcf North Dome Gas field. Iran discovered a 48-Tcf gas field at North Pars only 30 miles away and a third field, which may be an extension of the South Pars field. Iran is also completing the dual 13 Tcf Aghar-Dalan field development project which will supply gas via a 200-mile pipeline for reinjection into oil fields in the southern Fars region.[204] These discoveries significantly expand the areas where Iran has found gas. In the past, Iran's largest non-associated gas fields were the Sarakhs and Kangan fields located in northern and southern Iran, and most of Iran's associated gas production came from its Khuzestan region.[205]

Iran hopes to exploit such discoveries to make gas a major part of its export earnings. It announced a 20-year development program in 1990 that would boost its gas production to 10 Tcf per year by 2010. Part of this production increase will aid EOR reinjection projects and part will be exported to other countries. The plan calls for domestic sales of 260 billion cubic meters (bcm) a year by 2010, and exports of 50 bcm a year. The key areas of development are gas field developments, gas-fired power generation, expanded gas exports, and a greatly expanded pipeline network.[206]

This program again makes Iran dependent on foreign investment, although Iran has been able to finance some aspects of its program such

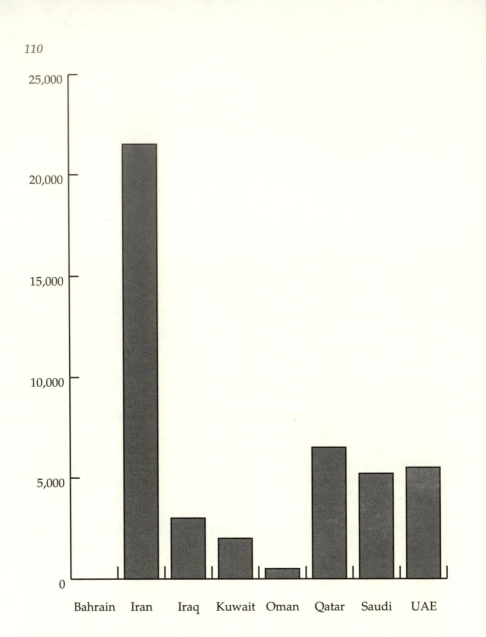

CHART FIFTEEN   Total Gas Reserves of the Gulf States (in Billions of Cubic Meters). *Source:* Adapted by Anthony H. Cordesman from IEA, *Middle East Oil and Gas,* Paris, OECD, IEA, 1995, Annex 2, and data provided by Bahrain and Oman. Bahrain's reserves are too small to show on the chart because of scale.

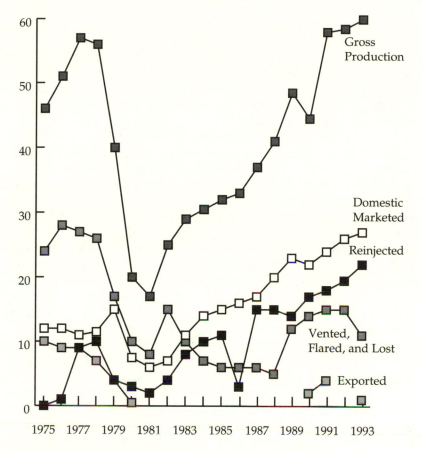

CHART SIXTEEN   Iranian Natural Gas Production (in Billions of Cubic Meters). *Source:* Adapted by Anthony H. Cordesman from International Energy Agency (IEA), *Middle East Oil and Gas,* Paris, 1995, pp. 252–256.

as the development of the 14 bcm Aghar-Dalan gas fields. Iran originally has $1.7-billion development plans for its South Pars field, based on a consortium composed of Italy's Saipem, TPL, and Japan's Mitsubishi. Consortium members canceled the agreement in January, 1994, however, due to Iranian financing problems. The contract then had to be awarded to NIOC's subsidiary, Petco (Petroleum Engineering and Development Company), which reduced development costs to only $900 million.[207]

In January, 1995, the NIOC announced that Royal Dutch Shell was negotiating to develop the large South Pars gas field, which ultimately is expected to produce 1 billion cubic feet (Bcf) per day of gas and 50,000 b/d of condensate. Shell completed a North Pars feasibility study in early 1994 with development plans that called for 3.6 Bcf per day of gas production. Approximately 1.2 Bcf of this output was be reinjected to the onshore Gachsaran, Bibi Hakimeh, and Binak oil fields. The other 2.4 Bcf would be sent to the more mature Agha Jari oil field. Talks stalled in January, 1995, however, when Shell asked for payment in crude oil rather than Iran's stipulation of natural gas.[208]

In March, 1995, the British firm John Brown signed a memorandum with Iran to participate in future South Pars development, but this seems to have been part of a revised NIOC plan that converted the Sotu Pars project to a scaled down effort which is broken up into smaller phases which will be funded through "buy-back" arrangements that will guarantee outside companies both recovery of their investment and a suitable rate of return.[209]

Iran needs major foreign investment if it is to be able to ship its gas exports. In January, 1995, Iran and Pakistan signed an agreement to ship up to 1.6 Bcf of South Pars gas via a 1,000-mile overland pipeline. Under the deal, Iran must provide at least $4.7 billion of the project's total $8.5-billion cost. Bidding for the construction contract began in July 1995, but the cost may well make the project impractical.

Iran is also examining ambitious projects to build pipelines from South Pars to India, and from northern Iran to Turkmenistan, Europe, Turkey, and the Ukraine. As of 1995, discussions were taking place over a proposed $4.5-$6 billion, 1,550-mile pipeline to carry Turkmen gas via Iran to Bulgaria or Turkey, and then to Western Europe. All of these projects present major financial uncertainties, and regional political uncertainties—as well as hostile pressure from the US. There have also been complications in getting payment for existing pipeline shipments. Iranian gas shipments to Azerbaijan through Iran's IGAT 1 pipeline were halted in 1993 because of non-payment, and work on an IGAT 2 pipeline to ship gas to the FSU was halted in 1993 for similar reasons.[210] It is far from clear that Iran can reach anything approaching its current goals for gas development and exports unless it creates radically improved incentives for foreign investment and reduces the political problems that it will surely face by creating pipeline agreements with the unstable countries to its north or ones that are vulnerable to political complications because of the India-Pakistan conflict.

These development problems will also affect domestic demand. Iran's domestic gas pipeline ships gas to about 3 million homes in 200 towns, and plans call for adding 85 towns and 1.7 million homes to the network by 1999. Gas-fired plants account for about 17,828 MW of power generation. Iran's plans call for an additional 18,000 MW by the end of 1998, with the majority being steam turbine or combine cycle plants that can use either oil or gas. There are few present prospects capable of meeting Iran's goals, but if gas was more reasonably priced the expansion of its domestic use might offer Iran a substantially more cost-effective use of resources than either massive pipeline projects or nuclear power plants. While reliable statistics are not available, gas is not so underpriced that domestic demand has been subject to the same distorted market conditions as demand for oil.

Oil, Gas, and Dual Containment

Iran's success or non-success in maintaining and expanding its oil and gas production will be a key factor in shaping its economic future and political stability. Iran remains a petroleum-dominated economy. It needs massive outside investment in its oil fields, gas fields, pipelines, refineries, and petroleum-related industries to rehabilitate its existing production capacity in order to approach its ambitious goals for the future. This explains why Iran held a conference in November, 1995 to attract such investment. It outlined 11 new oil development projects with a total value of around $6 billion, and it managed to attract some 40 European and Asian firms in spite of US pressure and the threat of US third party sanctions.[211]

So far, however, Iran has little prospect of attracting all of the investment it needs. Even Japanese companies who have shown a serious interest in the Iranian oil market have been reluctant to move ahead with pre-financing or other deals.[212] This failure is partly a result of pressure by the US and the threat of US sanctions against foreign companies. Most of Iran's problems, however, are self-inflicted rather than the result of US efforts at sanctions and containment. Iran's weal domestic economy has caused trouble in funding some of the activities that the government would like to self-finance, and Iran has failed to attract investment for several reasons. It needs to conduct far more direct and professional negotiations and stop attempting to change the terms of financing and negotiation in mid-stream.

Iran needs to provide more convincing evidence that its politics will not cause new crises and conflicts and its domestic politics will not lead to nationalizations or forced changes in the terms of an agreement. It needs to manage its debts and payments more effectively and without constant efforts to reschedule or slip payments due. It needs to offer substantially more attractive terms to outside investors, such as its new "buy back" programs. It needs to down-scale many projects or divide them into smaller phases to reduce investment cost and demonstrate feasibility. It seems probable that many technocrats in the NIOC understand these realities, but it is unclear that Iranian leaders and politics permit the NIOC to grant the necessary investment terms and incentives.

Unless Iran makes striking improvements in the financial terms it offers, it is likely to be vulnerable to US sanctions and financial pressures. Although most potential non-US investors are probably now deterred more by Iran's erratic financial terms and management of its negotiations than by US sanctions, even relatively marginal pressures on foreign companies and countries may be enough to make them shift investment funds to less controversial and risky opportunities. Japanese and French firms, and key foreign firms like Royal Dutch/Shell Group have already made this clear.[213]

At the same time, it must be stressed that the US government does not seem to be giving adequate attention to the potential cost of this aspect of "dual containment" in shaping its policy towards Iran. There are several major problems inherent in any US effort which increases Iran's structural economic problems:

- If Iran does offer new incentives and investment terms, it will take much more Draconian sanctions than the US is now imposing, and if it does not make such changes, the impact of US sanctions is likely to be limited.
- As is discussed in the following chapters, Iran can probably keep up its present military efforts, and programs to develop weapons of mass destruction, regardless of its problems with its petroleum sector.
- It is hard to see how strengthening economic sanctions can avoid increasing the West's problems with Iran, and aiding hard-line movements that demonize the US. It provides further ground for Iran to blame the US and outside powers for its failures to develop its oil and gas resources.
- Weakening Iran's oil and gas sector is unlikely to moderate its present or future behavior. If its plans to expand its exports fail and it is forced to seek maximization of oil and gas prices, Iran will be more prone to try to intimidate and threaten its neighbors, gaining revenues at their expense. In fact, Iran is more likely to be pragmatic in dealing with its Gulf neighbors if it enhances its oil and gas revenues.
- Weakening Iran's oil and gas sector increases the rationale for Iranian nuclear power plants, which inevitably eases Iran's problems in nuclear proliferation.

More broadly, the US has failed to address the conflict between its containment policy and its energy policy. US energy forecasts and policies call for a steady increase in Iranian oil and gas production, but Iran cannot easily sustain and expand its production to meet the goals projected in US estimates. The latest US forecasts of world dependence on oil exports are shown in Table Seven, and Charts Seventeen, Eighteen, and Nineteen, and they raise important questions about world energy balances if Iran cannot sustain its existing production capacity or make its planned increases in exports. These questions are particularly important, because US policy is also affecting the future ability of other "pariah states" like Iraq and Libya to meet their projected production levels.

There is no way to separate the economic dimension of containment from the political and military dimensions. US policy makers may well choose to argue that economic containment will have at least some impact on Iran's military build-up, thus offseting the potential cost of economic instability in terms of world oil prices, internal economic instability, and revanchism in reaction to US policy. The fact is, however, that dual containment has powerful negatives and economic sanctions that target the entire Iranian economy are a blunt instrument that may ultimately do more harm than good.

TABLE SEVEN Estimated Increase in World Oil Production by Region and Country

Country/Region	1990	1992	2000		2005		2010	
			Base Case	Range	Base Case	Range	Base Case	Range
OPEC	27.8	27.2	37.5	35.0–41.8	42.1	36.8–45.5	46.5	39.2–49.1
Middle East & Gulf								
Iran	3.2	3.6	4.3	4.2–4.7	5.0	4.5–5.4	5.4	4.9–5.7
Iraq	2.2	0.4	4.4	4.0–5.1	5.4	4.6–6.0	6.4	5.5–6.6
Kuwait	1.7	1.1	2.9	2.8–3.2	3.6	3.1–3.9	4.2	3.5–4.6
Qatar	0.5	0.4	0.6	0.5–0.7	0.6	0.5–0.7	0.6	0.5–0.6
Saudi Arabia	8.5	9.6	11.5	10.8–12.5	12.8	11.5–13.5	14.1	12.3–14.6
UAE	2.5	2.6	3.1	2.9–3.3	3.5	3.0–3.7	4.3	3.3–4.5
Total Gulf	18.6	17.7	26.8	25.2–29.52	30.9	27.2–33.2	35.0	30.0–36.6
Algeria	1.4	1.3	1.5	1.4–1.8	1.3	1.0–1.5	1.1	0.7–1.3
Libya	1.6	1.6	1.8	1.6–2.2	2.1	1.8–2.3	2.0	1.2–2.2
Total Middle East	21.6	20.6	30.0	—	34.3	—	38.0	—
Total OECD	20.1	20.6	20.3	18.4–21.5	19.7	16.6–21.1	19.4	15.5–21.1
US	9.7	9.7	8.2	7.3–8.6	8.2	6.6–8.9	8.6	6.4–9.5
North Sea	4.2	4.6	5.3	4.9–5.6	4.6	4.2–4.8	4.2	3.7–4.4
FSU**	11.5	9.1	7.8	7.3–8.5	9.4	8.3–10.7	10.9	9.2–11.5
Eastern Europe	0.3	0.2	0.2	0.2–0.3	0.2	0.1–0.2	0.2	0.1–0.2
Asia								
China	2.8	2.8	3.1	2.9–3.4	3.4	3.0–3.6	3.2	2.7–3.4
Indonesia	1.5	1.7	1.4	1.2–1.5	1.1	0.9–1.3	1.0	0.7–1.2
Australia	0.7	0.6	0.7	0.5–0.8	0.6	0.4–0.7	0.5	0.3–0.6
Other Asia	1.7	1.7	2.1	1.9–2.4	2.1	1.7–2.3	1.8	1.4–2.0

(continues)

TABLE SEVEN (*continued*)

Country/Region	1990	1992	2000		2005		2010	
			Base Case	*Range*	*Base Case*	*Range*	*Base Case*	*Range*
Latin America								
Venezuela	2.6	2.6	3.3	3.0–3.7	3.8	3.4–4.1	4.3	3.6–4.5
Mexico	3.0	3.1	3.2	3.0–3.4	3.3	2.9–3.5	3.3	2.8–3.5
Other	2.2	2.4	3.5	3.2–3.9	3.3	2.9–3.5	3.1	2.7–3.3
Sub-Saharan Africa								
Gabon	0.3	0.3	0.3	0.3–0.4	0.3	0.2–0.3	0.2	0.2–0.3
Nigeria	1.8	2.0	2.4	2.3–2.7	2.6	2.3–2.8	2.8	2.4–3.0
Other	1.8	1.9	2.1	1.8–2.5	2.0	1.5–2.2	1.9	1.4–2.1
World Total	69.6	67.4	78.6	72.5–86.6	84.2	72.6–91.4	88.8	73.7–94.7

*Less Syria and Egypt.
**Former Soviet Union.

Source: Adapted by Anthony H. Cordesman from EIA, *International Energy Outlook, 1995*, Washington, DOE/Eia-048(95), p. 29. The EIA, Oil Market Simulation Model Spreadsheet, 1994, data provided by the EIA Energy Markets and Contingency Information Division, and EIA, *International Energy Outlook, 1994*, pp. 11–20.

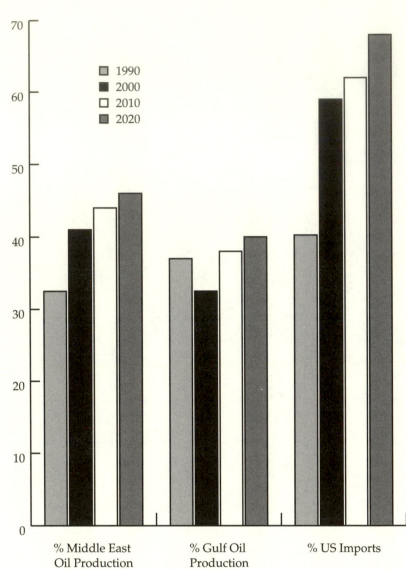

CHART SEVENTEEN   Middle East and Gulf Oil Production as a Percent of World Total versus Increase in Percentage of US Dependence on Oil Imports. *Source:* Adapted by Anthony H. Cordesman from EIA working estimate.

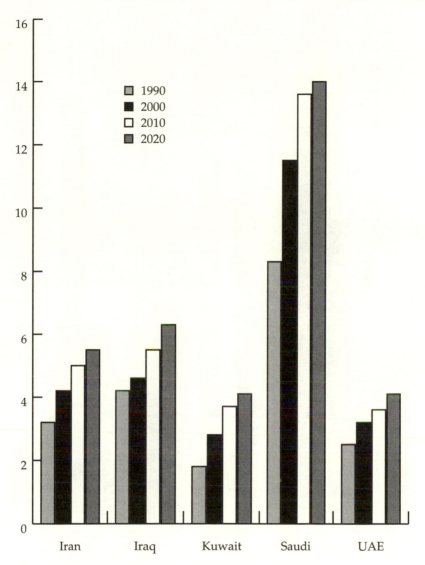

CHART EIGHTEEN   The Growing Strategic Role of Gulf Oil Producers (Average Daily Production in Millions of Barrels). *Source:* Adapted by Anthony H. Cordesman from EIA, *International Energy Outlook,* 1995, Washington, DOE/ EIA-048(95), p. 29.

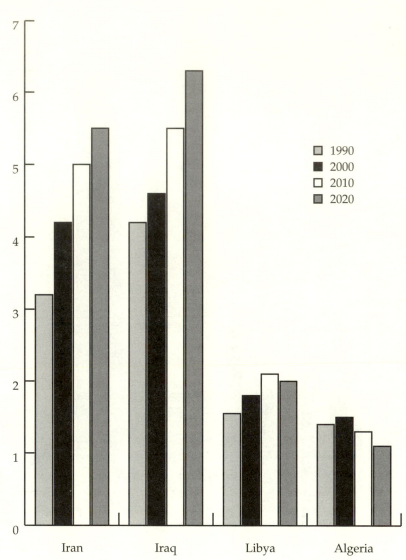

CHART NINETEEN   The Growing Importance of Radical and Potentially
Radical Middle East Oil Producers (Average Daily Production in Millions of
Barrels). *Source:* Adapted by Anthony H. Cordesman from EIA, *International
Energy Outlook,* 1995, Washington, DOE/EIA-048(95), p. 29.

6

Iran's External Relations and Regional Ambitions

The analysis of Iran's foreign policy and regional ambitions is a more familiar aspect of security analysis than its internal politics, internal security efforts, demographics, and oil. Once again, however, such an analysis has several major uncertainties, and reflects deep differences of opinion between the US and its allies. Further, such an analysis presents the problem that there is an inevitable gap between Iranian statements and actions, and Iran's foreign policy cannot be separated from its actions in supporting terrorism and extremism.

Iran's foreign policy continues to defy easy categorization. In the first decade of its existence, the Islamic Republic of Iran was a revolutionary state opposed to the regional status quo and the domination of the world by the two superpowers. Iran followed the almost predictable historic trajectory of revolutionary states that have destabilized the international system by seeking to bring about fundamental changes in the domestic political situation of other states and in the conduct of inter-state relations. Ayatollah Khomeini set the foreign policy agenda of the Islamic Republic during the first decade of its existence, both from the stand point of ideology and the issuing of important directives which dramatically affected Iran's relations with the outside world. Iran's defeat in the war with Iraq heralded the end of this militant attempt to 'export the revolution' by force.

The acceptance by Iran in July, 1988 of United Nations Security Council Resolution 598—calling for a cease-fire—constituted the revolutionary leader's single greatest submission to the logic of realpolitik, coming as it did in the wake of severe Iranian battlefield defeats between April and July. Iran emerged from the war with the recognition on the part of some of its political elite that militant confrontation with the outside world had been counterproductive. It became readily apparent that successful implementation of economic reforms and reconstruction depended on the adoption of a policy of openness towards the outside world and responsible diplomacy.

Under Rafsanjani, the basic policy guidelines of Iran's 'second republic' have stressed that the concrete needs of the post-war Iranian state were to have priority over the abstract goals of the revolution and that Iran would give up extremist rhetoric and ideological slogans. The pragmatists have articulated a set of foreign policy goals—development of 'normal' diplomatic relations with the outside world, improvement of access to western technology, and the integration of Iran into the world capitalist system in order to enhance its ability to reconstruct and develop the economy.

The end result was intended to be the transformation of the Islamic Republic into a success story—similar to the dynamic economies of Southeast Asia—which the rest of the Muslim world would try to emulate. In the mind-set of the pragmatists the transformation of the Islamic Republic into a success story at home would ultimately ensure that the Islamic Revolution would be 'exported' by peaceful means. These goals were not universally shared by the elite, however, and the pragmatists could not prevent the radicals, who viewed these objectives as a betrayal of the revolution, from criticizing and sabotaging them.

But the foreign policy of the 'second republic' has not lived up to expectations that the chastened and devastated Islamic Republic would be transformed into a 'normal' post-revolutionary state. The Islamic Revolution of Iran has not been able to bridge the gap between the logic of state interests and the ardor of revolutionary policies in any consistent manner. Residual revolutionary ideological fervor has had an impact on many of Iran's actions. As a result, Iran has lacked the capacity to engage in a consistent foreign policy or to restructure its foreign policy apparatus.

The formulation and execution of the foreign policy of the second republic has been hostage to a variety of factors. Iran has no personality of the stature of Ayatollah Khomeini to dominate the foreign policy arena. Neither Supreme Leader Khamenei nor President Rafsanjani have been able to rise above the constraints posed by a system in which policy is ultimately the outcome of compromise among various institutions and competing factions.

Once again Rafsanjani and Khamenei are divided when it comes to foreign policy. While Khamenei shares Rafsanjani's commitment to reconstruction and development, he has a genuinely conservative ideological outlook toward the outside world. This is symbolized by his exhortations for the Islamic Republic to combat Western political and economic domination of the Islamic world, post–Cold War US attempts at "hegemony," and the cultural onslaught against Iran itself. Iran's Supreme Leader routinely uses much stronger rhetoric than its president.

Rafsanjani's role in foreign policy has not lived up to the expectations of reformers or of the president himself. The enhancement of the powers of the president in 1989 was intended not only to strengthen his domestic authority, but also to bring greater direction to foreign policy. The elimination of the post of Prime Minister was intended to prevent the repetition of the struggles between the two executive posts as in the 1980s. Nonetheless, Rafsanjani has had to tread carefully in foreign policy matters, especially regarding relations with the USA.

Since 1989, radicals have kept a close watch for any hints of a diplomatic overture towards the "Great Satan," particularly as Rafsanjani was largely responsible for the infamous hostages for arms controversy in 1987. Rafsanjani has often had to rely on 'trial balloons'. His closest advisors and supporters have tested the waters with steps like calling for the release of Western hostages in Lebanon, a US-Iranian dialogue, or even the establishment of relations between the two countries. When the reaction has been negative, particularly on the part of Ayatollah Khamenei, Rafsanjani has avoided criticism by not being directly associated with the initiative in question.[214] Even so, Rafsanjani has not escaped severe criticism for advocating trade and commercial links with the USA, and has been reminded by Khamenei that "trade is not separate from politics and diplomacy."[215]

Iran's central national security policy making body is divided. The constitutional reforms of 1989 created a Supreme National Security Council (Article 176), headed by the presidency, which was intended to ensure better co-operation between the various institutions that play a role in the formulation of foreign policy, and to ensure co-ordination between national security matters and foreign policy. This succeeded in part. The measured deliberations of the SNSC—whose members include two representatives of the Supreme Leader, the head of the judiciary, the Chief of the General Staff, head of the Plan and Budget Organization, and the ministers of Interior, Foreign Affairs, and Intelligence—were reflected in Iran's adoption of prudent and careful policies in two areas of supreme import for the country's national security and foreign policy: the Kuwait crisis of 1990–1991, and the emergence of independent states on Iran's northern boundaries following the collapse of the Soviet Union. At the same time, the SNSC seems to have agreed to the assassination of opposition leaders and to have permitted or encouraged Iran's support of anti-Israel and other extremist movements.

The Foreign Ministry's stature and position was considerably damaged by the revolution, as hundreds of experienced diplomats were purged and replaced by semi-literate, revolutionary ideologues bent solely on exporting the revolution and alienating other countries. Under the 'second republic' the Foreign Ministry's position has improved during the past few years. The end of the war with Iraq in 1988 has removed the excessive focus on purely national security considerations, while the failure to export the revolution has given the Foreign Ministry the chance to practice more 'normal' diplomacy. Foreign Minister Ali Akbar Velayati—a medical doctor when he assumed the post in 1981, but now a veteran diplomat—also seems to have tried to bring about a measure of stability in Iran's foreign policy. He has purged many of the Foreign Ministry's ideologues, improved its research capabilities (partly through the creation of the affiliated Institute for Political and International Studies), and has given the Foreign Ministry a much higher visibility through his participation in international events. At the same time, the Foreign Ministry has been at least indirectly involved in some acts of terrorism.

It is extremely difficult to ascertain the exact roles of Iran's intelligence services and paramilitary forces—the Ministry of Information and Intelligence, Military Intelligence, and the Revolutionary Guards. It is equally difficult to determine the role Iran's senior leaders play in directing these actions and approving them. It is clear, however, that the activities of these organizations include scientific and technological espionage, covert acquisition of dual-use technology, spying on large expatriate Iranian communities in France, Germany and Scandinavia, and assassination of high profile Iranian dissidents in Western Europe. Western intelligence agencies and governments believe these activities are not operations conducted by 'rogue' elements within Iran, but that they are formulated at the highest levels of government, with their execution requiring the use of personnel from several ministries—including Foreign Ministry personnel in overseas missions—working in coordination with one another.

The Majlis presents another problem. Its role in foreign policy is supposedly limited to the functions of legislative oversight and the scrutiny of international agreements to ensure that they are not contrary to Iran's national interests and ideological principles. The Majlis, however, has shown it can put serious pressure on cabinet ministers. It has made Velayati's tenure more difficult by forcing him to 'explain' certain policies or initiatives. His presence at the Non-Aligned Conference in Cairo in June, 1994, for example, was attacked by radicals and certain Majlis members.[216]

Unofficial institutions—including tax-exempt religious 'charitable' organizations like the Bonyad-e-Musta'azafin and Bonyad-e-15 Khordad—still tend to intervene in the foreign policy arena. The former behaves as a law unto itself in Iran, providing funding to Islamic movements in the Middle East. The latter offered to pay the bounty for the killing of British author Salman Rushdie for blasphemy.

Such organizations do not come under the control of the President, nor of official organs like the Foreign Ministry. Thus, while Rafsanjani cannot revoke the *fatwa*—the religious edict condemning the British author to death—he tried unsuccessfully to dissolve the Bonyad-e–15 Khordad itself. Eventually, he bypassed the problem by declaring that no official organ of the state will carry out the sentence against Salman Rushdie. It is thus significant that the sixth anniversary of the issuance of the *fatwa* (February, 1995) passed by with little commentary on the part of the British or Iranian governments.

Different Views of Iran's External Relations and Regional Ambitions

The Clinton Administration's view of Iran's external relations and regional ambitions is clear, and the hardening of US attitudes towards Iran is reflected in recent statements of the Administration's view regarding Iran's treatment of its neighbors and other states in the region. The report on US security strategy for the Middle East prepared by the Office of the Secretary of Defense in the spring of 1995 refers to Iran as follows:[217]

> Iran harbors ambitions of establishing Iranian hegemony over the Persian Gulf and expanding its influence over radical Islamist forces. It has pursued these objectives through every means at its disposal, including subversion and terrorism, applying such tactics not only within the Gulf but also in places as distant as Egypt, Sudan, Algeria, Lebanon, the former Yugoslavia, and the newly independent Caucasian and Central Asian Republics. Tehran has been the most vocal and active critic of the Middle East peace process and provides support for some of the most violent opponents of peace, including Hamas. . . . It is obvious that Iran is assertively flexing its muscles vis-à-vis its smaller Gulf neighbors. Of even greater concern in the long run, Iran is also clearly dedicated to developing weapons of mass destruction, including chemical, biological, and nuclear weapons, a prospect that would have serious repercussions for regional stability.

In testimony to Congress in early 1995, Joseph S. Nye, Assistant Secretary of Defense for International Security Affairs, described the Iranian threat to its neighbors as follows:[218]

> it is quite clear that Iran harbors ambitions of establishing Iranian hegemony over the Persian Gulf and exporting its unique brand of radical Shi'ism. Iran has not hesitated to pursue these twin objectives through every means at its disposal, including subversion and terrorism. We see such tactics applied toward the realization of Iranian ambitions not only within the Gulf but far beyond it. . . .
>
> We are especially concerned about the recent sales of Russian Kilo submarines and tactical aircraft and Chinese and North Korean missiles to an

Iranian government that makes no secret of its desire to dominate maritime traffic in and out of the Persian Gulf. In this regard, we are also closely watching the Iranian military build-up on several islands whose ownership is disputed between Iran and the UAE—Abu Musa and Greater and Lesser Tunbs. Whatever the specific Iranian motivation for fortifying the islands, the creation by a hostile power of bases sitting aside the western approaches to the Straits of Hormuz is obviously a matter of serious concern for commercial traffic, our own naval presence, and the security of our Arab friends.

Even some governments and experts who agree that Iran is a significant threat to its neighbors, believe such US statements are too extreme and fail to provide adequate qualifications or perspective. They argue that the Clinton Administration is ignoring the fact that many of Iran's actions have sought accommodation with its neighbors, and that Iran has tended to place significant limits on its hostility towards its neighbors and the West.

Actions Speak Louder than Words

There are several practical problems in resolving such differences. Iranian government and quasi-official statements do little more than provide a constant series of claims to moderation that are intermingled with revolutionary rhetoric and threats. It is possible to analyze these statements at length, but they can be used to prove everything and nothing. About all that they "prove" is that Iran often makes moderate and well balanced foreign policy statements, while continuing to use much of the same revolutionary rhetoric as it did in the past.

Iran's actions towards its neighbors and other states are equally ambiguous and difficult to put into perspective. Iran has legitimate defense needs and recently has been a major victim of aggression. Iraq invaded Iran in 1980—just as Iraq invaded Kuwait in 1990. The result for Iran was eight years of bloody land warfare with Iraq, and two years of naval conflict with the West. The conflict also resulted in a series of major missile and air raids on Iranian cities and economic facilities, and the Iraqi use of massive amounts of chemical weapons against Iranian military forces.

While the West and Iran's neighbors may view Iran largely as a potential threat, Iran has reason to feel similarly threatened. It shares both a 1,448 kilometer border and a vital shipping channel—the Shatt al-Arab—with a hostile Iraq. Iran also has a 499 kilometer boundary with Turkey, who is currently fighting a civil war with its Kurds that has led to major Turkish incursions into Iraq, and considerable tension between Turkey and Iran. Roughly 7% of Iran's population is Kurdish, and Iran fought for more than five years to suppress Iraqi-backed Kurdish dissidents during the Iran-Iraq War.

Iran has a 35 kilometer border with Armenia and two stretches of border with Azerbaijan—a 432 kilometer stretch in the north and a 179 kilometer border in the northwest. The conflict between a "Christian" Armenia and a "Muslim" Azerbaijan threatens to involve Iran on religious grounds, and affects one of its largest minorities—24% of Iran's population is Azerbaijani. Iran has a 909 kilometer border with an unsettled Pakistan. Moreover, both countries are faced with a restive Baluchi minority which straddles their mutual borders and against whom the authorities in Tehran and Islamabad have cooperated militarily since the 1970s.

It has a 936 kilometer border with an Afghanistan that seems to be locked in a permanent state of civil war. Iran and Afghanistan have long disputed control of the water rights from the Helmand River, and Iran faces problems resulting from both Afghan refugees and the long standing tensions between Afghanistan's dominant Sunni tribes and the Shi'ite tribes, which make up roughly 15% of Afghanistan's population. Iran has a 992 kilometer border with Turkmenistan and a 740 kilometer coastline on the Caspian, both of which present new challenges as well as new opportunities. Iran also has a 2,440 kilometer coastline on the Persian Gulf and the Gulf of Oman, and must deal with many unsettled disputes over the control of islands in the Gulf, Gulf waters, and offshore oil and gas facilities.[219]

About the only thing that Iranian foreign policy and "revolutionary" statements have in common is that they usually emphasize these "threats" and the "defensive" nature of Iran's actions. At the same time, Iran's foreign policy cannot be separated from its support of extremism and terrorism. The practical issue for analysis, therefore, is what Iran's recent actions say about its intentions and capabilities, and the threat that it may pose in the future.

Iranian Relations with Other Gulf States

Iran has sent mixed signals in dealing with its southern neighbors. It reduced its support of Islamic extremist movements within the southern Gulf after the death of Khomeini, and has often stated that it is seeking to improve its relations with the Southern Gulf states. For example, it has avoided confrontations over oil policy, and has negotiated with states like Kuwait, Qatar, and Oman over improvements in relations, and the sharing of offshore oil and gas. In May, 1992, Iran gave Kuwait back six airliners that Iraq had seized and flown to Iran during the Gulf War (although only after trying to extract large fees).

States like Oman and Qatar have responded by steadily expanding their relations with Iran, as much as a deterrent to Iranian "adventures" as because of any belief in the moderation of the Iranian regime. Oman has held extensive talks with Iranian officials at both the political and military level, and has even discussed naval exercises with Iran—although Oman shapes it military forces primarily to deal with the risk of an Iranian threat to the Omani-controlled waters in the Straits of Hormuz, shipping traffic in the lower Gulf and Gulf of Oman, the Qu'oin Islands, and the Musandam Peninsula.

Oman has a particularly important need to avoid confrontation with Iran. The shipping channels through the Strait of Hormuz link the Persian Gulf and the Gulf of Oman, and are one of the world's most important strategic water ways. Roughly 17% of the world's oil production transited through the Strait in 1990, and this percentage could nearly double by the year 2010.

The geography of the Strait makes Iran a continuing potential threat. The Strait is about 60 to 100 kilometers (40 to 60 miles) wide and Oman's Musandam Peninsula faces Iran across the Strait, while both Oman and Iran have long coasts on the Gulf of Oman. Iran's main naval base at Bandar-e Abbas, and smaller bases on the islands of Qeshm, Larak, and Jazireh are all just across the Strait from Oman's small naval base at Ghanam (Goat) Island.

The main east-west shipping channels through the Strait pass just south of the mid-point in the Strait and Iran's 12 mile limit, and just north of Oman's Qu'oin islands (As Salmah, Didamar, and As Salamah Wabanatuha). These shipping channels are 30–35 kilometers long and 8–13 kilometers wide. They are divided into inbound and outbound channels about two kilometers wide, with depths of 75 to 200 meters—although a shallower route exists to the northeast of the Qu'oin Islands which is about 45–80 meters deep. Further, the Musandam Peninsula is separated from the rest of Iran by the UAE, and the Peninsula has very rough terrain and few significant airports. Its northern islands are vulnerable to an Iranian amphibious operation, and it is difficult for Oman to reinforce.

Oman is the only Gulf state with a coast and ports on the Indian Ocean. It has a total of 2,092 kilometers of coastline, and Oman's coastline on the Gulf of Oman about is 1,700 kilometers long and is located on the Gulf of Oman. The Gulf of Oman is an arm of the Arabian Sea that is bordered on the north by Iran and on the south by Oman. It is about 565 kilometers (350 miles) long and 320 kilometers (200 miles) wide. Like the Strait of Hormuz, the Gulf of Oman is a critical petroleum shipping route.

Qatar fears that Iran may reassert its past claims to more of Qatar's "North field" gas reserves in the Gulf. Nevertheless, Qatar has held extensive talks with Iran and relations have been good enough so that Qatar had to politely refuse an Iranian offer of military alliance. For example, Ali Akbar Nateq-Nouri, the speaker of the Majlis, visited Qatar in November 1995 and asked Qatar to pass on Iran's request to play a role in Gulf security and resolve the dispute over Abu Musa and the Tunbs to other members of the Gulf Cooperation Council. Nateq-Nouri stated that the Gulf countries, "together with Iran constitute one family. . . . This family should maintain peace in the region and in the case of differences, they must sit together and settle them with dialogue."[220] The Iranian Minister of Defense visited Qatar in May 1996, even though Qatar had just agreed to allow the US to base USAF fighters in Qatar.[221]

Kuwait also has reason to fear Iran, which is within a few minutes flying time of Kuwaiti territory. During the Iran-Iraq War Iran threatened Kuwait with air strikes, the support of terrorism and assassination attempts, anti-ship missile strikes, mine warfare, and other attacks on shipping. At the same time, Kuwait has expanded its dialogue with Iran both as a deterrent to Iranian "adventures" and as a counter-balance to Iraq. Kuwait has rejected US pressures to support a trade ban on Iran, and now imports about $87 million worth of goods a year from Iran while exporting less than $10 million. Kuwait signed a new trade compact with Iran in late December, 1995 calling for closer cooperation between chambers of commerce, expanded trade, and a joint trade fair in 1998.[222]

Iran's interaction with the states of the Arabian peninsula is dominated by long-standing ideological, political and strategic tensions with Saudi Arabia. As self-professed Islamic states, Iran and Saudi Arabia are ideological rivals for spiritual leadership of the Islamic world. Furthermore, the Saudis who are strict Wahhabi Sunnis have shown little but contempt for the Twelver Shi'ism of the Iranians, a feeling which is reciprocated by the latter. For several years now, political tensions between Riyadh and Tehran have been exacerbated by Iranian attempts to politicize the *hajj*—the pilgrimage to Mecca—with vociferous demonstrations against the 'enemies' of Islam—and by Saudi attempts to restrict the number of Iranian pilgrims. For the Saudis the *hajj* is an intensely spiritual and religious matter, for the Iranians it is an intrinsically political act. Finally, Saudi Arabia and Iran have quarreled about production quotas and pricing within the Organization of Oil Producing and Exporting Countries.

At the same time, Iran has maintained low-level contact with anti-regime Shi'ites in Bahrain, Kuwait, Saudi Arabia's Eastern Province, and the UAE. Iran's officials and media have aggressively attacked the Saudi royal family, and Iran has sponsored protests during the Haj. On

June 2, 1993, for example, it encouraged a massive anti-American protest by Iranian pilgrims in Mecca, in spite of a pledge not to cause such incidents.

The Problem of Abu Musa and the Tunbs

By the mid-1990s, the most serious issues affecting Iran's conduct towards its neighbors are Iran's actions in dealing with the UAE, and the extent to which Iran has or has not contributed to the current political upheavals in Bahrain.

In April, 1992, Iran became involved in a serious dispute with the United Arab Emirates over the control of Abu Musa and the Greater and Lesser Tunbs. These three islands are located in the lower Gulf north of Dubai and south of Qeshem island. They are north of the main shipping channels and west of the Straits of Hormuz—the entrance to the Gulf.[223] Control of the islands offers Iran a significant potential strategic advantage; it can threaten tanker traffic through the Gulf— which involves the movement of 20% of the world's oil and an average of 75 ship transits per day. It also improves Iran's ability to defend its key naval bases in the lower Gulf and affects competing claims to off-shore oil and gas rights.

This dispute between Iran and the UAE cannot, however, be blamed solely on Iran's revolutionary regime, nor can it be labeled as a simple act of aggression. The dispute involves complex territorial claims that long precede the emergence of the present Iranian regime. Iran and the UAE have had radically different views of the legal meaning of prior claims to the islands since the 19th century. Iran feels it had a right to the islands because it exerted at least indirect control over Abu Musa and the Tunbs before Britain seized control of the islands in 1887. The UAE feels that it has a right to the islands because Iran has not exerted mean-ingful control over the Tunbs in modern times, while the islands were under the control of the ruling family in Ras al-Khaimah. The UAE also argues that Abu Musa was under the control of the ruling Arab family in Sharjah, and that although the family had branches living in both Iran and Sharjah, the main branch was in Sharjah. Experts dispute the level of authority the ruling Qawasim family of Sharjah and Ras al-Khaimah exerted over the islands, and the fact that Qawasim paid intermittent tribute to Iran.

Such arguments remained moot as long as Britain controlled the Gulf. While the Shah's father made claims to the islands beginning in the 1930s, the British had treated the claims of Sharjah and Ras al-Khaimah as legit-imate for nearly a half century, and the British decision stood through force majeure.

This situation changed in 1968, however, when Britain announced it was withdrawing from the Gulf. This British decision left Ras al-Khaimah and Sharjah without a military protector, and the Shah acted to take advantage of the situation. On November 30, 1971—the day before British forces formally ceased to exert military control over the emirates and Ras al-Khaimah, and the United Arab Emirates gained independence—Iranian marines used hovercraft to seize Abu Musa and the Tunbs. This seizure of the islands resulted in several casualties, but none of the islands then had a large native population. The Greater Tunb is little more than a barren rock, and had no population at the time, except for a few visiting fishermen. The Lesser Tunb was so small that its only previous strategic importance had been as a shipping hazard. Abu Musa was the only island large enough to have a small port and a few square miles of territory, but it had no surface flat enough to serve as a runway. Its permanent population was well under 50, except for gangs of Arab laborers who mined the iron oxide on the island.

The Shah soon made it clear that Iran intended to exert full sovereignty over the islands. In fact, Iran's Prime Minister, Abbas Hoveida, informed the Iranian Majlis that full Persian sovereignty "had been restored following long negotiations with the British government," and that Iran, "in no conceivable way relinquished or will relinquish its incontestable sovereignty and right of control over the whole of Abu Musa island."[224]

The Shah did, however, provide compensation to the Emir of Sharjah for the seizure of Abu Musa and allowed some Arabs from the UAE to remain on the island.[225] The Shah also reached an agreement with Sharjah in 1971 that gave 55% of the affected oil and gas revenues to Iran and 45% to Sharjah. Iran has since claimed this agreement explains why it allowed UAE citizens to continue to live and work on the island. The UAE, however, has claimed that the Shah seized Abu Musa and the Tunbs through sheer force majeur, and that neither Sharjah nor Ras al-Khaimah ever agreed to accept Iran's control and sovereignty over the islands.[226] In any case, the Shah left several aspects of control over the islands unresolved.

The Shah did not aggressively pursue his claims to full sovereignty over the islands while he remained in power. Iran's new revolutionary government did little to change this situation during its first decade in power, perhaps because of its focus on the Iran-Iraq War. As a result, the issue of full sovereignty over the islands was left unresolved for more than twenty years. The UAE also continued to invest in economic operations in Abu Musa and provided visas for many of the workers on the island.

It came as a surprise to the UAE, therefore, when Iran suddenly reasserted full control of Abu Musa. Iran claimed it did so because it had not received a fair share of the offshore oil production from the island, although the Iranian media soon began to refer to the entire island as Iranian territory and as part of Hormuzgan province. Iran expelled 100 workers that had UAE, rather than Iranian, visas and expelled many of the Arab residents. Further, during April 25–May 4, 1992, Iran staged the largest amphibious exercise it had conducted since the end of the Iran-Iraq War. This exercise took place in the Straits of Hormuz at the same time that Iran was reasserting its control of Abu Musa. It lasted 11 days and practiced efforts to block the Straits to an outside invader (the US). The exercise covered an area of some 10,000 square miles of ocean, and involved 45 surface ships, 150 small craft, and an unknown number of Iranian Air Force aircraft.

The UAE reacted to these developments with a proposal to solve the sovereignty problem by leasing the entire island to Iran, and altering the sharing of oil in favor of Iran. Iran rejected this proposal, and the UAE reacted by renewing its claims to the Tunbs and obtaining support from the Gulf Cooperation Council (GCC) and Arab League. Iran countered by breaking off talks on the issue on September 28, 1992, and charging that the GCC states and Arab League states had become US plotters. President Rafsanjani of Iran declared the issue a US "conspiracy . . . to justify its illegitimate presence in the Gulf."[227]

The UAE and Iran have continued to take different positions on the dispute. The UAE has sought to refer the issue to the UN Security Council or the International Court of Justice in the Hague. Iran has reacted by expanding its military presence on the islands. There is some dispute over the scale of this build-up. In the spring of 1995, Secretary of Defense William Perry referred to the Iranian deployment of chemical weapons on the island, including 155 mm shells and an Iranian force of up to 6,000 as "very threatening." Some US experts believe, however, that Secretary Perry exaggerated the Iranian build-up and confused the deployment of poison gas with the deployment of non-lethal agents. They believe that the total Iranian presence on the islands and in the immediate vicinity has only reach temporary maximums of about 3,700 men.

It does seem, however, that Iran built up a garrison force of at least a battalion and possibly over 1,000 Naval Guards on Abu Musa and the Tunbs, deployed added artillery and 10 older tanks—which it placed in sheltered positions, deployed small stocks of CS gas, and created concrete ramps and emplacements that might be used for anti-ship missiles. There are reports that Iran has extended the runway on Abu Musa to the point where it can be used to handle B-727 and B-737 jets, has deployed Improved Hawk surface-to-air missiles, and is expanding the port to allow it to base large naval vessels. It has also improved the facilities on

Greater Tunb, installed a new generating plant, and deployed additional Naval Guards forces.[228]

The practical problem is to determine whether these Iranian actions are defensive, offensive, or simply ambiguous. The Clinton Administration officials have emphasized the aggressive aspects of the Iranian build-up, and the islands have a very strategic postion. The main east-west shipping channels through the Gulf pass within 10–15 kilometers on either side of the Tunbs, as well as the Island of Jazireh-ye Forur, about 50 kilometers to the east. Both the Tunbs and the deeper waters in this part of the Gulf are on the Iranian side of mid-point between Iran and the Southern Gulf, although the Tunbs are not within the 12 mile limit of Iran. Abu Musa is about 40 kilometers south of the smaller Tunb and 25 kilometers south of the east-bound tanker channel—which is the channel that passes to the south of the Tunbs. It is about 50 kilometers southeast of the Iranian Island of Jazireh-ye Sirri As a result, control of the Tunbs extends Iran's ability to threaten the tanker channels with missiles and hit and run naval raids, while control of Abu Musa ensures that tankers cannot shift to the south without passing equally near to an Iranian controlled Island.

It is important to note, however, that there are limits to the strategic value of these small islands, and that even Abu Musa is difficult to use as a survivable base for naval operations and siting anti-ship missiles in the face of attacks by US airpower. Further, while the three islands do have a strategic position near the main shipping channels in the lower Gulf, Iran has long had anti-ship missiles deployed in other positions near the Straits, which could attack any large vessels moving in and out of the Gulf.

Iran also possesses bases at Forur and Sirri, and at Qeshem, Hengam, and Larak—islands which are closer to the Strait of Hormuz, larger, and easier to defend. All five of these islands are also capable of staging mining and Naval Guards operations against shipping in the lower Gulf. Iran seems to have deployed Silkworm anti-ship missiles on Qeshem Island and on Sirri Island near the Strait of Hormuz. These missiles have ranges of up to 90 kilometers. There are reports that Iran has deployed advanced long-range anti-ship missiles like the Sunburst on Sirri, although such reports have never been confirmed by US experts.[229]

So far, Iran has not used the islands to take any actions that can clearly be labeled as aggressive. Iran did, however, act at a time when it claimed it was trying to improve its relations with the Southern Gulf states. As a result, some experts see Iran's actions as evidence that it cannot be trusted. Some experts also feel that Iran's actions reflect a continuing conflict between the influence of pragmatists and extremists in the Iranian government—although Rafsanjani visited Abu Musa shortly before the

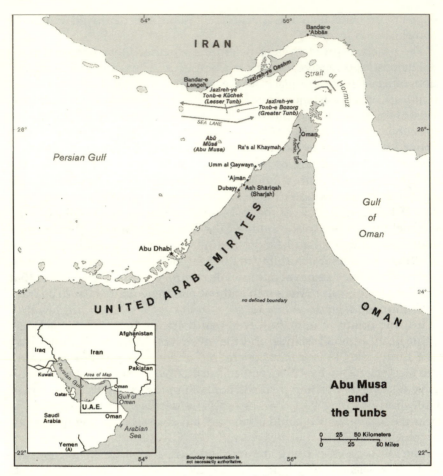

MAP THREE   Iran, the Strait, Abu Musa, and the Tunbs

seizure and almost certainly approved every step Iran has taken regarding the islands. In fact, the Iranian action in Abu Musa must be seen from a nationalist perspective and as one that has broad popular support in Iran.

Further, the UAE's position towards Iran is divided. Although Abu Dhabi has led the effort to regain UAE control over part of Abu Musa and the Tunbs, it permits Iranian dhows to operate out what approaches a free port in Abu Dhabi and enforces minimal security over the movement of such dhows. Dubai has large numbers of Iranians and former Iranians and reshipping to Iran is a major industry. Dubai exported $681 million worth of goods to Iran in the first nine months of 1995—even though Iran was attempting to reduce such exports by cracking down on smuggling and limiting the outflow of hard currency.[230]

Iran's Relations with Bahrain

Iran has long had troubled relations with Bahrain, and has made sporadic claims to it since the time of the Shah. Shah Reza made claims to Bahrain when he came to power in World War II and Iran protested Britain's transfer of its political agent in the Gulf from Bushehr to Bahrain when this took place in 1946. Iranian maps often showed Bahrain as part of Iran and the Iranian Majlis even passed laws applying to Bahrain—although they had no power or effect.

The Shah strongly reasserted Iran's claim to Bahrain in a note to the British government in early 1968, shortly after Britain had announced that it would leave the Gulf. This led to negotiations between Iran and Britain, which resulted in an agreement in late 1969 that the issue would be referred to the Secretary General of the United Nations, who would appoint a mission of inquiry to determine the wishes of the people of Bahrain. It was clear that this agreement would lead to Bahrain's independence under the Al Khalifas, but it served the Shah's interests by making it increasingly unlikely that Britain could unite Bahrain into a federation of Emirates that would unite most of the smaller states in the Southern Gulf.[231]

The Shah did not challenge Bahrain's sovereignty after the UN decided in favor of independence in 1970. In 1979, however, the Shah's fall and the rise of Khomeini created a new radical group that could appeal to Bahrain's Shi'ite majority, many of whose clergy trained in Iran. This, coupled with the many Iranian residents in Bahrain, gave the radicals in Tehran a natural conduit for influence.

Shortly after Khomeini's rise to power in 1979, he stated that Bahrain was part of Iran. He also sent "messengers" to Bahrain to promote Iran's religious revolution. This led to riots in Bahrain as early as August, 1979— when some 1,500 Shi'ite demonstrators rallied in Bahrain in favor of the Iranian revolution. As a result, Bahrain's security forces arrested many of the demonstrators, exiled some, and expelled at least one pro-Iranian Sheik, as well as several members of the Shi'ite clergy. Further Shi'ite protests, including some violent demonstrations against the US presence in Bahrain, occurred at the time of the student seizure of the US embassy in Tehran.[232]

These developments helped make Bahrain a strong supporter of Iraq at the start of the Iran-Iraq War. Bahrain allowed Iraq to disperse some of its aircraft in Bahrain and the Al Khalifa family made it clear that it supported Iraq's initial victory claims. This led to new protests in April, 1980. The security forces arrested at least 50 Shi'ite leaders and were forced to organize a new structure designed to control and infiltrate Shi'ite opposition. At the same time, Iran began actively to provide funds, training, and arms for its supporters in Bahrain.

The tensions between Bahrain and Iran reached a crisis point in mid-December, 1981, when Bahrain's government arrested 73 people, including

58 Bahraini nationals, 13 Saudis, 1 Kuwaiti, and 1 Omani, and eventually deported up to 300 others, all members of a Shi'ite group called the Islamic Front for the Liberation of Bahrain, who had planned a coup for Bahrain's national day on December 16, 1980. Many had trained in Iran and had smuggled in arms, men, and some $120,000 in cash from Iran. The group had obtained Bahraini police uniforms and planned to assassinate key members of the Al Khalifa family and government officials. They intended to declare an Islamic republic when their leader arrived from Iran.

The plot was discovered by an immigration official in Dubai who noted suspicious movements from Iran to Bahrain. Bahraini security officials then discovered that the Iranian chargé d'affaires in Manama was both importing equipment, like walkie-talkies, from London in his diplomatic pouch and funding the group. Another 13 members of the group were found to be operating in Saudi Arabia and others in the UAE. While the arrests of the group's members did not lead to public protests, the group was found to have received considerable support in the Diraz and Awali districts of Bahrain. The group was also found to have some 150–200 guerrillas training in Iran. The group also had ties to Hadi al-Modarasi, a Shi'ite mullah who had lived in Bahrain while the Shah was in power and who subsequently became the head of the Gulf Affairs Section of Iran's Revolutionary Guards.

These discoveries led Bahrain to be cautious in dealing with those it arrested for the coup attempt. Any signs of public demonstrations were carefully suppressed when the government held trials in 1982. The government expelled another 200–300 Shi'ites, rather than arrest them, and kept new arrests that it made in 1983 a secret. Bahrain also made a major effort to expand economic opportunities for Shi'ites, while it increased efforts to penetrate every Shi'ite group and cell. These government efforts largely contained violent protests and pro-Iranian actions, although low level sabotage and occasional incidents continued until the end of the Iran-Iraq War in 1988.[233]

Iran seems to have reduced its support of radical groups in Bahrain during the period immediately after the end of the Iran-Iraq War and the death of Khomeini. Anti-government Shi'ite activity in Bahrain was also limited during the Gulf War. Since 1992, however, Bahrain has experienced growing economic problems, which have led to serious internal unrest among Bahrain's Shi'ites. Some of this unrest has been supported by Iranian-trained, Bahraini Shi'ite clergy and students—many of whom were educated in Qom. Iran also continues to permit the Islamic Front for the Liberation of Bahrain to maintain an office in Tehran, and may be providing substantial funds to the group's main office in London—the location of most other Bahraini exile organizations.[234]

Bahraini officials increasingly see Iran as a primary cause of the problems that have emerged since 1994. Bahraini officials believe that Iran has actively supported the present Shi'ite unrest in Bahrain, and has active ties to a number of the more extreme Shi'ite clerics and members of the Islamic Front for the Liberation of Bahrain that have helped trigger demonstrations and riots. Bahrain also expelled a Iranian diplomat, Third Secretary Abdul-Rasool Dokoohki, for "activities incompatible with his diplomatic status" in early February, 1996.[235] They also arrested 44 Bahraini Shi'ites on June 3, 1996 for plotting to overthrow the government. Bahrain indicated that many of those arrested had at least some political ties to Iran, and had been trained in Iranian-funded camps in Lebanon, in Iran, or Afhganistan.

Bahraini government officials feel Iran directly encouraged protests and violence to precipitate broad social revolution, and they fear that may take more direct subversive or military action if the situation in Bahrain continues to deteriorate. They are concerned that Iran has used its theological schools to radicalize the Bahraini Shi'ite clergy that train there, that Iran seems to have trained cadres of Bahraini Shi'ites in revolutionary techniques, and that Iran may try to exploit the possible threat posed by the many Iranians living in Bahrain.[236]

Offshore Oil and Gas Claims

Iran has potential disputes over the control of or sharing of several offshore oil and gas zones in the Gulf. The vast offshore gas dome near Qatar is a key case in point. Iran initially made claims to 40% of the dome at a time outside experts felt that Iran had a claim to only about 10% of the waters over the dome. Qatar, in turn, argued that Iran had no claim to the North Field, although it acknowledged that it was developing at least one reservoir that extends into Iranian territory.

Since that time, Qatar seems to have reached a peaceful *modus vivendi* with Iran over the issue, although the rights to these gas resources might still be a source of Iranian claims and military action. Iran has also made past claims to offshore waters claimed by Kuwait, and to control over the Omani waters and Quoin Islands in the Straits of Hormuz.

Iranian Interference in Shi'ite Affairs in the Southern Gulf and the Iranian "Fifth Column"

Officials in other Gulf countries express differing views about the threat Iran poses in terms of its support for other Shi'ite and Islamic fundamentalist movements in the Gulf. Some officials feel that Iran has set up intelligence and surveillance networks in all the Southern Gulf states and Yemen, and that Iranian intelligence has, at the least, penetrated many of the Islamic extremist movements in the Southern Gulf—even if it does not exert control. They feel that Iran has actively surveyed potential targets for military or terrorist action, such as critical oil facilities, power plants, communications centers, and desalinization plants.

UAE and other Southern Gulf officials express concern over the fact that Iran has a potential "fifth column," created by the presence of nearly 100,000 Iranians in the UAE and the constant flow of dhow traffic between Iran and the UAE. They are concerned about the potential problems posed by the fact that some 16% of the UAE's population is Shi'ite, by Iran's potential claims over Gulf waters, and by the proximity of Dubai and the eastern emirates to Abu Musa and Iran.

Iran has often been hostile to Saudi Arabia, and Iran's media and some of its political leaders have vigorously attacked the Saudi royal family, causing repeated riots and other problems during the Haj. Some Saudi officials feel that Iran has also provided training, funds, and possibly arms for Shi'ite minorities in Saudi Arabia and other Gulf countries. Furthermore, they believe that Iran is indirectly encouraging Sunni extremist movements that would not otherwise support Iran's Shi'ite faith, or show any interest in dealing with Persian led movements. Few officials, however, cite specific Iranian actions and incidents.

Iran has also maintained an intelligence network in Kuwait since the Iran-Iraq War. During the war it supported and encouraged Kuwaiti Shi'ites and Iranian expatriates in numerous bombings, sabotage, and assassination attempts. Kuwait has made repeated efforts to destroy these networks and has expelled or imprisoned many of those it believes have ties to Iran. Though Iran has been much less hostile to Kuwait since 1989, it seems likely that it retains significant intelligence links to Shi'ite groups in Kuwait.

Given this background, it is not surprising that many Gulf states had adopted a "dual-track" diplomacy with Iran. On the one hand, they have maintained a dialogue with Iran, maintained relations, attempted to expand trade and encourage Iran's "pragmatists," "moderates," and "modernists." On the other hand, they have strengthen their military forces and ties to the US and used forum like the Gulf Cooperation Council to condemn Iran. The Foreign Ministers of the GCC provided a particularly strong condemnation of Iran at their meeting on June 2, 1996. This condemnation came only days before Bahrain announced that it had made 44 arrests to block an Iranian supported conspiracy.

The Foreign Ministers condemned Iran for interfering "in the internal affairs of Bahrain and other member countries," and for "repeated measures" concerning the strategic Gulf islands of Abu Musa and the Tunbs. They urged Iran "not to resort (to) or encourage acts of sabotage, and to respect the sovereignty and independence of council states." They condemned Iran for seeking to develop an arsenal that "exceeds its ordinary and legitimate defense needs."[237]

Iranian-Syrian Relations

Iran maintains close relations with Syria, and this relationship has many of the characteristics of a de facto alliance.[238] The two states are ideological opposites—Syria is an secular pan-Arab state and Iran is a revolutionary Persian Islamic state—but the two countries have cooperated closely since the first years of the Iranian revolution. The origins of this alliance can be found in the Camp David peace process between Egypt and Israel which threatened Syria's national security, a failed attempt at a rapprochement betweenIraq and Syria, and Iran's quest for allies in the Arab world.

Under the Shah, Iran was a supporter of the peace process. In October 1977, President Sadat met with the Shah of Iran in Tehran. The Shah told Sadat that Israel's Prime Minister Menachem Begin and Foreign Minister Moshe Dayan were prepared to negotiate with Egypt bilaterally and to bypass the Geneva peace process. A month later Sadat was in Jerusalem. In the interim a meeting took place between Sadat and Asad, in which Asad latter implored the Egyptian leader not to rush forward, not to recognize Israel even before detailed bargaining started, and not to break Arab ranks. Asad felt that the formal removal of Egypt from the Arab camp would leave the rest of the Arabs vulnerable to Israel military power and strategic designs.[239]

In spite of Asad's opposition, Sadat and Begin signed the Camp David accords in September 1978, and signed the Egypt-Israel peace treaty six months later. Asad was left out in the cold, although he then had the satisfaction of seeing the Shah fall the following year.

The Iranian revolution offered Asad a strategic counterweight he could use to avoid Syria's political marginalization in regional politics and to counterbalance Iraq's hostility.[240] Syria and Iraq did reach a short-lived reconciliation in January 1979, when Saddam Hussein visited Damascus. However, the fact that Asad and Saddam Hussein were both Ba'athists and Arab nationalists did little to bind them together. If anything, they were natural rivals and they had vastly different visions of the respective roles of their countries. As a result, the Syrian-Iraqi reconciliation did not survive an internal coup in Iraq in July 1979. During this coup, Saddam ousted his relative President Hasan al-Bakr, eliminated his pro-Syrian rivals, and emerged as Iraq's sole strongman. Asad quickly concluded that Iraqi inexperience and rhetoric could spell danger in the Arab-Israeli conflict, and that Iraq had begun to help the Muslim Brotherhood against his regime.

As a result, Asad turned to the new Islamic Republic of Iran. Even when Asad was trying to reach a reconciliation with Iraq, he had "judged it a supreme Arab interest to befriend" the Ayatollah Khomeni. Asad had long viewed the Shah as an American stooge, as a de facto ally of Israel, and a potential member of the Egyptian-Israeli peace axis. As a result, Asad had tried to convince his fellow Arabs—traditionally suspicious of

Iran—that the Ayatollah's Iran should be seen in a totally different way from the Pahlavi Iran.

The new Iranian regime was anti-Israel, anti-American. Unlike the Iraqi Ba'athists, Asad saw beyond the Arab heartland and included the periphery as critical to the balance of forces between the Arabs and Israel. As a result, it is easy to see why Asad proclaimed that the Iranian Revolution was a victory for the Arab world and an important step in the liberation of Palestine. This same logic led Asad's Foreign Minister, Abdel Halim Khaddam, to proclaim the Iranian revolution as the "most important event in our contemporary history. Syria supported it prior to its outbreak, during it, and after its triumph."[241]

There was truth in these claims. Asad had indeed began helping the Iranian revolutionaries long before their seizure of power. Some of Khomeini's early lieutenants and confidants, men like Ibrahim Yazdi, Sadegh Qotbzadeh, and Mustafa Chamran had sought refuge in Syria and gotten Syrian passports. When Khomeini was expelled from Iraq at the request of the Shah in October 1978, Asad offered the Ayatollah political asylum in Syria. While he did not accept it, having decided to wage revolution from Neuphle-le-Chateau outside Paris, Khomeini made sure to thank the Syrians publicly following his triumphant return to Tehran.

For their part when the Iranian revolutionaries seized power they set about looking for allies in the Arab world at the same time as they were seeking to subvert moderate Arab regimes. The euphoria with which Yasser Arafat of the PLO was greeted when he visited Tehran to take charge of the former Israeli mission and transform it into the PLO mission could not disguise the fact that the PLO was no substitute for an Arab state as an ally. Further, Iraq was out of the question: Ayatollah Khomeini nurished a deep-seated hatred for the Ba'athist system in Iraq which he saw as godless and as oppressing Iraq's Shi'ites.

Khomeini viewed the Arab states of the Gulf as godless monarchies and clients of the Great Satan. Libya was too far away and insignificant, and South Yemen was Marxist and anathema to the Islamic revolutionaries. Iran welcomed the support offered by Algeria, a staunch anti-imperialist country, but Algeria was not strategically relevant and was not a major actor in inter-Arab politics. In contrast, Syria had earned the gratitude of the revolutionaries for support rendered to the Iranian Revolution. Moreover, Syria was a key actor in the inter-Arab arena which the Iranian revolutionaries were keen to enter, and had impressive anti-imperialist and anti-Zionist credentials.

The resulting de facto alliance occurred in spite of a number of religious and ideological differences. The *Alawi* sect from which Asad comes is ostensibly an offshoot of Shi'ism that has long been despised by the majority Sunnis. Historically neither Sunnis nor mainstream Shi'ites considered the Alawis to be real Muslims. Indeed, it took a *fatwa*—a religious decree—by a noted Lebanese cleric in 1973 to state that the *Alawis* are were real Muslims. There was also an ideological dichotomy between Iran's Islamic universalism and Syria's secular Arab nationalism, although the two shared similar views regarding a wide range of regional and international issues: they both see Israel as a predatory and usurping state. Throughout the 1980s, both countries also criticized the two superpowers, although both concentrated their attacks on the US, they saw as helping impose Israeli domination over the region.

Their common hostility towards Iraq also deepened the bonds between Damascus and Tehran in the 1980s, during a time when Iran was engaged in a live and death struggle with its Iraqi neighbor. Syria did Iran a great service by closing the oil pipeline carrying Iraqi oil to the Syrian port of Baniyas in April 1982, and caused Iraq tremendous economic hardship in the process.

Iran's relations with Syria provided the Iranian government with access to Syrian-dominated Lebanon and ultimately with access to Lebanon's disenfranchised and economically impoverished Shi'ite population. Iran became deeply involved in Lebanese following the Israeli invasion of Lebanon in June 1982, which led to the political awakening of the Shi'ites in the south. Asad allowed the Iranians to send Revolutionary Guards and to help build a Shi'ite political party and guerrilla force, Hezbollah, as an alternative to the mainstream Shi'ite party, Amal. Thanks to Iranian financial and military help, Hezbollah gradually became an effective guerrilla organization which Syria then exploited to put pressure on Israel.

Iran's relations with Syria cooled somewhat in the aftermath of Iran's defeat in the Iran-Iraq War in 1988. Contrary to Syria's expectations, its partner was defeated by an Iraq which emerged as the foremost Arab military power and as the preeminent player in inter-Arab politics. Moreover, Iraq sought revenge for Syria's support of Iran and began giving aid to anti-Syrian forces in Lebanon, and Syria was somewhat isolated in an Arab world euphoric over the defeat of Iran. Syria reacted by trying to outflank Iraq by improving its relations with Egypt and the Arab states of the Gulf.

The Iraqi invasion of Kuwait helped to rebuild Syrian-Iranian ties. Both countries adamantly opposed to the Iraqi action, although problems remained in Iranian-Syrian relations because of Syria's role in the UN Coalition and the Damascus Declaration. Iran strongly objected to the Damascus Declaration as an Arab plan to implement a regional security arrangement in the Gulf which would have Egyptian and Syrian military support but exclude Iran. Iranian officials stated that neither Syria nor Egypt were *Persian* Gulf states and that both should be excluded from the area. The failure of the Damascus Declaration removed this source of tension soon after the cease-fire in 1991, but a new source of tension arose when Syria supported the UAE in its quarrel with Iran over the islands of Abu Musa and the Tunbs.

The Arab-Israeli peace process that began in Madrid in 1991 was also a source of tension. Iran feared that Syria would go the way of Egypt, the Palestinians, and Jordan, and that Iran would lose its most important ally in the Arab world. The failure of Syrian-Israeli talks during 1994–1996, and the election of a hard-line Israeli government under Benjamin Netanyahu, thus came as a relief to Tehran. It saw this vindication of its own 'principled' opposition to peace in contrast with the a sell-out by Egypt, the PLO, and Jordan.

As a result, the de facto alliance between Iran and Syria is largely a matter of mutual convenience. It currently serves the tactical and strategic interests of both states, but has not led to close ties between the two regimes. It could be seriously undermined by a breakthrough in the Syrian-Israeli peace negotiations or by the emergence of a new and more pro-Syrian regime in Iraq.

Iran's Actions in its Northern Border Area, Central Asia, and Afghanistan

Iran's dealings with its northern neighbors have led to similar concerns that Iran may be seeking to extend its Islamic influence over the region. Iran opened embassies in the Azerbaijan, Turkmenistan and Tajhikistan Republics in 1991, and made a major effort to support the Islamic revival in these countries. It revived the long dormant Economic Development Council that once existed between Iran, Turkey, and Pakistan in the mid-1960s. The Azerbaijan, Kyrgyzstan, Tajhikistan, Turkmenistan, and Uzbekistan republics joined this Council in a summit meeting on February 17, 1992. Iran announced at this meeting that it had signed a Caspian Sea cooperation pact with Azerbaijan, Russia, Kazakhstan, and Turkmenistan.

Since that time, Iran has competed with Turkey and Saudi Arabia in providing money and advisors to rival secular and Islamic elements. It has signed oil exchange agreements with one Asiatic republic and has compete actively for pipelines that pass through Iran. Iran opened a new rail link between Mashhad in Iran to Sarakhs on the Turkmenistan border in May, 1996, which connects with rail links to Tadzhen and the Central Asian rail network that links Russia and all of the Asiatic republics. Iran's Foreign Minister Ali Akbar Velayati called this link the "Silk Road for the 21st Century" during the opening ceremony, and Iran is seeking to create a trade route from the Asiatic republics to Northern Iran and eventually a new major port on Iran's coast on the Gulf of Oman.

None of Iran's actions seem particularly aggressive, however, and it is difficult to tell whether Iran has ambitions to dominate any of the former Soviet republics or is simply seeking economic and cultural influence. Iran and Russia have maintained a dialogue on political developments in the former Soviet republics. Although Russia has supported the secular, former communistic regimes in these countries, and Iran has supported the Islamic movements, there are few indications that Iran has provided direct military support or money to the various Islamic rebel groups.

Russia has also recently sought to strengthen its relations with Iran in dealing with the Caspian region. It held bilateral talks with Iran in late November, 1995, and sought both a common policy on dealing with the economic development and environmental situation in the Caspian, and cooperation over oil pipeline and shipping affecting Azerbaijan, Turkmenistan, and Kazakhstan. Iranian Deputy Foreign Minister Mahmud Vaezi visited Moscow in mid-February, 1996 and met with Yeltsin and Russian Foreign Minister Yevgeny Primakov. They discussed the civil conflict in Tajikistan, Caspian issues, and oil development and pipeline issues—focusing particularly on Azerbaijan. While this meeting scarcely reflected full agreement between Russia and Iran, it also hardly reflects tension or Russian fears of Iranian aggressiveness.[242]

Iran has valid commercial and cultural reasons for seeking an expansion of its influence in the region. The Muslim republics are major potential markets for Iranian gas and oil, and some of the non-Muslim republics like Ukraine are equally important potential markets. Iran so far has only had moderate success in creating such commercial ties—it had a total of $214 million worth of exports to the former Soviet republics in 1993, versus $518 million in imports. Iran is, however, expanding its rail and pipeline links to these republics in ways that could have strategic significance. Iran also continues to offer small concessional loans and other incentives for economic cooperation.[243]

The only sign of Iranian military or extremist action in Central Asia has been its provision of funds and arms to Islamic rebels in Tajhikistan in 1993. This civil war, however, has become a struggle between Russian backed ex-Communists and native religious groups, and was not provoked by Iran. Iran also issued warnings to Armenia that summer, redeploying Iranian troops to the border with Azerbaijan. However, this action in support of the Azerbaijanis was taken only when Armenian forces began to overrun southwestern Azerbaijan.[244] Iran was scarcely alone in supporting Islamic causes in this area, or provocative in trying to halt Armenian attacks on Azerbaijan. Turkey, for example, joined Iran in condemning Armenian attacks on the Azerbaijani enclave of Nagorno-Karabakh in May, 1992.

At the same time, Iran has had growing problems with Azerbaijan. A visit by Velayati to Baku on March 3, 1996 ended in Velayati having to leave without having a final press conference after Hassan Hassanov, the Azerbaijani Foreign Minister, accused Iran of aiding a Christian Armenia which had occupied a fifth of Azerbaijan and had "killed 30,000 Azeri (Shi'ite) Muslims and made a million others homeless." Velayati responded by charging that Azerbaijan had allowed "Israeli agents" to penetrate into Central Asia. This exchange of charges was important for several reasons:[245]

- It indicated that Iran was not supporting all Islamic causes in Central Asia, or even a largely Shi'ite Azerbaijan—although the regime of Azerbaijan is secular and not religious.
- There are nearly twice as many Azeris in northern Iran as in Azerbaijan, and Iran is under considerable pressure from its own Azeris to support Azerbaijan.
- Iran's actions favor the Turkic nationalists in the region over Shi'ite nationalists, and tend to reinforce Azerbaijan's exclusion of Iran from pipeline deals with Azerbaijan. They may also cause problems for oil swap deals between the two countries.
- It showed that Iran had just as many problems in playing the "great game" as any other nation, and that there was little risk of Iran dominating any regime in the area.

Iran's ties to Afghanistan are more controversial, but they cannot be separated from the problems Iran faces in dealing with Afghan refugees and the ethnic and religious civil war in that country. Iran and the UNHCR estimated that there were approximately 1.7 million Afghan refugees in Iran in late 1994. Many have been integrated into local society, while others live semi-nomadic lives or reside in government settlements. The UNHCR repatriated more than 110,000 refugees to Afghanistan in 1994 and is supervising the repatriation of many more.

Some experts believe that Iran has confined itself largely to supporting the Shi'ite and pro-Iranian Afghan tribes in western Afghanistan, and dealing with the problems of trying to remove more Afghan refugees from Iran.[246] Other experts feel that Iran has at least some role in sponsoring the "Afghani"—a mix of more than 20 camps in Afghanistan that used to train the Mujahideen to fight the Soviets and are now used to train militant Arabs, Kashmiris, Tajiks, and other Islamic extremists and dissidents. These camps are largely south and east of Kabul—in areas outside Iranian influence—and are under the control of Afghani leaders like Guldbuddin Hikmatyar and Abdul Rasul Sayyaf who do not support the Iranian version of Islamic revolution. Even so, some experts feel the graduates of these training camps move through Iran and the Sudan and may have some Iranian support and backing.[247]

In any case, Iran has had little recent success in encouraging pro-Iranian factions in Afghanistan—a failure which follows a long series of similar Iranian failures since the early 1700s. Western Afghanistan has been relatively free of Iranian influence since the Taliban militia captured Herat, and Iran was sufficiently concerned over the risk of a new influx of refugees to close its borders in late September 1995. Iran also held military exercises near the Pakistani border in March 1996 that seem to have included defensive exercises of a kind that would help Iran improve its control over its border area with Afghanistan. This may illustrate the fact that one aspect of the "great game" never changes. Anyone who attempts to control or exercise influence over Afghanistan invariably ends up a loser.[248]

Iran's Dealings with Pakistan

Iran's dealings with Pakistan have been troubled by the fact the two countries support different factions in Afghanistan, and by Pakistan's problems with religious extremists—some of which seem to have at least Iranian religious and political support. The Zafar (Victory) exercise that Iran held near the Pakistan border during March 5–10, 1996, does not seem to have been designed to intimidate Pakistan. Nevertheless, Pakistan cannot ignore the fact that a massive exercise was being held near its volatile Western Provinces that involved extensive nuclear, biological, and chemical warfare activity, and large numbers of Iranian ground and air forces.[249]

At the same time, there has been extensive dialogue between Pakistani and Iranian officials, mutual visits between senior military officers, and at least low level exchanges of data on nuclear and missile technology. Iran and Pakistan agreed in November, 1995, that they would set up a joint trade council and signed new agreements on shipping, maritime trade, and investment protection. They agreed that work on an Iran-Pakistan gas pipeline would start in 1996 and on a joint refinery project. It is also possible that they reached a covert agreement on Pakistani sales of military parts and equipment to Iran.

What Iran and Pakistan may find hard to resolve is their differences over the Taliban movement. Despite denials by Prime Minister Bhutto, the Taliban seems to be getting official and unofficial support from both Pakistan and Saudi Arabia and some Iranian's have expressed the fear that Pakistan is trying to compete with Iran in creating trade routes to Central Asia. However, Prime Minister Bhutto has stated, "We consider Iran a friend, a neighbor, a brother in Islam. . . . Neither the leadership, the governments, the peoples, nor the elected representatives of Iran and Pakistan can dream of the day when we would be rivals or compete with each other." She also has claimed, "Pakistan has decided not to give financial or military support to any faction of the Afghans."[250]

Iran and Pakistan also face somewhat similar problems with the US. While US policy towards Pakistan is far more friendly that it is toward Iran, Congressional restraints on US arms transfer and aid to Pakistan have led Pakistan to seek other areas of support and cooperation. Iran and Pakistan also have a growing incentive to cooperate in some areas of military technology, and both import missile equipment and other systems with China—creating a potential for three-way military cooperation.

Iran's Relations with Turkey

Iran's relations with Turkey have also been complex. Iran relies heavily on trade through Turkey, and has attempted to negotiate pipeline arrangements that would ship oil and gas from Central Asia, Azerbaijan, and Iran through Turkey to Europe. At the same time, it is clear that Iran supports Turkey's Islamic parties and has supported Kurdish separatist groups like the PKK against Turkey. This Iranian support include allowing the PKK to train in eight to nine camps in Iran, and the shipment of arms to the PKK. Iran provided major new shipments of arms to help the PKK rearm after Turkish military attacks on PKK bases in Iraq during the summer of 1995.

Iran has also made efforts to increase its influence with the Kurds in Iraq, and has worked with Syria to influence both Turkish and Iraqi Kurdish groups to oppose Turkey and the Kurdistan Democratic Party (KDP) and Patriotic Union of Kurdistan (PUK)—the Iraqi Kurdish groups that cooperate with the US. According to some reports, the Italaat branch of Iranian intelligence now has three offices in the Kurdish enclave in Iraq, including one in Arbil. Iran may also have begun encouraging Iraqi Kurdish extremists to attack the offices of the US Office of Foreign Disaster Assistance (OFDA) in the enclave. At least one abortive bombing attempt in 1995 may have links to Kurdish groups with ties to Iranian intelligence.[251]

The Policy Implications of Iranian External Relations

The evidence available on Iran's relations with the Southern Gulf states and its northern neighbors does not justify characterizing Iran as a highly aggressive state. At the same time, though, it scarcely justifies labeling Iran as moderate and ignoring the potential threat it poses to the Gulf. In short, the evidence does not support either those who "demonize" Iran or those who attempt to "sanctify" it.

On balance, the data available does not describe a nation which can best be dealt with as a pariah state. Iran does not seem so rigid and inflexible that political dialogue and economic incentives will have no effect. At the same time, Iran's dealings with extremist groups scarcely indicate that it is "misunderstood," or that it can be influenced by making concessions. Further, Iran's actions in dealing with Abu Musa and the Tunbs do make a strong argument for efforts to limit Iran's military build-up and for this aspect of military containment.

7

Iran's Support of Terrorism and Extremism in Other States

There is no way to separate Iran's foreign policy and overt actions in dealing with other states from the issue of Iranian support of terrorism and extremism. Most of the recent charges against Iran affect its relations with states outside the Gulf, its northern border area, Afghanistan, and South Asia. They affect Iran's relations with Arab states in the Levant and North Africa, its relations with the Sudan and Iraq, its actions in Europe, and its actions in dealing with Israel.

The US considers Iran to be the main sponsor of international terrorism and opposition to the Arab-Israeli peace process.[252] Washington accuses Tehran of providing military training and moral and financial support to extreme Islamist movements throughout the width and breadth of the Middle East. According to the State Department, Iran was involved in 45 significant terrorist incidents in 1987, 24 incidents in 1989, 10 in 1990, five in 1991, 20 in 1992, six in 1993, six in 1994, and at least six in 1995.[253] Iran is estimated to provide over $50 million dollars worth of support to groups such as Hezbollah in southern Lebanon, which is waging a guerrilla war against Israel, and its puppet the South Lebanon Army and Hamas, the violent Palestinian Islamist group in the West Bank and Gaza Strip.

These charges have been supported by other countries. Between late 1994 and mid-1995 a French court held a trial that sentenced Iranian nationals to jail terms for their role in the assassination of Shahpour Bakhtiar. French prosecutors concluded that the Iranian government was directly linked to the assassination; in fact they sentenced an Iranian civil servant, *in absentia*, to life in prison in June, 1995, for his alleged role in the assassination of Shahpur Bakhtiar.[254] France's Prime Minister Alain Juppe denounced Iran's terrorist activity in March, 1996. The German government has charged Ali Fallahiyan, the Iranian Minister of Information and Intelligence, with being responsible for the assassination of four Iranian Kurdish exiles at a bar in Berlin in 1992. The Swiss government has also issued warrants for Iranians for the killing of Kazem Rajavi that had clear links to the Iranian government.[255]

While some experts feel that these Iranian efforts are low level efforts that may be run by radical elements in the Iranian government, there are a few intelligence and counter-terrorist experts who seem to feel such operations go on without direct review by all of the most senior members of the Iranian government. Senior French, German, Israeli, and US experts all believe there are clear links between Iran's acts of terrorism and support of extremist groups and the Iranian Supreme Council for National Security, which includes Ayatollah Ali Khamenei, President Rafsanjani and Hojatolislam Ali Fallahiyan, the head of Iran's secret services. It is also clear that senior members of the Iranian Foreign Service and Ministry of Information are either actually intelligence agents or under their direct control.[256]

The Iranian government denies most ties to extremist or terrorist groups, claiming that these ties are defensive in character or protect the legitimate rights of Muslim, and by stating that it is the US which is the real "terrorist."[257]

Exporting the Revolution

Various experts have claimed that Iran has provided support to Islamic extremist groups in Algeria, Morocco, Tunisia, and Egypt. According to some sources, it has played a role in backing some of the more violent elements of the fundamentalist FIS movement in Algeria. The list of Iranian backed groups includes a wide variety of Shi'ite, Islamic, nationalist, and secular extremist organizations such as the Egyptian al-Gama'a al-Islamiyya, Kurdish Hezbollah, Lebanese Hezbollah, Palestinian Hamas, Palestinian Islamic Jihad, and Ahmed. Egyptian security experts believe that the Iranian National Security Council has directly approved and controlled at least some operations against Egypt and other states.[258]

There is little doubt that the main mission of the Quds forces in the Revolutionary Guards is the export of the revolution. These forces train foreign terrorists and activists in Iran. Quds forces, deployed in Lebanon, the Sudan, and other countries, both train and support violent local extremist movements. Similarly, Iran's Organization for the Liberation of Revolutionary Fighters (ORLF) conducts covert and overt operations, and has been associated with attacks on Jewish groups and Iranian Kurdish opposition leaders, and operations in France and Thailand.

The Clinton Administration does not cite Iranian responsibility for attacks in Algeria, Morocco, Tunisia, and Egypt in its most recent report on terrorism, but many US and European experts believe that Tehran's Ministry of Intelligence and Security (the MOIS or VEVAK) has supported extremist movements in these countries. The report does state, "Iran supports many . . . radical organizations that have engaged in terrorism. . . . Tehran continues to provide a safehaven to the terrorist Kurdistan Worker's Party (PKK) in Iran. The PKK—seeking to establish a Kurdish state in southeastern Turkey—in 1994 conducted a violent campaign against Turkish tourism, including attacks on tourist spots frequented by foreigners, while continuing unabated used of terrorism against Turkish citizens, including ethnic Kurds."[259]

US and British experts believe that Iranian agents have provided funds, and possibly explosives, to the Turkish Islamic Jihad and the Kurdistan Workers Party (PKK) in Turkey. They indicate one related car bombing killed a US Air Force sergeant on October 28, 1991. Iranian agents seem to have killed an anti-fundamentalist Turkish journalist—Ugur Mumcu—on January 24, 1993, and attempted to kill a Turkish-Jewish businessman on January 28, 1993.

As has been touched upon earlier, Iran has played an increasingly destabilizing role in the Kurdish area in Iraq. Revolutionary Guards forces have crossed into the Kurdish security zone to attack Iranian Kurds who took shelter in the area. Iran also helped to train and arm the "Afghan faction" of the Islamic Movement of Iraqi Kurdistan (IMIK), which opposed Talabani's PUK. The PUK defeated the IMIK in December, 1993, and drove it into Iran, but Iran's sponsorship of Shi'ite factions among the Kurds has helped to contribute to the Kurdish problem in Iraq. There are also some indications of Iranian and Syrian cooperation in aiding the PKK.

At the same time, a number of experts believe, for example, that Algerian, Bahraini, and Egyptian officials often exaggerate the role of Iran and other foreign governments in sponsoring domestic opposition movements to discredit these movements and cover up their own failures to govern and to achieve economic growth and reform. They believe that Iran's actions in Turkey are directed largely at suppressing Iranian dissidents and opposition movements, and that Iran's ties to the PKK are at least indirectly tied to Iran's long standing support of Shi'ite Kurdish movements and Iran's opposition to Turkey's suppression of its Kurdish dissidents. Thus, the debate is not so much one over whether Iran supports extremist groups or conducts intelligence operations and assassinations overseas, but rather one over the scale and importance of such Iranian efforts.[260]

It is also difficult to translate Iran's support of some overseas groups into terrorism. For example, Iran has been a major supplier of arms to Croatia and to the government of Bosnia. It sent 350 to 400 Revolutionary Guards to Bosnia to assist in weapons training, and sent arms through the port of Split and to airfields in Krk Island and Zaghreb. There is little doubt that US intelligence tracked these developments in detail and could have halted or at least sharply reduced them. It was politically convenient for the US to stand aside, however, as long as the Bosnia government had no other major source of military aid.

The US has reversed its position since the Dayton agreement, and made a major effort to force the same Iranians out of Bosnia it once tolerated. It has also suddenly discovered their potential as "terrorists."[261] At the same time, Foreign Minister Velayati has responded by lying about removing all Iranian and Iranian-sponsored paramilitary forces from Bosnia, and in saying that Iran only sent humanitarian workers to Bosnia that were never involved in the fighting.[262] There is an obvious difference between such shadow games and terrorism.

Iran's Support of the Sudan

Iran's relations with the Sudan are also a source of dispute. Many experts feel Iran plays a major role in supporting the Sudan's hard-line Islamic fundamentalist government, which is now led by extremists like Lt. General Omar Hassan al-Bashir and Sheik Hassan al-Tourabi. They believe that Iran continues to support the Sudan in its training of revolutionaries and extremists. To support this assertion, they point out that the Iranian ambassador to the Sudan was himself involved in the Iranian takeover of the US Embassy in Tehran, as well as creating the infrastructure for the military elements of the Hezbollah in the 1980s. These experts contend that Iran shipped at least $17 million worth of arms to the Sudan in 1991, and continued to provide arms in 1992 and 1993.

They go on to note that Hojatolislam Ali Fallahiyan and Mohsen Rezaii, the head of the Islamic Revolutionary Guards Corps, have visited the Sudan on several occasions. Further, experts in this camp cite reports in early 1995 that an Iranian delegation to the Sudan, led by Ali Natiq Nuri, the speaker of the Iranian Parliament, obtained Iranian naval basing rights at Port Sudan on the Red Sea. Among these experts there is a general consensus that Iranian support for religious extremism in the Sudan is contributing to the extension of the bloody civil war between the Sudan's Arab and non-Arab population, which is, in turn, steadily reducing the tolerance for Christian and secular elements in the northern Sudan. Such sources also indicate that Iran has provided training and support to Nafei Ali Nafel, the head of the Sudan's intelligence service.[263]

The US State Department reports that the Sudan has permitted Iran to use the Sudan as a secure transit point and meeting place for Iranian-backed extremist groups. Although the US indicates that it has no evidence that the government of the Sudan conducted or sponsored a specific action of terrorism in 1994—with or without Iranian support—it notes:[264]

> The list of groups that maintain a presence or operate in the Sudan is disturbing and includes some of the world's most violent organizations: the Abu Nidal Organization, the Lebanese Hezbollah, the Palestinian Islamic Resistance Movement (HAMAS), the Palestinian Islamic Jihad (PIJ), and Egypt's Islamic Group. The National Islamic Front of the Sudan also supports Islamic opposition groups from Algeria, Tunisia, Kenya, and Eritrea. . . . President Bashir stated publicly that it was the Sudan's duty to protect 'mujahideen' who sought refuge. . . . The Sudanese regime regularly denied there were terrorists in the Sudan, and it refused to investigate information the US ambassador supplied about the training of terrorists at the Merkhiyat Popular defense camp northwest of Khartoum.

Few experts doubt that Iran has ties to the Sudan and linkages to extremist and terrorist groups operating in the Sudan. What some experts do question is the extent of such ties and just how serious a role Iran plays in the control and direct sponsorship of terrorism. They also question reports of large scale military cooperation between Iran and the Sudan—such as reports that Iran has sent 1,000 to 2,000 Revolutionary Guards to assist the Sudan's military forces.[265]

Iran's Relations with Iraq

Iran's relations with Iraq are another area where it is difficult to separate Iran's legitimate defensive needs from terrorism and potential threats to other nations in the region. Iranian and Iraqi relations have been tense ever since the end of the Iran-Iraq War, and the threat of another war with Iraq is almost certainly a major factor in Iran's efforts to build-up its conventional forces and acquire weapons of mass destruction. At the same time, an Iranian rapproachment with Iraq also poses a potential threat to the stability of the region.

Iran and Iraq never reached a full cease-fire or peace settlement after the end of the Iran-Iraq War, and Iran has made claims for up to $100 billion in reparations from Iraq. Iran supported the UN Coalition during the Gulf War and seized the Iraqi aircraft that fled to Iraq during Desert Storm. Iran has returned some prisoners of war since 1990, but Iraq claims that Iran still holds up to 20,000 Iraqis captured during the Iran-Iraq War and that Iran is supporting several thousand Iraqi troops that fled to Iran after the uprisings that followed the Gulf War. Iran, in turn, claims that Iraq holds up to 5,000 Iranians, while Iraq claims it has none.[266]

Iraqi officials did meet with Iranian officials before the Gulf War in an effort to persuade Iran not to support the UN Coalition, but this effort failed and Iran confiscated the Iraqi aircraft that fled to Iran during the war. Iraqi and Iranian officials met again in October, 1993, but the talks produced little result. The only real change in relations between 1991 and 1993 was a growing black market in the border area that traded oil smuggled from Iraq for spare parts and food smuggled in from Iran.[267]

In September, 1994, the International Committee of the Red Cross (ICRC) issued a report on "unresolved humanitarian issues" from the Iran-Iraq war. The ICRC noted that the Iranian government violated the Third Geneva Convention by failing to identify combatants killed in action and exchanging information on those killed or missing. According to the report, the fate of almost 19,000 Iraqi prisoners of war (POWs) in Iran "remained unknown." The report criticized the Iranian government for obstructing ICRC efforts to register and repatriate POWs.[268]

In addition to these broad diplomatic tensions, Iran and Iraq have engaged in a low level conflict in which Iran has backed anti-regime efforts by Iraqi Shi'ites, and Iraq has backed the Iranian People's Mujahideen. During the Gulf War, Iran supported Iraqi Shi'ite military attacks on the People's Mujahideen camps in Iraq. Since that time, the People's Mujahideen has launched attacks on Iran from camps in Iraq, while Iran has attacked the People's Mujahideen camps in Iraq.

On April 9, 1992, Iran sent several F-4 fighters to strike People's Mujahideen bases in Iraq, losing one F-4. Iran claimed—with justification—that these strikes were in retaliation for Mujahideen ground attacks on two Iranian towns near the border on April 5, 1992. Iran also stated that it conducted the raids in response to other People's Mujahideen raids on Iran that had been designed to disrupt its parliamentary elections, sabotage pipelines, and strike at Iranian border posts.

Iran conducted new air raids on Iraq on May 25, 1993, and at least 12 Iranian aircraft struck two of the People's Mujahideen camps in Iraq. One of these bases was at Jalat, near Sulaymaniyah, about 55 miles from the border. The other was at Ashraf, about 65 miles northeast of Baghdad—a camp reported to have between 1,500 and 5,000 guerrillas. Iran stated that these air raids were in retaliation for Mujahideen attacks in Iran, intended to disrupt the Presidential elections, and for Mujahideen support of Iranian Kurdish rebels during the previous two weeks.

Iran held maneuvers on the Iraqi border in Khuzestan in May, 1993, and deployed an armored brigade, an IRGC force of about 8,000 men, helicopters, and fighters. Iraq retaliated by announcing in June, 1993, that it was deploying additional air and land units to the border area, although it is unclear if any major redeployments actually took place. On July 23, 1993, Iraq claimed that Iran conducted a major artillery assault on Mujahideen camps in Iraq, including a three hour bombardment by multiple rocket launchers in the area of Sulaymaniyah.[269]

In late fall of 1994, however, Iran's attitude towards Baghdad seemed to soften. Javad Larijani, the vice chairman of the Iranian Majlis's Foreign Affair Committee and an advisor to Rafsanjani, gave an interview in which he stated that no country was better placed to help Iraq repair its economy than Iran and that, "Iran and Iraq will set the course for the major issues of the Persian Gulf." Ali Akbar Nateq-Nouri—the speaker of the Iranian Parliament and a possible candidate for president in 1997— gave another interview, which seemed to advocate improving relations with Iraq as a counterbalance to US power.

These initiatives failed for reasons that are not entirely clear, but which seem to be related to attacks by the People's Mujahideen. In November, 1994, Iran announced that it fired four missiles at the Mujahideen camp at Ashraf and claimed it had inflicted heavy casualties. Iran indicated that the attack followed the cancellation of an Iranian diplomatic mission to Baghdad. Simultaneously, Iran strengthened its army deployments in the border area.[270]

The new hard line the US took towards Iran in 1995 seems, however, to have led Iran to make yet another attempt to improve its relations with Iraq. Iranian government radio began to call for an end to the UN sanctions on Iraq on February 20, 1995. Iran sent a delegation to Baghdad in May, 1995, that was led by Ali Koram, a senior advisor to Velayati. On May 26, Iran's Deputy Foreign Minister, Hossein Sheikholeslam, announced that arrangements had been made for Velayati to visit Baghdad. There were also news reports that Iran and Iraq had reached an agreement to exchange prisoners of war and that Iran had asked Iraq to extradite Masoud Rajavi, the leader of the People's Mujahideen, to Iran.[271]

Once again, the talks failed. In early July, Iran appears to have sent gunmen to assassinate three Peoples Mujahideen leaders in Baghdad. Iran also made statements on July 18, 1995, indicating that it was backing away from its attempts to improve relations with Iraq. Hassan Ruhani, the Secretary of Iran's Supreme National Security Council issued a statement that Foreign Minister Velayati had been invited to Iraq, but had rejected the invitation. Ruhani also stated that Iraq had not complied with many of the provisions of both the July, 1988 cease-fire and UN Security Council Resolution 598, and that no visit would take place until Iraq did so:[272]

> Most of the articles of the resolution have not been implemented yet. . . . The articles dealing with war reparations, reconstruction of war-stricken areas, repatriation of prisoners of war, and some other issues are not resolved. There is strong evidence substantiating that Iraqis are still holding some 5,000 prisoners of war.

The Iranian Armed Forces Command went further on July 30, 1995, and held a major military exercise called Beyt-ol-Muqaddas (Jerusalem) in the border area near Kermanshah in August. This exercise involved armored forces and exercises simulating nuclear, biological, and chemical warfare.

Iran accused Iraq of repeatedly violating the terms of the 1988 cease-fire during the first half of 1995 and of committing 80 violations from January 21 to June 22. It charged Iraq with planting mines and firing artillery shells into Iran, conducting reconnaissance overflights with planes and helicopters, and installing anti-aircraft equipment near the border. It also accused Iraq of provoking clashes with Iranian border guards and kidnapping Iranian civilians.[273]

Saddam Hussein, in turn, attacked Iran's leaders in a speech on August 8, 1995. He criticized them for keeping Iraqi POWs and Iraqi combat aircraft, and for snubbing Baghdad's peace overtures. Saddam charged that Iran had ignored 245 Iraqi calls for peace since the beginning of the Iran-Iraq War. In reporting Saddam's speech, the Iraqi media referred to 20,000 Iraqi prisoners, 22 IL-76 transports, five Boeing airliners, five other commercial aircraft, and over 100 combat aircraft.[274] In November 1995, Velayati made it clear that Iran would return only 22 of the aircraft that had fled Iraq during the Gulf War and implied these would all be civilian aircraft. This meant that Iran would not even return all of the civil aircraft that had flown to its territory. Iraq, in turn, contiuned to allow the People's Muajhideen to carry out military operations and exercises from locations near the border, and new exercises were held at the Ashraf Camp in March, 1996.[275]

These developments illustrate how hard it may be to achieve any rapprochment between Iran and Iraq, and indicate the lasting strategic importance of any such rapproachment. The history of Iranian-Iraqi relations to date appears to diminish the possibility of a "devil's bargain" between the two countries. No one, however, can afford to dismiss an Iranian and Iraqi strategic relationship, or "Molotov-Ribbentrop Pact," out of hand.

The Iranian Struggle Against the
People's Mujahideen and Other Opposition Groups

Several Iranian government agencies are responsible for internal and external security, including the Ministry of Intelligence and Security, the Ministry of Interior, and the Revolutionary Guards, a military force established after the revolution which is coequal to the regular military. The Iranian Ministry of Intelligence and Security (VEVAK)—directed by the Hojatolislam Ali Fallahiyan—is particularly powerful in terms of operations outside Iran, although Iranian military intelligence—currently directed by Brigadier General Abdollah Najaf—has branches overseas and seems to conduct clandestine operations, as well as aid in Iran's efforts to bypass foreign export controls and obtain military and dual-use technology.[276]

There is little doubt that these agencies are deeply involved in a battle of assassination and counter-assassination with People's Mujahideen representatives overseas. For example, VEVAK agents almost certainly caused the death of Kazem Rajavi, the head of the People's Mujahideen organization in Geneva on August 24, 1990; Mansour Amini, a People's Mujahideen supporter in Turkey on June 4, 1992; and Mohammed Hussein Naghdi, a leading member of the National Council of Resistance in Rome on March 16, 1993.

In 1993, the government of Switzerland requested the extradition from France of two Iranians indicted in the 1991 murder in Geneva of Karem Rajavi, the brother of the leader of the Mujahideen-e Khalq, Masud Rajavi. Instead, the French government expelled the suspects to Iran on December 29, 1993. The two were among 13 Iranians indicted by the Swiss government for the murder; the other 11 were at large at the time of the indictments. Ahmad Sadi Lahijani, a member of the Mujahideen-e Khalq, was assassinated in Ghalebeih, Iraq on May 29, 1994.[277]

Iranian agents killed a total of four dissidents in 1994 and seven in 1995. Most of the anti-dissident attacks in 1995 were conducted in Iraq. These attacks included the shooting of two People's Mujahideen member in Baghdad on May 17, killing two members of the Kurdish "Toilers" (Komelah) Party in Sulaymaniyah on June 5, and killing three members of the People's Mujahideen on July 10. Iran also seems to have played a role in the murder of Hashem Abdollahi, the son of a witness who helped convict two Iranians for murdering former Prime Minister Bakhtiar. This killing took place in Paris on July 10, 1995.[278]

At the same time, Iran's treatment of the People's Mujahideen cannot be dealt with as if Iran was simply committing acts of state terrorism against legitimate political dissidents. This is the impression given by a recent US State Department report on *Patterns of Global Terrorism*, which states:[279]

> Tehran seems to have maintained its terrorist activities at the level of 1993, when there were four confirmed and two possible attacks on dissidents living outside Iran. Iranian terrorist operations concentrate on Iranian dissidents, particularly members of the Mujahideen-e Khalq (MEK) and the Kurdish Democratic Party of Iran (KDPI). . . . Confirmed attacks on Iranian dissidents in the past year include the following: the 7 January killing of Taha Kirmenned, a dissident who was a member of the KDPI by gunmen in

Corfu, Turkey; the 10 January wounding of a member of the KDPI by a letter bomb in Stockholm, Sweden; the killing of a KDPI leader in Sulaymaniyah, Iraq, on 10 March; and the killing of two members of the MEK in
Qabbiyah, Iraq, while driving to Baghdad on 29 May.

The People's Mujahideen has a long history of terrorism dating back to
the murder of US officials in Iran during the time of the Shah. It began the
war of assassination with a long series of killings and bombings as it
attempted to seize power from Khomeini in the early 1980s. It also fought
and propagandized for Iraq during the Iran-Iraq War. The People's
Mujahideen has since continued this war from outside Iran and has
become little more than an Iraqi front. It has conducted many acts of terrorism in Iran and regularly deploys military forces in exercises near the
Iranian border. For example, it held an exercise involving over 1,000 men
near the boarder area in March, 1996. As a result, Iranian attacks on members of the People's Mujahideen, and Iran's air and Scud attacks on the
People's Mujahideen camps in Iran, must be seen as part of a two-sided
clandestine war and not as terrorism.[280]

Iran's attacks on MEK officials must, therefore, be viewed as acts of self
defense and not simply as acts of state terrorism.[281] In fact, the same US
State Department that attacks Iran for its strikes on the MEK recognizes,
"while the MEK has been victimized by Iranian terrorism, the group has
itself employed terrorist tactics."[282]

The same is true of at least some of the attacks by the VEVAK and other
Iranian security organizations on anti-regime Kurdish movements. Iran
almost certainly carried out the assassination of two leaders of the Kurdish Democratic Party of Iran (KDPI). They killed Abdul Rahman
Qassemlou and two associates in Vienna in 1989, after arranging a meeting to "negotiate" with members of the Iranian government. They went
on to kill his successor, Sadeq Sharafkandi, and three associates in Berlin
on September 24, 1992.

Iran seems to have been involved in a number of other attacks. A member of the Revolutionary Command of the Kurdish Democratic Party of
Iran, Taha Kermani, was assassinated in Corum, Turkey on January 4,
1994. Prior to his murder, Mr. Kermani was designated a refugee by the
UN High Commissioner for Refugees (UNHCR). A member of the Kurdish Democratic Party of Iran was assassinated in Sulaymaniyah, Iraq on
March 10, 1994. Osman Mohammed Amini, a member of the Revolutionary Command of the Kurdish Democratic Party of Iran, was murdered in
his apartment in Copenhagen on June 24, 1994. Three members of the
Mujahideen were killed by gunmen in Baghdad on July 10, 1995.[283]

Like the People's Mujahideen, however, the KDPI is a violent opponent of Iran which has often used terrorism and assassination in attack-

ing the Iranian regime, and Iraq has long provided support and arms for the KDPI. The KDPI helped instigate an ethnic civil war in northeastern Iran in the early 1980s and supported Iraq during part of the Iran-Iraq War. It also uses other countries as sanctuaries to attack Iranian officials. It must be noted, though, that Iran has denied Kurdish efforts to seek greater autonomy and has often been ruthless in suppressing legitimate and peaceful Kurdish opposition. According to some reports, the Iranian government razed 17 Kurdish villages in August, 1994.[284]

A distinction needs to be made between Iranian attacks that are part of a war with extremist groups and true acts of violence against legitimate peaceful opposition. There is no justification for attacks by the VEVAK, other Iranian security organizations, and other pro-Iranian groups with clear links to the Iranian government or moderate Iranian dissidents.

The most striking of these attacks was Iran's assassination of former Prime Minister Shahpour Bakhtiar and three bodyguards on August 8, 1991. In December, 1994, a court in France convicted three Iranians of the 1991 assassination of Bakhtiar and his assistant, Katibeh Fallouch. Defendants Ali Vakili Rad and Massoud Hendi were sentenced to life and 18 years, respectively. The prosecutor said the crime was organized from "within the heart of the Islamic Republic of Iran."[285] At 76, Bakhtiar was a spent force in Iranian politics, and scarcely a serious threat to the regime. Yet VEVAK agents set up the assassination using an extensive network of agents in France, killed Bakhtiar's secretary on August 6, 1991, and seem to have deliberately slit Bakhtiar's throat rather than simply shoot him.

Some US and European experts believe that the Iranian foreign service joined Iran's security organizations in directly supporting this assassination effort and then seeking the release of the terrorists involved. They believe that Ali Akbar Velayati, the Iranian Foreign Minister, and Hojatolislam Ali Fallahiyan, the director of the intelligence and security ministry, were personally involved in the planning and execution of Bakhtiar's assassination in 1991.[286]

There have been many other such attacks. Iranian intelligence agents and hard-liners have attacked or intimidated Iranian dissidents in France, Italy, Turkey, Switzerland, and other countries. A wide range of Western experts believe that Iranian agents killed the Japanese translator of Salman Rushdie's *Satanic Verses* on June 12, 1991, and attempted to kill the Italian translator nine days earlier. They also seem to be responsible for assassinating Fereydun Farokhzad, a radio personality, in Germany on August 4, 1992, Abd al-Rahman Boroumand, a Bakhtiar supporter, in Paris in April 1991; and Ali Mohammed Assadi, a monarchist opposition figure, in November, 1994. Iran has repeatedly issued diplomatic passports to those who have been involved in assassination efforts, and Britain, Germany, France, and Switzerland have expelled several would be Iranian assassins.[287]

Iran's death threats against Salman Rushdie are a particularly unpleasant example of such terrorism—although at least some Iranian leaders have tried to compromise on the issue.[288] These threats are further indications of the fact that Iranian security organizations fail to draw a line between attacking members of armed and violent opposition movements and attacking peaceful opposition leaders. It is difficult to believe that the Rafsanjani government does not approve such actions, and it is one thing to meet terrorism with counter-terrorism and quite another to meet moderation with murder.[289] Iran's killing of moderate and peaceful members of the Iranian opposition in Turkey, France, and other countries has no justification. Neither does the mindless persecution and butchering of innocent Bahais, or Iran's series of attacks and threats against writers and journalists.[290]

These actions by the VEVAK, IRGC, and other elements of Iran's security services and armed forces are also a warning that Iran's intelligence operations can pose a significant threat to Iran's neighbors, and to any power projecting armed forces into the region. It is clear from these actions that Iran can escalate to more serious levels of terrorism at any time. No analysis of Iranian contingency capabilities can ignore the fact that the US lost more men in the Marine Barracks bombing in Lebanon than it lost in combat during the entire Gulf War, and these losses were a powerful factor in the precipitous US withdrawal from Lebanon. While such a withdrawal would never have taken place if the US had the kind of clear strategic interests in Lebanon that it does in the Gulf, there is also little doubt that Iran played at least an indirect role in the Marine Corps Barracks bombing and that it has the capability to conduct or stimulate similar acts of unconventional warfare or terrorism in the future.

Iran's Opposition to Israel

There is no ambiguity regarding Iran's political hostility to Israel. The Iranian regime has issued many statements which effectively deny Israel's right to exist. Iran has been a vehement opponent of the Israeli-PLO peace settlement, and some leading Iranian religious and political figures have called for the use of armed violence to prevent it.

In October, 1991, Iran sponsored an "International Conference to Support the Islamic Revolution of Palestine" that included representatives of Hamas, the Hezbollah, PFLP-GC, and Abu-Musa. All of these groups have been associated with terrorist violence. Iranian officials have held high level meetings with Palestinian extremist groups in Damascus and hosted other meetings of the Hezbollah and Hamas in Iran. Several of these groups—including Hamas and Islamic Jihad—made statements acknowledging Iranian funding in 1993.[291]

Iran has strongly opposed each step forward in the peace process. Iranian radio referred to the Gaza-Jericho agreement between Israel and the PLO as "a stain of shame" and "unprecedented treachery." On the February 11, 1995, Iranians, marching at a rally in Tehran's Azadi Square marking the sixteenth anniversary of the overthrow of the Shah, chanted slogans like "death to America" and "death to Israel." President Rafsanjani reinforced this sentiment with a speech acknowledging Iran's encouragement of anti-Israeli Palestinian and Lebanese groups.[292] Iran vehemently attacked the Palestinian elections in January 1996, and charged that only 1 in 15 Palestinians had voted. It claimed that Arafat's victory in the elections was a fraud that did nothing more than "demonstrate the legitimacy of the combatant groups among the people of Palestine."

Iran also seems to have encouraged Hamas and Islamic Jihad to execute the wave of bombings that took place in the months before the Israeli election in May, 1996. Iran stepped up its arms shipments to the Hezbollah to 1996, in the months before the Israeli election. It sent 10 flights worth of arms in the 45 days before the Hizbollah began a major series of rocket attacks on Israel in April, 1996. These flights compared with one flight every three months in 1995, and Iran provided the Hizbollah with some 500–900 additional Russian-made Katyushas. Iran almost certainly encouraged the wave of Hizbollah rocket attacks on Northern Israel that helped lead to a major Israeli confrontation with Lebanon in early May 1996. These attacks were timed to both delay peace negotiations between Israel and the PLO, and to try to influence Israeli public opinion to vote for the Likud, rather than the Labor Party.[293]

Hassan Habibi, the Vice President of Iran, met in the Iranian Embassy in Syria with Emad al-Alami, the main leader of Hamas; Ramadan Abdullah Shalah, the leader of Islamic Jihad, and leaders of the Lebanese Hizbollah during the week between the first two major bus bombings in Jerusalem. Habibi was accompanied by Hussein Sheikhoeslam, an official in the Iranian Foreign Ministry and one of the men responsible for taking hostages at the US Embassy in Tehran in 1979. Sheikhoeslam is responsible for activities to promote Islamic revolutionary and resistance movements. The meeting discussed tactics Habibi and Sheikhoeslam evidently provided money to Hamas, Islamic Jihad, and the Hizbollah. Sheikhoeslam stated publicly after the meeting, "The Islamic Revolution is in for a glorious future. . . .

There is no peaceful solution. The Israelis must return to the countries they came from."[294]

Leading Iranian radicals like Mohtashemi and conservatives like Ayatollah Khamenei have adopted a common ideological view that the "usurper, Zionist administration must pack up. Jews can stay in Palestine, but the administration of Palestine belongs to the nation of Palestine and the Palestinians."[295]

Some Iranians have argued that Iran should do nothing to hinder the peace process which is flawed any way and will collapse as a result of its own contradictions. President Rafsanjani has said that while Iran does not support the peace process it will do nothing to undermine it:[296] "Practically speaking, we do not take any action against the peace plan. When we see this whole process is unjust we state our opposition as a matter of principle. But if the content of the peace plan is just, the substance is just, we shall go along with it."

Similarly, Foreign Minister Ali Akbar Velayati has stated that:[297]

> We do not believe that the recent developments (Arab-Israeli negotiations) are progressing in this direction (establishing of peace). There are conditions, and perhaps desires and objectives, promoted by the Zionist regime. According to this Zionist desire, if Israel fails to control the region by maintaining its occupation of the Arab territory under the well known international conditions and circumstances, it will seek to control the region by controlling economy and culture in the Arab and Muslim states. . . . We believe that there is an Arab and Islamic determination to resist it. My explanation for this issue is based on my conviction that there is no similarity or harmony between the Zionist state and other states in the region, particularly if we remember Israel's history which is replete with crime, aggression and the occupation of territory.

These statements, however, are often contradictory. Iranian President Hashemi-Rafsanjani also declared in February, 1996 that the Arab-Israeli peace process posed a "great danger to the Palestinian cause," and added that the "Islamic Republic of Iran, with its immense resources, possibilities and facilities and revolutionary spirit, is the staunch supporter of the Palestinian cause."[298] The Iranian government and media welcomed the attacks Hamas, Islamic Jihad, and Hezbollah made on Israel in 1996, and welcomed the devastating suicide bombings of February-March 1996 as "divine retribution."

Iran has strongly objected to the new contacts between Israel and moderate Arab states like Morocco and Oman. When Israeli Prime Minister Yitzhak Rabin visited Oman, a spokesman for the Iranian foreign ministry stated that, "Allowing occupiers to get a foothold in the region not only paves the way for the Zionist regime to come out of isolation, it also prepares the ground for creation of discord and infiltration into the ranks of Moslems. . . . [It is] detrimental to the unity of Moslem nations and the region's peace and security."[299]

What is harder to put into perspective is the scale of direct Iranian support for terrorist and violent acts against Israel and supporters of the peace process. US Secretary of State Warren Christopher has argued, "Iran is in a category all its own. . . . No other regime employs terror more systematically as an instrument of national policy—to destroy the peace process, to intimidate its neighbors, and eliminate its political opponents."[300] Christopher, as well as many US and Israeli officials, have indicated that Iran may have provided support for the May 17, 1992, bombing of the Israeli embassy in Buenos Aires and that it may have attempted to bomb the Israeli embassies in Colombia and Ecuador.[301]

A recent US State Department report on terrorism states that,[302]

> Iran is . . . the world's preeminent state sponsor of extremist Islamic and Palestinian groups, providing funds, weapons, and training. Hezbollah, Iran's closest client, could well have been responsible for the July 14, 1994 bombing of the Argentine Israel Mutual Association that left nearly 100 persons dead. This operation was virtually identical to the one conducted in March 1992 against the Israeli Embassy in Buenos Aires, for which Hezbollah claimed responsibility. Hezbollah had stated that it would seek retaliation against Israel for the kidnapping of a well known Lebanese Shi'ite terrorist and the Israeli air strike in June on a Hezbollah camp in Lebanon that killed more than 20 militants.
>
> Iran supports many other radical organizations that have engaged in terrorism. Tehran opposes any compromise with, or any recognition of, Israel and, as the peace process moves ahead, has worked to coordinate a rejectionist front to oppose the Israeli-PLO accords, particularly with the PIJ, the PFLP-GC, and Hamas, as well as Hezbollah.

Secretary Christopher has stated that, "Wherever you look, you will find the evil hand of Iran in this region." On May 1, 1995, Secretary Christopher hinted that the United States had direct evidence linking Iran to the July, 1994 bombing in Argentina—although the government of Argentina does not seem to accept such evidence and the State Department report on terrorism for 1995 only mentions, "Hizbollah, Iran's closest client, remains the leading suspect."[303]

There is little doubt that Iran has provided funds, and some arms and explosives, to the Palestinian Islamic Jihad, the Popular Front for the Liberation of Palestine—General Command, and Hamas with the deliberate aim of destroying the peace accords. Experts from a number of Western countries agree that Iran has helped to organize various pro-Iranian cells of the Hamas, Hezbollah, and other groups. Further, these experts agree that Iran maintains Revolutionary Guards cadres in Lebanon, and provides the Hezbollah with between $25 million and $60 million dollars a year. They note that Iran has begun to smuggle arms through Turkey and northern Iraq to the PKK and Hezbollah, as well as provide arms through Syria. Turkey intercepted three trucks full of munitions near the Cilvegozu border crossing with Syria, and another three trucks at Gurulek on the Turkish border with Iran in January, 1996. The trucks held 500,000 rounds of ammunition, plastic mines, TNT, 81 mm mortars, 1,696 mortar rounds, 168 RPG launchers, and more than 2,000 grenades and all six trucks were bound for Lebanon.[304]

Many Israeli and US experts go further. They believe that senior officials in the Iranian government directly approved acts of terrorism against Israelis, and various car bombings and attacks on Israeli embassies—although recent evidence casts growing doubt on the possibility Iran was directly involved in the attack that killed 86 people in the Jewish community center in Buenos Aires on July 18, 1994.[305] They believe that such operations against Israel and the peace process are directly reviewed by Iran's top leadership, including President Rafsanjani, Ayatollah Khamenei, Foreign Minister Velayati, Defense Minister Mohammed Forouzandeh, and the members of the Iranian National Security Council.

Some US and Israeli experts also believe that Iran has gone beyond supporting groups that oppose Israel and has begun to fund anti-peace and extremist movements within the Palestinian Authority.[306] These views have been supported by reports that Hussein Shaikholeslam, a senior Iranian intelligence officer with an Iranian Foreign Ministry position, provided support to Fahti Shqaqi, the leader of Islamic Jihad, when he attempted to assassinate Yasser Arafat in late 1995."[307]

Other experts have a different view. They argue that Iran's sponsorship of anti-Israeli extremist groups is largely indirect. They do not dispute the fact that Iran has provided some support to anti-Israeli extremists, but they do not believe there is strong evidence that Iran has actively organized or supported terrorist networks in attacks on Israel. They also doubt that Iran has direct control over the actions of the Hezbollah and other extremist groups attacking Israel and the peace process and feel that Syria has been much more directly involved in controlling and influencing Hezbollah's actions in attacking Israel. They fear that Israel and the US deliberately underplay Syria's role, and emphasize Iran's, because they wish to keep Syria active in the peace process.

Such experts all note that Iran's actions in Lebanon cannot be seen simply in terms of its opposition to Israel; Iran has long-standing ties to the Shi'ite movement in Lebanon dating back to the time Lebanese clergy played a major role in Iran's conversion to the Shi'ite faith. They feel that at least some Iranian actions which have been blamed on Iran's leadership have been taken independently by elements within the Ministry of Information and Intelligence, and military and Revolutionary Guards intelligence units. They also contend that Iran will accept any peace settlement reached by Syria, or which meets the needs of the Shi'ites in South Lebanon.

At least some French, German, and Swiss experts also feel that Iran has reduced its support of terrorism since 1991, concentrating instead on attacking Iranian dissident movements. Other experts believe, however, that such statements reflect policies which effectively allow Iran to conduct limited operations against dissidents on French, German, and Swiss soil as long as they do not attack other targets, encourage Islamist extremist factions in these countries, or injure civilians.[308]

These differences are partly differences of nuance. There is no disagreement over the fact that Iran effectively denies Israel's right to exist, claims both that the peace process is illegitimate and that those Arab leaders who support it oppose the true will of their peoples, or that Iran continues to support movements who use violence. At the same time, these differences are not minor ones from a policy point of view. Broad support for extremists and violent anti-Israeli groups is very different from organized and direct support of terrorism. Broad ideological opposition to Israel and the peace process is very different from a total and unchangeable commitment to rejectionism. The answers to these questions are critical in determining whether any dialogue or policy of constructive engagement with Iran is possible, or likely to produce meaningful results.

The Policy Implications of Extremism and Terrorism

Like Iran's internal politics and relations with its immediate neighbors, the evidence regarding Iran's support of terrorism and extremism does not validate either the position of those who "demonize" Iran or those who "sanctify" it. Iran does present the kind of threat that the Clinton Administration describes in its statements and reports on terrorism. At the same time, it does support terrorist and extremist activity and it is scarcely free of guilt.

Iran's opposition to Israel's existence, its support of extremist movements that oppose the peace process, and its activities in support of the Hezbollah in Lebanon present a particularly significant threat to the stability of the Middle East. Like Iran's support of Islamic extremist movements in the Southern Gulf, this aspect of Iran's conduct strongly reinforces the need for "military containment." It also limits what the US can hope to achieve through constructive engagement unless Iran is willing to change its conduct in return for better relations.

The US and Israel, however, need to be far more careful about what they define as "terrorism" when describing the scale of Iranian activity. Careless rhetoric both destroys credibility and the basis for negotiation and dialogue. It fails to recognize that the support of peaceful Islamic movements is legitimate, as is non-violent criticism of Israel and the US. It also makes it difficult to seek specific and well targeted changes in Iran's conduct, or to obtain the support of European and Asia states. Hyperbole is not a substitute for objectivity or integrity.

8

Iran's Conventional Military Forces

Like Iran's relations with its neighbors and its support of extremism, Iran's conventional military capabilities are key indicators of the character of the regime and the risk it poses to its neighbors. However, Iran cannot be analyzed simply in terms of its current military strength. It must be studied in the broader context of its military politics, the scale of its military expenditures and arms imports, its military demographics, and war fighting capabilities. It is also important to distinguish between Iran's capability to challenge the US and Southern Gulf states in a major regional contingency, and its capacity to intimidate the Gulf states and conduct more limited and less conventional forms of war.

The Control and Leadership of Iran's Military Forces

Iran has attempted to reform the overall organization of its military forces since the Ayatollah Ruhollah Khomeini's death but with only moderate success. The division of Iran's military forces into "regular" and "revolutionary" branches has long been a source of internal problems. Rafsanjani recognized this when he was appointed commander-in-chief during the Iran-Iraq War, but Khomeini blocked his efforts from June, 1988 to August, 1989, to merge the Islamic Revolutionary Guards with the Iranian regular army. After the war, Khomeini put a hard-line mullah in a position where he had authority nearly equal to that of Rafsanjani and gave him supervisory authority over the IRGC Minister Ali Shamkhani and IRGC Commander Mohsen Rezaii. These actions reinforced the feuding between Iran's regular forces and the IRGC that helped contribute to Iran's defeat at the hands of Iraq.[309]

Rafsanjani and Khamenei seem to have reached a working accord over the control of the armed forces since Khomeini's death. Khamenei automatically became the formal commander of the armed forces when he became leader and president on September 2, 1989. At the same time, Rafsanjani retains effective practical command as head of the Supreme Council for National Security. There does not seem to have been any major debate within the Iranian leadership over the need to change senior appointments to ease the tensions between the military factions. At the same time, the clergy has been less intrusive in shaping Iranian military developments.

The post-Khomeini changes in the leadership of the military and internal security forces seem to reflect an emphasis on cohesion, pragmatism, and effectiveness, rather than moderation. When Rafsanjani formed his own cabinet on August 19, 1989, he purged some extremists such as Interior Minister Ali Akbar Mohtashemi and Intelligence Minister Mohammad Reyshahri. He also appointed a number of leading technocrats to offices within the Ministry of Defense. At the same time, a number of the Ayatollah Ruhollah Khomeini's supporters and hard-line revolutionaries remain in senior positions. Further, Iran's Islamic Revolutionary Guards Corps has continued to remain under the command of Mohsen Rezaii (a strong revolutionary) and retains considerable independence, to the point where it sometimes seems to act independently from the central government.[310]

It is hard to determine which changes in Iran's command structure represent the result of jockeying for personal power, and which changes have been designed to achieve other goals.[311] At the end of the Iran-Iraq War Brigadier General Ismail Sohrabi was dismissed as chief of staff for the failure of Iranian forces to hold at Faw. A number of other Iranian regular army officers were also dismissed or arrested, and some may have been executed.[312] The Minister of the Revolutionary Guard, Mohsen Rafiqdust, was removed for incompetence in September, 1988—although he was then made military advisor to Rafsanjani and later held a critical position in the government as head of the Foundation for the Oppressed.[313] These changes, however, do not really seem to have punished those who were guilty of causing Iran's defeat. In most cases, the need to find a scapegoat, or personal politics, seems to have shaped the decisions.

Rafsanjani has since presided over a number of command changes that have eased divisions within the military, improved efficiency, and mixed the guard and regular military leadership to reduce the friction between the IRGC and regular forces. Two of these changes were especially important. The first was the abolition of the Ministry for the Revolutionary Guard in the fall of the 1989 and the creation of a Ministry of Defense and Armed Forces Logistics (MODAFL) under Akbar Torkan, a close supporter of Rafsanjani.

Ali Shamkhani was moved from the position of Minister of the Revolutionary Guard to commander of the navy in October, 1989, and Torkan was given a portfolio that combined the administrative apparatus of the regular forces and the IRGC. Torkan was a civilian with no clear ties to either the regular armed forces or the Guards and, therefore, was in a good position to be seen as relatively neutral.[314] This appointment marked the first meaningful attempt since the beginning of the revolution to set up a unified ministry of defense.

The second change was the transformation of the Supreme Defense Council into the Supreme Council for National Security in 1990–1991. Rafsanjani is the Secretary General of the Supreme Council for National Security, and has ensured that several of his loyalists play an important role in the Council. These loyalists include Iran's Foreign Minister, Ali Akbar Velayati.

Iran also adopted a broader military reform plan that called for the creation of a single chain of command during war; for a rationalization of the complex and unwieldy command system that had grown up around various subdivisions of the regular armed forces and Islamic Revolutionary Guards Corps; for the development of national defense industries; and for the acquisition of modern arms. Command of all the armed forces was placed under a single Office of the Joint Chiefs of Staff in 1988, which seemed to indicate that control of the regular forces and IRGC had been unified.

These changes, however, left the separate military branches of the IRGC intact, and the IRGC had enough political power to persuade Khamenei to reestablish its Central Headquarters Staff under Rezaii in 1989. The IRGC's joint staff was originally formed in late 1984 and now includes the commanders of the land, air, and naval branches of the IRGC.[315] The IRGC has created relatively modern command structures within each of its branches since 1989. At the same time, the creation of a single Office of the Joint Chiefs of Staff has only limited meaning. There is a joint staff at the top of the armed forces which combines elements from the regular forces and the IRGC, but both the regular armed forces and IRGC retain their own joint staffs under this combined staff. The end result is that the command structure still operates in parallel, with coordination only at the top.

Pragmatic professionals have been appointed to some senior positions. These include Brigadier General Ali Shahbazi's appointment as Chief of the Army Staff. Rafsanjani and Khamenei retained professionals like Brigadier General Mansoor Sattari as Air Force Commander, and Brigadier General Hussein Hansani-Sadi as Commander Armed Forces Ground Forces. This emphasis on professionalism has given the regular forces the most effective and stable command they have enjoyed since 1979.

Other measures seem to have been designed to improve political unity within the armed forces. The role of the Office of the Joint Chiefs of Staff was strengthened in 1992. The commander of this office was Hassan Firouzabadi, a civilian who has been associated with the Guards. The creation of this office and Firouzabadi's appointment not only created more unity at the top, but also marked another attempt to mix regular force and IRGC commanders. Firouzabadi announced the creation of a Supreme Council for Military Policy to help implement the creation of clear roles and missions and command structures for the armed forces.

Some of the internal security services—police, Gendarmerie, and Islamic Revolutionary Committees (*komitehs*)—were merged in 1991 and renamed the Law Enforcement Forces of the Islamic Republic. They are headed by Brigadier-General Reza Seyfollahi, who was appointed by the Supreme Leader Ayatollah Khamenei, but reports to the Minister of the Interior Ali Mohammad Besharati. These mergers have not, however, created a unified internal security structure or made day-to-day life easier or less repressive for many Iranians. The police forces may be more firmly under Rafsanjani's control, but the IRGC and Basij continue to operate with considerable independence. The VEVAK and various clerical groups also seem to operate independently, and often in ways that are more repressive than effective.

At the same time, added professionalism has not meant any clear trend in favor of moderates or the regular armed forces. Many regular army appointments come from the IRGC, or are influenced by it. Torkan was replaced as Minister of Defense by Mohammad Foruzandeh, a member of the IRGC, after Rafsanjani's reelection in 1993. Other senior radicals in critical security positions include Hojatolislam Ali Fallahiyan, head of the internal security services, Mohammad Gharazi, as Minister of Telecommunications, and Ali Larijani, Minister of Culture and Islamic Guidance. Some sources include Mohammed Ali Besharati, the Minister of the Interior and a protege of the Ayatollah Khamenei among this group.

The IRGC is also increasing its ability to act as an effective force. It has come a long way since the early 1980s when it was a disorganized militia. The Iran-Iraq War led to its transformation into a more professional force, and further developments have taken place since the death of Khomeini. While the Islamic Revolutionary Guards Corps remains under the control of Rezaii and most promotions seem to be decided by the IRGC's leadership, the IRGC adopted military ranks and uniforms similar to those of the regular military in 1991. At the same time its commander stipulated that henceforth promotion or advancement within the IRGC would be based on the following traditionally military criteria: (i) military skills and knowledge attained during the war with Iraq; (ii) the level of education of the IRGC member—the higher the level of one's education the greater the prospects for promotion; (iii) organizational, administrative, and managerial skills and level of experience in these areas. Ideological and spiritual fervor were no longer adequate qualifications.

Mohammed Baqer Zolqadr was made Chief of Staff of the IRGC Central Headquarters in 1989, and given special responsibility for enforcing discipline and requiring the IRGC to implement orders. Mustafa Izadi was appointed head of the IRGC ground forces in 1989 and Alireza Afshar was appointed commander of the Basij or volunteer forces in January 1990.[316] Hussein Dehqan, the former commander of the IRGC contingent in Lebanon was appointed the first head of the IRGC air forces in April, 1990. He was then replaced by Brigadier General Hosein Jalali in early 1992, in what seems to have been an effort to give the air forces more professional leadership.[317] Hussein Alai was replaced as head of the IRGC naval forces by Ali Shamkhani in 1990 (who now heads both the regular navy and IRGC naval forces), and Brigadier General Hossein Mantequei is the commander of the IRGC's missile forces and seems to command its long-range missiles and weapons of mass destruction.[318]

There will almost certainly continue to be rivalry between the IRGC and regular forces. However, the political importance of any remaining political splits between the Iranian regular army and the IRGC— as distinguished from a struggle for power within the armed forces— may be limited. The regular forces are no longer the forces once shaped by the Shah. It has been more than a decade and a half since the Shah's fall. Most of Iran's current military manpower have no Western training or history of loyalty to the former monarch. It is the product of the revolution which it fought for during the Iran-Iraq War.[319] More recently, the unexpected promotion of Hasan Firuzabadi, a civilian, to the post of Chief of Staff of the armed forces in May 1995 with the rank of Major-General was bound to strain regime ties with the armed forces, particularly in light of the fact that Firuzabadi outranks the two most senior officers in the Iranian armed forces, Major-General Mohsen Rezaii of the IRGC and Major-General Ali Shahbazi, chief of staff of the regular army.[320]

This mix of political and military developments has probably improved the government's control over Iran's internal security—in spite of Iran's economic and social problems. The regular forces are more closely aligned with the government. The IRGC and internal security forces are better disciplined and better organized than before—although they still have not reached the standard of the regular forces. The People's Mujahideen and other opposition groups have little military power, and the regime does not seem to face any major ethnic challenges—although it has some low level problems with Kurdish nationalists.

Iranian Military Expenditures

Iran's overall military effort is one key measure of the threat Iran may pose to the region. It is important to note in this context that US advocates of dual containment have been careful to avoid accusing Iran of a massive military build-up. A recent report on US security strategy for the Middle East by the Office of the Secretary of Defense refers to current military developments in Iran as follows:[321]

> While Iran's conventional military capability will remain limited throughout the 1990s, recent purchases such as submarines, attack aircraft, and anti-shipping missiles, and the build-up of Iranian forces on several disputed islands near the Strait of Hormuz suggested that it is actively seeking the capability to menace merchant ships moving in and out of the Gulf. It is obvious that Iran is assertively flexing its muscles vis-à-vis its smaller Gulf neighbors.

Joseph S. Nye, Assistant Secretary of Defense for International Security Affairs provides a similar description of the Iranian conventional military threat:[322]

> While Iran's overall conventional military capability is limited and will remain so throughout the 1990s, recent purchases demonstrate its desire to develop an offensive capability in specific mission areas that endanger US interests. . . . We are especially concerned about the recent sales of Russian Kilo submarines and tactical aircraft and Chinese and North Korean missiles to an Iranian government that makes no secret of its desire to dominate maritime traffic in and out of the Persian Gulf. In this regard, we are also closely watching the Iranian military build-up on several islands whose ownership is disputed between Iran and the UAE—Abu Musa and Greater and Lesser Tunbs. Whatever the specific Iranian motivation for fortifying the islands, the creation by a hostile power of bases sitting aside the western approaches to the Straits of Hormuz is obviously a matter of serious concern for commercial traffic, our own naval presence, and the security of our Arab friends.

The best data currently available on Iran's military expenditures and arms transfers are the unclassified DIA data available from reporting by the US Arms Control and Disarmament Agency (ACDA). These data are shown in Table Eight. It is important to note that these data have significant uncertainties, because they involve estimates that attempt to convert some aspects of Iranian military expenditures—like manpower costs and arms transfers—to a context specific dollar value.

There is no agreement within the US government over the size of Iranian military expenditures. For example, the US Central Intelligence Agency (CIA) estimated in 1993 that Iran spent $13 billion on defense in 1992, while the ACDA figures shown in Table Eight indicate that Iran's

TABLE EIGHT   Iranian Annual Military Expenditures and Arms Imports

	Military Expenditures ($ Millions)		Arms Imports ($ Millions)	
	$ Current	*$94 Constant*	*$ Current*	*$94 Constant*
1983	4,864	—	875	—
1984	6,059	8,386	2,700	3,737
1985	6,772	9,044	1,900	2,537
1986	8,836	11,490	2,600	3,381
1987	7,487	9,436	2,000	2,521
1988	6,926	8,406	2,600	3,155
1989	5,929	6,886	1,500	1,742
1990	6,394	7,117	1,800	2,003
1991	6,154	6,597	2,100	2,251
1992	3,964	4,133	360	375
1993	4,705	4,502	1,000	1,021
1994	3,042	3,042	390	390
1995	*3,350*	—	*390*	—
1996	*3,800*	—	*650*	—

Source: Adapted by Anthony H. Cordesman from ACDA, *World Military Expenditures and Arms Transfers, 1994–1995,* Washington, GPO, 1996, Tables I & II, and Richard F. Grimmett, *Conventional Arms Transfers to the Third World, 1987–1995,* Washington, Congressional Research Service, CRS-95-862F, August 4, 1995, pp. 57–58, 67–69. Data for 1994 and 1995, and all data in italics, estimated by Anthony Cordesman.[323]

expenditures totaled only $3.9 billion. Similarly, US intelligence experts felt in 1994 that Iran had spent up to $8 billion on military forces in 1993, while ACDA estimated only $4.9 billion. The CIA issued revised estimates in 1995 that stated it could not make accurate conversions of expenditures in Iranian Rials to dollars, but indicated that Iran had reported it had spent 1,785 billion Rials on defense in 1992, including $808 million in hard currency, and 2,507 billion Rials in 1993, including $850 million in hard currency.[324]

The IISS has produced somewhat different figures. It estimates that Iran's economic problems and defeat in 1988 reduced Iran's defense spending from $9.9 billion in 1987/88, to $5.8 billion in 1989/90, $3.2 billion in 1990, $5.8 billion in 1991, $1.8–2.3 billion in 1992, $4.86 billion in 1993, $2.3 billion in 1994, and $2.46 billion in 1995.[325] These IISS estimates, however, do not seem to include some key procurement expenses and many of Iran's expenditures on weapons of mass destruction.

Any estimate of the burden military expenditures have placed on Iran's economy and total government budget are even more uncertain, and Iranian official economic statistics have little reliability. Iran reported total military expenditures of only $1.8 billion in 1992 and $1.2 billion in

1993, versus a GDP that is estimated at $71 billion in 1992. The US CIA, on the other hand, estimated that Iran spent $13 billion on defense in 1992, or 13–14% of its annual GDP. This level of effort may be correct. Iran seems to have spent about 20% or more of its GDP—and over 50% of its central government expenditures—on defense during much of the Iran-Iraq War. It seems to have spent 10% to 15% of its GDP on military forces and equipment since 1988.[326]

Chart Two has already shown a US estimate of the trends in Iran's GDP relative to the trends in Iran's military expenditures. Chart Twenty uses the same source to show the trends in Iran's military expenditures and arms imports relative to its total central government expenditures and total export earnings. It illustrates trends which indicate that the Iranian government is sharply increasing its total budget, with virtually all of this increase going to the civil sector. Chart Twenty-One provides a detailed estimate of the trends in military expenditures and arms exports alone, and also indicates that Iran's economic crisis has forced Iran to reduce its military effort sharply.

The data in these charts and Table Eight indicate that Iran's real defense spending is now less than one third of the level it reached during the Iran-Iraq war, they also indicate that Iranian military expenditures still total over $2.0 billion. To put such spending levels in context, ACDA estimates that Egypt's total spending during 1990–1993 averaged around $1.5 billion. Iraq's expenditures averaged around $10 billion during 1988–1991, but no recent figures are available. Kuwait's spending reached peaks of $15 billion a year during 1990–1992, but dropped to $3.6 billion in 1993. Turkey spends between $6 billion and $7 billion. The UAE spends around $2 billion annually, and Saudi Arabia spends well over $20 billion.[327]

Such data scarcely indicate that Iran's military spending is large enough to support a major military build-up. In fact, they indicate that Iran is spending too little to maintain its present force structure; "recapitalize" it to replace the equipment lost to combat, age, and war or modernize its current force structure. It also seems likely from such figures that Iran's economic crisis is forcing it to make increasingly painful choices between guns and butter.

However, current Iranian spending levels are sufficient for Iran to continue to pose a significant threat to its neighbors. While Iran may not have been able to fund the military build-up it would like, it has concentrated its resources in areas that pose a serious threat to its neighbors and the West. Iran has steadily built up its ability to threaten Gulf shipping and to acquire and deliver weapons of mass destruction. This build-up of its ability to threaten Gulf shipping is described in the following chapters, as are its missile and biological, chemical, and nuclear weapons programs. It is also important to note that none of the estimates of Iranian

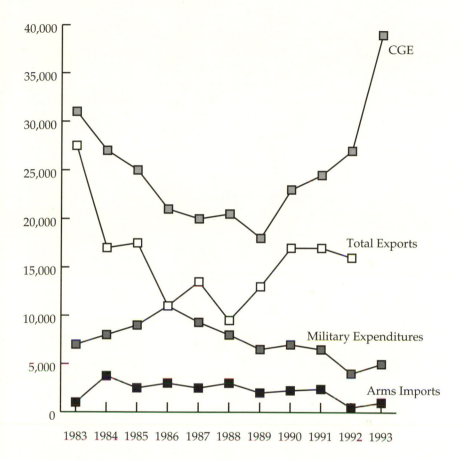

CHART TWENTY   Iranian Central Government Expenditures, Military Expenditures, Total Exports, and Arms Import Deliveries: 1983–1993 (Constant $93 Millions). *Source:* Adapted by Anthony H. Cordesman from ACDA, *World Military Expenditures and Arms Transfers, 1993–1994,* ACDA/GPO, Washington, 1995.

military spending described above attempt to account for Iran's efforts to produce biological, chemical, and nuclear weapons—programs which cost at least several hundred million additional dollars per year, and which may total over $500 million a year in dollar equivalent value.

Further, Iran continues to discuss much larger spending efforts. While it is almost impossible to validate the recent military spending claims of the Iranian government, or translate them into constant dollars, Rafsanjani's military spending request for the 1996–1997 budget totaled 5.9 bil-

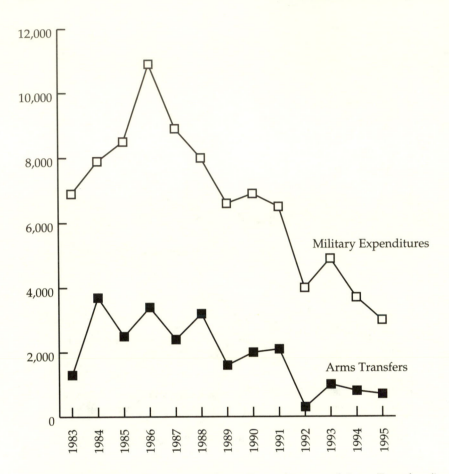

CHART TWENTY-ONE   Iranian Military Expenditures and Arms Transfers (in Constant 1993 Dollars). *Source:* Adapted by Anthony H. Cordesman from ACDA, *World Military Expenditures and Arms Transfers, 1993–1994,* ACDA/GPO, Washington, 1995, Tables I & II. Data for 1994 and 1995, and all data in italics, estimated by Anthony H. Cordesman.

lion Rials (roughly $3.9 billion in January 1996 $US). On paper, this request is a major increase over Iran's 1994–1995 budget ($2.3 billion) and a 31% increase over its 1995–1996 budget request ($2.46 billion).

This level of increase would still produce a budget significantly lower than the comparable estimates of $4.86 billion for 1993–1994, and there is no way to know where the money will be spent or how much of a real increase it represents given the inability to accurately translate figures in Rials into comparable levels of purchasing power. Nevertheless, Rafsanjani made the request in the context of a civil budget that called for new sacrifices for Iran's future, speeches which condemned American "aggressiveness" in the Gulf, and estimates of oil revenues that only totaled 51.5% of Iran's revenues—the lowest percentage in recent history. Such a request is, at a minimum, a warning that Iran may be funding more guns at expense of desperately needed butter.

The problems Iran faces in paying for both guns and butter could increase some aspects of the threat Iran poses to its neighbors. Unless oil prices rise sharply for other reasons, a combination of military expenditures and domestic needs may push Iran towards progressively stronger efforts to persuade its neighbors to cut production and raise oil prices. While Iran has recently cooperated with Saudi Arabia and other OPEC states in attempting to stabilize oil prices and set production quotas, it will be under steadily increasing economic pressure to try to force its southern Gulf neighbors to cut their production. Iran has also talked about raising production capacity to 4.5 million barrels per day by 1994 and 5 million barrels per day by 1995, and investing $5 billion in on-shore and off-shore oil drilling, exploration, and development. It is uncertain whether Iran can actually produce at these levels, but its investment will serve little purpose if it simply cuts prices.[328]

Iran may well find it harder and harder to fund its ambitions, and its only way of obtaining more revenue may be to raise its oil revenues. This problem may become even more serious once Iraq is allowed to resume its oil exports. Mere reports that Iraq would resume exports of even 1.5 million barrels a day put significant downward pressure on oil prices in the early winter of 1993. As a result, Iran may try to intimidate its neighbors and use the threat of force or unconventional warfare to put pressure on the southern Gulf states.

Iranian Conventional Arms Transfers

While the total value of Iran's arms transfers may have dropped significantly since the Iran-Iraq War, Iran's ability to import advanced arms and military technology has improved. Iran's opposition to Iraq's invasion of Kuwait may not have affected US policy, but it gave Iran new respectability and better access to the world's arms markets.

At the same time, Iran has also had to use many of its arms imports to replace aging or inadequate equipment, or make up for war time losses. Throughout the Iran-Iraq War, Iran was heavily dependent on the PRC, North Korea, and Eastern Europe and could only obtain low to moderate quality systems from these suppliers. It could not replace, modernize, or even maintain many of the Western-supplied arms it received before the Shah's fall. It then lost 40% to 60% of its major land force equipment during the final battles of the Iran-Iraq War.[329]

TABLE NINE   Iranian Arms Transfers by Major Supplier: 1983–1994 (in millions of current US dollars)

	1983–1986	*1987–1990*	*1991–1994*
Agreements			
Soviet Union	10	2,500	1,200
China	1,845	3,400	400
United States	0	0	0
Major West			
European	865	200	100
All Other European	3,835	2,100	100
All Others	2,385	2,000	900
Total	8,940	10,200	2,700
Deliveries			
Soviet Union	100	1,100	2,400
China	1,165	2,500	1,100
United States	0	0	0
Major West			
European	460	500	100
All Other European	3,285	1,900	0
All Others	2,250	1,800	300
Total	7,260	7,800	3,900

Note: Values of covert US sales to Iran in 1985–1986 are not included.

Source: Adapted by Anthony H. Cordesman from material provided by the US Government and Richard F. Grimmett, *Conventional Arms Transfers to the Third World, 1983–1990*, Washington, Congressional Research Service, CRS-91-578F, August 2, 1991, *Conventional Arms Transfers to the Third World, 1984–1991*, Washington, Congressional Research Service, CRS-92-577F, July 20, 1991, and *Conventional Arms Transfers to the Third World, 1987–1994*, Washington, Congressional Research Service, CRS-95-862F, August 4, 1995. 0 = data less than $50 million or nil. All data are rounded to the nearest $100 million. Major West European includes Britain, France, Germany, and Italy.

The Quantity of Iran's Arms Transfers

Table Nine and Chart Twenty-Two provides further data on Iran's recent arms orders and deliveries from given groups of suppliers. When the data in Table Five and Chart Twenty-Two are combined with those shown in Table Eight, they indicate just how much Iran's arms imports have declined since the Iran-Iraq War.

According to the estimates in Table Nine and Chart Twenty-Two, Iran took delivery on $7.6 billion worth of arms during the four year period between 1987–1990—the time between the final years of the Iran-Iraq War and the Gulf War. It received $1.1 billion in deliveries from Russia, $2.5

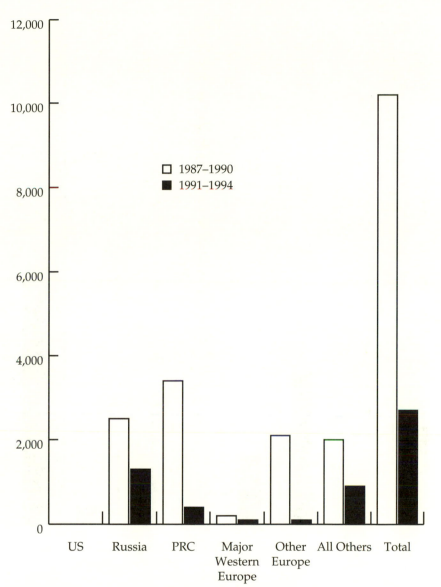

CHART TWENTY-TWO   Iranian Arms Sales Agreements by Supplier Country: 1987–1994—Part One ($Current Millions). *Source:* Adapted by Anthony H. Cordesman from work by Richard F. Grimmett in *Conventional Arms Transfers to Developing Nations, 1987–1994,* Congressional Research Service 95-862F, August 4, 1994, pp. 56–57.

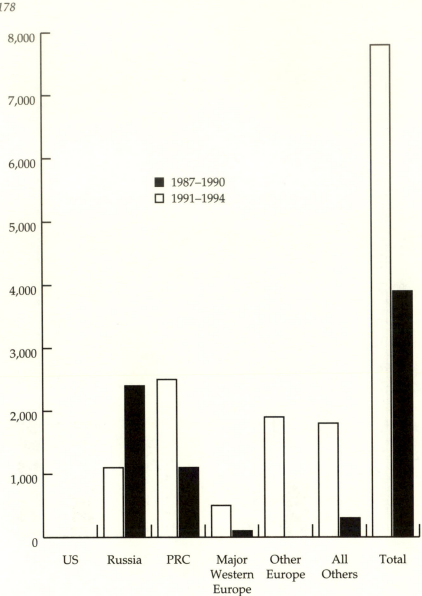

CHART TWENTY-TWO   Iranian Arms Deliveries by Supplier Country: 1987–1994—Part Two ($Current Millions). *Source:* Adapted by Anthony H. Cordesman from work by Richard F. Grimmett in *Conventional Arms Transfers to Developing Nations, 1987–1994*, Congressional Research Service 95-862F, August 4, 1994, pp. 56–57.

billion from China, $500 million from Western Europe, $1.9 billion from other European states (mostly Eastern Europe), and $1.8 billion from other countries (mostly North Korea).[330]

Chart Twenty-Two and Table Nine also show that the volume of arms transfers to Iran dropped sharply during the four year period from 1991–1994, with Iran taking delivery of only $3.9 billion worth of arms.[331] Despite some reports of a massive Iranian military build-up during the 1990s—deliveries during 1991–1994 were only worth about 52% of the value, even in current dollars, of the deliveries that Iran had received during the previous four years. It received $2.4 billion in deliveries from Russia, but only $1.1 billion from China, $100 million from Western Europe, and $300 million from other countries (mostly North Korea).[332]

Another US estimate, covering the period from 1992–1994, estimates that Iran received a total of $1,765 million worth of arms during this three year period, $1,000 million from Russia, $40 million from Germany, $525 million from China, $20 million from other Middle Eastern countries, $30 million from East European countries, $110 million from other East Asian countries, and $40 million from other states.[333]

Iran's new arms agreements dropped even more in value. They went from $10.2 billion during 1987–1990 to $2.7 billion during 1991–1994—a decline of 74%. Such expenditures scarcely indicate that Iran's recent arms import programs are "aggressive," although many of the reductions may be more the result of Iran's economic crisis than its desires.[334] One US estimate projects that Iran will acquire a total of $7.7 billion worth of arms during the period from 1994–2000, or about $1.1 billion a year worth of arms.[335] There is no way, however, to know if Iran's arms imports will rise to this level or exactly what Iran will buy.

The Quality of Iran's Arms Transfers

It is important to note that the cuts in the quantity of Iranian arms transfers have been partly offset by important changes in the quality of Iran's arms transfers. After the Iran-Iraq War, Iran was able to increase its arms orders from Russia, and deliveries increased from $1.1 billion during 1987–1990 to $2.4 billion in 1991–1994. Iran was able to import first line tanks like the T-72 and aircraft like the MiG-29 and Su-24 from the Russian Republic. During 1991–1994, Iran was able to obtain nearly $3.4 billion worth of deliveries from Russia.

Iran also found it easier to acquire equipment and supplies for its biological and chemical weapons efforts, and received increased—if still limited—imports of high technology for its nuclear weapons program.[336] This new access to arms is summarized in Table Ten, which shows major recent Iranian military modernization by service and type of weapon.

TABLE TEN   Key Iranian Equipment Developments

Land
- Russian and Polish T-72 Exports
- Iranian Zulfiqar MBT (prototype) and upgrade T-54/T-54 "Sfir-74"
- Russian BMPs
- Domestic APC modifications (Cobra, Boraq)
- Modified "Babr 400" HET
- Russian and Asian AT-2s, AT-3s, and AT-4s
- Chinese and 15+ North Korean 146mm self-propelled weapons
- Russian 2S1 122mm self-propelled howitzers
- Russian BM-24 240mm, BM-21 122mm and Chinese Type 63 107mm MRLs
- Iranian Hadid 122mm–40 round MRL
- Iranian Arash and Noor rockets (variants of Chinese and Russian 122mm rockets)
- Iranian Fajer and Haseb rockets (variants of Chinese 107mm rocket)
- Iranian Shahin 1 and 2, Oghab and Nazeat (2 versions) long-range rockets

Air/Air Defense
- MiG-29s with refueling, may be receiving 15–20 more from Russia
- Possibly received AA-8, AA-10, and AA-11s from Russia
- Su-24s (probably Su-24D version), may be receiving 6 to 9 more from Russia
- Possibly received AS-10, AS-11, AS-12, AS-14/16s from Russia
- Su-25s (formerly Iraqi)
- Iran is trying to purchase more Su-25s, as well as MiG-31s, Su-27s, and Tu-22Ms
- Iran is considering imports of Chinese F-8 fighter and Jian Hong bomber
- Chinese F-7M fighters with PL-2, PL-2A, and PL-7 AAMs
- Iran claims to have fitted F-14s with IHawk missiles adapted to the air-to-air role
- IHawk, 50–55 SA-2 and HQ-23 (CSA-1), 25 SA-6, and 10–15 SA-5 launchers
- Reports in July 1995, that Russia might have agreed to sell SA-10s to Iran
- Chinese FM-80 launchers and a few RBS-70s
- Large numbers of SA-7s, HN-5s, SA-14s and possibly SA-16s
- HN-5 light SAMs
- Rapier and 10–15 Tigercat fire units
- ZSU-23-4

Sea
- Russian Type 877EKM Kilo-class submarines, possibly with 1,000 modern magnetic, acoustic, and pressure sensitive mines
- North Korean midget submarines
- US Mark 65 and Russian AND 500, AMAG-1, KRAB anti-ship mines
- Reports that Iran is negotiating to buy Chinese EM-52 rocket-propelled mine
- Iran claims to be developing non-magnetic, acoustic, free-floating, and remote controlled mines. It may have also acquired non-magnetic mines, influence mines, and mines with sophisticated timing devices.
- Wake-homing and wire-guided Russian torpedoes

(continues)

TABLE TEN   (*continued*)

- Silkworm (HY-2) sites with 50–60 missiles—Iran working to extend range to 400km
- Chinese CS -801 (Ying Jai-1 or SY-2) or CS-802 (YF-6) SSMs
- Boghammer fast interceptor craft

Missiles
- Possibly 250–300 Scud Bs with 8–15 launchers
- Chinese CSS-8 missiles with 25–30 launchers
- Reports that China is giving Iran technology to produce M-9 class missile
- Iran-130 missile (?)
- North Korean Scud Cs with 5–14 launchers
- Iran appears to be planning to purchase 150 North Korean No Dong 1s
- Iran is also interested in North Korea's developmental Tapeo Dong 1 or Tapeo Dong 2

CBW
- Chemical weapons (sulfur mustard gas, hydrogen cyanide, phosgene and/or chlorine; possibly Sarin and Tabun)
- Biological weapons (Anthrax, hoof and mouth disease, and other biotoxins)
- Nuclear weapons development (Russian and Chinese reactors)

Source: Based on interviews, reporting in various defense journals, and the IISS, *Military Balance*, various editions.

Iran cut its orders from China from $3.4 billion during 1987–1990 to $400 million in 1991–1994, and deliveries dropped from $2.4 billion during 1987–1990 to only $100 million in 1991–1994. However, the end of the Iran-Iraq War allowed Iran to reduce orders for wartime replacements and munitions, however, and to concentrate on acquiring more advanced Chinese weapons and technology, such as anti-ship missiles, ballistic missile production capability, and anti-aircraft missiles.[337]

At the same time, Iran has had even more severe problems in obtaining equipment, munitions, and spare parts from Europe and the West. Iran cut its orders from Europe from $2.3 billion during 1987–1990, to $200 million in 1991–1994, and deliveries dropped from $2.5 billion during 1987–1990, to $1,100 million in 1990–1993. During 1991–1994, it received only $100 million worth of deliveries from Western Europe, no major deliveries from Eastern Europe and no deliveries from the US. This left it without the parts and munitions necessary to support and modernize the Western-supplied equipment obtained during the Shah's reign.[338]

Iran's shift to arms imports from Russia carried disadvantages as well as advantages. These imports meant Iran had to convert to a third major supplier of arms in the course of about 15 years. This has forced

Iran to move from dependence on the West, to dependence on Asia, to dependence on Russia, creating serious problems in conversion and standardization.

Iran's force structure is still heavily based on Western supplied equipment, which is not interoperable with Russian and Asian equipment. While much of Iran's military equipment from Asia is based on older Soviet designs, it is not standardized with its new Russian supplied equipment in terms of most parts, detailed maintenance procedures, training, and some aspects of tactical operations. This sharply increases Iran's problems in interoperability, sustainability, training, and operations.

Further, Iran's ability to obtain arms from Russia is uncertain. Russia has a strong economic incentive to sell to Iran, but only if it can obtain oil or hard currency. As a result, Iran's economic problems seem to have been a key reason why new arms agreements with Russia dropped from $2.5 billion in 1987–1990 to $1.2 billion in 1991–1994.

Russia must also make hard strategic choices. It has little reason to build up a significant military power on the border of its former Asiatic republics. It must consider the impact of sales to Iran on its relations with the US, because the US has put strong pressure on Russia not to make major arms sales to Iran. Russia seemed to agree not to make such sales in a meeting between Clinton and Yeltsin in September, 1994, which was formalized during a meeting between Vice-President Gore and Viktor Chernomyrdin on June 29, 1995. Russia also appeared to strengthen its controls on the transfer of "dual-use" technology during the Clinton-Yeltsin summit meeting in Moscow in May, 1995.

There does not, however, seem to be any formal Russian-US agreement as to exactly what kind of items Russia will not export to Iran. Russia has stated that any cut-off of exports will only apply to new orders. Since Russia has never defined the nature of Iran's existing orders, this leaves considerable leeway as to what Russia may or may not deliver in the future. For example, Russia is actively discussing the sale of such advanced technology as an SA-10/SA-12-based air defense system, and Russia and Iran have discussed the sale of up to 1,000 T-72 Exports and a similar number of BMPs. There also are growing forces in Russia that advocate much larger sales to Iran. These include some of the new hard-line supporters of Yeltsin like Oleg Soskovets, the Chairman of Yeltsin's re-election campaign. These advocates of arms sales also include all of Yelstin's opponents.[339]

This shift in Russian politics is reflected in recent debates which have focused on US sales of F-16 fighters to Central Europe, and the Western "monopoly" of arms sales to the Gulf. On a visit to Tehran in October, 1995, Russian Defense Minister Pavel Grachev announced, "Russia will allow no country to decide partners for Russia." A Russian Ministry of Foreign Trade official also announced on February, 1996 that Iran was planning to buy $1 billion worth of military related equipment during the next two years, and that Iran had accounted for more than 85% of Russian sales to the Gulf in recent years. The spokesman indicated that Iran had bought $437 million worth of exports in 1994, with $104 million in military technology and arms and $330 million in equipment and services. She indicated that Russian military-related sales might total $4 billion over the next decade. Russia has since indicated that Iran is seeking a long-term cooperation agreement on arms and paid $380 million on its past debts to Iran in 1995—$250 million in oil and $150 million in cash.[340]

Iran also has sought advanced arms through other sources—including India, Belarus, and Poland. In its 1994 declaration to the UN arms register, it stated that it had imported 20 T-72 Export tanks from Russia in 1994 and 34 from Poland. Iran has kept up the smuggling system it developed during the Iran-Iraq War to buy arms illegally, and has obtained arms and technology from a number of West European countries. Iran also has turned to Latin America for arms and technology, and has bought arms from Brazil.[341]

The Problem of Iran's Aging Weapons Inventory

Iran's efforts to import arms must also be evaluated in terms of (a) Iran's losses during the Iran-Iraq War; (b) the fact that most of its weapons are either low grade PRC and North Korean exports, or Western supplied systems that have seen hard service in combat and are now 15–25 years old; and (c) Iran is limited access to the spare parts and technical support required to maintain, repair and modernize such systems.

The problems Iran faces because of its continuing dependence on major Western-supplied systems are summarized in Table Eleven. Iran has tried to deal with these problems by "cannibalizing" some weapons to keep others in operation. It has often been unable, however, to obtain key parts, forcing Iran to resort to worn, low quality spare parts obtained from Third World suppliers. One reason for this is that many key parts for Western-supplied equipment are no longer in supply because the original manufacturer has either halted production, or has modified the system so much since the 1960s and 1970s, that the equipment must be extensively modified or rebuilt to use the new or available parts and subassembly. The result has been the inability of Iran to upgrade or modernize most of its Western-supplied systems to anything approaching Western standards for 10–20 years.

Iran attempted some creative ways to work around these problems. The recent history of Iranian military maintenance services, however, reveals a less than impressive record. Under the Shah, standards were

TABLE ELEVEN Iranian Dependence on Decaying Western Supplied Major Weapons

Weapon		
Type	Number	Comments
Land Forces		
Chieftain tank	240–260	Worn, underarmored, underarmed, and underpowered. Fire control and sighting system now obsolete. Cooling problems.
M-47/M-48	150–260	Worn, underarmored, underarmed, and underpowered. Fire control and sighting systems now obsolete.
M-60A1	150–160	Worn, underarmored, underarmed, and underpowered. Fire control and sighting systems now obsolete.
Scorpion AFV	70–80	Worn, light armor, underarmed, and underpowered.
M-114s	70–80	Worn, light armor, underarmed, and underpowered.
M-109 155mm SP	150–160	Worn. Fire control system now obsolete. Growing reliability problems due to lack of updates and parts.
M-107 175mm SP	20–30	Worn. Fire control system now obsolete. Growing reliability problems due to lack of parts.
M-110 203mm SP	25–35	Worn. Fire control system now obsolete. Growing reliability problems due to lack of parts.
TOW ATGM	100s	Serious quality problems in remaining missiles.
AH-1J Attack helicoptor	100	Worn, avionics and weapons suite now obsolete. Growing reliability problems due to lack of updates and parts.
CH-47 Transport helicoptor	35–45	Worn, avionics and weapons suite now obsolete. Growing reliability problems due to lack of updates and parts.
Bell, Hughes, Boeing, Agusta, Sikorsky helicoptors	350–445	Worn, growing reliability problems due to lack of updates and parts.

(continues)

TABLE ELEVEN *(continued)*

Type	Number	Comments
Air Force		
F-4D/E FGA	55–60	Worn, avionics now obsolete. Critical problems due to lack of updates and parts.
60 F-5E/FII FGA	60	Worn, avionics now obsolete. Serious problems due to lack of updates and parts.
F-5A/B	10	Worn, avionics now obsolete. Serious problems due to lack of updates and parts.
RF-4E	8	Worn, avionics now obsolete. Serious problems due to lack of updates and parts.
RF-5E	5–10	Worn, avionics now obsolete. Serious problems due to lack of updates and parts.
F-14 AWX	60	Worn, avionics now obsolete. Critical problems due to lack of updates and parts. Cannot operate some radars at long ranges. Phoenix missile capability cannot be used. (May be in storage.)
P-3F MPA	5	Worn, avionics and sensors now obsolete. Many sensors and weapons cannot be used. Critical problems due to lack of updates and parts.
Key PGMs	—	Remaining Mavericks, Aim-7s, Aim-9s, Aim-54s are all long past rated shelf life. Many or most are unreliable or inoperable.
IHawk SAM	150–175	Worn, electronics, software, and some aspects of sensors now obsolete. Critical problems due to lack of updates and parts.
Rapier SAM	30	Worn, electronics, software, and some aspects of sensors now obsolete. Critical problems due to lack of updates and parts.
Navy		
Babar DE	1	Worn, weapons and electronics suite obsolete, many systems inoperable or partly dysfunctional due to critical problems due to lack of updates and parts.
Samavand DDG	5	Worn, weapons and electronics suite obsolete, many systems inoperable or partly dysfunctional due to critical problems due to lack of updates and parts.

(continues)

TABLE ELEVEN (*continued*)

Weapon		Comments
Type	*Number*	
Alvand FFG	3	Worn, weapons and electronics suite obsolete, many systems inoperable or partly dysfunctional due to critical problems due to lack of updates and parts.
Bytander FF	2	Obsolete. Critical problems due to lack of updates and parts.
Hengeman LST	4	Worn, needs full scale refit.

Source: Estimate made by Anthony H. Cordesman based on the equipment counts in IISS, *Military Balance, 1995–1996,* "Iran," and discussions with US experts. Note that different equipment estimates are used later in the text. The IISS figures are used throughout this chart to preserve statistical consistency.

poor to mediocre and maintenance services relied heavily on foreign contractors and extensive foreign resupply. Since the fall of the Shah, the
cumulative effect of the revolution, Iran-Iraq War, lack of adequate technical training, and low technical standards of some elements of the Revolutionary Guards has led to steady equipment losses through age, wear,
and attrition. These pressures have also forced Iran to mix its aging, Western-supplied equipment with a wide mix of equipment from non-Western sources, most of which is inferior and not interoperable. This lack of
standardization within Iranian forces has steadily created additional
training, battle management, and logistic support problems.

Iran has shown it can buy some Western spares, upgrades, weapons systems, and dual use technologies on the black market. It has also used the
complex mix of overt and covert purchasing offices it established during
the Iran-Iraq War. Among these are the State Procurement Organization,
Aviation Technology Affairs (ATA), Foreign Procurement Management
Center, Defense Support Organization (Saziman Poshtiban Defa), Qods
Research Centre, Lavson Ltd., National Iranian Oil Company (NIOC),
together with various fronts and subsidiaries. These organizations are particularly important components of Iran's covert purchasing system. Iran
has had some success in using them to buy older US equipment, which it
can use to obtain spare parts for the repair of its US weapons.

Iran has also used these organizations to get high technology components like radar testing devices, navigation and avionics equipment, fiber
optics, logic analyzers, high speed computers, high speed switches, precision machinery, jet engines, tank engines, and remote sensors. It has
aggressively sought out chemical protection and detection gear, refueling
technology, early warning radar technology, and avionics conversion
equipment—although it is not clear if it has been able to deploy such
equipment in its forces.

Despite these procurement efforts, Iran has achieved only limited
overall progress in making its more sophisticated Western-supplied
weapons fully operational, and in giving them sustainability in
extended combat. Further, Iran faces an uncertain future in terms of
access to Western and Russian arms, technology, and spare parts. The
Bush and Clinton Administrations have made steadily more serious
efforts to persuade European states, Russia, and the PRC to limit arms
transfers to Iran. The US has put heavy pressure on Russia, Poland, the
Czech Republic, Slovakia, and Germany to limit their arms transfers of
dual-use items, and has been joined in such efforts by Britain. The European Community strengthened its controls in June, 1993, and began to
examine additional sanctions. This led Iran to turn to new sources of
parts and support like Belarus and India, but it is unclear how successful such efforts will be.[342]

Iran's Military Industries

Iran is expanding its military industries. While there is no way to estimate the size of Iran's effort with any precision, some experts believe
it may be spending as much as several hundred million dollars a year
in manufacturing conventional arms in Iran, and an even larger
amount on missiles and weapons of mass destruction.[343] According to
Akbar Torkan, former Minister of Defense and Armed Forces Logistics,
Iran has merged its plans for the Iranian regular army and forces into
one system to make them more efficient, and has tripled its output of
arms since 1979.[344]

In the late 1980s, Iran claimed to have at least 240 state-owned arms
plants under the control of the Ministry of Defense and Armed Forces
Logistics, Defense Industries Organization, IRGC,[nbs]and the Reconstruction Jihad Ministry during the Iran-Iraq War. Iran also claimed to
have some 12,000 privately owned workshops, which employed a total of
about 45,000 people, and that it planned to expand their operations to a
level that would employ 60,000 people within the coming five years.

The central direction of these organizations and their R&D efforts has
improved steadily since 1989, although it is still divided into three main
organizations: the Ministry of Defense, Islamic Revolutionary Guards
Corps, and Construction Jihad. Iran has also shifted away from a procurement strategy based on imports, and military industries dependent
on foreign parts and technical support, to one that emphasizes self-sufficiency. It has had significant technical support from China and North
Korea, and Iran has had at least some recent Russian, Pakistani, Argentine, Brazilian, Indian, Taiwanese, and German help in expanding these
facilities. In addition, Iran has created a more effective organization for
managing its military industries called the Defense Industries Organization (DIO). This organization supervises the Iran Aircraft Industry, Iran
Helicopter Industry, and some aspects of the Iran Electronics Industry.
Iran also has a parallel military industrial complex under the control of
its Revolutionary Guards.[345]

Iranian plants can build ammunition, mortars, light anti-tank weapons,
small arms, and automatic weapons. They have doubled their output since
the end of the Iran-Iraq War, and now produce nearly 50 types of munitions,
including tank rounds artillery shells, and rockets. They can probably meet
between 50% and 75% of Iran's needs in a major regional contingency and
its output is steadily building up Iran's reserves. They make most of Iran's
assault rifles, mortars up though 120 mm, and anti-tank rocket launchers.

These plants can rebuild armored weapons and a number of Western,
former Soviet bloc, North Korean and Chinese weapons systems. These
plants hold the capability to make spare parts for Iran's Western-supplied

tanks and other armored vehicles, and limited production of a light wheeled APC called the Boraq—a system somewhat similar to the BTRs, which Iran first acquired during the time of the Shah.

Iran had not made heavy artillery weapons in the past, but it can recondition and repair such weapons. It also claimed in May, 1996, to have produced a self-propelled version of a Russian 122 mm gun that it called the Thunder-1, with a firing range of 15,200 meters and a road speed of 65 kilometers per hour.[346] It has long made a 12 tube multiple rocket launcher. Iran has a growing capability to produce moderate technology military electronics, and makes military radios and low-technology RPVs like the 22006, Baz, and Shahin.

Iran now has the necessary technical sophistication to rebuild the jet engines for many of its American fighters and helicopters, as well as produce parts and modifications for some of its radars, missile systems, avionics, ships, and armored personnel carriers. It can also manufacture long-range rockets, and has upgraded some of Iran's F-4s, F-14s, and C-130s—although with mixed success. They have adapted a number of Chinese supplied anti-ship missile systems for use on patrol craft and Western supplied ships, and have launched at least one Iranian-made landing craft.[347]

Iranian officials have, however, made exaggerated claims about the production capabilities of these facilities. They have claimed to be able to mass produce Scud missiles and tanks. They have even gone so far as to assert that Iran no longer needs major arms imports. For example, Ali Akbar Nateq-Nuri, the speaker of the Majlis, proclaimed on January 1, 1995, "Thanks to God, we stand today in such a position that we have reached self-sufficiency within the defense industries. This issue has caused fear and concern for the global powers, especially the USA. . . . It is a great honor for the armed forces that we do not depend on outside countries for military purchases."[348] Similarly, Iran's current Minister of Defense and Armed Forces Logistics, Mohammed Forouzandeh, has declared, "Iran has reached self-sufficiency in arms . . . and ammunition production and can be the best source for supplying other states. . . . We are today exporting arms and ammunition to 14 other countries, and even transferring technology for making some weapons."[349]

In reality, Iran cannot currently mass produce a single sophisticated guided missile system, or advanced conventional weapon, unless it imports some of the major parts needed to assemble one. It does not approach self-sufficiency in arms and military technology, and has no prospect of doing so in the foreseeable future.

Iran may, however, be able to acquire significant additional capabilities in several key areas. Iran is giving the funding of a long range missile and weapons of mass destruction plants high priority, and is obtaining significant support from North Korea and China.[350] Iran would be able to produce tanks, if it acquired T-72 assembly plants from Russia and Poland, and might also be able to improve significantly its ability to manufacture sophisticated avionics, missile control systems, and other advanced military avionics.

Iran's Military Manpower

The trends in Iran's total military manpower, and comparisons of this manpower with the manpower of other Gulf forces, are shown in Charts Twenty-Three to Twenty-Six. Iran's current military capabilities are heavily influenced by its demographics and the size of its total military manpower. Iran is by far the most heavily populated Gulf state, giving it a major potential advantage in building up its military forces. Iran's total pool of manpower is about 14,639,000, counting the male population from 15–49. The CIA estimates that 8,704,000 males are fit for military service and that 615,000 reach military age each year.[351] The IISS estimates that there are 3,844,000 males between the ages of 13 and 17, another 3,159,000 between the ages of 18 and 22, and a total of 4,828,000 between the ages of 23 and 32.[352]

At the same time, sheer manpower numbers have little importance in modern warfare, and Iran can no longer draw on the kind of revolutionary and patriotic fervor that existed during the early years of the Iran-Iraq War. Iran's manpower base has deep ethnic divisions, and its ability to transform its manpower numbers into military power is severely limited by its economic problems and access to arms imports. The idea that developing countries can take advantage of cheaper manpower is also often a myth. This may be true of guerrilla and infantry combat, and some forms of unconventional warfare, but it has little application to sophisticated military operations. Skilled manpower is costly to train, retain, and employ effectively and countries like Iran are poorly organized to carry out effective manpower management. While salaries may be low, the overhead costs of military productivity in Third World forces usually raise the cost of performing technically skilled and military leadership tasks above those of developed countries. This makes it difficult or impossible to use military manpower effectively in some demanding technical tasks and complex military operations.

Iran currently does not maintain an active manpower base proportionate to its total population, and would have difficulty in doing so because of a combination of cost, internal divisions within Iran's forces, and the shock of Iran's bloody battles and defeats in the Iran-Iraq War. Iran's active strength is now about 359,000, including 293,000 full time actives in the regular forces, and 120,000 Revolutionary Guards. This compares

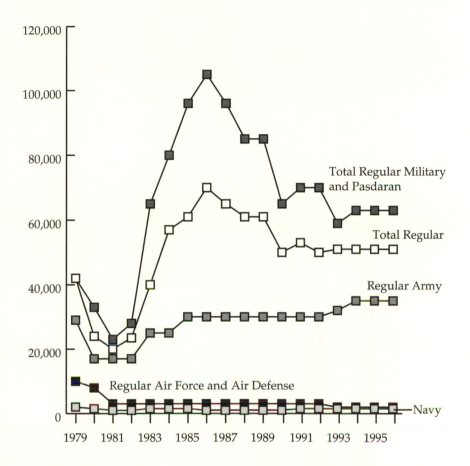

CHART TWENTY-THREE Trends in Iranian Military Manpower: 1979–1996.
Source: Adapted by Anthony H. Cordesman from various editions of the IISS, *Military Balance.*

with 382,000 men for Iraq—which has less than one-third of Iran's total population. The regular army has about 320,000, including 220,000 full time actives in the regular forces and 100,000 Revolutionary Guards versus 350,000 for Iraq. The Iranian Air Force and air defense force has about 55,000 men, the regular Iranian Navy has about 18,000 men, and the Iranian Naval Guards total about 20,000 (including 2,000 in IRGC naval air and marine forces). Iran also has roughly 90,000 Basij militia and more than 45,000 gendarmerie and border guards, but these paramilitary forces pose little threat to Iran's neighbors.[353]

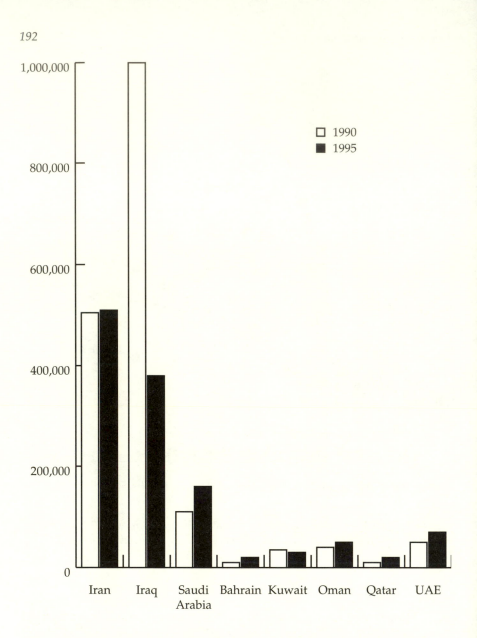

CHART TWENTY-FOUR   Total Active Military Manpower in All Gulf Forces 1990–1995. *Note:* Iran includes active forces in Revolutionary Guards. Saudi Arabia includes active in National Guard. *Source:* Adapted by Anthony H. Cordesman from various sources and the IISS, *Military Balance.*

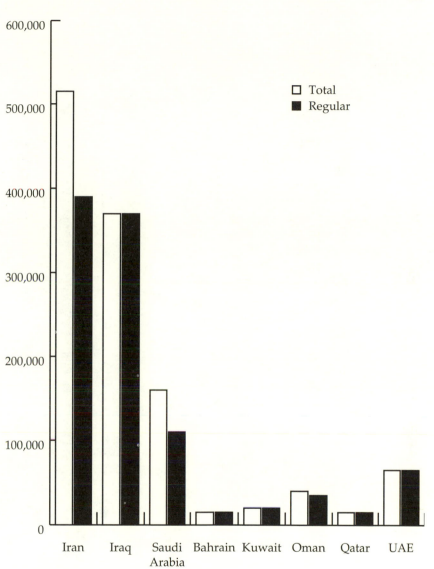

CHART TWENTY-FIVE   Total Active Military Manpower in All Gulf Forces—
1996. *Note:* Iran includes active forces in Revolutionary Guards. Saudi Arabia
includes active in National Guard. *Source:* Adapted by Anthony H. Cordesman
from the IISS, *Military Balance, 1995–1996.*

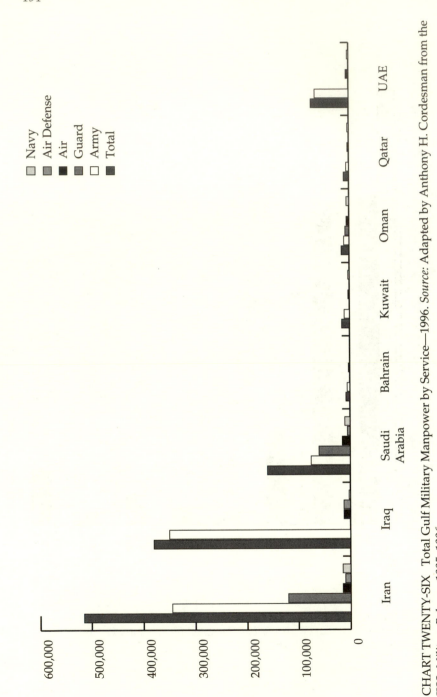

CHART TWENTY-SIX Total Gulf Military Manpower by Service—1996. *Source:* Adapted by Anthony H. Cordesman from the IISS, *Military Balance, 1995–1996.*

9

The Threat from
Iranian Land Forces

Military expenditures, arms imports, and total military manpower help measure Iran's military potential, but they are not measures of its contingency capability. It is the mission capabilities of Iran's military services, which largely determine the kinds of threats Iran can pose in the region and whether these threats will increase in the future.[354]

Iran's land forces have been in a constant state of change since the end of the Iran-Iraq War and it is difficult to make accurate estimates of their strength. Iran's army and Revolutionary Guards units have suffered from the combined impact of revolution, a Western embargo on arms transfers, and the Iran-Iraq War. Iran's ground forces also took far greater losses during the Iran-Iraq War than the Iranian Air Force or navy, particularly during the war's final battles. Iran's defeats in the land battles of 1988 were so severe that they led to the disintegration of some elements of the Pasdaran and even Iran's main regular army units. These defeats also caused massive losses of weapons and equipment.

While Iran's exact losses are disputed, it is clear that Iran lost over half of its operational armor between February and July 1988. Iraq seems to be correct in claiming to have captured some 1,298 Iranian tanks and heavy armored fighting vehicles, 155 other armored fighting vehicles, 512 armored personnel carriers, large amounts of artillery, 6,196 mortars, 8,050 RPGs and recoilless rifles, 60,694 rifles, 322 pistols, 501 pieces of heavy engineering equipment, 6,156 pieces of communications gear, 16,863 items of chemical warfare defense equipment, and 24,257 caskets.[355] The degree of disintegration in Iran's land forces at the end of the Iran-Iraq War is reflected in the fact that much of this captured equipment showed no sign of combat damage or wear. Much was abandoned in the field, either out of panic, or because of supply problems.

Iran's Current Major Combat Formations

Iran has, however, rebuilt some of its capabilities. According to the IISS and various US experts, the Iranian regular army had a strength of 12 division equivalents in 1996, and around 42–45 maneuver brigades. These formations included 4 armored divisions (two with three brigades and two with four brigades), 6 infantry divisions, and two special forces divisions. They also included the following independent brigades or groups: 1 armor unit, 1 infantry unit, 3 commando units, 2 airborne/special forces units, 1 air defense unit, 5 artillery units, and 4 army aviation units.

The full Iranian Army order of battle is not available, but includes the Lord of the Martyrs 21st, Khorasan 77th, and Qasvin 16th divisions. Most regular army divisions have three brigades, but only battalion-sized units have standardized tables of organization and equipment (TO&Es). Even the four armored divisions have different strengths and equipment mixes and many divisions have a hybrid structure and mix equipment from different supplier countries.

Iran's relative Army manpower strength is shown in Chart Twenty-Seven. The 220,000 active men in the Iranian Army are largely conscripts. Iran's reserves have a potential strength of about 350,000 men, but most of these men have little call-up training and no clear mobilization assignment.[356]

The Iranian Army is normally deployed in three army-sized formations north to south along the border with Iraq. Iran seems to have been able to move some units away from the southern border since Iraq has concentrated its forces to deal with the domestic threat posed by its Shi'ites in the south and Kurds in the north, but tensions between the Iranian government and the Kurds have forced Iran to maintain strong forces in the northwest.

Many of the army's key deployment locations and casernes are the same as during the time of the Shah. They include Zahedan in the southeast; Mashhad and Gorgan in the northeast; Tehran, Qazvin, and Sarab in the north-central region; Kharramabad, Isfahan, and Shiraz in central Iran; Orimiyah, Maragheh, and Sanandaj in the northeast; Kermanshah in west-central Iran; and Ahwaz and Shushtar in the southeast. Army aviation is headquartered at Tehran, Mashhad, and Shiraz. Officer training takes place at the Tehran Military Academy, infantry and armor training takes place at Shiraz, signal training takes place at Tabriz, and aviation training takes place at Isfahan.[357]

Iranian Land Forces Armor

Estimates of the current equipment holdings of Iran's land forces are uncertain, and it is not possible to distinguish the holdings of the Iran-

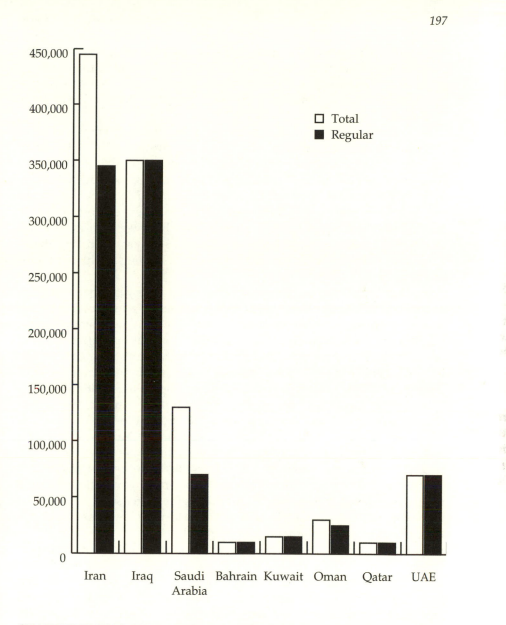

CHART TWENTY-SEVEN   Total Active Military Manpower in Gulf Armies in 1996. *Note:* Iran includes active forces in Revolutionary Guards. Saudi Arabia includes active National Guard.

ian regular army from those of the Islamic Revolutionary Guards Corps. Chart Twenty-Eight provides a rough indication of the trends in Iranian armored weapons strength, and Charts Twenty-Nine to Thirty-Six show how Iran's armored weapons strength ranks relative to other Gulf powers.

Iran seems to have had an inventory of around 1,250-tanks in early 1995. Additional deliveries raised this total to around 1,350–1,360 tanks by January, 1996, and the core of Iran's inventory of main battle tanks consisted of about 150 M-47/M-48s and 160 M-60A1s, 250 Chieftain Mark 3/5s, 75 T-62s, 225 T-72s, and 500 T-54s, T-55s, and T-59s.[358] Only part of this inventory, however, is fully operational. Some experts estimate that Iran's sustainable *operational* tank strength may be fewer than 1,000 tanks. Further, its Chieftains and M-60s are at least 16–20 years old, and the T-72 is Iran's only tank with advanced fire control systems, sights, and anti-armor ammunition.

Iran has claimed to have developed a world class main battle tank. It announced in late December, 1994 that it had spent a total of $10 billion on military forces in the preceding five years, and claimed to have begun production of a new main battle tank called the Zulfiqar, after two and one-half years of development. Prototypes of this tank were first shown in April, 1994, and while some sources report it is based upon the T-72, the pictures of the prototype show a design closer to the M-48/M-60. The tank uses welded steel construction for its hull and turret, has a box-shaped hull, and its suspension is similar to that of the M-60. There is as yet, however, no evidence that Iran can manufacture the advanced armor, engines, suspensions, or guns for a first line main battle tank of any type. Its main armament seems to be a 125 mm gun with a fume extractor and possibly an automatic loader. The gun is in a narrow mantlet and does not have a coaxial machine gun. This makes the turret somewhat similar to that of the Brazilian Osorio MBT. Two prototypes have been seen, differing largely in the commander's cupola.[359]

As a result, Iran is currently dependent on its holdings of the export version of the T-72 Export for anything approaching an advanced tank. The T-72 Export performed badly in Iraqi hands during the Gulf War and lacks the thermal sights, night vision systems, fire control systems, and advanced armor to compete with first line Western tanks like the M-1A1/2, Challenger, Le Clerc, or Leopard 2.

Iran seems to have about 1,000 operational armored personnel carriers and armored infantry fighting vehicles. These appear to include 70–80 operational British-supplied Scorpions, more than 300 BMP-1s, 100 BMP-2s, some 230–240 M-113s and other Western APCs, and 300–320 BTR-50s and BTR-60s. Iran has an unknown number of British Chieftain bridging tanks and may have another 100–150 BMPs in the process of repair or

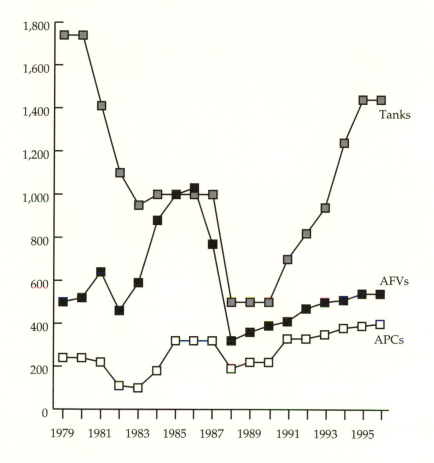

CHART TWENTY-EIGHT   Trends in Iranian Armored Weapons: 1979–1996.
Source: Adapted by Anthony H. Cordesman from various editions of the IISS, *Military Balance.*

delivery.[360] Iran's BMPs are its only modern AFVs and they total only about 20% of Iran's holdings of other armored vehicles. They also have significant ergonomic problems, limited night vision capabilities, and poor weapons system performance. Iran has claimed to have developed an advanced APC called the Boraq.[361]

Iran has large holdings of anti-tank guided weapons. It has TOW and Dragon weapons supplied by the US, and seems to have introduced Soviet and Asian versions of the AT-2, AT-3, and AT-4 into its forces. It also has large numbers of RPG-7 and Western 3.5" rocket launchers.

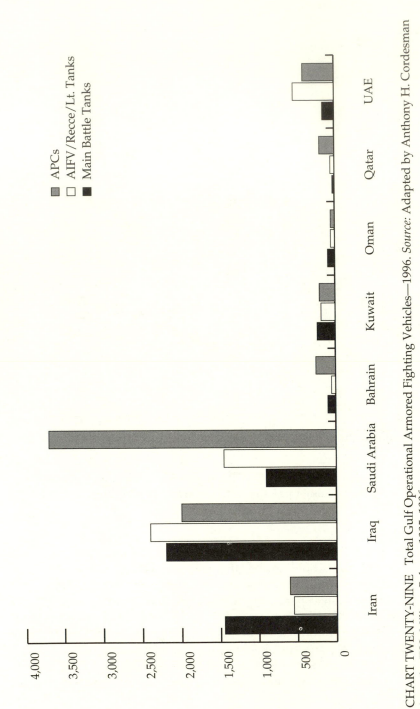

CHART TWENTY-NINE Total Gulf Operational Armored Fighting Vehicles—1996. *Source:* Adapted by Anthony H. Cordesman from the IISS, *Military Balance, 1995–1996.*

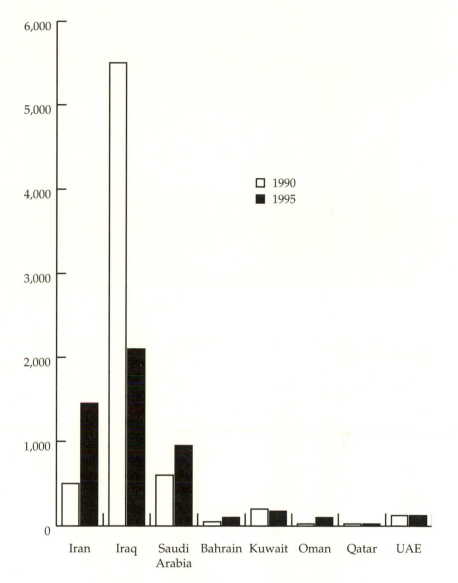

CHART THIRTY   Total Operational Tanks in All Gulf Forces, 1990–1995.
Note: Iran includes active forces in Revolutionary Guards. Saudi Arabia includes active National Guard. *Source:* Adapted by Anthony H. Cordesman from various sources and the IISS, *Military Balance.*

Total Operational Main Battle Tanks

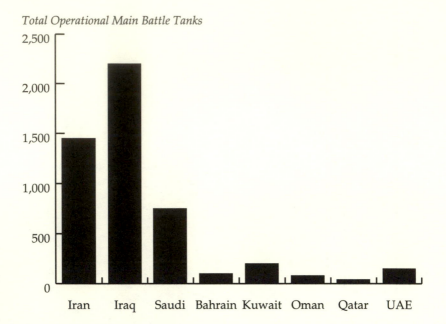

Operational Modern Tanks: T-72, M-84, M-60A2/A3, M-1A1/2, Challenger, Leopard/ OF-40, Le Clerc

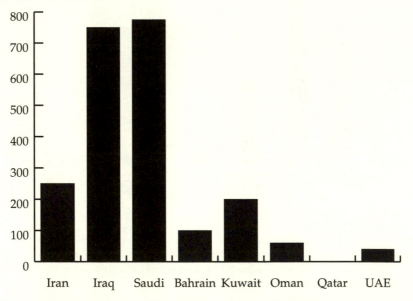

CHART THIRTY-ONE   Gulf Tanks in 1996. *Source:* Adapted by Anthony H. Cordesman from the IISS, *Military Balance, 1995–1996.*

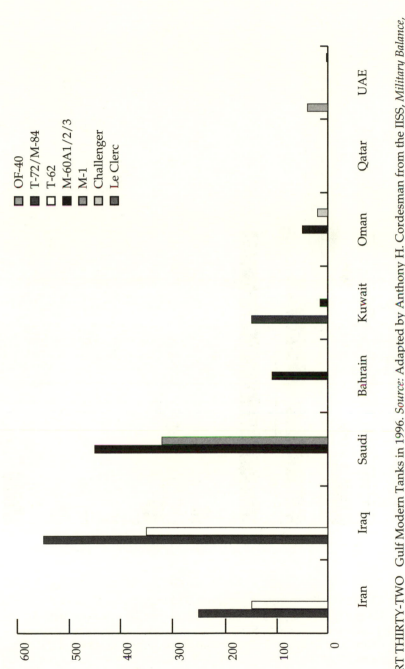

CHART THIRTY-TWO Gulf Modern Tanks in 1996. *Source:* Adapted by Anthony H. Cordesman from the IISS, *Military Balance, 1995–1996.*

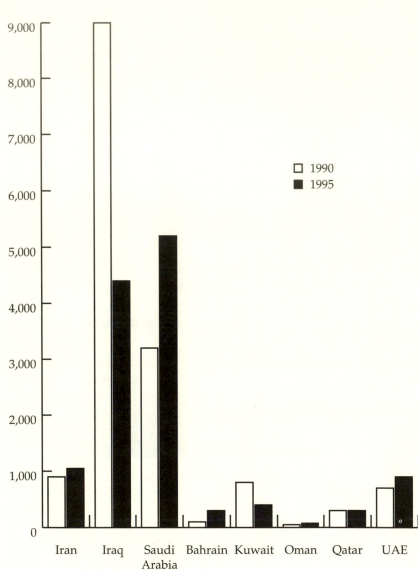

CHART THIRTY-THREE   Total Operational Other Armored Vehicles (Lt. Tanks, Scout, AIFVs, APCs, Recce) in Gulf Forces, 1990–1995. *Note:* Iran includes active forces in Revolutionary Guards. Saudi Arabia includes active National Guard. *Source:* Adapted by Anthony H. Cordesman from various sources and the IISS, *Military Balance.*

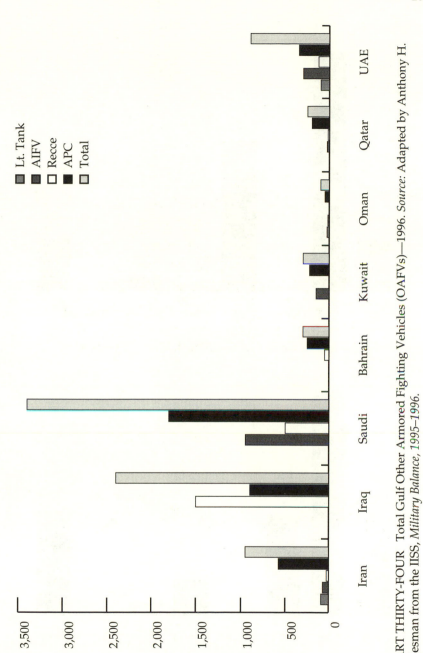

CHART THIRTY-FOUR Total Gulf Other Armored Fighting Vehicles (OAFVs)—1996. *Source:* Adapted by Anthony H. Cordesman from the IISS, *Military Balance, 1995–1996.*

Total

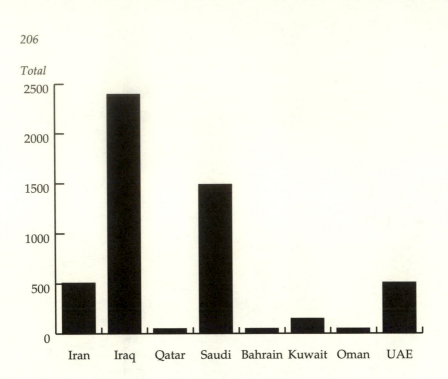

Total Advanced or Modern Types: Scorpion, BMP-1, BMP-2, BMP-3, M-2

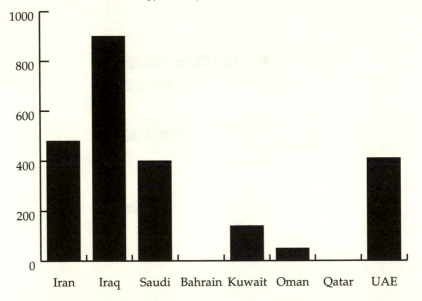

CHART THIRTY-FIVE   Gulf Armored Infantry Fighting Vehicles, Reconnaissance Vehicles, Scout Vehicles, and Light Tanks in 1996. *Source:* Adapted by Anthony H. Cordesman from the IISS, *Military Balance, 1995–1996.*

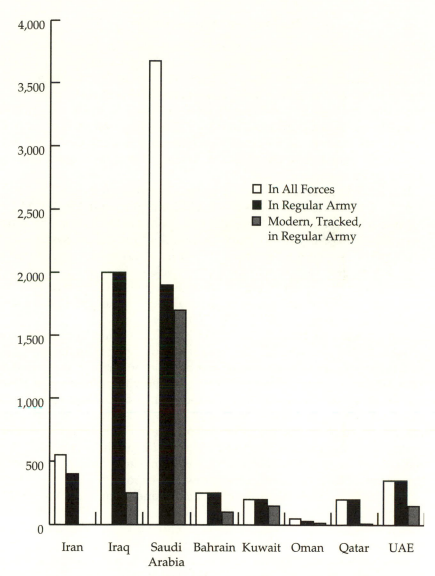

CHART THIRTY-SIX Armored Personnel Carriers (APCs) in Gulf Armies—
1996. *Note:* Iran includes active forces in Revolutionary Guards. Saudi Arabia
includes active National Guard. *Source:* Adapted by Anthony H. Cordesman
from the IISS, *Military Balance, 1995–1996.*

Iranian Land Forces Artillery

Chart Thirty-Seven provides a rough indication of the trends in Iranian artillery strength, and Charts Thirty-Eight to Forty-One show how Iran's artillery strength ranks relative to other Gulf powers. Iran has 2,000–2,500 medium and heavy artillery weapons and multiple rocket launchers. This high total reflects the continuing Iranian effort to build-up artillery strength that began during the Iran-Iraq War when Iran used artillery to support its infantry and Islamic Revolutionary Guards Corps in their attacks on Iraqi forces. Iran has had to use artillery as a substitute for armor and air power.

Iran's holdings of self-propelled weapons appear to include 25–35 M-110 203 mm howitzers, 20–30 M-107 175 mm guns, and 150–160 M-109 155 mm howitzers. These US-supplied weapons are badly worn, have not been modernized in over 15 years, lack modern fire control systems and artillery radars, and total less than 10% of Iran's artillery strength. Iran is now attempting to compensate for its lack of modern artillery and artillery mobility by replacing its US self-propelled weapons with Chinese and North Korean systems. Iran also has 60 Soviet 2S1 122 mm self-propelled howitzers, and 9 M-1978 170 mm weapons.

Iran appears to have 20–25 M-115 towed 203 mm howitzers, and 130–140 M-101A1 towed 105 mm howitzers surviving from the arms that Iran imported from the US during the time of the Shah. It also seems to have 80–90 Austrian GHN-45 155 mm gun/howitzers. Iran's non-Western holdings of towed artillery weapons include 1,000–1,1050 North Korean, Chinese, and Soviet M-46 and Type 59-1 towed 130 mm guns; and 550 Soviet, North Korean, Polish, and Czech D-30 122 mm gun-howitzers. They also include 30–35 D-20 towed 152 mm howitzers, 100 People's Republic of China 122 mm towed howitzers, and other former Soviet bloc, PRC, and North Korean towed weapons.[362]

Iran has 880–890 multiple rocket launchers, including some M-1989 240 mm multiple rocket launchers, 700 Chinese Type 63 107 mm multiple rocket launchers, 100 Soviet BM-21 and 5 Soviet BM-11 122 mm launchers, and 9 M-1989 240 mm towed multiple rocket launchers.

Iran has also produced at least 50 multiple rocket launchers. These include the 122 mm 40 round Hadid rocket launcher system, which mounts the launcher on a 6 X 6 truck, and the entire load can be salvo-fired in 20 seconds. Maximum range is about 20.4 kilometers, and a hydraulic crane is fitted so the launcher can be re-loaded in about 8–10 minutes. It is not clear how many Hadid launchers are currently deployed among Iranian forces. In addition, Iran is producing a variant of Chinese and Russian 122 mm rockets called the Arash and Noor, as well as variants of the Chinese 107 mm rocket called the Fajer and Haseb. Some of these rockets have chemical warheads.

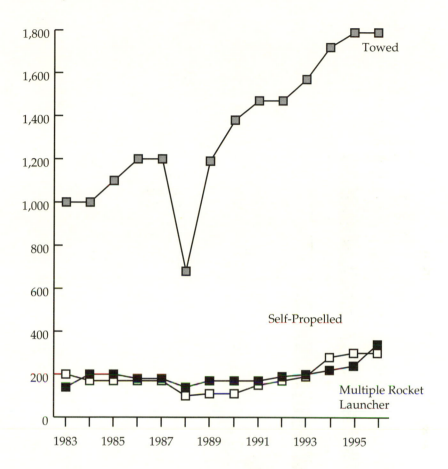

CHART THIRTY-SEVEN   Trends in Iranian Artillery Weapons: 1979–1996. *Source:* Adapted by Anthony H. Cordesman from various editions of the IISS, *Military Balance.*

The Iranian land forces also operate the Shahin 1 and 2, Oghab, and Nazeat long-range rockets. The Shahin 1 is a trailer-launched 333 mm caliber unguided artillery rocket with a solid propelled rocket motor, a maximum range of 13 kilometers, and a 190 kilogram conventional or chemical warhead. The Shahin 2 is an improved version of the Shahin 1 with a maximum range of 20 kilometers, and a 190 kilogram warhead. The Shahin evidently can be equipped with three types of warheads: a 180 kilogram high explosive warhead, a warhead using high explosive submunitions, and a warhead that uses chemical weapons.

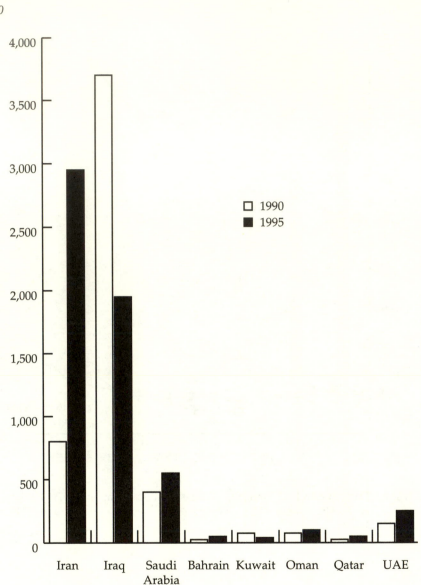

CHART THIRTY-EIGHT   Total Operational Self-Propelled and Towed Tube Artillery and Multiple Rocket Launchers in Gulf Forces, 1990–1995. *Note:* Iran includes active forces in Revolutionary Guards. Saudi Arabia includes active National Guard. *Source:* Adapted by Anthony H. Cordesman from various sources and the IISS, *Military Balance, 1995–1996.*

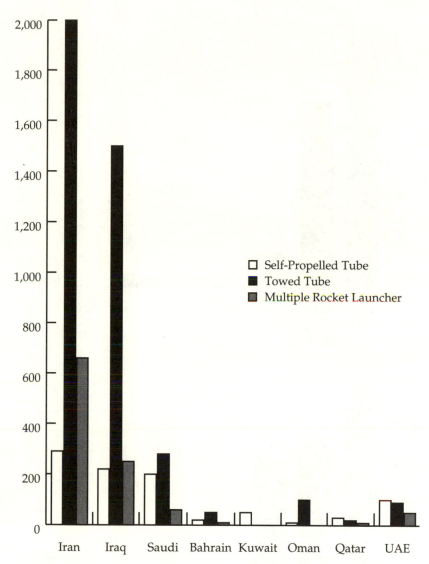

CHART THIRTY-NINE   Total Operational Gulf Artillery Weapons—1996.
Source: Adapted by Anthony H. Cordesman from the IISS, *Military Balance,*
1995–1996.

Total Operational Towed Artillery

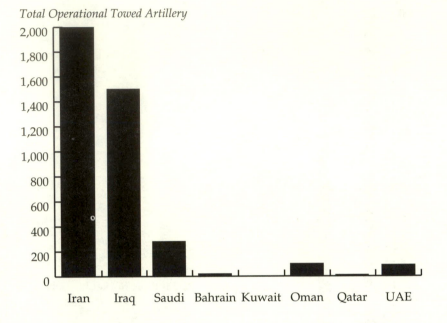

Total Operational Self-Propelled Artillery

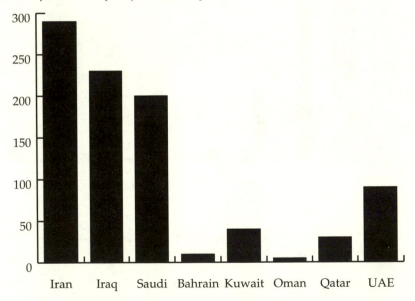

CHART FORTY   Gulf Tube Artillery Weapons in 1996. *Source:* Adapted by
Anthony H. Cordesman from the IISS, *Military Balance, 1995–1996.*

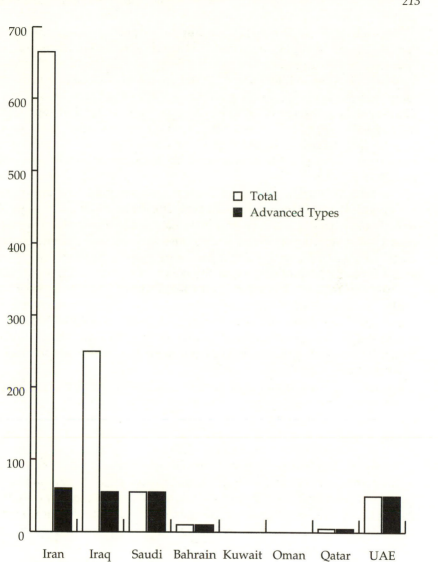

CHART FORTY-ONE   Total Operational Gulf Multiple Rocket Launchers—1996.
Source: Adapted by Anthony H. Cordesman from the IISS, *Military Balance,*
1995–1996.

The Oghab is a 320 mm caliber unguided artillery rocket which is spin stabilized in flight, has a maximum range of 34 kilometers, and a 70 kilogram HE fragmentation warhead—although chemical warheads may be available. While it may have a chemical warhead, it lacks the range and/or accuracy to hit anything smaller than large area targets like assembly areas and cities. It has an operational CEP that has proved to be in excess of 500 meters at maximum range.[363] Further, Iran has no way to target accurately the Oghab or any other long range missile against mobile or point targets at long ranges, other than a limited ability to use RPVs.[364]

The Nazeat is a TEL launched system with conventional and possibly chemical and biological warheads. The full details of this system remain unclear, but it seems to be based on Chinese technology and uses a solid fuel rocket, with a simple inertial guidance system. Nazeat units are equipped with communications vans, meteorological vans, and a global positioning system for surveying the launch site. There are two variants of the Nazeat solid fueled rocket system—a 355.6 mm caliber rocket with 105 kilometers range and a 150 kilogram warhead, and a 450 mm caliber rocket with a reported range of 130–150 kilometers and a 250 kilogram warhead. Both systems have maximum closing velocities of Mach 4–5, but both also appear to suffer from poor reliability and accuracy.[365]

Iran bought large numbers of mortars during the Iran-Iraq War for the same reasons it bought large numbers of towed tube artillery weapons. It had some 3,500 weapons in 1996, of which approximately 1,200 were medium and heavy mortars. Iran had at least several hundred of its heavy mortars mounted in armored vehicles.

These artillery weapons give Iran considerable ability to mass fires against relatively static area targets, but towed artillery is an anachronism in modern maneuver warfare operations, and Iran has only limited artillery fire control and battle management systems, counter-battery radar capability, and long-range target acquisition capability (although it does have some RPVs) to support its self-propelled weapons. Iran has actively sought more modern fire control and targeting systems since the mid-1980s, but it is unclear how many it obtained or put in service. Most of its artillery units are only effective against slow moving mass targets at ranges of less than 10–15 kilometers, or for harassment and interdiction fire.

The Army has some 1,700 anti-aircraft guns, including 14.5 mm ZPU-2/4s, 23 mm ZSU-23-4s and ZU-23s, 35 mm M-1939s, 37 mm Type 55s, and 57 mm ZSU-57-2s. It also has large numbers of SA-7s.

Iranian helicopter holdings are uncertain. According to the IISS, the Iranian Army retains 100 AH-1J Sea Cobra attack helicopters, and 40

CH-47C, 130 Bell-214A, 35 AB-214C, 40 AB-205A, 90 AB-206, 12 AB-212, 30 Bell 204, 5 Hughes 300C, 9 RH-53D, 10 SH-53D, 10 SA-319, and 45 UH-1H transport and support helicopters out of the original total supplied by the West. Most experts agree, however, that the operational readiness of Iranian helicopters is low, perhaps only about 25% of inventory, and Iran has little sustained sortie capability. The IISS estimates that the army's fixed wing aircraft included 40 Cessna 185, 310, and O-2A aircraft, 19 F-27s, 8 Falcon 20s, 15 PC-16s, and 5 Strike Commanders.

Iranian Army communications are relatively limited. They consist largely of aging VHF radio with some HF and UHF capability. Iran still relies heavily on manually switched telephone systems. It has Chinese and Western encryption systems and some digital voice, fax, and telex encryption capability.

The Islamic Revolutionary Guards Corps[366]

The Islamic Revolutionary Guards Corps (IRGC) remains under the command of Major General Mohsen Rezaii. US experts believe that the IRGC had a total manning of around 120,000 in 1996, of which roughly 100,000 men were in the land forces. It was organized into eleven internal security regions, with most of its forces assigned to the conventional military mission and internal security mission. Unlike the regular army, which is organized as a national force, the IRGC is organized along territorial lines.

The IRGC has 15–20 "divisions." These include two "armored divisions," and the IRGC has set the goal of creating mechanized "divisions." The full order of battle of the IRGC is not available, but it includes the Karbala-25, Imam Hussein 14, Holy Prophet 27, Vali-ye-Asr 7, and Ashura 31 divisions, and seems to include the 10th Special Forces Division, 8th Najaf-e Ashraf unit, and 41st Saraollah unit. Most of its divisions, however, have manning levels less than those of brigades in the Iranian regular army, and many have less firepower than Iranian regular army combat battalions. The IRGC does not have any armored formations larger than brigade size, and even these units seem to be far less heavily armored than Iranian regular army armored brigades

The IRGC has some 25–35 independent "brigades"—including armored, infantry, special forces, paratroop, air defense, artillery, missile, engineer, and border defense units. These brigades have manning equivalent to battalions in the regular forces.[367]

The armored elements of the IRGC are slowly expanding, and some have T-72s and armored fighting vehicles. Other IRGC units, with T-54 tanks, are reported to be upgrading their tanks with T-72 engines and laser range finders. This conversion is called the Safir-74 (Messenger 74), and supposedly upgrades tanks captured from Iraq with what Rezaie has stated are "major changes in engine power, transmission, firepower, and internal fire extinguishing system." It is supposed to have better target acquisition capability against mobile and static targets and better armor. Iran has claimed that the components for this conversion are manufactured in Iran, but it is unclear whether this is true, how many of Iran's 190 T-54s and T-55s are in the IRGC, and how many have been converted.[368]

Rezaie and other leaders of the IRGC have called for more armor, including large numbers of T-72s. Most IRGC land forces are still largely infantry forces, however, and the IRGC is only slowly being upgraded. The Iranian regular army receives most of Iran's new heavy weapons and it will be sometime before even the best IRGC units can rival the regular forces in firepower and maneuver capability.

Like the Iranian Army, the IRGC possesses numerous anti-tank weapons, including Dragon, TOW, and AT-3 ATGMs, 3.5" rockets, and RPG-7s. It also has about 1,500 air defense guns, large numbers of small and man-portable surface-to-air missiles, and increasing numbers of the HN-5 light surface-to-air missiles. Iran's holdings of such weapons are uncertain, but it seems to be importing both Chinese and Russian short-range air defense missiles.[369] The IRGC seems to be the principle operator of Iran's land-based surface-to-surface missile forces. Both the Iranian regular army and IRGC have offensive and defensive chemical warfare capabilities.

Iran has conducted a number of recent "urban warfare" exercises that indicate the IRGC is being trained for internal security missions. The "Ashura" exercise in June 1995 involved elements from a wide range of Revolutionary Guards units, and involved operations in a nearly 400 square kilometer area in the Neinava Region southwest of Tehran, although Iranian claims that the exercise involved 450,000 men were grossly exaggerated.

It is interesting to note that normally such exercises are presented to the Iranian people as being defensive and in preparation for a possible US invasion, but sometimes they have been described in a different manner. Moshen Rezaie, the commander of the Revolutionary Guards stated that the exercises "will convey a clear message to our enemies, that is our ability to defend the liberty and independence of Iran. . . . [They will] also assure the friends of the Islamic Republic that Iran possesses the most reliable defensive power to maintain peace and security in the region and that it could *exploit its capabilities to consolidate friendly relations in the region and the world.*"[370]

The Quds Forces

About 5,000–10,000 men in the IRGC are assigned to the unconventional warfare mission. These latter forces include the Quds troops, which operate outside the border and have bases inside and outside of Iran. The Quds troops are divided into specific groups or "corps" for each country or area in which they operate. For example, there is a corps for Lebanon, for the Sudan, and for Africa. The budget for this part of the IRGC is a classified budget directly controlled by Khamenei, and which is not reflected in the Iranian general budget.

The Quds forces have a main training center at Imam Ali University which is based in the Sa'dabad Palace in Northern Tehran. Troops are trained to carry out military and terrorist operations, and are indoctrinated in ideology. The University is chaired by Mohammed Shams, a general in the Iranian Army. The commander of the Quds is General Ahmad Vahidi, who used to head the information department in the IRGC General Command and had the mission of exporting the revolution. The Imam Ali University trains Egyptian, Saudi, and Lebanese as well as Iranians. There are other training camps in the Qom, Tabriz, and Mashhad governates, and in Lebanon and the Sudan.

Iran's Paramilitary Forces

Iran's paramilitary and internal security forces seem to have relatively little warfighting capability. The Basij (Mobilization of the Oppressed) is a popular reserve force of about 90,000 men with an active and reserve strength of up to 300,000 and a mobilization capacity of nearly 1,000,000 men. It is controlled by the Islamic Revolutionary Guards Corps, and consists largely of youths, men who have completed military service, and the elderly. During the Iran-Iraq War, the Basiij was organized into poorly trained and equipped infantry units which were often used in Iran's human wave assaults. Since the war, the Basij has been restructured into a pool of men that can be called up in wartime. This pool consists of up to 740 battalions with about 300–350 men each, which are composed of three companies or four platoons plus support.

The primary mission of the Basij now seems to be internal security, and monitoring the activities of Iranian citizens. The Basij's actions vary with the political climate and the jurisdiction, however, and the Basij perform a "round out" role in providing manpower to build-up the strength of IRGC units in an emergency.

Organized Basij units are equipped with small arms, and can act as a force to secure rear areas or deal with ethnic forces or popular riots. Further, they provide a potential base for the expansion of the IRGC in time of crisis and war. The Basij is also used for civil projects or activities where the regime seeks to mobilize youth for a single task or propaganda purposes. The Basij includes a large home guard force which serves some of the same purposes, but which is a static militia force tied to local defense missions.

Iran claimed to have integrated many of its other internal security forces in 1991. They total of about 45,000–60,000 men and are now said to be part of the Ministry of Interior. These forces are comprised of the former Gendarmerie, other police elements, and border guards. The border guards are organized as a paramilitary police force with light utility vehicles, light patrol aircraft (Cessna 185/310 and AB-205 and AB-206s), 90 coastal patrol craft, and 40 harbor patrol craft. They keep order throughout the rural areas of Iran and deal with ethnic and tribal security problems. The border guards have a regional organization, and some military training and equipment. This equipment includes automatic weapons, mortars, and light anti-tank weapons. A Tribal Basij force has existed for many years, which may either be part of the Gendarmerie or the IRGC.[371]

These paramilitary forces seem unlikely to offer Iran much advantage in wars against its neighbors, and Iran seems to have experienced some problems with the loyalty of some of these forces in late 1993—leading to the arrests of a number of officers in October.[372] Though human wave attacks have failed in the past and can only be used in border areas, Iran lacks the equipment to waste it on such untrained and low quality forces in other combat roles. These forces can, however, provide rear area security and a manpower pool to draw upon in an extended conflict. They offer Iran improved internal security, and should be adequate to deal with most ethnic threats. The best trained forces of the Iraqi-backed People's Mujahideen are a possible exception.

As has been discussed earlier, however, Iran's intelligence forces may pose a significant threat to Iran's neighbors and other states. In addition to Iran's main intelligence service—the VEVAK—Iran has other intelligence elements within the Foreign Ministry, IRGC, and the Iranian armed forces. Iran supports other states and extremist movements in a number of unconventional warfare and terrorist roles, and US experts believe there is considerable evidence that they have done so with the direct knowledge of Iran's foreign minister and senior leadership.[373]

The Warfighting Capabilities of Iranian Land Forces

Iranian capabilities for land warfare seem likely to improve during the coming decade. Even with Iran's economic crisis, its land forces are likely to build up to about 500,000 full time actives in its regular forces by 2000–2005. Iran is likely to add another 120,000 additional men in its Islamic Revolutionary Guards Corps (Pasdaran Inquilab), plus substantial additional manpower in its Basij (Popular Mobilization Army) and internal security forces. A combination of the regular and Revolutionary Guards forces seems likely to give Iran about 400,000–500,000 full time actives—and Iran has the capacity to develop significant reserves. Iran's current equipment holdings are also likely to increase. Iran is likely to acquire an inventory of around 1,500–1,900 tanks by 2000–2005. It is likely to have about 1,800–2,100 operational armored personnel carriers and armored infantry fighting vehicles, and 2,500–3,000 medium and heavy artillery weapons and multiple rocket launchers.

At the same time, much will depend on Iran's ability to pay for arms imports, the future structure of Iran's land forces, Iran's strength relative to Iraq, and whether Iran can develop a significant capability to project power across the Gulf.

The split between the Iranian regular army and the IRGC remains a critical problem that currently helps to prevent Iran from concentrating its total mix of land forces into standardized, well-manned, well-equipped, and well-trained land units that can conduct effective armored maneuvers or combined arms operations. The regular forces and IRGC have carried out joint exercises in recent years, but they appear to be making limited progress. Iranian exercises usually seem designed as much to intimidate neighboring states and in particular Iraq rather than to improve military effectiveness.

Iranian ground forces have, however, steadily increased the size and tempo of their armored warfare and nuclear, biological, and chemical warfare exercises. They also have increased the number of land-air and land-air-naval exercises. The Beyt-ol-Muqaddas (Jerusalem) series in August, 1995, and Zafar (Victory) series in March, 1996, still had a political character, but they involved more demanding training than Iran's show piece exercises of the early 1990s.

Iran held the largest military exercise in its peacetime history during May 23–24, 1996. Iran claimed that the exercise involved 200,000 men, 10 full divisions, six full brigades, 100 army helicopters, 1,700 field guns and tanks, and more than 700 armored and tracked vehicles. The air force commander of the exercise stated that it was designed to, "create fear in the hearts of enemies and increase the combat readiness of the armed forces. Iran also claimed that the exercise involved Iranian made Zulfiqa tanks and Kobra APCs.[374]

The exercise did not involve all of the forces Iran claimed, and many aspects were poorly structured. It did, however, involve over 100,000 men and was a joint exercise involving all of Iran's military services. These forces held extensive exercises near the Iraqi border, and over a large area in the Koush-e Nosrat desert south of Qom. Like many of Iran's other recent exercises, the exercise indicated that there is less political tension between the regular forces and the IRGC, in part because most personnel who served under the Shah have left the regular forces and in part because of the influence the leaders of the Revolutionary Guard have had on senior regular army appointments.

Even if Iran's land forces do not remain divided, however, their mix of equipment is likely to retain so many different types and generations that it will be difficult to support and maintain. Iran has no way to standardize its equipment, ammunition and missiles rapidly. Even if Iran has a well structured plan to create modern standardized armored, mechanized, and artillery forces, it still lacks a reliable supplier and/or the funds to make the massive integrated purchases it needs. Its purchases of the T-72 may be a step towards this end, but Iran would need deliveries of around 1,500–2,000 T-72s to meet all of its requirements.

Iran also needs to acquire modern armored infantry fighting vehicles for its first line units and standardize on a given type. This would entail a total of 2,000 relatively modern armored vehicles. In addition, Iran needs much larger inventories of self-propelled artillery, improved antitank weapons and short-range air defenses, together with a much stronger support and logistic training system to sustain mobile armored warfare and fast moving offensive operations.

Iran faces other major challenges in improving the quality of its land forces. Most of its tanks lack modern fire control systems, armor, night and thermal vision devices, and guns and ammunition equal to those of the most advanced neighboring states. Sustainability and power projection capabilities are limited, as are battlefield recovery and repair capabilities. Overall night warfare capabilities are limited, and Iran has only limited ability to move artillery rapidly, mass and shift fires, and acquire beyond-visual-range targets. Communications, command, and control systems are obsolete and unreliable. Helicopter and combined operations training with fixed wing aircraft are of very limited quality at best.

Virtually all of Iran's land force equipment holdings must be modernized or reconditioned to recover from the combined impact of a cut-off of Western weapons and equipment, the wear of eight years of war, and the massive losses of 1988. Iran needs improved tank and artillery rounds, remotely piloted vehicles (RPVs) that are integrated into division or brigade level operations, improved mobile short range air defense systems (SHORADS) and man-portable surface-to-air missiles, tank transporters, secure communications, night vision and improved sights, modern fire control systems, and tracked support equipment. It would also greatly benefit from advanced training and simulation technology.

The Iranian regular army almost certainly understands these requirements. It has learned from the Iran-Iraq War and Gulf War that a reliance on mass, rather than quality, is ineffective. It has sought to give its existing unit strength more armor and artillery, strengthen the firepower and mobility of selected specialized independent brigades, and give its infantry divisions added artillery strength and armored infantry fighting vehicles. Even so, the preceding analysis has shown that it will be well beyond the year 2000 before Iran's land forces can acquire anything like the full mix of modern equipment they need.

It is likely to be even longer before Iran can use such equipment effectively. The Iranian Army is short of trained technicians, officers, and non-commissioned officers. Iran is only beginning to rebuild the level of training and discipline it had when the Shah fell. In spite of some recent large scale exercises—like the Martyr Reysali Delvari, Naser, Val Fajr, Velayat, Victory and Fatah series of exercises—its land forces are only beginning to shift from a focus on defense in depth against an Iraqi invasion, to tactics emphasizing a maneuver force. The Victory 4 exercise in the spring of 1993 marked the first recent multi-service exercise involving amphibious and heliborne assaults of the kind that would give Iran the capability to project power across the Gulf, but it was not particularly impressive. While there were follow-on exercises in 1994 and 1995, these exercises lacked the scale and content that would indicate Iran has the ability to do much more than launch limited raids or attack small islands and oil facilities in the Gulf.

The regular army has just started to train a portion of its forces effectively for combined operations, high tempo combined arms operations, and power projection and amphibious warfare missions.[375] Conscript training, junior officer and non-commissioned officer training is poor to mediocre, and medium to large scale unit training is also poor.

Regular army formations differ sharply in size, force mix, and equipment and are difficult to supply and support. Many units are badly under strength, and some combat and support units only have about 65–80% of the strength needed to fully man them. Iran's high command remains divided, and its logistic system is compartmented and ineffective. Many Iranian combat units have low overall manpower strength, and some of Iran's units lack the manpower and equipment to be employed in anything other than static defensive battles. Logistics, combat engineering, and support capabilities are limited and dependent on reinforcement from the civil sector for any sustained operations.

The land units of the IRGC remain an ambivalent force that often seem to conduct themselves as an independent actor in Iranian politics. The training of the IRGC has improved, and it has conducted more realistic large scale exercises with the Army, Navy, and Air Force—some involving missile, amphibious, and unconventional warfare exercises in the Gulf.[376] There are also some elite IRGC units capable of performing demanding special forces, commando, infiltration, and unconventional warfare missions. This reflects the IRGC's considerable capability for unconventional warfare and terrorism, and the IRGC has held increasingly larger amphibious exercises in recent years. For example, the Ra'ad (Thunder) series of exercises held around Kharg Island during December 23–26, 1995, could be seen as either defensive or offensive in character. So could the Saeqe-2 (Thunderbolt 4) exercises held in late November, 1995.

The IRGC land forces, however, have many defects. The IRGC is poorly organized and poorly trained for conventional war fighting. It is relatively lightly equipped, and its ideology is a poor substitute for proper equipment, discipline, standardization, and coherent organization. Iran's land forces clearly lack the capability to sustain large-scale armored thrusts deep into the territory of a well-armed regional power like Iraq, and are not capable of significant amphibious operations in the face of opposition by a power like the US. Iran is just beginning to acquire significant offensive and power projection capabilities, and could do little more than exploit an Iraqi civil war, or rush battalion-sized forces to support a coup attempt in an exposed country like Bahrain.

It is difficult to translate these trends into war fighting capabilities, because so much depends on how long Iran is cutoff from resupply, the extent to which the Southern Gulf states acquire serious military capabilities, and the strength of Western power projection forces. Even today, however, the problems in Iran's ground forces do not preclude them from defending against a weakened Iraq. Iran would probably be much more capable of successful defensive operations against Iraq today than it was in 1988. Given Iraq's diminished strength, it is unlikely that even an Iraqi attack into Iran, led by the Republican Guards, could achieve more than limited initial gains.

Iran is well deployed to fight Iraq, and might be able to conduct limited armored offensives in the Iran-Iraq border area. It is unclear that Iran could take significant amounts of Iraqi territory along the border area, or seize the Shi'ite areas in southeastern Iraq without a massive popular uprising, but much would depend on how well Iraqi forces fought and their loyalty to Saddam Hussein. In the future, much will also depend on how rapidly Iraq can recover from the Gulf War and when it can begin to rebuild and modernize its land forces. Iraq should be able to defend against an Iranian invasion through the year 2000, but this defense would be heavily dependent on Iraqi unity and the willingness of Iraqi Shi'ites to fight for the central government. Iraq is also likely to become significantly more vulnerable to an Iranian invasion after 2000, if it does not begin to receive significant supplies of parts, munitions, and new arms.

Iran's land forces currently present only a limited threat to the Southern Gulf states, unless a change in a Southern Gulf regime should allow Iran to build-up a significant military presence in the Southern Gulf. Iranian land forces could currently support the seizure of islands and off-shore oil facilities in the Gulf, defeat any Kurdish uprising, and play a significant role in low intensity combat in Iran's northern and eastern border areas.

It is also impossible to rule out a sudden or surprise Iranian attack in support of an uprising against a southern Gulf regime that might produce success out of all proportion to the size and effectiveness of the Iranian forces deployed. Iran has a number of land units that should perform well in unconventional warfare missions in support of any popular uprising. It could deploy brigade-sized forces relatively rapidly across the Gulf, if it was allowed to make an unopposed amphibious and air assault. Under these conditions, it could intervene in a civil war in Bahrain, or another of the smaller Gulf states.

Iranian land forces could easily defeat the Iranian Kurds or any other internal opposition force. They are also capable of intervening at the brigade and division level in a conflict like the war between Azerbaijan and Armenia, and in Afghanistan. They have very limited capability, however, against Turkey's first line forces.

Iranian conventional land warfare capabilities will only improve to the extent the build-up of Iranian forces outpaces that of its neighbors. In addition, Iran's freedom of action in the Gulf will be heavily dependent on the reaction of US naval and air forces and the position taken by Iraq. It is far from clear that Iran's conventional land warfare capabilities will improve faster than those of its neighbors, particularly if Iran's land forces remain split between the regular forces and those of the Revolutionary Guards.

As a result, Iran may be more of an indirect threat to its neighbors and the West than a threat in terms of a major regional conflict. Iranian land forces, particularly the IRGC, can already play a significant role in training, equipping, and supporting guerrilla and terrorist forces in countries like Lebanon, the Sudan, and Bosnia. They can covertly project power in terms of supporting radical or extremist movements in other states. All of these capabilities will improve as Iran builds up and modernizes its land forces.[377]

10

The Threat from Iranian
Air and Air Defense Forces

Iran's air force has gone through a decade and a half of revolution and war, and its current operational strength is as hard to estimate as the operational strength of Iran's ground forces. While Iran had 85,000 men and 447 combat aircraft in its air force at the time the Shah fell from power, it steadily lost air strength from 1980 to 1988. As Chart Forty-Two shows, the air force suffered combat losses in the Iran-Iraq War and many aircraft gradually ceased to be operational once Iran was cut off from its US suppliers. In addition, the Iranian Air Force has lacked effective foreign technical support for fifteen years. The air force was also purged of some of the pilots, technical personnel, and other officers that served under the Shah, during the first few years of the Khomeini regime.[378]

The Iranian Air Force

Iran's air strength has improved significantly, however, since 1988. By 1996, the Iranian Air Force and air defense force have built themselves back to a total inventory of around 260–300 combat aircraft. The Air Force also had an independent surface-to-surface missile brigade. The Iranian Air Force had a strength of about 55,000 men, with 35,000 men in the air force plus 20,000 more in its land-based air defense forces. The relative current strength of the Iranian Air Force is show in Table Twelve and Charts Forty-Two to Forty-Five.

The Iranian Air Force had 18 combat squadrons comprised of nine fighter ground-attack squadrons, with 4/55-60 F-4D/Es, 4/60 F-5E/FIIs, and 1/27-30 Su-24s; and seven air defense squadrons, with 4/60-65 F-14s, 2/30-35 MiG-29s, and 1/25-30 F-7Ms. Iran has claimed that it is modernizing its F-14s by equipping them with IHawk missiles adapted to the air-to-air role, but it is far from clear that this is the case or that such adaptations can have more than limited effectiveness.[379]

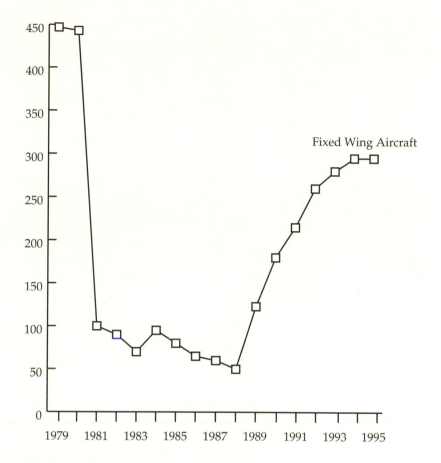

CHART FORTY-TWO   Trends in Iranian Operational Major Combat Aircraft, 1979–1996. *Source:* Adapted by Anthony H. Cordesman from various editions of the IISS, *Military Balance.* No useful estimate is possible of armed helicopter strength.

Iran also had a reconnaissance squadron with 3–8 RF-4Es, and possibly 5–10 additional RF-5EIIs. It operated 5 P-3F maritime reconnaissance aircraft, 1 RC-130 and other intelligence/reconnaissance aircraft, together with large numbers of transports and helicopters. Iran also had 5 MiG-29, 20–25 F-5B and F-5FII, 5 FT-7, 10 EMB-312 Tucano, 7 T-33, 26 Beech F-33A/C and some Chinese F-6 combat capable trainers in inventory, although the operational status of these aircraft is unclear.[380]

The Iranian Air Force was organized largely into multi-role squadrons that can perform both air defense and attack missions—

TABLE TWELVE   Advanced Combat Aircraft by Type in Gulf Forces

	Number	Type
Bahrain	24	Total Fixed Wing Combat
	16	F-16C/D
Iran	295	Total Fixed Wing Combat
	30	Su-24D
	30	MiG-29
Iraq	353	Total Fixed Wing Combat
	30	Su-20
	1	Su-24D
	12	Su-25
	38	Mirage F-1EQ5/200
	12	MiG-29
	15	MiG-25
	4	MiG-25R
Kuwait	76	Total Fixed Wing Combat
	40	F/A-18C/D
	8	Mirage F-1/CK
Oman	46	Total Fixed Wing Combat
	(19)	Jaguar (SO) Mark 1, T-2
Qatar	12	Total Fixed Wing Combat
	6	Mirage F-1EDA/DDA
Saudi Arabia	295	Total Fixed Wing Combat
	42	Tornado IDS
	24	Tornado ADV
	98	F-15C/D
	5	E-3A
UAE	97	Total Fixed Wing Combat
	9	Mirage 2000E
	22	Mirage 2000EAD
	6	Mirage 2000DAD
	8	Mirage 2000RAD

Note: Older aircraft with inferior avionics are not included. Supersonic flight performance is not regarded as more than a marginal measure of combat performance.
Source: Adapted by Anthony H. Cordesman from the IISS, Military Balance, 1995–1996.

although this is not true of its F-14 and Su-24s. The IRGC also had some air elements. The IRGC operates some of Iran's PRC-made fighters and displayed some of the Iraqi fighters that Iran is absorbing into its forces at a recent air show in Tehran. The IRGC seems to be expanding its air capabilities, although it is not clear what combat formations exist within the IRGC, or whether the IRGC will become a direct competitor with the regular air force.

Total Fixed Wing Combat Aircraft

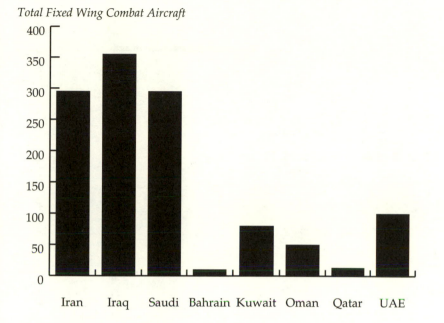

Operational Modern and Advanced Combat Aircraft: MiG-25, MiG-29, F-14, F-15, F-16, F/A-18, Mirage F-1, Mirage 2000

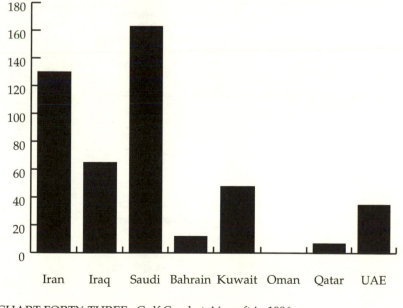

CHART FORTY-THREE   Gulf Combat Aircraft in 1996.

228

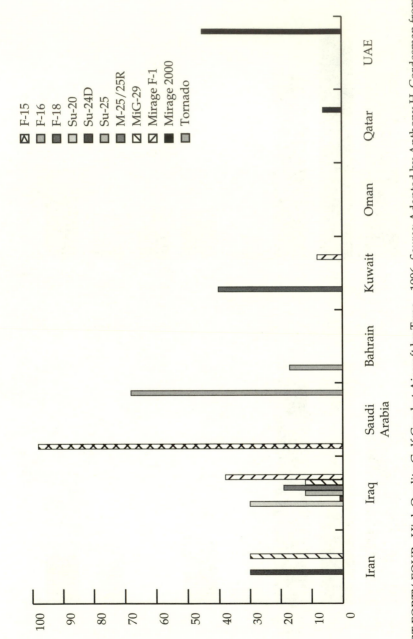

CHART FORTY-FOUR   High Quality Gulf Combat Aircraft by Type—1996. *Source:* Adapted by Anthony H. Cordesman from the IISS, *Military Balance, 1995–1996.*

Total Armed Helicopters

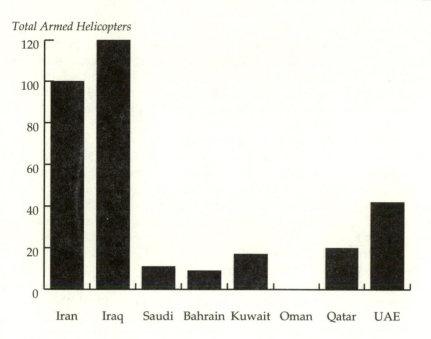

Modern Attack Helicopters: AH-64, Mi-25, Mi-24, SA-330, SA-342, AS-332F

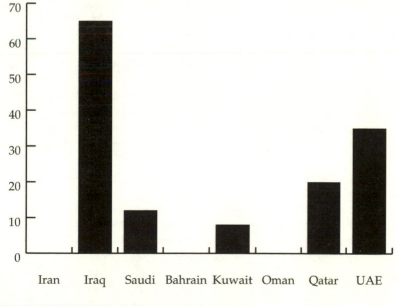

CHART FORTY-FIVE   Gulf Attack Helicoptors.

The Iranian Air Force was based principally at Bandar Abbas, Bushehr, Dezful, Doshan, Tehran (Tapeh, Ghaleh Morghi, Mehrabad), Hamadan, Isfahan, Shiraz, Tabriz, and Zahedan. Its fighter attack units were based at Bandar Abbas, Bushehr, Dezful, Mehrabad, Hamadan, and Tabriz. Its air defense units are based at Doshan, Tapeh, Mehrabad, and Shiraz. Shiraz provides interceptor training and is the main base for transport aircraft.[381]

Force quality and readiness, however, remained a major issue. Brigadier General Mansour Sattari, then Chief of Staff of the Iranian Air Force, claimed in 1994 that the air force had "reached self sufficiency in all fields, including pilot training, missiles, radar, air defenses, maintenance and repair, manufacture of parts and basic repair of facilities. . . . We constantly patrol the international waters and have a watchful eye on the moves of foreign warships there. . . . If the foreigners pose any threat, we will meet them with all our might."[382]

These claims were little more than whistling in the dark. Many of Iran's operational aircraft have only limited operational capability. As few as 50% of Iran's US-supplied combat aircraft may be operational, and few of Iran's operational US-equipped squadrons can long support sustained sortie rates higher than one per aircraft every three to four days. An estimate by the US Office of Naval Intelligence indicated that Iran had only 175 operational combat aircraft in 1996. Roughly 44% of these aircraft were "second generation" aircraft like the Chinese F-7 and US F-5, 22% were "third generation" aircraft like the F-4 and F-14, and 34% were "fourth generation" aircraft like the Su-24 and MiG-29. The same estimate indicated that Iran's operational strength had only increased from 150 aircraft in 1985 to 175 in 1995, and that Iran's strength would drop to 125 aircraft in 2005.[383]

Furthermore, some US-supplied aircraft may lack the operational avionics necessary to fire air-to-air and air-to-surface missiles properly. For example, Iran has lost the capability to make use of most of the long-range air defense capabilities of the F-14. It has kept the plane flying by reverse-engineering critical parts, but its Phoenix missiles have not been operational since 1980, and efforts to adapt it to use other missiles have failed.

Iran's success in obtaining other parts and spares for its US-supplied aircraft has been limited. Iran has had some successes, but failed in covert efforts, such as attempting to buy compressor blades for the F-5's engines in the UK and surplus F-5s from Vietnam.[384] These problems helped lead Akbar Torkan to state that, "Our equipment is mostly American: F-4, F-5, F-14 fighter jets. Our transport aircraft are also American: C-130s, Boeing 747s, and 707s. We have a very good fleet: 14 707s, 12 747s, and 53 C-130s. This should be enough to see us through the next 30 years. . . . We have

72 F-14s. . . . For closer support we have F-5 fighters and for deep strikes we have F-4 fighters. This is a very good configuration. We have 750 helicopters. . . . Unfortunately, because our fleet is mainly made up of American products, providing spares is very difficult."[385]

Iran also has a severe pilot problem. Many of its US-trained pilots were purged at some point during the Revolution. Its other US-trained pilots and ground-crew technicians are aging to the point where many should soon retire from service, and have not had advanced air-to-air combat and air attack training for more than 15 years. While Iran practices more realistic individual intercept training using its US-supplied aircraft than Iraq, it fails to practice effective unit or force-wide tactics and has shown no capability to fly large numbers of sorties with its US supplied aircraft on even a surge basis.

There is some debate over exactly how many new aircraft Iran is obtaining from the People's Republic of China, from the former Soviet Union, and from other sources. According to many experts, Iran imported 30 F-7M fighters from the Chinese by mid-1993, out of a possible total order of 50–72, but did not take further deliveries. As was the case in Pakistan, Iran found the F-7M to be inferior in performance and extremely difficult to maintain. The People's Republic of China also sold Iran PL-2 and PL-2A air-to-air missiles (Chinese copies of the Sidewinder) and PL-7 air-to-air missiles (Chinese copies of the Matra Magic R-550) with these aircraft.

A few experts believe that Iran made larger purchases of Chinese fighters, and that it took delivery of over 50 Chinese-made F-6 fighters between 1987 and mid-1992. These experts also believe that Iran had nearly 70 Chinese-made F-7s in operation by mid-1994. US experts believe these estimates are incorrect and that Iran does not have the F-6 operational in combat units.

Regardless of which estimate is correct, purchases of the F-7M will do little to affect the regional balance. It is a marginal copy of the MiG-21, with poor ground attack performance and limited air-to-air combat capability against first line fighters of any potential opponent. It is also difficult to upgrade and overhaul.[386] What could be more significant are reports that Iran is considering major imports of the more advanced F-7 attack variant, F-8 fighter, Jian Hong 7 bomber, and/or F-10. The F-10 is a developmental fighter derived from the Israeli Lavi; if it is successful, it will be the first truly modern Chinese-made fighter.[387]

Iran's most important source of new aircraft has been Russia. Iran's new MiG-29s and Su-24s are far superior in quality to the aircraft it has obtained from the Chinese, and Iran may have signed agreements that would give it a total of 50 MiG-29s, 36 Su-24, and the necessary support equipment.[388] These deliveries can greatly improve Iranian capabilities.

Iran's 30–35 MiG-29s are late model MiG-29As or MiG-29Bs, and Iran has claimed to have given them refueling capability.[389] These aircraft are designed for forward area air superiority and escort missions, including deep penetration air-to-air combat. Their flight performance and flying qualities are excellent, and are roughly equivalent to that of the best Western fighters.[390] They have relatively modern avionics and weapons, and an advanced coherent pulse-Doppler radar with look-down/shoot-down capabilities that can detect a fighter sized (2 square meter) target at a range of 130 kilometers (70 nautical miles), and track it at 70 kilometers (38 nautical miles).

The MiG-29 also has a track-while-scan range of 80 kilometers (44 nautical miles) against a 5 square meter target and is designed to operate with the radar off or in the passive mode, using ground-controlled intercept.[391] It has an infrared search and track system collimated with a laser range finder, a helmet-mounted sight, internal electronic countermeasure systems, SPO-15 radar warning receiver, modern inertial navigation, and the modern Odds Rod IFF. The range of the infrared search and track system is 15 kilometers (8.2 nautical miles) against an F-16-sized target. The maximum slant range of the laser is 14 kilometers (7.7 nautical miles) and its normal operating range is 8 kilometers (4.4 nautical miles).

The MiG-29 can carry up to six air-to-air missiles, a 30 mm gun, a wide mix of bombs, and 57 mm, 84 mm, and 240 mm air-to-ground rockets. A typical air combat load would include 250 rounds of 30 mm gun ammunition, 335 gallons of external fuel, 4 AA-8 Aphid infrared guided missiles, and 2 AA-10 Alamo radar-guided medium-range air-to-air missiles. Iran may have acquired AA-8, AA-10, and AA-11 Archer air-to-air missiles from Russia.

The MiG-29 does, however, have a number of ergonomic problems. The cockpit frames and high cockpit sills limit visibility. The cockpit display is fussy and uses outdated dials and indicators similar to those of the F-4. There is only a medium angle heads-up display and only partial hands-on system control. The CRT display is dated, and the cockpit is cramped. The helmet mounted sight allows the pilot to slave the radar, IRST, and heads up display (HUD) together for intercepts and covert attacks using off-boresight cueing, but the weapons computer and software supporting all combat operations are several generations behind those in fighters like the F-15C.[392] This makes it doubtful that even a well-trained MiG-29 pilot has the air-to-air combat capability of a well-trained pilot flying an F-16C/D, F-15C, F/A-18D, or Mirage 2000 in long range missile or beyond visual range combat, or in any form of combat when only the other side has the support of an AWACS type aircraft.

The Su-24 is a twin seat, swing wing strike-attack aircraft that its roughly equivalent in terms of weight to the F-111, although it has nearly twice the thrust loading, and about one-third more wing loading. The Su-24 can carry payloads of up to 25,000 pounds and operate on missions with a 1,300 kilometer radius when carrying 6,600 pounds of fuel. With a more typical 8,818 pound (4,000 kilogram) combat load, it has a mission radius of about 790 kilometers in the Lo-Lo-Lo profile, and 1,600 kilometers in the Lo-Hi-Lo profile. With extended range fuel tanks and airborne refueling by an aircraft like the F-14, the Su-24 can reach virtually any target in Iraq and the southern Gulf.[393]

Although it is not clear what variant of the SU-24 has gone to Iran, it seems likely to be the Su-24D, which includes a sophisticated radar warning receiver, an improved electronic warfare suite, an improved terrain avoidance radar, a bean, satellite communications, an aerial refueling probe, and the ability to deliver electro-optical, laser, and radar-guided bombs and missiles.[394]

The Su-24D is an excellent platform for delivering air-to-surface missiles and biological, chemical, and nuclear weapons. The air-to-ground missiles it can carry include up to three AS-7 Kerry radio command guided missiles (5 kilometers range), one AS-9 Kyle anti-radiation missile with passive radar guidance and an active radar fuse (90 kilometers range), three AS-10 Karen passive laser-guided missiles with an active laser fuse (10 kilometers range), three AS-11 Kilter anti-radiation missiles with passive radar guidance and an active radar fuse (50 kilometers range), three AS-12 Kegler anti-radiation missiles with passive radar guidance and an active radar fuse (35 kilometers range), three AS-13 Kingposts, and three AS-14 Kedge semi-active laser-guided missiles with an active laser fuse (12 kilometers range). It can also carry demolition bombs, retarded bombs, cluster bombs, fuel air bombs, and chemical bombs. Some experts believe that Russia has supplied Iran with AS-10, AS-11, AS-12, and possibly AS-14/AS-16 air-to-surface missiles.

Iran's purchase of Russian aircraft has the major additional benefit of enabling the Iranian Air Force to use some of the Iraqi aircraft that fled to Iran during the Gulf War. There is some question about the exact number of aircraft involved, and how many are flyable. Some sources report as few as 106 combat aircraft, but Iraq has officially claimed that they total 139 aircraft. The author's estimate, based on conversations with various experts, is 24 Mirage F-1s, 22 Su-24s, 40 Su-22s, 4 Su-17/20s, 7 Su-25s, 4 MiG-29s, 7 MiG-23Ls, 4 MiG-23BNs, 1 MiG-23UB, and 1 Adnan. This is a total of 112 combat aircraft—the total usually counted by the IISS. The transport and support aircraft include 2 B-747s, 1 B-707, 1 B-727, 2 B-737s, 14 IL-76s, 2 Dassault Falcon 20s, 3 Dassault Falcon 50s, 1 Lockheed Jetstar, 1 A-300, and 5 A-310s. This is a total of 31 aircraft.[395] Velayati has already made it clear that Iran will not return the combat aircraft even if the UN lifts its sanctions on Iraq, and has discussed to possible return of only 22 of the 31 civil aircraft.[396]

Iran has already begun to fly Iraqi MiG-29s and Su-24s, obtained Russian support at training facilities in Iran, and is in the process of absorbing all of Iraq's flyable MiG-29s, Su-24s, and possibly its Su-20/Su-22s into its force structure.[397] This could give Iran up to 90 additional combat aircraft, if it can continue to obtain suitable support from Russia. Iran probably cannot operate Iraqi Mirage F-1s effectively without French technical assistance, which currently seems highly unlikely. The 8–12 Iraqi MiG-23s are sufficiently low in capability so that Iran may be unwilling to pay for the training and logistic burden of adding this type to its inventory. The seven Su-25s are a more attractive option since they are specially equipped for the close air support mission but it would be very expensive for Iran to operate a force of only seven aircraft.

Iran is also reported to have discussed buying Tu-22M (Tu-26) bombers from Russia and other states of the former Soviet Union, as well as buying Su-25 close support aircraft, MiG-31 fighters, and Su-27 attack aircraft. Reports of efforts to buy the Tu-22M seem to be correct, and Iran evidently sought 10–15 such bombers—although the exact configuration it wanted is unclear. Unlike the obsolete Soviet Tu-16 and Tu-22—or the even more obsolete Chinese H-5 and H-6—the Tu-22M is a modern bomber with a maximum range near 2,500 miles, good-range payload, adequate avionics, and reasonable low altitude flight performance. Any Russian sale of such aircraft would significantly improve Iranian offensive capability.

Iran has moderate airlift capabilities for a regional power. Its air transport assets include one tanker/transport squadron with 4 B-707s, and five transport squadrons with 9 B-747Fs, 11 B-707s, 1 B-727, 20 C-130E/Hs, 3 Commander 690s, 15 F-27s, and 5 Falcon 20As. Its helicopter strength includes 2 AB-206As, 39 Bell 214Cs, and 5 CH-47 transport helicopters.

The Warfighting Capabilities of Iranian Air Forces

It is clear from Iran's imports that it is seeking to obtain first line air defense and long-range strike fighters. Also evident is Iran's intention to rebuild a high technology air force that can provide both effective air defense and the ability to strike deep into Iraq, the southern Gulf states, and any other neighboring power. If Iran can obtain additional imports of 50–100 first line combat aircraft, it may be able to achieve near parity with a decaying Iraqi Air Force by 2000, *if* Iraq continues to face an embargo on all shipments of aircraft, parts, and air munitions. However, Iran has only a limited current prospect of keeping its US-supplied

aircraft operational much beyond the late 1990s, and may find it difficult to convert to Russian fighters fast enough to offset its losses of US
types.[398]

There is little evidence that Iran can currently sustain high sortie rates
for more than one-third to one-half of its present combat aircraft for more
than a matter of days. More generally, the Iranian Air Force is still organized to fight at the squadron level. There is little sign that it is organized
to fight effectively, using mass and technology effectively in air defense,
close air support, or interdiction missions. Iran also lacks the training,
advanced training facilities, and sensors to compete with the West in
beyond-visual-range and dog-fight combat.

There are a wide range of areas where Iran needs to improve its training and technology—even if it gets more MiG-29s and Su-24s, and aircraft like the Su-27, Su-25, and MiG-31. These areas include acquiring
some form of airborne warning and air control system (AWACS), modern air-to-air missiles to replace its US inventory, modern, remotely
piloted vehicles (RPVs), and improved electronic countermeasure, and
airborne refueling technology. Iran also needs support in repairing and
reconditioning its captured Iraqi fighters, in rehabilitating and improving its F-4s, and in recovering the beyond-visual-range air combat capability of its F-14s. In addition, it must find ways of integrating its fighters into an effective air control and warning system, integrating their
operations with those of its ground-based air defense system, while
avoiding the many war fighting limitations of over-dependence on
ground-controlled intercepts.

Iran also needs to either recondition and upgrade its RF-4Es and RC-
130E/Hs, or acquire modern reconnaissance and intelligence aircraft.
Furthermore, it needs to recondition and improve the sensors and
weapons on the army's AB-206B and AH-1J attack helicopters, as well as
recondition its force of transport helicopters. Iran needs spares, support
organization, and training to achieve dramatic improvements in sortie
rates and sustainability. Additional air bases, for the purpose of reducing the air force's vulnerability through greater aircraft dispersal are also
necessary.

At some point in the near future, Iran must also make a clear decision
between trying to maintain a hybrid air force and standardizing on Russian aircraft. Continued reliance on aging US aircraft presents obvious
risks, and there are no near-term prospects that the US will relax its constraints on the sale of parts and new equipment. In contrast, an Iranian
Air Force based on Russian attack aircraft like the Su-24 and Su-27, close
support aircraft like the Su-25, Tu-22M bombers, advanced Russian air-
to-surface weapons like the AS-9, AS-10 and AS-14, air defense aircraft
like the MiG-29 and MiG-31, and air-to-air missiles like the AA-8, AA-10,

and AA-11, could be quite effective. Such an air force would take 5–8 years to create, however, and would be extremely costly. Iran also faces the risk of creating new supply problems with Russia. In addition, Russia has so far failed to provide any Third World state with effective advanced air combat and air-to-ground training and the associated equipment, training and technical support to fight effectively as a coherent modern air force.

Like all other Gulf air forces—and most Third World air forces, the Iranian Air Force is still a collection of small individual formations, rather than a unified force. It lacks cohesive air battle tactics, mission planning, and C⁴I/BM organization. It trains on a formation level, and rarely operates even as integrated squadrons. It does conduct joint training with the other services, but in the form of limited sorties in set piece exercises. In many of these exercises, the Iranian Air Force has indicated it lacks the force cohesion and training to operate in the air defense mode or attack mode in even local operations.

This mix of strengths and weaknesses leaves the Iranian Air Force with limited to moderate war fighting capability. For all its problems, the Iranian Air Force is not limited to the highly individualized "knights of the air," or World War I type of training, characteristic of some Southern Gulf air forces. It has more effective force-on-force capabilities than any Gulf air force except the Royal Saudi Air Force, and has steadily improved its air combat and exercise training since the end of the Gulf War. It has conducted increasing larger and more realistic joint exercises with land forces, land-based air defense forces and naval forces. Its annual Pirouzi series of air-naval exercises also indicate that the Iranian Air Force would now be considerably more effective in supporting naval and amphibious operations than in the early 1990s.

The Iranian Air Force can now conduct limited air attacks against all of its neighbors, and can deliver precision-guided weapons, chemical weapons, and possibly biological weapons. It can sustain limited numbers of daily attacks on hostile Kurdish camps and the bases of the People's Mujahideen. It can selectively attack shipping in the Gulf and could assist the naval forces in limited operations there, unless it met US or Saudi resistance. It could also assist Iran's land forces in any new fighting with Iraq. It might not be able to win air superiority over the Iranian border area, but could do a much better job of defending Iranian territory than it did during the Iran-Iraq War.

The Iranian Air Force is strong enough to deter offensive strikes from any southern Gulf air force, except for the Saudi Air Force. It can also probably penetrate the air space of all southern Gulf countries, except Saudi Arabia, at least to the extent of conducting selective slash and run attacks on key military depots or bases. It could probably even execute at least one successful mass surprise attack on a Saudi target before the Saudi Air Force could fully organize its air defenses, although much would depend on the activity of the Saudi E-3A force and the readiness of Saudi F-15Cs.

The future capabilities of the Iranian Air Force are difficult to estimate. The Iranian Air Force and air defense force are likely to expand to around 35,000 men by the year 2000–2005, but it is unclear that the air force will increase its total inventory much above 300 aircraft. It is going to need to replace its 4/55-60 F-4D/Es, 4/60 F-5E/FIIs, 4/60-65 F-14s, and 1/25-30 F-7Ms no later than 2010, and there is little prospect that Iran could rebuild its US-supplied fighters without direct US support. It also needs to replace its 5–10 RF-5EIIs, 3–8 RF-4Es, and probably its 5 P-3Fs and RC-130s, with more modern intelligence and reconnaissance aircraft. The most logical replacements would be to seek greater than 150 MiG-29s, or some more advanced Russia dual-role fighter, and over 100 Su-24s, or some other advanced Russian strike aircraft. Iran has had good reason to examine other types of Russian aircraft like the Su-25 close support aircraft, MiG-31 fighters, and Su-27 attack aircraft, and to seek advanced Russian reconnaissance and intelligence aircraft.

It will not be enough, however, simply to buy advanced fighters, attack aircraft, and reconnaissance aircraft. Iran lags far behind the West and its most advanced neighbors in the ability to command an air force in large-scale battle. If Iran is to compete effectively with Saudi and US forces in air combat it will also need an AWACS-like aircraft, advanced beyond-visual-range missiles and combat capabilities, advanced stand-off air attack ordnance, a new C^{4}I/BM system, and much more advanced electronic warfare capabilities. Iran also has a strong incentive to modernize its naval aviation capabilities, replace its P-3s with a new maritime patrol aircraft, and seek out an advanced bomber with anti-ship missile capabilities like the Tu-22M (Tu-26) bombers from Russia and other states of the former Soviet Union,

The practical problems are whether Iran can obtain such aircraft from Russia, whether Iran can afford them in sufficient numbers, can manage the complex conversion from US to Russian aircraft efficiently, and can convert from an air force organized to fight at the squadron, or small flight level, to one that can conduct coherent force-wide operations and fight modern joint warfare. The problems Iran faces go far beyond modernizing its air order of battle, and require fundamental changes in its ability to conduct force-on-force warfare. It is far from clear that Iran can accomplish all these tasks in the near to mid-term. Iran is also unlikely to obtain any assistance from the US and Europe as a substitute for Russia. Further, Chinese capabilities are unlikely to evolve to the point where

China can be an adequate supplier of aircraft, munitions, and technology before 2010.

In the interim, Iran will continue to lag behind the rate of modernization in Saudi Arabia, and has no foreseeable near to mid-term hope of challenging a combination of US, British, and Saudi air power. The Iranian Air Force could, however, deploy quickly to a friendly air base in the southern Gulf—in the event of a coup or other change in the political posture of that state—although it would take several weeks for Iran to deploy enough support equipment and stocks to support more than limited squadron sized operations from such a base. While the Iranian Air Force could not compete with the Turkish or Pakistani air forces, it might be able to fly combat support and offensive missions over the territory of Azerbaijan, or the other former Soviet republics near the Iranian border. Such operations would, however, have to be squadron sized and Iran could only fly relatively low sortie rates.

Iranian Ground-Based Air Defenses

Iranian ground-based air defenses play a critical role in shaping Iranian willingness to take risks and use conventional military forces. As long as Iran is vulnerable to the kind of air offensive the UN Coalition conducted against Iraq during Desert Storm, it is likely to be restrained in the risks it will take. Much depends, however, on how Iran perceives its vulnerability to air attack and the attrition levels it can inflict on attacking aircraft. This perception will be shaped in part by Iran's ability to modernize its fighter forces, but Iran has no near-term prospect of acquiring an airborne defense platform similar to the E-3A airborne warning and air control system (AWACS) operated by the Saudi and US air forces, or match the West in airborne electronic warfare capabilities. Iran's success in modernizing its ground-based air defenses will, therefore, probably be as important in influencing its willingness to take military risks as its acquisition of aircraft.[399]

In 1996, Iran seemed to have assigned about 20,000 men to land-based air defense functions, including 14,000–16,000 regulars and 5,000–8,000 IRGC personnel. It is not possible to distinguish clearly between the major air defense weapons holdings of the regular air force and IRGC, but the air force appeared to operate most major surface-to-air missile systems and its total holdings seem to include 30 Improved Hawk fire units (150+ launchers), 50–55 SA-2 and HQ-23 (CSA-1) launchers (Chinese-made equivalents of the SA-2), and 25 SA-6 launchers. The air force also had three Soviet-made long range SA-5 units with a total of 10–15 launchers—enough for six sites. The relative strength of Iran's land-based air defenses is shown in Table Thirteen.

TABLE THIRTEEN   Gulf Land-Based Air Defense Systems

Country	Major SAM	Light SAM	AA Guns
Bahrain	None 40+ RBS-70	? 18 Stinger 7 Crotale	
Iran	12/150 I Hawk 3/? SA-5 45 HQ-2J (SA-2) ? SA-2	SA-7 *HN-5* 30 Rapier 15 Tigercat	1,500 Guns ZU-23, ZSU-23-4, ZSU-57-2, KS-19, FM-80 (CH Crotale)
Iraq	SA-2 Roland SA-3 SA-7 SA-6 SA-8	5,500 Guns ZSU-23-4 23mm, M-1939 37mm SA-9 SA-13 SA-14, SA-16	ZSU-57-2 SP, 57mm, 85mm, 100mm, 130mm
Kuwait	4/24 I Hawk	6/12 Aspede	6/2×35mm Oerlikon
Oman	None Blowpipe	2 VAB/VD 20mm 34 SA-7 *28 Javelin* 28 Rapier	4 ZU-23-2 23mm 12 L-60 40mm
Qatar	None Blowpipe	? *12 Stinger* 9 Roland	
Saudi Arabia	128 I Hawk	Crotale Stinger *500 Redeye* 68 Shahine mobile 40 Crotale 73 Shahine static	92 M-163 Vulcan 20mm 50 AMX-30SA 30mm 128 35mm guns 150 L-70 40mm (in store)
UAE	5 I Hawk Bty.	20+ Blowpipe *10 SA-16* 12 Rapier 9 Crotale 13 RBS-70 100 Mistral	48 M-3VDA 20mm SP 20 GCF-BM2 30mm

Source: Adapted by Anthony H. Cordesman from the IISS, *Military Balance, 1995–1996.*

Iran's holdings of lighter air defense weapons include 30 Rapier fire units in five squadrons, 5–10 Chinese FM-80 launchers, 10–15 Tigercat fire units, and a few RBS-70s. Iran also hold large numbers of man-portable SA-7s, HN-5s, SA-14s, and possibly SA-16s, plus about 2,000 anti-aircraft guns—including some Vulcans and 50–60 radar-guided and self propelled ZSU-23-4 weapons.[400] It is not clear which of these lighter air defense weapons were operated by the army, the IRGC, or the air force. The IRGC clearly had larger numbers of manportable surface-to-air launchers, including some Stingers which it had obtained from Afghanistan. It almost certainly had a number of other light air defense guns as well.

During the Iran-Iraq War, Iran's major surface-to-air missiles were redeployed to cover the Iraqi border, its major cities, and its ports in the Gulf. There are no authoritative data on how Iran deployed these air defenses, but Iran seems to have deployed its new SA-5s to cover its major ports, oil facilities, and Tehran. It seems to have concentrated its Improved Hawks and Soviet and Chinese-made SA-2s around Tehran, Isfahan, Shiraz, Bandar Abbas, Kharg Island, Bushehr, Bandar Khomeini, Ahwaz, Dezful, Kermanshah, Hamadan, and Tabriz, although some IHawks seem to have been deployed on Abu Musa and the Tunbs.

Since that time, Iran's air defense forces have steadily increased the number of surface-to-air missile sites along the Gulf coast and on islands in the Gulf, and Iran made major increases in such deployments during 1994 and 1995. Iran had only three major (Hawk, SA-6, SA-5) missile sites in 1992. It now has nine to twelve major sites, but these sites are still too widely space to provide more than limited are defense for key bases and facilities, and many lack the missile launcher strength to be effective. This is particularly true of Iran's SA-5 sites, which provide long-range medium to high altitude coverage of key coastal installations. Too few launchers are scattered over too wide an area to prevent relatively rapid suppression.[401]

Iran also lacks the missile strength, low altitude coverage, command and control assets, sensors, resistance to sophisticated jamming and electronic countermeasures, and systems integration capability necessary to create an effective air defense net. Its missiles and sensors were most effective at high to medium altitudes against aircraft with limited penetrating and jamming capability.

Iran faces serious problems in modernizing its air defense system to correct these weaknesses—many of which date back to the time of the Shah. Although Iran bought modern surface-to-air missiles at the time of the Shah, it never integrated these missiles into an effective land-based air defense system. It had not made its air control and warning system fully operational at the time the Shah fell, and had experienced serious problems in operating some of its largely British-supplied radars.

Once the Shah was deposed, Iran had no way of purchasing the equipment needed to improve or properly maintain its Western-supplied radars, communications system, and software. It also lost many of its Western-trained operators, technicians, and commanders during the purges following the revolution. This reduced its ability to use its Western-supplied equipment effectively. In spite of limited deliveries as a result of the Iran-hostage deal, Iran has never been able to find a source of parts, equipment, and technical expertise that has allowed it to support its Western-supplied systems properly.[402] Many of the Western-supplied surface-to-air missiles in Iran's order of battle are not fully operational, and Iran is forced to rely on inadequate radars, data processing systems, and command and control links to support its missile units.[403]

Iran has responded by obtaining the SA-2, CSA-1, SA-6, and SA-5 from the PRC, Russia, and Central Europe. Iran has acquired some Soviet warning and battle management radars, command, and communications equipment. It has deployed the SA-5 to several of its bases on the Gulf coast, including Bandar Abbas, and has obtained some new Soviet radars as part of the sale of SA-5 missiles. There are credible reports that Iran is seeking to import three more batteries of SA-5 missiles from the former Soviet Union, more CSA-1s, and further deliveries of Russian and Chinese radars. There are also reports that Iran may be paying North Korea for assistance in creating a network of underground command centers in 18 sites—although such reports are uncertain.[404]

These transfers of surface-to-air missiles and sensors from Russia and the People's Republic of China have helped improve Iran's land-based capabilities, but they have not been adequate to meet all of its needs. They have given Iran improved capability against regional air forces without sophisticated jammers and anti-radiation missiles, but they scarcely give Iran a modern integrated air defense system that can resist attack by a power like the US.

The Warfighting Capabilities of Iranian Land-Based Air Defense Forces

In the short-term, Iran requires substantial deliveries of added equipment to make its Western supplied weapons fully operational, much more advanced heavy surface-to-air missiles, and a considerably more advanced C⁴I/BM system. Iran must also find a reliable source of Hawk parts to make its current missiles functional. Iran also needs to rehabilitate and improve its radar-guided anti-aircraft guns and most of its short-range air defense systems. In addition, it is necessary for Iran either to modernize or replace its Rapiers, Tigercats, and FM-80s, and to replace its obsolescent mix of different systems of radars and command and control equipment.

However, improving the capabilities of its Western systems and further purchases of SA-2 and SA-5 systems cannot give Iran the range of capabilities it needs. The SA-2, CSA-1, SA-6 and SA-5 are highly vulnerable to active and passive countermeasures. Even the latest versions of the

Improved Hawk does not approach the Patriot in performance capability, and the Improved Hawks in Iranian hands are nearly 17 years old. If Iran is to create the land-based elements of an air defense system capable of dealing with the retaliatory capabilities of Western air forces, it needs major improvements in its electronic warfare capabilities, and a modern, heavy surface-to-air missile system that is part of a larger and better integrated air defense system.

Iran has boasted of its electronic warfare and battle management capabilities. In fact, Khamenei has claimed, "Today, one of the most sophisticated military tools—to which the Americans would never even conceive Iran could have access—is being built in workshops of the Islamic Revolutionary Guards Corps and mass produced by Iranian experts . . . (The US) with all its intelligence apparatus and spy networks is unaware of this."[405] Iran has been able to improve some aspects of its electronic warfare capabilities using European and Russia equipment—some imported by its covert purchasing network—but it has shown no signs of having anything approaching an adequate electronic warfare capability for its air defense forces, any more than it has for its air forces, land forces, or navy. Further, US experts indicate that Iran's electronic warfare exercises are primitive and very poorly structured and integrated.

Such a system will not be easy for Iran to obtain either. No European or Asian power can currently sell Iran either an advanced ground-based air defense system, or an advanced heavy surface-to-air missile system. The US and Russia are the only current suppliers of such systems, and the only surface-to-air missiles that can meet Iran's needs are the Patriot, SA-10, SA-12a and SA-12b.

Iran has no hope of getting the Patriot system from the US, making Russia the only potential source of the required land-based air defense technology. This explains why Iran has sought to buy the SA-10 heavy surface-to-air missile/anti-tactical ballistic missile systems and a next generation warning, command, and control system from Russia. The SA-10 (also named the Fakel 5300PMU or Grumble) has a range of 90 kilometers or 50 nautical miles. It has a highly sophisticated warning radar, tracking radar, terminal guidance system and warhead, and has good electronic warfare capabilities. The SA-10 is a far more advanced and capable system than the SA-2, SA-3, SA-5, or SA-6.[406]

Much depends on Russian willingness to make such sales in the face of US pressure. Reports surfaced in July, 1995, that Russia might have decided to sell Iran the SA-10. If true, this is a significant development since Russia has the capability to provide the SA-10 or SA-12 quickly and in large numbers, as well as support it with a greatly improved early warning sensor system, and an advanced command and control system for both its fighters and land-based air defenses.

Such a Russian system would still have important limits. Russia has not fully completed integration of the SA-10 and SA-12 into its own air defenses, has significant limitations on its air defense computer technology, and relies heavily on redundant sensors and different, overlapping surface-to-air missiles to compensate for a lack of overall system efficiency. A combination of advanced Russian missiles and an advanced sensor and battle management system would still be vulnerable to active and passive attack by the US.

It would also take at least three to five years for Iran to deploy and integrate such a system fully, once Russia agreed to the sale. Its effectiveness would also depend on Russia's ability to both provide suitable technical training, and to adapt a Russian system to the specific topographical and operating conditions of Iran. A Russian system cannot simply be transferred to Iran as an equipment package. It would take a major effort in terms of software, radar deployment and technology—and considerable adaptation of Russian tactics and siting concepts—to make such a system fully combat effective. As a result, full-scale modernization of the Iranian land-based air defense system is unlikely to occur before 2005 under the most optimistic conditions, and will probably lag well beyond 2010.[407]

An advanced land-based Russian air defense system would, however, give Iran far more capability to defend against retaliatory raids from Iraq or any Southern Gulf air force. It would allow Iran to allocate more fighter/attack aircraft to attack missions and use its interceptors to provide air cover for such attack missions. It would also greatly complicate the problem of using offensive US air power against Iran, require substantially more US forces to conduct a successful air campaign, and probably greatly increase US losses.

11

The Threat from Iran's Naval Forces

Most Gulf nations have treated sea power as an afterthought, but the Iranian Navy and Naval Branch of the Islamic Revolutionary Guards Corps are likely to play a critical role in Iranian military action in the Gulf. Any Iranian intervention in a Gulf state that does not involve the cooperation of a southern Gulf government and free access to ports and air fields, would require some kind of amphibious operation. Naval forces are equally essential to a wide spectrum of other possible conflicts that affect the islands in the Gulf, control of the Straits of Hormuz, unconventional warfare using naval forces, attacks on coastal targets in Iraq and the southern Gulf, and Western and southern Gulf naval operations in the Gulf.[408]

As a result, it is not surprising that Iran has given the modernization of its naval forces a high priority since the end of the Iran-Iraq War. Iran has obtained missiles from the Chinese, some additional ships, midget submarines from North Korea, and submarines from Russia. Iran has also received significant logistic and technical support from Pakistan.[409] It has improved its naval training, acquired additional mine warfare capability, and repaired some of its ships. It has stepped up training and exercise activity, most notably in the Lightning 3, Val Fajr 1 and 2, Fatah 3, and Naser series of exercises. Iran has also bought new missiles and ships, purchased submarines from Russia, and improved its ports and strengthened their air defenses. Furthermore, it has conducted combined arms training exercises with the land forces and air force.[410]

These efforts have done more to improve Iran's capabilities to threaten Gulf shipping and offshore oil facilities, and its capability to support unconventional warfare, than they have to allow it to act as an effective navy. Iranian naval forces still have many limitations, but the military capability of Iranian naval forces should not be measured in terms of the ability to win a battle for sea control against southern Gulf and/or Western forces. Iran's forces are likely to lose any such battle if Western forces are involved for the foreseeable future. It is Iran's ability to conduct limited or unconventional warfare, or to threaten traffic through the Gulf, that gives it the ability to threaten or intimidate its neighbors.

Iran's Surface Navy

In 1996, Iran's regular Navy, the naval elements of the Islamic Revolutionary Guards Corps, and the Iranian marines totaled around 38,000 men—with about 18,000 regulars and 20,000 men in the Iranian Naval Revolutionary Guard forces. While some sources list Iran as having three Marine Brigades, it is not clear how the marine units are structured, trained, or equipped.[411]

While most Iranian major surface ships have limited operational capability, the strength of the Iranian Navy is impressive by Gulf standards. According to various estimates, Iran's operational inventory includes 2 submarines with a third in delivery, 2 destroyers, 3 frigates, 10 missile combatants, 2 corvettes, 26 light patrol and coastal combatants, 3 mine warfare ships (including one training ship), 9 armed helicopters, and 8 amphibious ships and craft. Iran also has a small marine force and large numbers of naval revolutionary guards. In addition, Iran had 5–7 Silkworm (HY-2) anti-ship missile sites to defend its ports and cover the Straits of Hormuz. The relative strength of Iran's Navy is shown in Chart Forty-Six.

Most of the regular navy is based at Bandar Abbas, the only large Iranian port far enough away from Iraq to be relatively secure from Iraqi air attack during the Iran-Iraq War. This port is the home of Iran's destroyers, frigates, and two Kilo-class submarines. Iran does not conduct extensive patrols in the Gulf of Oman, but does hold occasional exercises there, and is expanding its base at Chah Bahar in the Gulf of Oman. Iran has another large naval base at Bushehr, where it deploys most of its guided missile patrol boats. It has operated hovercraft forces out of the oil port at Kharg Island since the time of the Shah, and has a moderate force at its Western port of Bandar Khomeini, which covers the waters opposite Iraq and the entrance to the Shatt al-Arab. It has small bases at Bandar Anzali and Noshahr on the Caspian. Noshahr is used for training Islamic Revolutionary Guards Corps forces in unconventional warfare.

Opinions differ as to how much of Iran's surface force is fully operational. Iran is clearly able to operate some of its British-made Saam-class fast attack craft. According to some reports, it can also operate most of the weapons systems on at least one destroyer, two frigates, six to ten fast attack craft (FAC), seven large patrol boats and 40 coastal patrol boats. Furthermore, these experts suggest an ability to

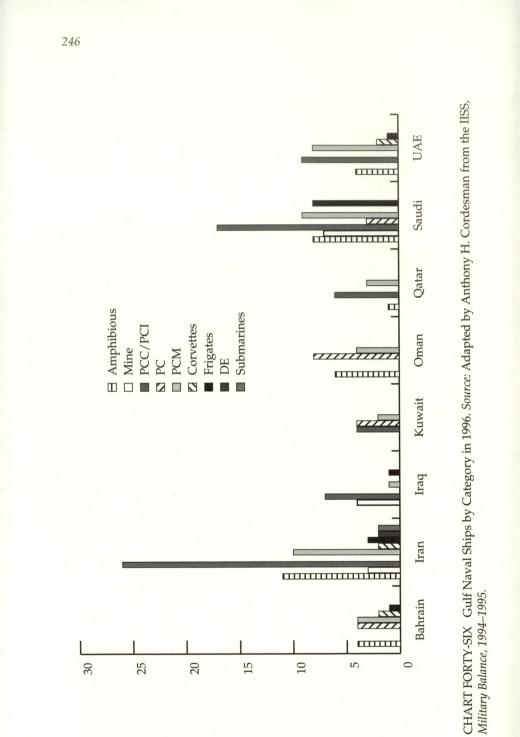

CHART FORTY-SIX Gulf Naval Ships by Category in 1996. *Source:* Adapted by Anthony H. Cordesman from the IISS, *Military Balance, 1994–1995.*

CHART FORTY-SIX (*continued*)

	Bahrain	Iran	Iraq	Kuwait	Oman	Qatar	Saudi	UAE
Submarines		2						
DE		2						
Frigates	1	3	1				8	1
Corvettes	2	2						2
PCM	4	10	1	2	4	3	9	8
PC	4			4	8		3	
PCC/PCI		26	7	4		6	17	9
Mine		3	4			1	7	
Amphibious	4	11			6		8	4

operate a maximum of 14 Hovercraft and 57 amphibious assault ships, logistic ships, and small patrol boats. If these reports are true, Iran has a total operational force of more than 80 vessels, although it would lack adequate air defense and anti-ship missile capabilities for its major surface ships.[412]

All of Iran's major surface vessels are obsolescent or obsolete, although they could be updated in Western shipyards. They include two Sumner-class (Babr-class) destroyers—the *Babr* and *Palang*. These ships displace 3,200 tons fully loaded and are capable of speeds of 31 knots. Each is armed with four paired elevating Standard SM-1MR surface-to-surface missile launchers, two twin 5" gun mounts, 6 Mark 32 torpedo tubes, and an Agusta AB 204AS helicopter. The Standard is still a potentially effective missile, with command guidance and semi-active radar homing and a maximum range of 46 kilometers. Iran's missile suites, however, have not been modernized in 20 years and all of Iran's Standard missiles have now aged beyond their normal shelf life. It is doubtful these ships have much effectiveness. These two ships still patrol, but it is unclear that they can use their anti-ship missiles and anti-submarine mortars effectively. These ships were originally laid down in 1943 and 1944, have not been refitted since 1971–1972, and possess weapons systems, sensors, and equipment that are over twenty years old.

Iran has one British-supplied 2,288-ton Battle-class ship called the *Damavand*. The *Damavand* is a British guided missile destroyer that displaces 3,360 tons fully loaded, has a speed of 31 knots, and is armed with four paired elevating Standard SM-1MR surface-to-surface missile launchers, two twin 5" gun mounts, a single Contraves RTN-10X Sea Hunter fire control radar, and a quadruple Sea Cat ship-to-air missile launcher. The *Damavand* had relatively modern air and sea search radars, and modern commercial grade ESM and EW gear, when it was first transferred to Iran. However, its main refitting took place in 1966 and its Standard missiles were added in South Africa in 1974–1975. Its Sea Cats no longer seem to be operational and it is unclear whether its Standards and electronics are fully operational. The *Damavand* does not patrol regularly and is no longer is counted as part of Iran's operational strength.[413]

Iran has three British-supplied Vosper Mark 5 Saam-class frigates—called the *Alvand*, *Alborz*, and *Sabalan*—each 1,100-ton frigates with maximum speeds of 39 knots. Each is armed with one five-missile Sea Killer Mark II surface-to-surface missile launcher and one Mark 8 4.5" gun mount. The Sea Killer has a relatively effective beam-riding missile with radio command or optical guidance, a maximum range of 25 kilometers, and a 70 kilogram warhead. These Alvand-class ships, however, were last refitted in 1977, and the operational readiness of their missiles and more sophisticated electronics is uncertain. There are some indications that Iran may have removed some of the missile launchers and replaced them with a BM-21 multiple rocket launcher to provide added fire support capability. Further, the *Sabalan* was extensively damaged in combat with the US Navy in 1988, during an engagement where the US sank its sister ship. It is not clear that it is really operational.[414]

Iran has two US PF-103 (Bayandor-class) corvettes called the *Bayandor* and the *Naghdi*. These ships are 900-ton vessels, with two 76 mm guns and a maximum speed of 18 knots. They were laid down in 1962, and delivered in 1964. Neither has sophisticated weapons systems or sensors, although one was reengined and given 20 mm guns in place of a 23 mm gun and depth charge rack in 1988.[415]

The rest of Iran's larger surface vessels consist of 10 French-made Combattante II (Kaman-class) fast attack boats armed with missiles and one 76 mm gun. These boats displace 275 tons, have maximum speeds of 37.5 knots, and are Iran's most modern Western-supplied combat ships. These ships were delivered during 1974–1981, and were originally equipped with four US Harpoon missiles. The combat capability of the anti-ship missile systems on the surviving boats is uncertain. Their Harpoons may not be operational, but at least two have been successfully converted to carry four CS-801/CS-802s, and all may be converted in the future.[416]

Iran has 10 to 15 large patrol craft and fast attack craft. The operational ships of this type in the Iranian Navy seem to include one captured Iraqi Bogomol (possible), three North Korean Chaho-class fast attack craft, three US Cape-class large patrol craft, and three Improved PGM-71 Parvin-class large patrol craft. These vessels are armed with guns ranging from 23 mm to 40 mm and the Chaho-class ships also have one BM-21 40 barreled rocket launcher. Most of these craft are operational and can be effective in patrol missions. They lack, however, sophisticated weapons systems or air defenses, other than machine guns and SA-7s, SA-14s, and possibly SA-16s.

Iran also ordered ten 68-ton Chinese Hegu (Hudong)-class fast attack craft or missile patrol boats for the naval branch of its Iranian Revolutionary Guards Corps in 1992. These ships are improved version of the Russian Osa II missile boat, and all 10 were delivered by March 1996. These vessels are 27 meters in length, carry four anti-ship missiles, and have two twin 25 mm guns. These vessels are equipped with search radars, but do not have a major anti-air missile system. These vessels are armed with the CS-801s and the more capable CS-802 missile, and Iran now has at least 40 CS-802s.

The CS-802 first became public in 1989. It has a 0.36 meter diameter and a weight of around 715 kilograms. It is a turbofan-powered missile with a range of 70–75 miles (120 kilometers), cruises at an altitude of around 20–30 meters, and can carry warheads of up to 363 pounds (165 kilograms). It has an over-the-horizon capability because it can be remotely targeted with a separate tracking and targeting radar.[417]

There are some indications that the Hegu-class ships may be used for the offshore defense of islands like Abu Musa and oil facilities in the Gulf. They seem to have been transferred to the Naval Branch of the IRGC, and Iran appears to be deploying them to Sirri and Abu Musa.[418]

Iran has 5–6 BH-7 and 7–8 SRN-6 Hovercraft. About half of these Hovercraft may be operational. They are capable of speeds of up to 60–70 knots, although their normal cruising speed is about half that. The BH-7 can carry 53.8 tons of cargo, and the SRN-6 can carry 10 tons. They are lightly armed and vulnerable, but their high speed makes them useful for many reconnaissance and unconventional warfare missions, and they can rapidly land troops on suitable beaches.

Iranian Mine Warfare Capabilities

Mine warfare, amphibious warfare, anti-ship missiles, and unconventional warfare offer Iran other potential ways of compensating for the weakness of its conventional air and naval forces. Iran's mine warfare vessels include 2–3 Shahrock-class MSC 292/268 coastal minesweepers (1 used for training in the Caspian Sea). The *Shahrock* and *Karkas* are known to be operational. They are 378-ton sweepers that can be used to lay mines as well as sweep, but their radars and sonars date back to the late 1950s and are obsolete in sweeping and countermeasure activity against modern mines. Iran has 1–2 Cape-class (Riazzi-class) 239-ton inshore minesweepers and seems to have converted two of its Iran Ajar-class LSTs for mine warfare purposes. Many of its small boats and craft can also lay mines.

Both the Iranian Navy and the naval branch of the IRGC are expanding their capability for mine warfare. While Iran has only a limited number of specialized mine vessels, it can also use small craft, LSTs, Boghammers, helicopters, and submarines to lay mines. Iran has a wide range of Soviet, Western, and Iranian-made moored and drifting contact mines, and US experts estimate that Iran has at least 2,000 mines.

Iran has both moored and bottom influence mines, and can place such mines in tanker routes—as it did during the Iran-Iraq War. They can be located near the Straits of Hormuz to deter commercial traffic, in narrow zones of operation to threaten warships, or in the Gulf of Oman—where sweeping and defensive coverage would be even more difficult than in the Persian Gulf. While such activity would be more a harassment than a serious war fighting capability, it could be combined with the use of land-based anti-ship missiles, commando raids, and submarine deployments. This would give Iran considerable leverage in terms of a cumulative threat to tanker and other shipping in the Gulf, and one that would be difficult to target, counter, and destroy.

Iran has significant stocks of US Mark 65 and Soviet AMD 500, AMAG-1, and KRAB anti-ship mines, has bought Chinese-made versions of the Soviet mines. It has claimed to be making its own non-magnetic, acoustic, free-floating and remote controlled mines, and has Chinese assistance in developing the production facilities for such mines.[419] It may have acquired significant stocks of non-magnetic mines, influence mines, and mines with sophisticated timing devices from other countries.

Even obsolete moored mines have proved difficult to detect and sweep when intelligence does not detect the original laying and size of the mine-field, and free floating mines can be used to present a constant hazard to shipping. Bottom-influence mines can use acoustic, magnetic, or pressure sensors to detect ships passing overhead. They can use multiple types of sensor/actuators to make it hard to deceive the mines and force them to release, they can be set to release only after a given number of ships pass, and some can be set to attack only ships of a given size or noise profile. Such mines are extremely difficult to detect and sweep, particularly when they are spaced at wide intervals in shipping lanes.

There also are reports that Iran has negotiated with China to buy the EM-52 or MN-52 rocket-propelled mine. The EM-52 is a mine that rests on the bottom until it senses a ship passing over it, and then uses a rocket to hit the target. It can be set to fire only after it has sensed given numbers of ships passing over it, and some reports claim it can operate to depths of 110 meters (363 feet). The maximum depth of the Straits of Hormuz is 80 meters (264 feet), although currents are strong enough to displace all but firmly moored mines.[420] Combined with modern submarine laid mines and anti-ship missile systems like the CS-801/802, HY-2, and SS-N-22, the EM-52 would give Iran considerable capability to harass Gulf shipping and even the potential capability to close the Gulf until US naval and air power could clear the mines and destroy the missile launchers and submarines.

Mines can be used throughout the Gulf, and in parts of the Gulf of Oman. The southern Gulf states may develop effective mine sweeping capabilities to clear concentrated fields in limited areas, but Iran could use such mines throughout the Gulf, and tanker companies and captains are unlikely to take their ships into harm's way in the face of even limited risks. It is also difficult for even the most advanced Western mine counter measure systems to detect and sweep modern mines. The US ships damaged by mines during the Gulf War were all operating in waters that had supposedly been swept, and even the best trained and equipped minesweeping teams have serious problems in sweeping non-magnetic mines, large areas with loose mines, and bottom mines or other mines which are timed to activate only after several ships have passed, or at fixed intervals.

Iranian Amphibious Warfare Capabilities

Iran has significant amphibious assets by Gulf standards, including four Hengam-class (Larak-class) LST amphibious support ships (2,940 tons loaded), 3 Iran Hormuz-class (South Korean) LSTs (2,014 tons loaded), and 1 Iran Ajar-class LST (2,274 tons loaded). Iran also has 3 1,400 ton LCTs, 1 250 ton LSL, at least 6—and possibly more than 12—nine ton LCUs, and about 50 small patrol craft. Each Hengam-class ship could carry 227 troops, nine tanks, and one helicopter; each Iran Hormuz-class could carry 140 troops and 8–9 tanks. The Ajar-class could carry 650 tons, but were converted to mine laying.

Unlike Iraq, Iran has sufficient support ships to sustain "blue water" operations and support an amphibious task force. It has one Kharg-class 33,014 ton replenishment ship, two Bandar Abbas-class 4,673 ton fleet supply ships and oilers, one 14,410 ton repair ship, two 12,000 ton water tankers, seven 1,300 ton Delva-class support ships, 5–6 Hendijan-class support vessels, two floating dry-docks and 20 tugs, tenders, and utility craft to help support a large naval or amphibious operation.

These ships give Iran the capability to deploy about 800 to 1,200 troops, and 30–50 tanks in an amphibious assault, and Iran has held extensive amphibious warfare exercises since 1992. These include exercises like the Great Khaibar exercise in September, 1995, which was centered on the Straits of Hormuz and Hengam Island, and which involved IRGC naval and marine units and Navy commands operating from Iranian Navy landing ships.[421] Iran does, however, lack the air and surface power to support a landing in a defended area, or a movement across the Gulf in the face of significant air/sea defenses. Iran would also probably gain more from using commercial ferries and roll on-roll off ships to move Iranian forces across the Gulf to a friendly port.

The Iranian Navy's air capability consists of two to three operational P-3F Orion maritime patrol aircraft out of an original inventory of five. According to reports from the Gulf, none of the surviving P-3Fs have fully operational radars and their crews often use binoculars. It also has up to 12 Sikorsky SH-3D ASW helicopters, two RH-53D mine laying helicopters, and seven Agusta-Bell AB-212 helicopters equipped with

Italian-made Sea Killer missiles. It uses air force AH-1J attack helicopters, equipped with French AS-12 missiles, in naval missions, and has adapted Hercules C-130 and Fokker Friendship aircraft for mine laying and patrol missions.[422]

Iranian Anti-Ship Missile Forces

Iran's lack of a modern long-range anti-ship missile, suitable targeting capability, and competitive electronic warfare capability is a major weakness in its war fighting capability. Iran seems to have expended virtually all of its Harpoon missiles during the Iran-Iraq War. Further, its Standards and the rest of its remaining US-supplied naval, air-to-air, and air-to-surface missiles have now aged well beyond their normal life cycle. Iran does not have a single reliable US-supplied missile in its naval or air inventory, and all of Iran's Western-supplied systems are so unreliable that some experts feel they can no longer be rated as operational in any form.

These problems explain Iran's interest in upgraded versions of the Chinese CS-802, the Russian SS-N-22, and Russian TU-22M bombers, equipped with long range anti-ship missiles. All of these purchases are ways of compensating for Iran's current lack of and advanced sea-based anti-ship missile capability.[423]

The Naval Branch of the Revolutionary Guards plays a major role in Iran's anti-ship missile capabilities. The Guards have operated Iran's Chinese-supplied Silkworm surface-to-ship missiles, since they were first delivered during the Iran-Iraq War, although these units may have support from the Iranian Navy. It also operates Iran's ten new 68-ton Chinese Hegu (Hudong)-class fast attack craft, which are equipped with CS-802 missiles.

The Silkworm is designated the HY-2 or Sea Eagle 2 by the People's Republic of China. It is a copy of the Soviet CSS-N-2 "Styx" missile, and is made by the China Precision Machinery Import and Export Corporation (CPMIEC). It is a very large missile with a 0.76 meter diameter and a weight of 3,000 kilograms. It has an 80–90 kilometer range and a 450 kilogram warhead.[424] It climbs to 145 meters (600') after launch and then drops to a cruise profile at 30 meters (100'). There are two variants. One uses radar active homing at ranges from the target of eight kilometers (4.5 nautical miles). The other is set to use passive IR homing and a radar altimeter to keep it at a constant height over the water.[425] Iran fired at least eight Silkworms against targets in Kuwait during the Iran-Iraq War, three of which were hits.

In 1996, the IRGC had four to five operational land-based anti-ship missile units, with three to six Silkworm launchers each. Iran had at least

50–60 Silkworm missiles, and some experts believe as many as 300.[426] These units were deployed near Iran's naval base at Chah Bahar, Bandar Abbas, Qeshem Island, and at Khuestak and Sirri Island near the Straits of Hormuz, to cover the entrance to the Gulf.

The IRGC has steadily increased its number of anti-ship missile sites since 1994, and also has presurveyed dispersal sites, and mobile missile launders. The Guards have formed at least one new unit using Chinese-supplied CS-801 anti-ship and ship-to-ship missiles, and there are reports that Iran is seeking to acquire much longer range anti-ship cruise missiles from either the People's Republic of China or the former Soviet Union. Iran has at least 60–100 CS-801 (YF-6) anti-ship missiles from the Chinese and may be using these to refit its surface fleet as well as to equip some shore based facilities and the Naval Branch of the IRGC. The Silkworm is a long-range, mobile anti-ship missile, and Iran has established fixed and pre-surveyed launch sites near the straits of Hormuz and in a number of other locations—including positions near Iraq and Kuwait. There are now four known launch sites for such missiles, versus one in 1990.[427]

The CS-801 anti-ship missile, also called the Yinji (Hawk) missile, is a solid fueled missile that began test flights in 1986. It is roughly equivalent to the French Exocet, and can be launched from land, ships and aircraft. It has a range of approximately 74 kilometers in the surface-to-surface mode, and uses J-Band active radar guidance. It has a 512 kilogram warhead and cruises at an altitude of 20–30 meters.

In late 1995, Iran publicly tested the CS(C)-802 anti-ship missile and US sources indicated that it had taken delivery on 40 such missiles. The CS-802 is an upgraded CS-801 that was first exhibited in 1988. It has many characteristics similar to the CS-801, but uses a turbojet propulsion system with a rocket booster instead of the solid fueled booster in the CS-801. As has been discussed earlier, it has a range of 70–75 missiles, has a warhead of up to 363 pounds, and can be targeted by a radar deployed on a smaller ship or aircraft operating over the radar horizon of the launching vessel.[428]

The CS-802 missile was fired at a "sea target" from a launch site near the Iranian naval base at Jask on November 28, 1995, as part of the Saeqer-4 (Thunderbolt 4) exercise. Jask is on Iran's southeast coast near the Straits of Hormuz, and the Iranian press release announcing the firing referred to it as the first operational testing of "advanced missile systems" by the Iranian Navy. Iran carried out another test in January 1996.[429]

Iran has also sought to buy more advanced anti-ship missiles from Russia, North Korea and China, and possibly even Chinese-made missile armed frigates. There is no way to know how many Iranian ships will acquire effective new anti-ship and anti-air missiles, or when any new types of missiles and ships might be delivered. Iran will have to make some such order by the late-1990s to keep up its present strength, however, its major Western-supplied ships cannot be made fully modern and operational without a comprehensive refit, which can only be accomplished in Western shipyards.[430]

Some sources have claimed that Iran has bought eight Soviet-made SS-N-22 "Sunburn" or "Sunburst" anti-ship missile launch units from Ukraine, and has deployed them near the Straits of Hormuz—although US experts have seen no evidence of such a purchase and doubt that Iran has any operational holdings of such systems. The "SS-N-22" is a title that actually applies to two different modern long-range supersonic sea skimming systems—the P-270 Moskit (also called the Kh-15 or 3M80) and P80 or P-100 Zubi/Onika. Although the performance of these systems is not as advanced as some descriptions in the Western press might indicate, the deployed versions have a maximum range of up to 100–120 kilometers. They have relatively sophisticated guidance systems, are harder to intercept than the CS-801/802 or HY-2, and are more resistant to countermeasures. If Iran should have such systems, they would be the only systems in the Gulf designed to defeat the defense on US Aegis ships.[431]

There are unverified reports that Iran is working on a version of the Silkworm with a range of up to 400 kilometers. It is unclear how it will target such a system without remote surveillance and a targeting platform. It is also unclear whether Iran is attempting to build a longer-range anti-ship system, or is using this development effort to build a land attack system. Furthermore, it is important to note that China is developing two follow-on supersonic missiles with cruise speeds of Mach 2.0 that could directly replace the HY-2 with little or no warning. The missiles are the HY-3 and C-101, and use ramjet propulsion and active radar terminal homing.[432]

Finally, Iran announced in May 1996 that it had fired a new missile called the Tondar during naval exercises. It is unclear whether this was an Iranian assembled Chinese CS-801 or CS-802 missile or a new system. It was clear, however, that the Revolutionary Guards forces were firing anti-ship missiles in the area around Kharg Island and had strengthened their anti-ship missile deployments to cover the Northern Gulf as well as the lower Gulf.[433]

Iran's Submarine Forces

Iran has attempted to offset the weakness of its major surface forces by emphasizing unconventional forms of naval warfare. It appears to have purchased or assembled one to three 27 ton midget submarines from North Korea in 1988. These submarines can dive to 300 feet, have a compartment for divers, and carry two side cargoes of 5 tons, or 14 limpet mines. It is, however, unclear as to whether Iran has been able to operate them successfully.[434]

Iran has also obtained two Type 877 EKM Kilo-class submarines, which it has named the *Tareq* and the *Noor*. The Iranian Navy's commander, Rear Admiral Ali Shamkani, announced in November, 1995 that a third submarine is expected to be delivered in 1996.[435]

Iran signed an agreement in early 1992 to buy these submarines from the United Admiralty Sudomeh shipyard in St. Petersburg at a cost of $600 million each. It subsequently sent crews for training to a Russian controlled naval base in Latvia. The first Kilo was transferred to Iran in November, 1992, and was commissioned as the Tareq-901. The ship completed its work-up exercise in the Gulf of Oman in the winter of 1992/1993. The US reacted by sending the nuclear attack submarine *Topeka* into the Gulf as a show of strength. The Topeka was the first US nuclear submarine deployment into the Gulf, and demonstrated the seriousness of US concern regarding Iran's acquisition of the Kilo.[436] The second Kilo was delivered to Iran in late July, 1993.[437]

The Kilo is a relatively modern and quiet submarine which first became operational in 1980. The Iranian Kilos are Type 877EKM export versions that are about 10 meters longer than the original Kilos and are equipped with advanced command and control systems. Each Type 877EKM has a teardrop hull coated with anechoic tiles to reduce noise. It displaces approximately 3,076 tons when submerged and 2,325 tons when surfaced. It is 73.2 meters long, 10.0 meters in beam, has a draught of 6.6 meters, and is powered by three 1,895 HP generator sets, one 5,900 SHP electric motor and one six-bladed propeller.

Each Kilo has six 530 mm torpedo tubes in the box, and can carry 12 homing and wire guided torpedoes or 30–40 mines. Some reports indicate that Iran bought over 1,000 modern Soviet mines with the Kilos, and that the mines were equipped with modern magnetic, acoustic, and pressure sensors. There is a remote anti-aircraft launcher with one preloaded missile in the sail and Soviet versions have 10 SA-16 manportable surface-to-air missiles stored inside. It has a maximum surface speed of 10 knots, a maximum submerged speed of about 17 knots, a minimum submerged operating depth of about 30 meters, a maximum diving depth of 300 meters, and a crew complement of 45. The submarine also has a surface cruise range of 3,000–6,000 nautical miles and a submerged cruise range of 400 nautical miles—depending on speed and combat conditions.[438]

These submarines give Iran a way of operating in the Gulf and in the Gulf of Oman that potentially reduces the vulnerability of its naval forces to air and surface attack. Equally important, Iran's mini-submarines provide the potential ability to hide in the shallow depths and currents near the Straits. Submarines can be used to fire torpedoes against slow moving tankers and launch mines near ports, long before they can operate effectively against hostile combat ships. Iran has already shown that it can use helicopters to communicate with its submarines using dipping sonars, and that it can improve its ability to target the submarines using shore based radars and patrol aircraft.[439]

At the same time, many Third World countries have found submarines to be difficult to operate, and Iran has had to turn to India for help in developing batteries that are reliable in the warm waters of the Gulf. Some reports indicate these problems were severe enough to make Iran cancel its order for a third Kilo submarine. Other reports indicate that Iran solved its problems in operating both Kilos by importing batteries from India, and that India is now providing Iran with continuing technical support in operating the submarines. Iran announced that it had conducted full scale naval maneuvers, which included its Kilo submarines for the first time, beginning on March 5, 1995. Iran also indicated that it had test fired advanced wake-homing and wire-guided Russian torpedoes. Some reports indicate that Iran will receive its third Kilo in late 1995, or that it is only delaying the purchase of a third because of a lack of hard currency.[440]

Iran does face operational problems in using such submarines. Many areas of the Gulf do not favor submarine operations. The Gulf is about 241,000 square kilometers in area, and stretches 990 kilometers from the Shatt al-Arab to the Straits of Hormuz. It is about 340 kilometers wide at is maximum width, and about 225 kilometers wide for most of its length. While heat patterns disturb surface sonars, they also disturb submarine sonars, and the advantage seems to be slightly in favor of sophisticated surface ships and maritime patrol aircraft.

The deeper parts of the Gulf are noisy enough to make ASW operations difficult, but large parts of the Gulf—including much of the southern Gulf on a line from Al Jubail across the tip of Qatar to about half way up the UAE—are less than 20 meters deep. The water is deeper on the Iranian side, but the maximum depth of the Gulf—located about 30 kilometers south of Qeys Island—is still only 88 meters. This means that no point in the Gulf is deeper than the length of an SN-688 nuclear submarine. The keel to tower height of such a submarine alone is 16 meters. Even smaller coastal submarines have maneuver and bottom suction problems, and cannot hide in thermoclines, or take advantage of diving for concealment or self-protection.

The Straits of Hormuz are about 180 kilometers long, but have a minimum width of 39 kilometers, and only the two deep water channels are suitable for major surface ship or submarine operations. Each of these channels is only about 2 kilometers wide. Further, a limited flow of fresh water and high evaporation make the Gulf extremely saline. This creates complex underwater currents in the main channels at the Straits of Hormuz and complicates both submarine operations, and submarine detection. There are some areas with considerable noise, but not of a type that masks submarine noise from sophisticated ASW detection systems of the kind operated by the US and UK. Further, the minimum operating depth of the Kilo is 45 meters, and the limited depth of the area around the Straits can make submarine operations difficult.

Submarines are easier to operate in the Gulf of Oman, which is noisy enough to make ASW operations difficult, but such deployments expose the Kilos to operations by US and British nuclear attack submarines. It is unlikely that they could survive for any length of time if hunted by a US or British navy air-surface—SSN hunter-killer team. On the other hand, no southern Gulf navy now has advanced detection gear. Saudi Arabia is seeking to upgrade the limited ASW sensors on its Al Madinah-class frigates. Bahrain and the UAE are considering improving their ASW assets.[441]

The effectiveness of the Iranian Kilos thus depends heavily on the degree of Western involvement in any ASW operation. If they did not face the US or the UK, the Iranian Kilos could operate in or near the Gulf with considerable impunity. If they did face US and British forces, they might be able to attack a few tankers or conduct some mining efforts, but are unlikely to survive extended combat. This makes the Kilos a weapon that may be more effective as a threat than in actual combat. Certainly, they have already received the attention of the southern Gulf states and convinced them that they must take Iran more seriously.

The Naval Branch of the Revolutionary Guards

The strength of the naval element of the Islamic Revolutionary Guards Corps is sometimes estimated at 20,000 men, but the actual total could be as little as 12,000–15,000. It operates Iran's land-based anti-ship missiles and coastal defense artillery. The naval branch of the IRGC operates Iran's 10 new 68-ton Chinese Hegu (Hudong)-class fast attack craft fast patrol boats and many of its CS-801 and CS-802 anti-ship missiles.[442]

It has training facilities and five bases in the Gulf, including the islands of Sirri, Abu Musa, Al Farisyah, and Larak, and the Halul oil platform. Most of these facilities seem to be relatively small, although the IRGC has established more extensive positions on Abu Musa, increased its troop presence from 150 to several thousand men, deployed Silkworm anti-ship missiles, and dug in tanks and artillery to support its fortifications.

While any such estimates are uncertain and it is not possible to distinguish between the holdings of the navy and the IRGC, Iran had 47 barges and service craft, 2 floating docks, about 100 coastal patrol craft, 35–40 Boghammer 41 foot craft, 35 Boston Whaler 22 foot craft, and large numbers of river craft. The Naval Guards were definitely equipped with the Boghammer Swedish-built fast interceptor craft, as well as small launches equipped with anti-tank guided missiles, and at least 30 Zodiak rubber dinghies to carry out rocket, small arms, and recoilless rifle attacks. They were also armed with machine guns, recoilless rifles, and man and crew portable anti-tank guided missiles.

The naval branch of the Islamic Revolutionary Guards Corps provides one of the largest unconventional warfare capabilities of any maritime force in the world.[443] It currently operates Iran's 32–36 up-engined Boghammer craft (6.4 tons), 35 or more Boston Whaler craft (1.3 tons), and numerous River Roadsted patrol and hovercraft. The Boghammer fast interceptor craft is particularly important to IRGC exercises and operations. Built by Boghammer Marine of Sweden, it can reach speeds of up to 69 knots, has a range of up to 926 kilometers, and has a 1,000 pound equipment load. The Boghammers and other fast patrol boats are unarmed, but crews can be equipped with heavy machine guns, grenade launchers, and 106 mm recoilless rifles.

The Boghammers, the other smaller fast patrol boats, and light craft like Iran's Zodiacs are extremely difficult to detect by radar in anything, but the calmest sea state. Iran bases them at a number of offshore islands and oil platforms, and they can strike quickly and with limited warning. There are key concentrations at Al Farisyah, Halul Island (an oil platform), Sirri, Abu Musa, and Larak, with a main base at Bandar Abbas. The Naval IRGC also has naval artillery, divers, and mine-laying units. It had extensive stocks of Scuba equipment, and an underwater combat center at Bandar Abbas.[444] Iran is also improving the defenses and port capabilities of its islands in the Gulf, adding covered moorings, more advanced sensors, and better air defenses.

The relative role of the IRGC and regular navy is unclear, although the IRGC seems to concentrate on coastal defense and unconventional warfare while the regular navy plays a more conventional "blue water" role. Some experts believed the naval branch of the IRGC would be merged with the regular navy when Admiral Ali Shamkani was made commander of both forces in 1989. However, they were still an independent force in 1996 with their own island bases and a facility at Noshahr Naval Academy on the Caspian Sea.

In addition to the 10 Hegu (Hudong)-class fast attack craft, the naval branch of the IRGC seemed to operate some of Iran's 11 US Mark III-class (41.6 ton), 6–20 US Swift Mark II-class (22.9 ton), 20 operational PBI type (20.1 ton), 3 Sewart type (9.1 ton), and 12 Enforcer type (4.7 ton) coastal patrol craft.[445] The PBI-type vessel has been sighted with crude installations of unguided Tigercats, which have a maximum range of six kilometers, and the IRGC is operating some of the new missile patrol boats Iran has acquired from the PRC.

Iranian Naval Warfighting Capabilities

These new forms of sea power offer Iran the ability to threaten tacitly and actively the flow of oil through the Gulf, and thereby the economic life blood of Iraq and its southern Gulf neighbors. Iran can threaten or attack shipping near the Straits, until decisive action is taken to destroy Iran's anti-ship missile units, mine warfare capabilities, submarines, and ability to use smaller ships. Iran can also take advantage of the long shipping routes through the Gulf. It has the ability to launch mines, naval or air strikes, and anti-ship missile strikes from positions along the entire length of the Gulf and the Gulf of Oman and to threaten or harass Gulf shipping. While strategists sometimes focus on "closing the Straits," a bottle does not have to be broken at the neck, and low-level mine and unconventional warfare strikes on shipping that are designed to harass and intimidate may allow Iran to achieve its objectives much more safely than escalating to all-out attacks on the flow of oil.

Iran's surface force cannot hope to challenge the combined power of US naval and air forces on a sustained basis. Iran can, however, use systems like anti-ship missiles, mines, and submarines to threaten US freedom of action and ability to deploy vulnerable high value targets, like carriers, in Gulf waters. As a result, it might take several weeks to defeat Iran's ability to attack Gulf shipping decisively, once the US deployed major naval and air forces, although much of Iran's naval power might be destroyed in a matter of days.

As for power projection, Iran cannot project power by land without crossing Iraq, but it can carry out small amphibious operations. This allows Iran to pose a tacit or active threat to the southern Gulf states, particularly small vulnerable states like Bahrain and the UAE—although Iran's capability to conduct such operations is currently limited. Unless the Southern Gulf states and US permit Iran to use ferries or commercial ships to conduct unopposed landings or transfers of troops, the Iranian Navy and IRGC are very limited in capability. While they can only conduct small landing operations, these operations would be highly vulnerable unless they achieved total surprise.

There is no way Iran could sustain them once US naval and air counterattacks began.

If Iran was to strike across the Gulf in force, the Iranian Navy and Naval Guards would need much more effective air-cover, a stronger surface fleet, and better night vision and targeting systems for their small craft, additional amphibious ships and hovercraft. Large scale assaults would also require Iran to use commercial ships with roll-on roll-off capability. At the same time, Iran can already use small elements of its naval forces to deploy mines and other unconventional warfare forces covertly, to supply arms to radical movements in the southern Gulf, seize undefended islands, and threaten or attack offshore oil operations, ports, and desalinization facilities.

The Iranian Navy is scarcely equal to Western navies in training and proficiency, but is the only Gulf Navy—aside from Oman—to conduct extensive and meaningful training. It operates jointly with the naval arm of the IRGC, and has steadily increased its number of exercises in recent years. It conducted 36 exercises in 1993, and 49 exercises in 1994, and planned a total of 57 exercises in 1995. It has slowly improved its amphibious, missile deployment, combined arms, interdiction, mine warfare, electronic warfare, and underwater warfare training.[446]

In addition to the limits imposed by Iran's ships and weaponry, these training efforts still have many tactical limitations. Nevertheless, such training efforts give Iran a much higher overall level of proficiency than most Southern Gulf navies. While some Southern Gulf navies have more modern ships and more advanced Western-supplied equipment, they fail to train effectively. The Southern Gulf navies are more showpiece forces than fighting forces. In spite of additional exercises with the US and British navies, most have shown little—if any—improvement in real-world war fighting proficiency since their virtual non-performance in the Gulf War.

As a result, Iran's present naval warfare capabilities can threaten and intimidate, and can cause significant initial or short-term damage to shipping in the Gulf, as well as offshore and coastal facilities in the Southern Gulf. Iran cannot, however, hope to engage in sustained naval warfare as long as the US commits major naval and air forces, and the Southern Gulf states are willing to provide bases and facilities to resist Iranian pressure. Iran would have to build up a very different navy to challenge a coalition of US, Britain, and the Southern Gulf states directly—or even US air and naval power acting with limited Southern Gulf support.

Iran would have to rebuild the technical base for its navy, and create an effective war fighting capability. To do this, it would need to replace or rebuild most of its surface fleet, and develop adequate training and joint warfare tactics and doctrine. It would also need to obtain anti-ship missiles that are competitive with those of southern Gulf, US, and British naval forces, as well as more advanced torpedoes, better mine laying capability, and advanced mines like bottom and moored influence and smart mines. In addition, Iran would need to modernize and expand the coverage of its shore-based missiles, and deploy them in enough locations and a mobile enough form to make them more survivable. Further, Iran would require improved C^4I/BM and electronic warfare systems, advanced land-based and surface ship based sensor systems, rebuilt and modernized P-3s or the purchase of a replacement, new or modified air defense and anti-ship missiles, and suitable electronics for its surface forces. Finally, Iran would need better, or modified, naval helicopters, and advanced exercise and training technology. It is currently very unlikely that Iran can obtain such capabilities before the year 2010, and there are few indications it is seeking them.

12

Conventional Warfighting Options and Policy Implications

There is no easy way to summarize Iran's conventional war fighting options. They involve a complex mix of strengths and weaknesses, and Iran's capabilities do not lend themselves to a simple order of battle comparison with the forces of other states, or a simple emphasis on a major regional conflict.

In broad terms, the preceding analysis of Iran's land, air, and naval forces indicates that it will be some years before Iran can become a major conventional military threat to its Southern Gulf neighbors, and that it has no near term prospect of being able to challenge the combined conventional war fighting capabilities of the West and the Southern Gulf states directly. Geography alone makes Iran different from Iraq. Iran can only launch a massive land attack by crossing through Iraq, making it much more dependent on naval, air, and power projection forces in exerting power in the Gulf .

The previous analysis has also shown, however, that direct conventional warfighting threats to the Southern Gulf are only part of the story. Iran can pose a wide variety of other kinds of threats to the Southern Gulf, and it is not possible to dismiss the risk of another round of fighting between Iran and Iraq.

Iran can use a wide range of combinations of conventional military force, unconventional military force, terrorism, and proxies to attack, threaten, or intimidate its neighbors. It can also apply such mixes of force in a wide range of contingencies. These include:

- Intervention in a civil war or military upheaval in Iraq involving religious issues, or a situation where Iraq appears vulnerable.
- A military response to Iraqi incursions into Iran, or attacks on People's Mujahideen forces and camps based in Iraq.
- Intervention in a Kurdish uprising in Iraq, suppression of a Kurdish uprising in Iran, or a military response to the spillover of the Kurdish conflicts in Turkey or Iraq.

- An Armenian military incursion into Iran, or an Armenian defeat of Azerbaijan which threatens its existence or takes on a religious character.
- Ethnic/religious conflicts with secular governments in the Islamic republics of the former Soviet Union, such as Tajikistan.
- Covert or overt support of a coup in Bahrain, or Shi'ite uprising in Saudi Arabia or any other Gulf state.
- Military threats or action in the Gulf in response to a major crisis in oil prices, and/or a struggle over oil quotas—including possible escalation to the deployment of submarines and the use of anti-ship missiles and mines.
- Covert intervention or open use of IRGC forces in a major military encounter between Israel and the Shi'ites in Lebanon.
- Systematic expansion of military training, arms, and funding for Hamas in the West Bank and Gaza, and assassination and bombing attacks on Israeli embassies and citizens.
- Support of a religious coup in an accessible neighboring state, or conflict between an "Islamic" force and peace-keeping or secular forces.
- Response to a military challenge to Iranian control of the Tunbs and Abu Musa.
- An air or naval clash in the Gulf over oil rights or shipping lanes.
- Use of force to assert Iran's claims to off-shore gas fields claimed by Qatar, or an "energy grab" to attack other off-shore or on-shore oil and gas fields or facilities.
- A major clash between Israel and the Palestinians and/or Syria after the failure of the current peace settlement.
- Attacks on US citizens or forces to try to eliminate the US presence in the Gulf, or weaken US support of Israel.
- A military response to a crisis over the transfer of chemical, biological, or nuclear weapons material and technology to Iran, or the transfer of long range missile systems.

Many of the above contingencies involve potential conflicts over what may be considered to be legitimate Iranian national interests. Nevertheless, they form an impressive list of risks that cannot be disregarded until Iran has a far more moderate and stable regime than it does today. Coupled to the fact that Iran currently has ample capability to defend against Iraq, this makes a strong case for military containment. Unlike political and economic containment, limiting the flow of arms to Iran will not affect the welfare of its people or limit its strategic value as an oil power. If anything, it will free resources for economic development. The West and its allies also have nothing to gain from aiding Iran in a military build-up that will force the West into matching efforts at power projection and deterrence or put further pressure on the Southern Gulf states to build-up their military forces.

A distinction does need to be made, however, between the kind of arms transfers that are increasing Iran's capability to threaten its neighbors and destabilize the region, and the kind of arms transfers Iran needs to maintain defensive military capabilities. As the previous analysis has shown, it is the nature of the particular arms transfer that will determine its impact on Iran and the region, and not simply the volume of arms.

13

Iran and Weapons
of Mass Destruction

There is another important dimension to Iran's military capabilities. Iran has long sought weapons of mass destruction, and the means to deliver them—although its efforts have never compared in scale to those of Iraq. Iran has lacked the resources to finance such a massive world-wide purchasing effort, and its revolutionary turmoil has limited its access to foreign technology and the efficiency of its industrial base. Iran has, however, sought long-range missiles, produced chemical weapons, developed biological weapons, and made efforts to acquire nuclear weapons.

Given the limitations of Iran's conventional forces, these efforts to acquire weapons of mass destruction are probably the most threatening aspect of Iran's present and future military capabilities. This has been reflected in many of the recent US statements about the threat from Iran. A recent report on US security strategy for the Middle East by the Office of the Secretary of Defense refers to this threat as follows:[447]

Iran harbors ambitions of establishing Iranian hegemony over the Persian Gulf and expanding its influence over radical Islamist forces. . . . It is obvious that Iran is assertively flexing its muscles vis-à-vis its smaller Gulf neighbors. Of even greater concern in the long run, Iran is also clearly dedicated to developing weapons of mass destruction, including chemical, biological, and nuclear weapons, a prospect that would have serious repercussions for regional stability.

Joseph S. Nye, Assistant Secretary of Defense for International Security Affairs, stated in early 1995 that:[448]

Iran is . . . clearly dedicated to developing weapons of mass destruction, including chemical, biological, and nuclear weapons, a prospect that would have serious repercussions for regional stability and perhaps for our ability to protect our interests in the area. In another forum, I would be prepared to discuss the details. . . . I would merely note that we learned in Iraq that a country can pursue a clandestine program in violation of its commitments and international norms. This experience makes us skeptical about the ability of normal inspections to detect similar programs in Iran.

Iran's current efforts to acquire long-range delivery systems and chemical, biological, and nuclear weapons are summarized in Table Fourteen, along with the similar efforts of Iraq and Israel that are now locking the Middle East into a process of creeping proliferation. This table also, however, reflects the current capabilities of Iraq and Israel, the two nations that are a major force behind Iran's efforts to acquire weapons of mass destruction. Iran's efforts cannot be viewed as if they were inherently aggressive or can be separated from the efforts of the other major powers in the Gulf and the Middle East. Iraq has already made extensive use of chemical warfare against Iran during the Iran-Iraq War, and has conducted extensive ballistic missile and attack aircraft strikes. Israel posseses nuclear armed missiles that can target any population center or area target in Iran. These potential threats may well lead Iran to continue to develop weapons of mass destruction even if its present regime should change in character.

It is also import to put Iran's efforts in perspective. Although Iran already has a significant capability to wage chemical warfare, this capability is not yet large or lethal enough to pose a major threat to the southern Gulf, so long as the Southern Gulf states have the support of US forces. Iran also faces a wide range of problems in improving its capabilities, and particularly in developing nuclear weapons. These problems include:

- *"Weaponizing" chemical, biological, and nuclear weapons.* Iran faces difficulties in developing the capability to load a biological or chemical agent, or nuclear device, into a bomb or warhead that will work safely, effectively, and reliably. Regardless of the theoretical lethality of a weapon of mass destruction, much depends on how well it can actually perform in combat.
- *"Weaponizing" different types of delivery systems.* It is relatively easy to fire chemical rounds at line-of-sight ranges and artillery or multiple rocket launchers can fire enough of a chemical agent to be effective even if the warhead design is poor. Firing chemical and other weapons of mass destruction at beyond-visual-range (BVR) targets does, however, require sophisticated reconnaissance and intelligence systems, and effective warheads to produce highly lethal effects. Long range attacks with aircraft and cruise missiles present

TABLE FOURTEEN   Iranian, Iraqi, and Israeli Weapons of Mass Destruction Programs and Related Delivery Systems

Iran
Delivery Systems
- Used regular Scud extensively during Iran-Iraq War. Fired nearly 100 Scud B missiles during 1985–1988. Scud missiles were provided by Libya and North Korea.
- Has 6–12 Scud launchers and up to 200 Scud B (R-17E) missiles with 230–310 km range.
- Has new long range North Korean Scuds—with ranges near 500 kilometers.
- Has created shelters and tunnels in its coastal areas to store Scud and other missiles in hardened sites and reduce their vulnerability to air attack.
- Can now assemble missiles using foreign made components.
- Developing an indigenous missile production capability with both solid and liquid fueled missiles. Seems to be seeking capability to produce MRBMs.
- May cooperate with Syria in developing capability to manufacture missiles.
- Probably has ordered North Korean No Dong missile which can carry nuclear and biological missile ranges of up to 900 kilometers. Can reach virtually any target in Gulf, Turkey, and Israel, although CIA now estimates deliveries will only begin in 1997–1999.[449]
- Has recently bought CSS-8 surface-to-surface missiles (converted SA-2s) from China with ranges of 130–150 kilometers.
- May have place order for PRC-made M-9 missile (280–620 kilometers range). More likely that PRC firms are giving assistance in developing indigenous missile R&D and production facilities.
- Has Chinese sea and land-based anti-ship cruise missiles. Iran fired 10 such missiles at Kuwait during Iran-Iraq War, hitting one US-flagged tanker.
- Su-24 long-range strike fighters with range-payloads roughly equivalent to US F-111 and superior to older Soviet medium bombers.
- Iranian made IRAN 130 rocket with 150+ kilometers range.
- Iranian Oghab (Eagle) rocket with 40+ kilometers range.
- New SSM with 125 mile range may be in production, but could be modified FROG.
- F-4D/E fighter bombers with capability to carry extensive payloads to ranges of 450 miles.
- Can modify HY-2 Silkworm missiles and SA-2 surface-to-air missiles to deliver weapons of mass destruction.
- Large numbers of multiple rocket launchers and tube artillery for short range delivery of chemical weapons.
- Experimenting with cruise missile development.

Chemical Weapons
- At least two major research and production facilities.
- Made limited use of chemical weapons at end of the Iran-Iraq War.

(continues)

TABLE FOURTEEN   *(continued)*

- Began to create stockpiles of cyanide (cyanogen chloride), phosgene, and mustard gas weapons after 1985. Include bombs and artillery.
- Was able to produce blister (mustard) and blood (cyanide) agents by 1987; used them in artillery shells against Iraqi troops.
- Production of nerve gas weapons started no later than 1994.
- Has produced a minimum of several hundred tons of blister, blood, and choking agents. Some are weaponized for support of ground troops. Others are used in chemical bombs.
- Has increased chemical defensive and offensive warfare training since 1993.
- Seeking to buy more advanced chemical defense equipment.
- Has sought to buy specialized equipment on world market to develop indigenous capability to produce advanced feedstocks for nerve weapons.

Biological Weapons
- Extensive laboratory and research capability.
- Weapons effort documented as early as 1982.
- Bioresearch effort sophisticated enough to produce biological weapons as lethal as small nuclear weapons. Working on toxins and organisms with biological warfare capabilities.
- Has biological support structure capable of producing many different biological weapons. Has evolved from piecemeal acquisition of biological equipment to pursuing complete biological production plants.
- Seems to have the production facilities to make dry storable weapons. This would allow it to develop suitable missile warheads and bombs and covert devices.
- May be involved in active weapons production, but no evidence to date that this is the case.
- Some universities and research centers may be linked to biological weapons program.

Nuclear Weapons
- In 1984, revived nuclear weapons program begun under Shah.
- Received significant West German and Argentine corporate support in some aspects of nuclear technology during the Iran-Iraq War.
- Limited transfers of centrifuge and other weapons related technology from PRC, possibly Pakistan.
- Stockpiles of uranium and mines in Yazd area.
- Seems to have attempted to buy fissile material from Kazakhstan.
- Has sought heavy water research reactors with no application to peaceful lightwater power reactor development.
- Has sought to obtain uranium enrichment and spent fuel reprocessing technology whose main applications are in weapons programs.
- Russian agreement to build up to four reactors, beginning with a complex at Bushehr—with two 1,000–1,200 megawatt reactors and two 465 megawatt reactors, and provide significant nuclear technology.

(continues)

- Chinese agreement to provide significant nuclear technology transfer and possible sale of two 300 megawatt pressurized water reactors.
- No way to tell when current efforts will produce a weapon, and unclassified lists of potential facilities have little credibility. We simply do not know where Iran is developing its weapons.
- IAEA has found no indications of weapons effort, but found no efforts in Iraq in spring of 1990. IAEA only formally inspects Iran's small research reactors. Its visits to other Iranian sites are not thorough enough to confirm or deny whether Iran has such activities.
- Timing of weapons acquisition depends heavily on whether Iran can buy fissile material—if so it has the design capability and can produce weapons in 1–2 years—or must develop the capability to process Plutonium or enrich Uranium—in which case, it is likely to be 5–10 years.

Iraq
Delivery Systems
- Delivery systems at the time of the Gulf War included:
  - Tu-16 and Tu-22 bombers.
  - MiG-29 fighters.
  - Mirage F-1, MiG-23BM, and Su-22 fighter attack aircraft.
  - A Scud force with a minimum of 819 missiles.
  - Extended range Al-Hussein Scud variants (600 kilometer range) extensively deployed throughout Iraq, and at three fixed sites in northern, western, and southern Iraq.
  - Developing Al-Abbas missiles (900 kilometer range) which could reach targets in Iran, the Persian Gulf, Israel, Turkey, and Cyprus.
  - Long-range super guns with ranges of up to 600 kilometers.
- Iraq had long-range strike aircraft with refueling capabilities and several hundred regular and improved, longer-range Scud missiles, some with chemical warheads.
- Iraq fired 84 Al-Husayns, 3 Al Husyan-Shorts, and 1 Al-Hijrarah (with a cement warhead) during the Gulf War.
- The Gulf War deprived Iraq of some of its MiG-29s, Mirage F-1s, MiG-23BMs, and Su-22s. Since the end of the war, the UN inspection regime has also destroyed many of Iraq's long-range missiles.
- Iraq, however, maintains a significant delivery capability consisting of:
  - HY-2, SS-N-2, and C-601 cruise missiles, which are unaffected by UN cease-fire terms.
  - FROG-7 rockets with 70 kilometer ranges, also allowed under UN resolutions.
  - Multiple rocket launchers and tube artillery.
  - Several Scud launchers
  - US experts believe Iran may still have components for several dozen extended-range Scud missiles. UN experts believe Iraq is concealing up to 6–7 Scud launchers and 11–24 missile assemblies.

(*continues*)

TABLE FOURTEEN *(continued)*

- Iraq has focused its missile programs around the Scud B. During the late 1980s, it began to enlarge the fuel tanks of its Scuds and reduce the weight of its warheads to extend their range beyond the normal 300 kilometer maximum range of the Scud. It also developed a capability to manufacture Scud variants in Iraq, and was working on production facilities for a development of the solid-fueled Argentine Condor missile called the Badr 2000.
- Iraqi missile programs at the time of the Gulf War included:
  - Scud Bs with a maximum range of 300 kilometers.
  - Al Husayns with a 600–650 kilometers range.
  - Al Husayn-Shorts (a variant of the Al Husayn) with a 600–650 kilometers range
  - Al Hijarahs with a 600–650 kilometers range
- Iraqi developmental missile programs at the time of the Gulf War included:
  - Al Fahd. A conversion of the SA-2 with an intended 300 kilometer range. Abandoned in the R&D phase.
  - Extended-range Al Fahd. A 500 kilometer range missile abandoned in the development phase after exhibition at the 1989 arms show in Baghdad.
  - Al Abbas. A longer version of the Al Husayn with a lighter warhead which was intended to have a 900 kilometer range. Abandoned during R&D.
  - Badr 2000. A solid-propellant two-stage missile based on the Condor with a range of 750–1,000 kilometers. Was in R&D when Gulf War began. Facilities were constructed to begin missile production.
  - Tammouz 1: a missile based on the Scud with an SA-2 sustainer for a second stage. It had an intended range of 2,000 kilometers but was not carried through to advanced R&D.
  - Al Abid: A three stage space vehicle with a first stage of 5 Al Abbas airframes. Test launch in December, 1989.
- Iraq also engaged in effort to develop a solid fueled missile with a similar range to the Tammouz.
- Clear evidence that at least one Iraqi long-range missile design was to have a nuclear warhead.
- Iraq attempted to conceal a plant making missile engines from the UN inspectors. It only admitted this plant existed in 1995, raising new questions about how many of its missiles have been destroyed.
- Iraq produced or assembled 80 Scud missiles in its own factories. Some 53 seem to have been unusable, but 10 are still unaccounted for.
- Had design work underway for a nuclear warhead for its long range missiles.
- In addition, Iraq has admitted to:
  - Hiding its capability to manufacture its own Scuds.
  - Iraq claims to have manufactured only 80 missile assemblies, 53 of which were unusable. UNSCOM claims that 10 are unaccounted for.
  - Developing an extended range variant of the FROG-7 called the Laith. The UN claims to have tagged all existing FROG-7s to prevent any extension of their range beyond the UN imposed limit of 150 kilometers for Iraqi missiles.

(continues)

TABLE FOURTEEN   *(continued)*

- Experimenting with cruise missile technology and ballistic missile designs with ranges up to 3,000 kilometers.
- Flight testing Al-Hussein missiles with chemical warheads in April 1990.
- Initiating a research and development program for a nuclear warhead missile delivery system.
- Successfully developing and testing a warhead separation system.
- Indigenously developing, testing, and manufacturing advanced rocket engines to include liquid-propellant designs.
- Conducting research into the development of Remotely Piloted Vehicles (RPVs) for the dissemination of biological agents.
- Attempting to expand its Ababil-100 program designed to build surface-to-surface missiles with ranges beyond the permitted 100–150 kilometers.
- Starting an indigenous 600mm supergun design effort.
- US and UN officials conclude further that:
  - Iraq is concentrating procurement efforts on rebuilding its ballistic missile program using a clandestine network of front companies to obtain the necessary materials and technology from European and Russian firms.
  - This equipment is then concealed and stockpiled for assembly concomitant with the end of the UN inspection regime.
  - The equipment clandestinely sought by Iraq includes advanced missile guidance components, such as accelerometers and gyroscopes, specialty metals, special machine tools, and a high-tech, French-made, million-dollar furnace designed to fabricate engine parts for missiles.
- Jordan found that Iraq was smuggling missile components through Jordan in early December, 1995.
- US satellite photographs reveal that Iraq has rebuilt its Al-Kindi missile research facility.
- Iraq retains the technology it acquired before the war and evidence clearly indicates an ongoing research and development effort, in spite of the UN sanctions regime.
- The fact that UN Security Council Resolution 687 allows Iraq to continue producing and testing short range missiles (less than 150 kilometers range) has meant it can retain significant missile efforts. Iraq's on-going rocket and missile programs include:
  - Luna/Frog-7. A Russian unguided rocket with a 70 kilometer range currently in service and in limited production.
  - Astros II. A Brazilian unguided rocket with a 60 kilometer range currently in service and in limited production.
  - SA-2. A Russian surface-to-air missile which China has demonstrated can be converted into a 300 kilometer range surface-to-surface missile.
  - SA-3. A Russian surface-to-air missile which has some potential for conversion to a surface-to-surface missile.
  - Ababil-50. An Yugoslav-designed Iraqi-produced 50 kilometer range artillery rocket with very limited growth potential.

(continues)

TABLE FOURTEEN   *(continued)*

- Ababil-100. An Iraqi 100–150 kilometer range system with parallel solid-fuel and liquid fuel development programs which seems to be used as a "legal" test-bed and foundation for much longer range missile programs once sanctions are lifted. Many of the liquid fueled programs are compatible with Scud production.
- Limited stocks of French and Chinese produced land and air launched cruise missiles.

Chemical Weapons
- Produced several thousand tons of chemical weapons from 1984 on. Used chemical weapons extensively against Iran and its own Kurdish population in 1988.
- Use of Tabun gas against Iranians beginning in 1984 is first confirmed use of nerve agents in war.
- Had roughly 1,000 metric tons of chemical weapons on hand at the time it invaded Kuwait, split equally between blister agents and nerve agents.
- UN destruction efforts at Samara destroyed over 27,000 chemical bombs, rockets, and artillery shells, including 30 Scud missile warheads. About 500 tons of mustard and nerve agents, and thousands of tons of precursor chemicals were burned or chemically neutralized.
- In revelations to the UN, Iraq admitted that, prior to the Gulf War, it:
  - Maintained large stockpiles of mustard gas, and the nerve agents Sarin and Tabun.
  - Produced binary Sarin filled artillery shells, 122mm rockets, and aerial bombs.
  - Manufactured enough precursors to produce 490 tons of the nerve agent VX. These precursors included 65 tons of choline and 200 tons of phosphorous pentasulfide and di-isopropylamine.
  - Tested Ricin, a deadly nerve agent, for use in artillery shells.
  - Had three flight tests of long range Scuds with chemical warheads.
  - Had large VX production effort underway at the time of the Gulf War. The destruction of the related weapons and feedstocks has been claimed by Iraq, but not verified by UNSCOM.
- The majority of Iraq's chemical agents were manufactured at a supposed pesticide plant located at Samara. Various, other production facilities were also used, including those at Salman Pak, Muthanna, and Habbiniyah. Though severely damaged during the war, the physical plant for many of these facilities has been rebuilt.
  - Iraq possessed the technology to produce a variety of other persistent and non-persistent agents.
- The Gulf War and subsequent
  - UN inspection regime may have largely eliminated these stockpiles and reduced production capability.

(continues)

TABLE FOURTEEN (continued)

- US experts believe Iraq has concealed significant stocks of precursors. It also appears to retain significant amounts of production equipment dispersed before, or during, Desert Storm and not recovered by the UN.
- Iraq has developed basic chemical warhead designs for Scud missiles, rockets, bombs, and shells. Iraq also has spray dispersal systems.
- Iraq maintains extensive stocks of defensive equipment.
- The UN maintains that Iraq is not currently producing chemical agents, but the UN is also concerned that Iraq has offered no evidence that it has destroyed its VX production capability and/or stockpile.
- Further, Iraq retains the technology it acquired before the war and evidence clearly indicates an ongoing research and development effort, in spite of the UN sanctions regime.

Biological Weapons
- Systematically lied about biological weapons effort until 1995. First stated that had small defensive efforts, but no offensive effort. In July, 1995, admitted it had a major offensive effort. In October, 1995, finally admitted major weaponization effort.
- The August, 1995 defection of Lieutenant General Hussein Kamel Majid, formerly in charge of Iraq's weapons of mass destruction, led Iraq to reveal the extent of its biological weapons program.
- Iraq reported to the UN in August, 1995 that it had produced 90,000 liters of Botulinium toxin, 8,300 liters of Anthrax, and significant quantities of other agents.
- Iraq has, however, continued to lie about its biological weapons effort.
- It has claimed the effort is headed by Dr. Taha, a woman who only headed a subordinate effort. It has not admitted to any help by foreign personnel or contractors. It has claimed to have destroyed its weapons, but the one site UNSCOM inspectors visited showed no signs of such destruction and was later said to be the wrong site. It has claimed only 50 people were employed full time, but the scale of the effort would have required several hundred.
- Reports indicate that Iraq tested at least 7 principal biological agents for use against humans.
  - Anthrax, Botulinum, and Aflatoxin known to be weaponized.
  - Looked at viruses, bacteria, and fungi. Examined the possibility of weaponizing Gas Gangrene and Mycotoxins. Some field trials were held of these agents.
  - Examined foot and mouth disease, haemorrhagic conjunctivitis virus, rotavirus, and camel pox virus.
  - Conducted research on a "wheat pathogen" and a Mycotoxin similar to "yellow rain" defoliant.
  - The "wheat smut" was first produced at Al Salman, and then put in major production during 1987–1988 at a plant near Mosul. Iraq claims the program was abandoned.

(continues)

TABLE FOURTEEN *(continued)*

- The defection of Hussein Kamel prompted Iraq to admit that it:
  - Imported 39 tons of growth media for biological agents obtained from three European firms. According to UNSCOM, 17 tons remains unaccounted for. Each ton can be used to produce 10 tons of bacteriological weapons.
  - Imported type cultures which can be modified to develop biological weapons from the US.
  - Had a laboratory- and industrial-scale capability to manufacture various biological agents including the bacteria which cause anthrax and botulism; Aflatoxin, a naturally occurring carcinogen; clostridium perfringens, a gangrene-causing agent; the protein toxin ricin; tricothecene mycotoxins, such as T-2 and DAS; and an anti-wheat fungus known as wheat cover smut. Iraq also conducted research into the rotavirus, the camel pox virus, and the virus which causes haemorrhagic conjunctivitis.
  - Created at least seven primary production facilities including the Sepp Institute at Muthanna, the Ghazi Research Institute at Amaria, the Daura Foot and Mouth Disease Institute, and facilities at Al-Hakim, Salman Pak Taji, and Fudaliyah. According to UNSCOM, weaponization occurred primarily at Muthanna through May, 1987 (largely Botulinum), and then moved to Al Salman. (Anthrax). In March, 1988 a plant was opened at Al Hakim, and in 1989 an Aflatoxin plant was set up at Fudaliyah.
  - Manufactured 6,000 liters of concentrated Botulinum toxin and 8,425 liters of anthrax at Al-Hakim during 1990; 5,400 liters of concentrated Botulinum toxin at the Daura Foot and Mouth Disease Institute from November, 1990 to January 15, 1991; 400 liters of concentrated Botulinum toxin at Taji; and 150 liters of concentrated anthrax at Salman Pak. Produced 1,850 liters of Aflatoxin in solution at Fudaliyah.
  - Produced 340 liters of concentrated clostridium perfringens, a gangrene-causing biological agent, beginning in August, 1990.
  - Produced 10 liters of concentrated Ricin at Al Salam. Claimed abandoned work after tests failed.
  - Relocated much of its biological weapons effort after Coalition strikes on its facilities at Al Kindi and Salman Pak to Al Hakim and other facilities. This makes tracking the weapons effort extremely difficult.
  - Had at least 79 civilian facilities capable of playing some role in biological weapons production still extant in 1995.
- Extensive weaponization program
  - Conducted field trials, weaponization tests, and live firings of 122mm rockets armed with anthrax and Botulinum toxin from March, 1988 to May, 1990.
  - Total production reached at least 19,000 liters of concentrated Botulinum (10,000 liters filled into munitions); 8,500 liters of concentrated Anthrax (6,500 liters filled into munitions); and 2,500 liters of concentrated Aflatoxin (1,850 liters filled into munitions).
  - Weaponized at least three biological agents for use in the Gulf War. The weaponization consisted of 100 bombs and 15 missile warheads loaded with

(continues)

TABLE FOURTEEN *(continued)*

Botulinum; 50 R-400 air-delivered bombs and 10 missile warheads loaded with anthrax.

- Also had 16 missile warheads loaded with Aflatoxin, a natural carcinogen. The warheads were designed for operability with the Al-Hussein Scud variant.
- A total of at least 166 bombs were filled with some biological agent. Iraq produced at least 191 bombs and missile warheads with biological agents.
- Developed and stored drop tanks ready for use for three aircraft or RPV s with the capability of dispersing 2,000 liters of anthrax. Development took place in December, 1990. Claimed later that tests showed were ineffective.
- Tested ricin, a deadly protein toxin, for use in artillery shells.
- The UN claims that Iraq has offered no evidence to corroborate its claims that it destroyed its stockpile of biological agents after the Gulf War. Further, Iraq retains the technology it acquired before the war and evidence clearly indicates an ongoing research and development effort, in spite of the UN sanctions regime.
- UN currently inspects 79 sites—5 used to make weapons before war; 5 vaccine or pharmaceutical sites; 35 research and university sites; thirteen breweries, distilleries, and dairies with dual-purpose capabilities; eight diagnostic laboratories.
- Retains laboratory capability to manufacture various biological agents including the bacteria which cause anthrax, botulism, tularemia, and typhoid.
- Many additional civilian facilities capable of playing some role in biological weapons production.

Nuclear Weapons
- Sought to buy a plutonium production reactor similar to the reactor France used in its nuclear weapons program in early 1970s.
- Contracted with France to build Osirak and Isis reactors in 1976, as part of Tuwaitha complex near Baghdad.
- Osirak raid in June 1981 prevented from acquiring reactors for weapons use. Led Iraq to refocus efforts on producing highly enriched uranium.
- Inspections by UN teams have found evidence of two successful weapons designs, a neutron initiator, explosives and triggering technology needed for production of bombs, plutonium processing technology, centrifuge technology, Calutron enrichment technology, and experiments with chemical separation technology.
  - Iraq used Calutron, centrifuges, plutonium processing, chemical defusion, and foreign purchases to create new production capability after Israel destroyed most of Osiraq.
  - Iraq established a centrifuge enrichment system in Rashidya and conducted research into the nuclear fuel cycle to facilitate development of a nuclear device.
- After invading Kuwait, Iraq attempted to accelerate its program to develop a nuclear weapon by using radioactive fuel from French and Russian-built reactors.

(continues)

TABLE FOURTEEN   *(continued)*

- Made a crash effort beginning in September, 1990 to recover enriched fuel from its supposedly safe-guarded French and Russian reactors, with the goal of producing a nuclear weapon by April, 1991. The program was only halted after Coalition air raid destroyed key facilities on January 17, 1991.
- Iraq conducted research into the production of a radiological weapon, which disperses lethal radioactive material without initiating a nuclear explosion.
  - Orders were given in 1987 to explore the use of radiological weapons for area denial in the Iran-Iraq War.
  - Three prototype bombs were detonated at test sites—one as a ground level static test and two others were dropped from aircraft.
  - Iraq claims the results were disappointing and the project was shelved but has no records or evidence to prove this.
- UN teams have found and destroyed, or secured, new stockpiles of illegal enriched material, major production and R&D facilities, and equipment—including Calutron enriching equipment.
- UNSCOM believes that Iraq's nuclear program has been largely disabled and remains incapacitated, but warns that Iraq retains substantial technology and established a clandestine purchasing system in 1990 that it has used to import forbidden components since the Gulf War.
- Iraq still retains the technology developed before the Gulf War and US experts believe an ongoing research and development effort continues, in spite of the UN sanctions regime.
- A substantial number of declared nuclear weapons components and research equipment has never been recovered. There is no reason to assume that Iraqi declarations were comprehensive.

Israel
Delivery Systems
- New IRBM/ICBM range high payload booster in development with South Africa. Status unknown.
- Up to 50 "Jericho I" missiles deployed in shelters on mobile launchers with up to 400 miles range with a 2,200 pound payload, and with possible nuclear warhead storage nearby. Unverified claims that up to 100 missiles are deployed west of Jerusalem.
- Jericho II missiles now deployed, and some were brought to readiness for firing during the Gulf War. These missiles seem to include a single stage follow-on to the Jericho I and a multistage longer range missile. The latter missile seems to have a range of up to 900 miles with a 2,200 pound payload, and may be a cooperative development with South Africa. (Extensive reporting of such cooperation in press during October 25 and 26, 1989.)
- Jericho II missile production facility at Be'er Yakov.
- A major missile test took place on September 14, 1989. It was either a missile test or failure of Ofeq-2 satellite.
- Work on development of TERCOM type smart warheads. Possible cruise missile guidance developments using GPS navigation systems.

(continues)

TABLE FOURTEEN   (*continued*)

- F-15, F-16, F-4E, and Phantom 2000 fighter-bombers capable of long range refueling and of carrying nuclear and chemical bombs.
- Lance missile launchers and 160 Lance missiles with 130 kilometers range.
- MAR-290 rocket with 30 kilometers range believed to be deployed.
- MAR-350 surface-to-surface missile with range of 56 miles and 735 lb. payload believed to have completed development or to be in early deployment.
- Israel seeking super computers for Technion Institute (designing ballistic missile RVs), Hebrew University (may be engaged in hydrogen bomb research), and Israeli Military Industries (maker of "Jericho II" and Shavit booster).

Chemical Weapons
- Mustard and nerve gas production facility established in 1982 in the restricted area in the Sinai near Dimona. May have additional facilities. May have capacity to produce other gases. Probable stocks of bombs, rockets, and artillery.
- Extensive laboratory research into gas warfare and defense.
- Development of defensive systems includes Shalon Chemical Industries protection gear, Elbit Computer gas detectors, and Bezal R&D air crew protection system.
- Extensive field exercises in chemical defense.
- Gas masks stockpiled, and distributed to population with other civil defense instructions during Gulf War.
- Warhead delivery capability for bombs, rockets, and missiles, but none now believed to be equipped with chemical agents.

Biological Weapons
- Extensive research into weapons and defense.
- Ready to quickly produce biological weapons, but no reports of active production effort.

Nuclear Weapons
- Director of CIA indicated in May, 1989, that Israel may be seeking to construct a thermonuclear weapon.
- Estimates of numbers and types of weapons differ sharply.
- At least a stockpile of 60–80 plutonium weapons. May have well over 100 nuclear weapons assemblies, with some weapons with yields over 100 Kilotons, and some with possible ER variants or variable yields. Stockpile of up to 200–300 weapons is possible.
- Possible facilities include production of weapons grade Plutonium at Dimona, nuclear weapons design facility at Soreq (south of Tel Aviv), missile test facility at Palmikhim, nuclear armed missile storage facility at Kefar Zekharya, nuclear weapons assembly facility at Yodefat, and tactical nuclear weapons storage facility at Eilabun in eastern Galilee.

(*continues*)

TABLE FOURTEEN   *(continued)*

Missile Defenses
- Patriot missiles with future PAC-3 upgrade to reflect lessons of the Gulf War.
- Arrow 2 two-stage ATBM with slant intercept ranges at altitudes of 8–10 and 50 kilometers and speeds of up to Mach 9, plus possible development of the Rafale AB-10 close in defense missile with ranges of 10–20 kilometers and speeds of up to Mach 4.5. Tadiran BM/C4I system and "Music" phased array radar. Israel plans to deploy two batteries of the Arrow to each with four launchers, to protect up to 85% of its population.[450]

Advanced Intelligence Systems
- The Shavit I launched Israel's satellite payload on September 19, 1989. It used a three stage booster system capable of launching a 4,000 pound payload over 1,200 miles or a 2,000 pound payload over 1,800 miles.
- Ofeq 2 launched in April, 1990—one day after Saddam Hussein threatens to destroy Israel with chemical weapons if it should attack Baghdad.
- Launched first intelligence satellite on April 5, 1995, covering Syria, Iran, and Iraq in orbit every 90 minutes. The Ofeq 3 satellite is a 495 pound system launched using the Shavit launch rocket, and is believed to carry an imagery system. Its orbit pass over or near Damascus, Tehran, and Baghdad.[451]

Source: Prepared by Anthony H. Cordesman, Co-Director, Middle East Program, CSIS.

challenges in terms of developing proven bomb and warhead designs that ensure safety, reliability, accurate targeting and navigation. Other factors that must be considered are the proper dissemination of biological and chemical agents, height of burst, and weather conditions for the use of biological, chemical, and nuclear weapons.

- *Developing effective warheads for ballistic missile systems.* Although ballistic missiles have the advantage that they are harder to defend against than aircraft, they involve major challenges in terms of operational reliability, accuracy, and targeting. It is extremely difficult to disseminate biological and chemical agents effectively within the narrow time window allowed by the closing velocity of a ballistic missile, and the weapons package necessary to do so can use up much of the useful payload of such a missile.
- *Obtaining fissile material.* The design of a nuclear weapon is well within Iran's technical capabilities, and Iraq and Pakistan have shown that developing nations can manufacture the high explosive lenses, triggering devices, and neutron initiators necessary to make functional nuclear weapons. It is far more difficult, however, to enrich uranium or process plutonium unless highly enriched material can be purchased from another state.

- *Developing small nuclear devices with reliable fusing.* Nuclear weapons present challenges in weight reduction and ensuring precisely the correct height of burst to get the right effect. The cost and scarcity of nuclear fissile material creates challenges in terms of the risk a warhead package will fail to explode or a missile will not hit its intended target. Biological weapons require the safe storage of dry or wet agents, and high technology fuses and agent dissemination systems.
- *Safety is also a major issue, particularly with biological and nuclear devices.* The risk of accidents or misfires on friendly territory is very real. The technology to ensure the safety and arming of a warhead only after a missile has performed properly on launch is complex and involves further weight penalties. No technology currently exists that can reliably disarm a missile warhead by remote command, or on a fail-safe basis, once a missile has completed its initial boost phase and apogee.

All of these problems can be solved with time at a cost affordable to Iran, and it is clear that the threat posed by Iran's weapons of mass destruction will become steadily more serious. Iran might also change the military balance in the Gulf relatively rapidly if it acquired highly lethal biological agents or a few nuclear devices. Warfighting capability is not the only measure of power. Weapons of mass destruction produce unpredictable changes in the perceptions of both the attacker and defender in terms of political decisions and war fighting.

While much of the discussion of weapons of mass destruction focuses on casualty and physical damage effects, they have major psychological, political, and tactical effects that may prove to be more important than lethality in a given contingency. Relative willingness to take risks and deal with the real-world outcome of uncertainty becomes critical, as do the relative value assigned to human life, the predictability of weapons effects, the nature of retaliation, and the protection of troops, civilians, and potential target areas.

Weapons of mass destruction can radically change crisis behavior, perceptions of the risks of escalation, acceptance of new levels of conflict, and acceptance of given kinds of conflict termination. They can do so in ways where decision-makers and military commanders have at best a limited understanding of the technical capabilities and effectiveness of the weapons involved. They affect the transparency and predictability of war. This is particularly true in the case of the Gulf, since neither Iran nor Iraq have anything approaching the intelligence assets necessary to obtain near-real time data on the actual impact of such weapons. In addition, there is simply too little empirical data available for either side to predict short-term or long-term damage effects.

Iran's Long Range Missile Programs

Iran has long had attack aircraft that can deliver weapons of mass destruction at very long ranges. It has also steadily improved its long-range missile forces since the beginning of the Iran-Iraq War. In addition to rockets like the Oghab, Shanin, and Nazeat, Iran has imported several effective surface-to-surface missile systems.[452] These systems now consist of the Scud B, North Korean variants of the Scud, and the Chinese CSS 8, and Iran is seeking to either import longer range systems or manufacture them in Iran.[453] A comparison of Iran's missiles with the other missile systems in the Middle East is provided in Table Fifteen, and the range of Iran's missile systems is shown in Map Four. Iran is also building tunnels along its Gulf coastline that can be used as missile shelters to reduce vulnerability to air and missile attack. These tunnels could be used to store a significant number of Scuds or follow-on systems, and possibly to provide a rapid deployment and launch capability.[454]

The Scud B

Iran's primary holdings of such missiles consist of the Soviet-designed Scud B (17E) guided missile. Iran has had these missiles since the early 1980s, and fired nearly 100 Scud Bs against Iraq during 1985–1988.

The Scud B has a maximum range of 180–190 miles (290–310 kilometers) with its normal conventional payload, and a maximum flight time of 325 seconds.[455] The Scud missile is 11.25 meters long, 85 centimeters in diameter, weighs 6,300 kilograms, and has a warhead weighing about 1,000 kilograms, of which 800 kilograms are high explosive and 200 are the warhead structure and fusing system.[456] It has a single stage storable liquid rocket engine and is usually deployed on the MAZ 543 eight wheel transporter-erector-launcher (TEL). It has a strap-down inertial guidance, using three gyros to correct its ballistic trajectory, and uses internal graphite jet vane steering.[457]

Iran seems to have purchased an estimated 200–300 Scud Bs from North Korea between 1987 and 1992. Israeli experts estimate that Iran had at least 250–300 Scud missiles, and at least 8–15 launchers on hand in 1995. All of these Scuds have been obtained from other countries, and Iran's claims during the Iran-Iraq War that it was able to actually manufacture Scuds were false. Iran currently can assemble missile systems manufactured by other countries, but it has not yet demonstrated

TABLE FIFTEEN   Possible Missile Delivery Systems*

Type	User Country	Nominal Range (Kilometers)	Maximum Payload (Kilograms)
Shorter-Range			
SS-21 Scarab A	Syria, Yemen	70	480
SA-2 Variant	(Iraq? Egypt?)	80	130
Ababil-100	Iraq	100–150	?
MGM-52 Lance	Israel (Iran?)	130	450
Iran 130/Mushak 120	Iran	130	190
CSS-8 M78610	Iran, Iraq	150	190
Al Faith	Libya	200	?
Scud B	Afghanistan, Iran, Egypt, Libya, Syria, UAE, (Yemen, Iraq?)	300	985
Project T	Egypt	450	985
Intermediate Range			
Jericho (YA-1)	Israel	500	500
Scud "C" Variant	Iran, Syria (Libya?)	500–550	500
Al Husayn	Iraq	600–650	500
Al Husayn (Short)	Iraq	600–650	?
Al Hijrah	Iraq	600–650	?
Jericho 2 (YA-3)	Israel	1,500	1,000
Badr 2000	(Iraq? Egypt? Libya?)	750–1,000	?
CSS-2 (DF-3)	Saudi Arabia	2,800	2,150

Note: *Excludes modifications of cruise missiles, heavy air-to-surface missiles, anti-ship missiles, other surface-to-air missiles, and RPVs/UAVs, or possible developments of such systems. Egypt, Israel, Iran, Iraq, Libya, and Syria have systems with the capability to be modified for the land attack role and/or some development capability to create such systems.

Source: Adapted by Anthony H. Cordesman from Office of the Secretary of Defense, *Proliferation: Threat and Response,* Washington, Department of Defense, April 1996; *Jane's Defense Weekly,* April 17, 1996, pp. 42–43; and IISS *Military Balance, 1995–1996.*

any capability to produce whole missiles or major assemblies like the booster.[458]

Missile Production Facilities

Iran has bought missile production equipment from a wide range of sources, including Europe, the FSU, Canada, the US, and Asia. It has

MAP FOUR   The Range of Current and Future Iranian Ballistic Missile Systems. *Source:* Office of the Secretary of Defense, *Proliferation: Threat and Response,* Washington, Department of Defense, April 1996, p. 17.

obtained extensive support from North Korea and the People's Republic of China, which have supplied new missiles and are helping Iran develop its own missile technology and production capabilities. This is part of a two-track acquisition effort where Iran is acquiring complete missiles from North Korea while it improves its capability to assemble missiles in Iran, and acquires the capability to produce entire liquid and solid-fueled missiles.

China agreed on October 4, 1994, that it would observe the limits imposed by the Missile Technology Control Regime and would not transfer such missiles or technology to any other state. It seems, however, to have defined such compliance in narrow terms. China agreed to refrain from selling Iran missile systems which violate the MTCR, but it simultaneously undermined the spirit of the accord by ignoring restrictions on the transfer of components and manufacturing equipment.

China seems to have provided extensive technical support, specialized computerized tools, and dozens to hundreds of guidance systems—although some of these guidance systems may have been used for relatively simple Iranian rocket systems like the Nazeat—a system somewhat similar to the Russian FROG.

There have been reports that China is actively involved in giving Iran the technology it needs to produce either an extended range Scud or an M-9 class missile. This would be significant because the M-9 is a modern developmental Chinese single-stage solid fueled missile with a range of about 600 kilometers, a 500–600 kilogram warhead, and a CEP of 600–1,000 meters.[459] US experts do not, however, believe there is evidence to support such reports.

Iran has bought 150–200 CSS-8 missiles and 25–30 launchers from the People's Republic of China in 1989. The CSS-8 is a surface-to-surface conversion and upgrade of the Soviet-designed SA82 surface-to-air missile. It has a range of approximately 150 kilometers (65 miles). There is some uncertainty as to whether such a sale is permitted under the guidelines of the Missile Technology Control Regime (MTCR), to which China has agreed to adhere. The MTCR sets a range limit of 150 kilometers for such sales.[460]

There are reports that Iran has at least two rocket and missile assembly plants, a missile test range and monitoring complex, and a wide range of smaller design and refit facilities.[461] The largest plant is said to be a North Korean-built facility near Isfahan, although this plant may use Chinese equipment and technology. There are no confirmations of these reports, but this region is the center of much of Iran's advanced defense industry, including plants for munitions, tank overhaul, and helicopter and fixed wing aircraft maintenance. Some reports say the local industrial complex can produce liquid fuels and missile parts from a local steel mill.

A second missile plant is said to be located 175 kilometers east of Tehran, near Semnan. Some sources indicate this plant is Chinese-built and began rocket production as early as 1987. It is supposed to be able to build 600–1,000 Oghab rockets per year, if Iran can import key ingredients for solid fuel motors like ammonium perchlorate. The plant is also supposed to produce the Iran-130. Another facility may exist near Bandar Abbas for the assembly of the Silkworm. China is said to have built this facility in 1987, and is believed to be helping the naval branch of the Guards modify the Silkworm to extend its range to 400 kilometers. It is possible that China is also helping Iran develop solid fuel rocket motors and to produce or assemble missiles like the CS-801 and CS-802. There have, however, been reports that Iran is developing extended range Scuds with the support of Russian experts, and of a missile called the Tondar 68, with a range of 700 kilometers.

Still other reports claim that Iran has split its manufacturing facilities into plants near Pairzan, Seman, Shiraz, Maghdad, and Islaker. These reports indicate that the companies involved in building the Scuds are also involved in Iran's production of poison gas and include Defense Industries, Shahid, Bagheri Industrial Group, and Shahid Hemat Industrial Group.[462]

There is no way to reconcile the different unclassified estimates of Iran's current missile production facilities. It does seem likely, however, that Iran's plants have the ability to assemble large numbers of North Korean and PRC supplied systems rapidly and that Iran is developing the capability to build whole missiles and produce major components. This will allow it to design and produce indigenous variants.

Iran's main missile test range is said to be further east, near Shahroud, along the Tehran-Mashhad railway. A telemetry station is supposed to be 350 kilometers to the south at Taba, along the Mashhad-Isfahan road. All of these facilities are reportedly under the control of the Islamic Revolutionary Guards Corps.[463]

The "Scud C"

Iran has succeeded in acquiring a longer range North Korean missile system—often referred to as a "Scud C"—although Iran formally denied this long after the transfer became a reality. Hassan Taherian, an Iranian foreign ministry official, stated in February, 1995, "There is no missile cooperation between Iran and North Korea whatsoever. We deny this."[464]

A senior North Korean delegation traveled to Tehran to close the deal on November 29, 1990, and met with Mohsen Rezaii, the commander of the IRGC. Iran either bought the missile then, or placed its order shortly thereafter. North Korea then exported the missile through its Lyongaksan Import Corporation. Iran imported some of these North Korean missile assemblies using its B-747s, and seems to have used ships to import others.[465] Iran probably had more than 60 of the longer range North Korean missiles by 1995, although one source reports 170. Iran seems to have set a goal of several hundred such missiles by the late 1990s.[466] Iran may also have begun to test its new North Korean missiles, firing from a mobile launcher at a test site near Qom about 310 miles (500 kilometers) to a target area south of Shahroud. There are also reports that units equipped with such missiles have deployed as part of Iranian exercises like the Saeqer-3 (Thunderbolt 3) exercise in late October, 1993.[467]

Currently, Iran appears to have 5–10 Scud C launchers, each with several missiles. This probably includes four new North Korean TELs received in 1995.[468] North Korea seems to have completed development of this missile in 1987, after obtaining technical support from the People's Republic of China. While it is often called a "Scud C," it seems to differ substantially in detail from the original Soviet Scud B, and seems to be based more on the Chinese-made DF-61 than on a direct copy of Soviet technology.

The missiles have a range of around 310 miles (500 kilometers), a payload of at least 500 kilograms, and relatively good accuracy and reliability. They give Iran the ability to strike all targets on the southern coast of the Gulf and all of the populated areas in Iraq, although not the West. With these missiles, Iran can also reach into part of eastern Syria, the eastern third of Turkey, and can cover targets in the border area of the former Soviet Union, western Afghanistan, and western Pakistan.[469]

The North Korean sale of this missile may make a significant change in Iran's ability to deliver weapons of mass destruction for other reasons. North Korea normally deploys the missile with a chemical warhead, and may have tested biological warheads as well. Neither Russia, nor the People's Republic of China, seem to have transferred the warhead technology for biological and chemical weapons to Iran or Iraq when they sold them the Scud missile and CSS-8. However, North Korea may have sold Iran such technology, and if it did so, Iran would be able to deploy far more effective warheads than Iraq had at the time of the Gulf War. Such a technology transfer would save Iran years of development and testing work in obtaining highly lethal biological and chemical warheads.

Possible Acquisition of the No Dong 1

Some experts believe that Iran and Syria—and possibly Pakistan—are cooperating in acquiring and producing a longer range North Korean missile called the No Dong 1. This missile is a single-stage liquid-fueled missile, with a range of up to 1,000 to 1,300 kilometers (620 miles) and a 1,200–1,750 pound warhead. The missile is about 15 meters long—four meters longer than the Scud B. It has an estimated theoretical CEP of 700 meters at maximum range, versus 900 meters for the Scud B, although its practical accuracy could be as wide as 2,000–4,000 meters. It has an estimated terminal velocity of Mach 3.5, versus 2.5 for the Scud B, which presents added problems for tactical missile defense. The missile may be transportable on a copy of the MAZ-543P TEL, although some experts question this supposition because the No Dong is so big.

The No Dong missile seems to be nearing final development in North Korea, possibly with substantial aid from military industries in the People's Republic of China. It underwent flight tests at ranges of 310 miles (500 kilometers) on May 29, 1993, and some sources indicate that Iranians were present at the tests. A number of experts believe Syria and Iran will buy major assembly and production facilities for the No Dong 1, as well as missiles or missile parts. Iran seems to be planning to acquire at least 150 such missiles, although some reports have surfaced that Iran is having financing problems in obtaining North Korean support, or that the missile may not enter full-scale production in North Korea for two to three more years.[470]

Iran may also be interested in developmental North Korean IRBMs called the Tapeo Dong 1 or Tapeo Dong 2, which was detected by US intelligence in early 1994. This Tapeo Dong missile has an estimated maximum range of 2,000 kilometers, and the Tapeo Dong 2 may have a range up to 3,500 kilometers. Both are liquid fueled missiles which seem to have two stages. Unlike the No Dong, the Tapeo Dongs must be carried to a site in stages and then assembled at a fixed site. The No Dong transporter may be able to carry both stages of the Tapeo Dong 1, but some experts believe that a special transporter is needed for the first stage of the Tapeo Dong 1, and for both stages of the Tapeo Dong 2.[471] There are reports that Iran is seeking full scale manufacturing capability for such systems, although it is unclear that Iran and North Korea have reached a financing agreement on any aspect of the No Dong program.

Possible Cruise Missiles

It is possible that Iran is developing a cruise missile with Chinese and other foreign assistance. Iran has experience with similar systems and fired at least 10 Chinese-made, land-based anti-ship cruises missiles at targets along the Kuwaiti coast during 1987–1988—hitting targets like Kuwait's sea island and a US-flagged oil tanker.

While Iran has no capability to develop and deploy a missile as sophisticated as the Tomahawk (TLAM)-like missile, US studies indicate that Third World nations like Iran and Iraq may be able to build a cruise missile about half the size of a small fighter aircraft and with a payload of about 500 kilograms by the years 2000 to 2005. Such missiles would cost only 10% to 25% as much as ballistic missiles of similar range, and both the HY-2 Silkworm and C-802 could be modified relatively quickly for land attacks against area targets.[472]

Building an entire cruise missile would be more difficult. The technology for fusing CBW and cluster warheads would be within Iran's grasp. Navigation systems and jet engines, however, would still be a major potential problem. Current inertial navigation systems (INS) would introduce errors of at least several kilometers at ranges of 1,000 kilometers and would carry a severe risk of total guidance failureyprobably exceeding two-thirds of the missiles fired. A differential global positioning system (GPS) integrated with the inertial navigation system (INS) and a radar altimeter, however, might produce an accuracy of 15 meters. Some existing remotely piloted vehicles (RPVs), such as the South African Skua claim such performance. Commercial technology is becoming available for differential global positioning system (GPS) guidance with accuracies of 2 to 5 meters.

There are commercially available reciprocating and gas turbine engines that Iran could adapt for use in a cruise missile, although finding a reliable and efficient turbofan engine for a specific design application might be difficult. An extremely efficient engine would have to be matched to a specific airframe. It is doubtful that Iran could design and build such an engine, but there are over 20 other countries with the needed design and manufacturing skills. While airframe-engine-warhead integration and testing would still present a challenge and might be beyond Iran's manufacturing skills, it is inherently easier to integrate and test a cruise missile than a long-range ballistic missile. Further, such developments would be far less detectable than developing a ballistic system if the program used coded or low altitude directional telemetry. Iran could also bypass much of the problems inherent in developing its own cruise missile by modifying the HY-2 Silkworm for use as a land attack weapon and extending its range beyond 80 kilometers, or by modifying and improving the CS-801 (Ying Jai-1) anti-ship missile. There are reports that the Revolutionary Guards are working on such developments at a facility near Bandar Abbas.[473]

Such cruise missile systems could reach a wide range of targets. A longer range cruise missile system with a 500 kilometer range—deployed in Iran's border areas—could cover most of Iraq, eastern Turkey, all of Kuwait, the Gulf coast of Saudi Arabia, Bahrain, most of Qatar, the northern UAE, and northern Oman. A system with a 1,200 kilometer range could reach Israel, the eastern two-thirds of Turkey, most of Saudi Arabia, and all of the other southern Gulf states including Oman. Such a system could also be programmed to avoid major air defense concentrations at a sacrifice of about 20% of its range.

Iranian Delivery System Warfighting Capabilities

It is important to stress that missile capabilities will not determine Iranian warfighting capability. Missiles may be the highest technology available, but there are no rules preventing Iran from using aircraft, unconventional delivery systems, proxies, or terrorists. Table Sixteen shows the range-payload capability of typical strike-attack aircraft in the Middle

TABLE SIXTEEN   Possible Air Delivery Systems[*]

Type	Cruise Speed (KM/HR) Low[***]	High	Nominal Range (Kilometers)[**] Low	High	Maximum Payload (Kilograms)
A-4	—	810	—	1,230	4,500
Alphajet	740	710	170	890	2,800
F-4	—	890	—	840	5,900
F-5	—	860	—	310	3,200
F-14	—	980	—	950	4,500
F-15	—	980	—	1,440	10,700
F-16	—	920	550	930	5,400
F/A-18	—	900	—	740	7,700
Hawk	920	780	—	185	2,950
Jaguar	960	880	—	850	4,750
MiG-21[****]	880	800	—	480	1,500
MiG-23[****]	960	950	450	950	3,000
MiG-27	960	890	390	600	4,500
MiG-29	960	890	—	1,150	—
Mirage F-1	980	980	640	—	4,000
Mirage III	970	950	830	—	1,810
Mirage 5/50	970	950	630	—	4,200
Mirage 2000	—	950	—	690	6,300
Q-5/A-5 Fantan	—	—	400	600	2,000
Su-17/20/22	950	950	430	680	4,000
Su-24	930	950	320	1,130	8,000
Tornado IDS	—	820	—	1,390	6,800
Tu-16	—	750	—	2,180	9,000
Tu-22 (Blinder)	—	750	—	1,500	10,000
Tu-22M (Backfire)	—	860	—	4,430	12,000

Notes: [*]Excludes modifications of cruise missiles and RPVs/UAVs, or possible developments of such systems. Egypt, Israel, Iran, Iraq, Libya, and Syria have systems with the capability to be modified for the land attack role and/or some development capability to create such systems.

[**]Low level radar-avoidance approach.

[***]Low = Lo-Lo-Lo profile, high = Hi-Lo-Hi profile. Excludes refueling and one-way missions would more than double range. Trade-offs can be made between range and payload in most cases. Some air defense fighters are included which could be used for such missions because of exceptional flight performance.

[****]Performance varies sharply with specific variant.

Source: Adapted by Anthony H. Cordesman from Office of the Secretary of Defense, Proliferation: Threat and Response, Washington, Department of Defense, April 1996 and IISS Military Balance, 1995–1996.

East, and Iran already has F-4s, F-5s, F-14s, Su-24s, and MiG-29s. It is also important to note that the performance of the aircraft in Table Sixteen will be notably greater if they are only flown one-way and/or are used in suicide missions. Further, converting an aircraft into a remotely piloted vehicle carrying a weapon of mass destruction and homing in on the target using a GPS and autopilot, with limited command guidance, is well within Iran's technical capabilities.

Iran also does not need new ballistic or cruise missile systems to pose a threat. Iran already has the capability to launch missile attacks against Iraq, to hit coastal area targets in much of the southern Gulf, and may also be able to use chemical warheads. The volume of such attacks is likely to be very similar to those Iraq launched during the Gulf War, or against Iran during the "war of the cities." The lethality would depend on the warhead, and much depends on the weaponization technology Iran has received from North Korea and/or the People's Republic of China.

Iran is currently limited by its lack of both sophisticated long-range targeting capability and missile systems whose accuracy is limited to attacking only area targets. Iran can, however, pose a major threat in terms of intimidation and popular fear using conventional warheads. It may also be able to use missiles with chemical and biological warheads to destroy or incapacitate military area targets, paralyze war fighting capabilities, or even attack large complexes of particular buildings and facilities. Such missile attacks would be vulnerable to point defense by the improved Patriot, and US air power could probably break up large scale attacks with strikes against Iran's missile launch facilities. Currently, however, the US has no way of preventing Iran from confronting it with the same iScud huntî problems encountered by the Coalition during the 1991 Gulf War. It would be almost impossible for US air units to hunt out and destroy enough of Iran's missile capabilities to halt all attacks. As a result, the US might well be forced to deter Iranian missile strikes by escalating its attacks on other high value Iranian targets.[474]

Iran's acquisition efforts also seem likely to give it a growing capability to launch missile attacks to ranges of over 600 kilometers after the year 2000. By that time Iran may well have guidance systems accurate enough to use against relatively small area targets like airfields and the assembly areas in ports. It may also have missile warheads with relatively efficient chemical and biological warheads. Much will depend on the precise level of technology involved, but Iran could easily develop a mobile force with 20–50 launchers and several hundred missiles by the years 2000–2005. Given the level of dual use technology available, it seems possible Iran could equip such missiles with biological warheads possessing lethalities close to those of small nuclear weapons—which would allow it to launch devastating attacks against cities, critical civil facilities, oil and gas facilities, and military area targets. Iran should also have the capability to deploy shorter range missiles with chemical and biological warheads for use against other military targets ranging from land force combat formations to large ships, like carriers.

Depending on how Iran chose to deploy its missiles, it could develop a significant launch-on-warning or launch-under-attack capability which the US might not be able to preempt, even in a surprise attack. It is doubtful that any "leakproof" defense system could be created to deal with such attacks, although wide area missile defense systems like THAAD or Aegis might have significant capability to degrade such attacks. This would place new emphasis on US ability to deter Iranian missile strikes by escalating its attacks on other high value Iranian targets, or by threatening the use of US nuclear weapons.

Iranian Chemical Weapons[475]

Both Iran and Iraq have signed the Geneva Protocols of 1925, prohibiting the use of poison gas. Both nations have also signed the Biological Warfare Convention of 1972, banning the development, production, and deployment or stockpiling of biological weapons.[476] Nevertheless, Iran began a crash effort to produce chemical weapons in the early 1980s, in response to Iraq's use of chemical weapons against Iran. Rafsanjani described chemical weapons as follows during this period:[477] "Chemical and biological weapons are poor man's atomic bombs and can easily be produced. We should at least consider them for our defense. Although the use of such weapons is inhuman, the war taught us that international laws are only scraps of paper."

The Islamic Revolutionary Guards Corps, with support from the Ministry of Defense, was put in charge of developing offensive chemical agents in 1983. Iran began producing limited batches of chemical agents in 1984. It then covertly obtained substantial imports of production equipment, the necessary feedstocks to produce such weapons, and outside technical support. This effort took several years and Iran did not make extensive use of chemical weapons during the Iran-Iraq War. Iran was, however, able to produce limited quantities of blister (mustard) and blood (cyanide) agents beginning in 1987.[478] These gas agents were loaded into bombs and artillery shells, and used sporadically against Iraq in 1987 and 1988.[479]

Iran had chemical weapons plants in operation at Damghan and Parchin no later than March, 1988, and may have begun to test fire Scuds with chemical warheads as early as 1988–1989. Iran did not succeed in producing nerve gas during the Iran-Iraq War, but it may have started producing nerve agents like Sarin and Tabun in the early 1990s.

The exact status of Iran's current chemical war fighting capabilities is unknown, but Iran has clearly established a significant chemical weapons production capability of 25 to 100 tons per year, including mustard gas and dusty mustard gas, phosgene gas, and blood agents like cyanogen chloride, or one of the cyanides.[480] This already gives Iran a significant capability to conduct a chemical war near its borders, to launch limited long-range air raids using chemical bombs, and to use chemical weapons in unconventional warfare. Iran is also steadily improving its chemical warfare production capabilities with Chinese equipment and technical assistance.[481]

While the chemical warheads for Iran's missiles are probably still of limited sophistication, Iran has had time to develop usable artillery, rocket warheads, and bombs. Iran probably has storable binary weapons, or will soon introduce them into inventory, and there are recent indications Iran is seeking to buy equipment to support its forces in conducting nerve gas warfare.[482] A recent report by German intelligence indicates that Iran has made major efforts to acquire the equipment necessary to produce Sarin and Tabun, using the same cover of purchasing equipment for pesticide plants that Iraq used for increasing its Sa'ad 16 plant in the 1980s. German sources note that three Indian companies—Tata Consulting Engineering, Transpek, and Rallis India—have approached German pharmaceutical and engineering concerns for such equipment and technology under conditions where German intelligence was able to trace the end user to Iran.[483]

British, German, and US experts believe that Iran now has stockpiles of between several hundred and 2,000 tons of various lethal chemical agents. They believe that Iran has chemical warheads for its 155 mm artillery shells, 122 mm rockets, bombs, and mines, and may have chemical warheads for some of its longer range rockets and guided missiles. Furthermore, US experts believe Iran has at least one chemical warhead assembly plant near Damghan and regularly ships such weapons to other storage sites by rail. A wide variety of experts believe Iran also has some capabilities to manufacture nerve gas now and that Iran is seeking to produce its own precursors to avoid dependence on controlled imports. Israeli experts have claimed that Iran is already stockpiling nerve gas weapons.[484]

Iranian chemical warfare capabilities will grow steadily with time, and they will not be subject to the limitations Iraq faces because of UN inspection and sanctions. Iran may have little practical experience in large scale chemical operations, but chemical weapons do give Iran new capabilities to intimidate the southern Gulf states and deter the West. Further, chemical weapons do not have to be delivered by missiles or aircraft. As is the case with biological weapons, devices can be smuggled into a target area.

Agents can be dispersed by man-portable devices or even grenades. They can be used as terrorist or unconventional warfare weapons for delivery into any building with central air conditioning. A passenger airliner could be used to fly a line and disperse agents as an aerosol. Chemical devices could be smuggled in and detonated in commuter centers, stadiums, or other crowded areas.

Iran does, however, face serious problems in making any attributable offensive use of chemical weapons in a war where US forces are engaged, or where Iran faces a combination of states with major conventional air strike capabilities. If Iran uses chemical weapons, it could destabilize and/or escalate a conflict in ways in which Iran would face massive conventional retaliation. If Iran had any major success in attacking civilian targets, or Western forces, in the southern Gulf with chemical weapons, it would at least face the possibility of theater nuclear retaliation.

Iranian Biological Weapons[485]

Iran seems to have begun developing biological weapons as early as 1982. Reports surfaced that Iran was working on the production of mycotoxins—a relatively simple biological agent that requires only limited laboratory facilities.[486] US intelligence sources reported in August 1989, that Iran was trying to buy two new strains of fungus from Canada and the Netherlands that can be used to produce mycotoxins. German sources indicated that Iran had successfully purchased such cultures several years earlier.[487] The Imam Reza Medical Center at Mashhad Medical Sciences University and the Iranian Research Organization for Science and Technology were identified as the end users for this purchasing effort, but it is likely that the true end user was an Iranian government agency specializing in biological warfare.

Many experts now believe that the Iranian biological weapons effort is under the control of the Islamic Revolutionary Guards Corps, who are known to have tried to purchase suitable production equipment for such weapons. It is clear that Iran conducted covert operations linked to biological weapons research and production in Germany and Switzerland in the 1990s. Iran has also conducted extensive research on more lethal active agents like Anthrax, hoof and mouth disease, and biotoxins. In addition, it has repeatedly approached various European firms for the equipment and technology necessary to work with these diseases and toxins.

Little is known about the exact details of Iran's effort to *weaponize* and produce such weapons. There are some reports that Iran has developed effective aerosol weapons and weapons designs with ceramic containers. Such uncertainties make it harder to determine the actual nature of Iran's current and probable future war fighting capabilities than is the case with chemical and nuclear weapons. Iran may encounter continuing difficulties in developing effective ballistic missile warheads using biological agents, but it should be able to meet the technical challenges both in improving its targeting and in finding effective ways to disperse agents from cruise missile warheads and bombs. Iran may already have the technology to disperse agents like anthrax over a wide area by spreading them from a ship moving along a coast or out of a large container smuggled into a city or industrial complex. It also seems likely that Iran will be able to create a significant production capability for storable encapsulated biological agents by the year 2000.[488]

It is impossible to do more than guess at Iran's war fighting doctrine for using biological weapons. Its leadership and military planners may well go on acquiring such weapons without making specific plans to use them. As for deterrence, Iran would be subject to the same threat of retaliation as with its use of chemical weapons. At the same time, the level of conflict would be more intense, making such retaliation even more likely.

Even the possibility that Iran has biological weapons gives it an enhanced capability to deter and intimidate the southern Gulf and the West. Iran could make overt use of biological weapons in much the same way as chemical weapons, but also has incentives to make covert use of biological weapons, because they are particularly well suited to unconventional warfare, or "terrorism."

While biological weapons are fundamentally different in character from both chemical and nuclear weapons, highly effective biological weapons can be as lethal as small nuclear devices. A recent study by the Office of Technology Assessment that compared the impact of a 12.5 kiloton nuclear weapon dropped in the center of Washington with the minimum and maximum effect of using a single aircraft to deliver 300 kilograms of Sarin and 30 kilograms of anthrax spores. The results indicate that the nuclear weapon would cover 7.8 square kilometers and produce prompt deaths of 23,000–80,000; the nerve gas would cover 0.22 square kilometers and kill 60–200, and the anthrax spores would cover 10 square kilometers and kill 3,000 to 10,000. Such calculations depend upon the scenario, the time of day, and the weather. They assume a sophisticated bomb or missile warhead. Such data are, however, a warning of the potential risks posed by biological weapons.[489]

Further, it must also be stressed that biological weapons do not have to be delivered by sophisticated weapons systems; they can be smuggled into a target area. Agents can be dispersed by man-portable devices or even grenades, and can be delivered by the cooling system of any building with central air conditioning. Unlike chemical weapons, biological agents are lethal enough to be dispersed from the roof tops or heights in urban areas, and wet agents can be placed in reservoirs. A passenger air-liner could be used to disperse agents as an aerosol, or spores could be covertly dispersed in commuter centers, stadiums, or crowded areas. Ships moving along the coasts of cities have been found to be ideal plat-forms for slowly dispersing anthrax spores.

Iranian Nuclear Weapons[490]

The US has expressed deep concern regarding Iran's search for nuclear weapons. In early 1995, Secretary of State Warren Christopher stated:[491]

> In terms of its organization, programs, procurement, and covert activities, Iran is pursuing the classic route to nuclear weapons which has been fol-lowed by almost all states that have sought a nuclear weapon. . . . Iran's efforts to acquire nuclear weapons also pose enormous dangers. Every responsible member of the world community has an interest in seeing those efforts fail. There is no room for complacency. Remember Iraq.

Christopher is also quoted as saying that Iran has tried for years to buy heavy water reactors to produce plutonium, is "devoting resources" to enriching uranium to weapons grade levels, and has "scoured" the states of the former Soviet Union for nuclear materials, technology, scientists, and technicians.[492]

Most Western experts do not believe Iran has been able to fund the kind of massive program that Iraq established, and Iran has often found it difficult to obtain nuclear technology. Few Western experts seem to support a recent report by a former member of the US National Security Council staff that Iran had developed a $10 billion dollar plan to acquire nuclear weapons.[493] Iran also does not have anything approaching Iraq's manpower base of several thousand nuclear technicians. Some estimates indicated that Iran had less than 500 nuclear physicists, engineers, and senior technicians in the late 1980s—compared to around 7,500 in Iraq.

The Revitalization of Iran's Nuclear Effort

Most Western experts do believe, however, that Iran's revolutionary gov-ernment revitalized the nuclear weapons program begun by the Shah during the Iran-Iraq War. Further, they believe that Iran has engaged in many of the weapons design and fuel cycle activities necessary to build a nuclear weapon. These experts assert that the Iranian government began to revitalize the Shah's massive nuclear effort in the mid-1980s, after Iraq used chemical weapons in the Iran-Iraq War. They contend that this is why Iran strengthened the Atomic Energy Organization that the Shah

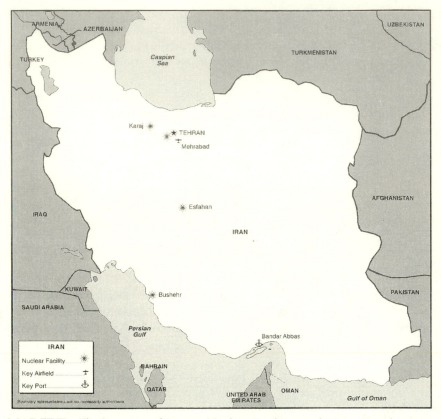

MAP FIVE   The Location of Iranian Nuclear Facilities and Major Transhipment
Centers. *Source:* Office of the Secretary of Defense, *Proliferation: Threat and
Response,* Washington, Department of Defense, April 1996, p. 15.

had formed in 1974, provided new funds to the Amirabad Nuclear
Research Center in Tehran, and formed a new nuclear research center at
the University of Isfahan in 1984 with French assistance.[494]

Further, these Western experts believe that Iran's efforts to acquire
nuclear weapons accelerated in the late 1980s—although it is not possible
to separate such efforts definitively from efforts to acquire nuclear power
generating facilities. Iran's Yazd Province has significant uranium
deposits (at least 5,000 tons) in the Shagand region, and Iran announced
in 1987 that it had plans to set up a yellow cake plant in Yazd Province.[495]
This facility was under construction by 1989 and Iran may have begun to
build a uranium processing or enrichment facility at Pilcaniyeu.[496] Iran
may also have opened a new uranium ore processing plant close to its

Shagand uranium mine in March, 1990, and it seems to have extended its search for uranium ore into three additional areas. Iran may have also begun to exploit stocks of yellow cake that the Shah had obtained from South Africa in the late 1970s while obtaining uranium dioxide from Argentina by purchasing it through Algeria.[497]

Iran began to show an interest in laser isotope separation (LIS) in the mid-1980s, and held a conference on LIS in September, 1987.[498] On February 7, 1990, the speaker of the Majlis publicly toured the Iranian Atomic Energy Organization and opened the new Jabir Ibn al Hayyan laboratory to train Iranian nuclear technicians.[499] Reports then surfaced that Iran had at least 200 scientists and a work force of about 2,000 devoted to nuclear research.[500]

Iran sought foreign support from a range of sources. Pakistan signed a nuclear cooperation agreement with Iran in 1987. Specialists from Iran's Atomic Energy Organization began to train in Pakistan, and Dr. Abdul Kadr Khan, who has directed much of Pakistan's effort to develop nuclear weapons material, visited Tehran and Bushehr in February, 1986, and January, 1987.[501] Iran also strengthened its nuclear research ties to the People's Republic of China. The two countries signed a formal nuclear research cooperation agreement in 1990, although cooperation had begun as early as 1985—after Iran had suffered its first major chemical attacks from Iraq and had started to give its nuclear effort high priority. Iranian nuclear engineers appear to have begun training in China, and China seems to have transferred nuclear research technology for reactor construction and other projects, and possibly some technology for LIS, to an Iranian facility at Isfahan.[502]

Iran signed an agreement with China's Commission on Science, Technology, and Industry for National Defense on January 21, 1991, to build a small 27-kilowatt research reactor at Iran's nuclear weapons research facility at Isfahan. This reactor was evidently to be plutonium fueled, and may have come on line in 1994.[503] On November 4, 1991, China stated that it had signed commercial cooperation agreements with Iran in 1989 and 1991, and that it would transfer an electromagnetic isotope separator (Calutron) and a smaller nuclear reactor, for ìpeaceful and commercialî purposes. These facilities are only suitable for research use and have little value in producing a nuclear weapon, but US experts believe that China has also provided Iran with data on chemical separation and other enrichment technology, as well as the design for facilities to convert uranium to uranium hexaflouride to make reactor fuel. They also believe that China has helped Iran in processing Yellowcake.[504]

Iran conducted experiments in uranium enrichment and centrifuge technology at its Sharif University of Technology in Tehran. Sharif University was also linked to efforts to import cylinders of fluorine suitable for processing enriched material, and attempts to import specialized magnets that can be used for centrifuges, from Thyssen in Germany in 1991. Italian inspectors seized eight steam condensers bound for Iran that could be used in a covert reactor program in 1993, and high technology ultrasound equipment suitable for reactor testing at the port of Bari in January 1994. Iran seems to have conducted research into plutonium separation and Iranians published research on uses of tritium that had applications to nuclear weapons boosting. Iran also obtained a wide range of US and other nuclear literature with applications for weapons designs.[505]

Other aspects of Iran's nuclear research effort also have some potential weapons applications. Iran is operating an Argentine-fueled five megawatt light water highly enriched uranium reactor at the University of Tehran. It is also operating a Chinese-supplied neutron source research reactor, and subcritical assemblies with 900 grams of highly enriched uranium, at its Isfahan Nuclear Research Center. This Center is experimenting with a heavy water zero-power reactor, a light water sub-critical reactor, and a graphite sub-critical reactor. In addition, it may have experimented with some aspects of nuclear weapons design.[506]

Chinese and Russian Reactor Deals

Iran also sought larger reactors. It negotiated with Spain to repair and complete the reactors that the Shah had begun at Bushehr, as well as with Kraftwerke Union and CENA of Germany in the late 1980s and early 1990s. It also attempted to import reactor parts illegally from Siemens in Germany and Skoda in Czechoslovakia.[507] When these attempts failed, Iran turned to China and Russia. On September 10, 1992, during his visit to Beijing, Rafsanjani is reported to have finished negotiations dealing with the purchase of one or two 300–330 megawatt reactors from the People's Republic of China. The sale of one such reactor was announced by Iran's Minister of Defense during the visit and led to immediate US protests to the People's Republic of China.[508]

As a result the sale was deferred, but China became more willing to sell to Iran as Chinese-US relations deteriorated. On July 4, 1994, Iran and the PRC announced that they had signed an agreement for the PRC to build a 300 megawatt reactor near Tehran.[509] Since that time, Iran has expressed an interest in buying two 300 megawatt pressurized water nuclear reactors from China, similar to the Chinese plant at Qinshan in Zhejiang Province. At least one of these reactors was evidently to be sited near Esteghial, near Bushehr on the Gulf Coast.[510] Iranian officials indicated in mid-May 1995, that Iran had already made an $800–$900 million down payment on the deal. Reports also surfaced in September, 1995 that China was helping Iran develop Calutron production facilities at Karai, about

160 kilometers northeast of Tehran, and the State Department indicated that China was help Iran develop gas diffusion facilities near Isfahan in April, 1996.[511]

There are, however, major uncertainties regarding such deals between Iran and China. The Chinese nuclear industry is still in the developmental stage, and China has had serious problems in bringing some of its reactors on line and keeping them operating. The reactor at Qinshan also uses a Japanese-made reactor vessel and German primary cooling pumps, and it is not clear if these will be exportable to Iran.[512] Further, there have been reports that China is willing to cancel the sale as a result of negotiations with the US. Coupled to Iran's financial problems, Iran's ability to consummate its deal with China is uncertain.[513]

Iran conducted similar negotiations with Russia and began to seek nuclear reactors from Russia in the mid-1980s. Reports surfaced that Russia had signed a contract to sell two nuclear reactors to Iran in the late 1980s—although the existence of any such contracts was not made public and no tangible steps seemed to follow. Negotiations continued, however, and on November 20, 1994, Iran announced that Russia had agreed to a $780 million deal to complete a reactor at Bushehr that German companies had begun during the time of the Shah.[514] Iran signed this agreement with Russia on January 8, 1995.[515]

The nuclear facility involved is about 730 miles south of Tehran, and 15 miles from the city of Bushehr. It is the site of two incomplete 1200 megawatt reactors that Siemens had begun to construct in 1976. Although work stopped in 1979 with the fall of the Shah, Iran has long kept the facility active, and some 300–400 Iranians normally live on the site and maintain it. Facilities exist to house some 2,000 workers at the site, with a capacity for supporting up to 2,000 more. As a result, Russia has already been able to deploy some 150 technicians to the reactor site. It plans to begin major shipments of material in 1995. It also plans to deploy up to 2,000 Russian workers and train some 500 Iranian technicians.[516]

Russia is scheduled to complete work on the first reactor by the year 2000.[517] The completion date and the cost of the contract depend, however, on whether Russia will be able to make the desired use of the existing facilities at the site, and whether Russia can tailor its VVER-1000 reactor design to fit these facilities. Iran had invested about $6 billion in the facility by the time the Shah fell. Construction of the main buildings and steel containment vessel for one of the reactors at Bushehr had reached 85% of completion at the time of the Shah's fall, and construction for the other was partially finished.[518]

Both reactor facilities were damaged during the Iran-Iraq War, however, and the Russian VVER-1000 is physically different from a Siemens 1,300 megawatt reactor. Further, Siemens had not yet installed the reactors themselves and the steam generators which produce steam for the turbines.[519] In September 1994, Russian technicians and experts inspected the site and concluded that corrosion was extensive, that their work would be hampered by the absence of the German technical documentation, and that it would be necessary to modify the outdated 1970s design and redesign the buildings to take a Russian water-moderated water-cooled reactor with a capacity of 1,000 megawatts, the VVER-1000.[520] As a result, Russia may only be able to use some of the remaining buildings and control facilities. Past efforts to export reactor designs have also led to significant delays and cost escalation, and that it would be necessary to modify the outdated of facilities designed for another reactor.[521]

The current project at Bushehr may only be the first step in a far more ambitious Iranian effort. Iran has shown an interest in purchasing another VVER-1000 reactor for use at Bushehr, and sources differ as to whether Iran is seeking to purchase two V1213 VVER 440 power reactors and another large research reactor, or a total of five large 1,300 megawatt reactors.[522] Some US experts believe that Iran is now seeking to buy four to five light water reactors from Russia, including two 1000 megawatt reactors and two 463 megawatt reactors, at a cost in excess of $5 billion that can be used to produce substantial amounts of fissile material for nuclear weapons. They also believe that Iran has aggressively sought to buy highly enriched and/or fissile material from the former Soviet Union, as well as the services of Soviet nuclear weapons designers.[523]

Iran has claimed that it needs to provide 20% of its electric power from nuclear generators to reduce its use of exportable oil and gas. Such claims, however, present a serious economic credibility problem. Reactors that cost billions of dollars in hard currency seem to make limited economic sense in a country with vast supplies of natural gas that can be used to generate electricity at 18% to 20% of the cost of nuclear electricity at market price conditions. The credibility of such claims are undermined further by Iran's policy of underpricing oil to the point where the increase in domestic consumption is cutting into its export capacity.

President Rafsanjani further undercut the argument that Iran needed nuclear power to allow gas to be exported by announcing that Iran had "endless" gas reserves and over 150 years of oil reserves in a speech to the Majlis on June 1, 1996. Rafsanjani announced the discovery of a new gas field of at least 9 trillion cubic feet and estimated Iran's oil reserves at 93 billion barrels.[524] It also makes only limited economic sense for Iran to concentrate all of the reactors in one area so far away from Iran's cities and industrial facilities in the north.

Some experts do, however, argue that Russia has priced its initial contracts so far below the normal world market price for such reactors that they might be economical, even for a nation with Iran's gas resources.

Such experts also argue that Iran has little experience with the true life cycle cost of nuclear reactors, and may be reacting to price quotes that give it a false impression of the economics involved.

It is impossible to state categorically that Iran's reactor purchases would be part of a nuclear weapons effort. Russia is selling light water reactors which are less suited to producing plutonium than the heavy water reactors Iran sought initially. Russia has repeatedly denied that it will give Iran any assistance in developing nuclear weapons. It repeatedly indicated that it will take back the plutonium-bearing spent fuel in the reactor, and has announced that Iran has signed a $30 million deal with Iran to provide fuel for the reactors and reprocess spent fuel in Russia.[525]

Mohammed Sadegh Ayatollahi, Iran's representative to the IAEA, has stated, "We've had contracts before for the Bushehr plant in which we agreed that the spent fuel would go back to the supplier. For our contract with the Russians and Chinese, it is the same." According to some reports, Russia would reprocess the fuel at its Mayak plant near Chelyabinsk in the Urals, and could store it at an existing facility, a Krasnoyarsk-26 in southern Siberia.[526]

There are also serious differences between the US and Russia over whether Russia initially agreed to provide centrifuge and other enrichment technology as part of the deal. The US claimed that Victor Mikhaliov, the head of Russia's Atomic Energy Ministry, had proposed the sale of a centrifuge plant in April 1995. The US then indicated that it had persuaded Russia not to sell Iran centrifuge technology as part of the reactor deal during the summit meeting between Presidents Clinton and Yeltsin in May, 1995. Russia subsequently stated, however, that it never planned to sell centrifuge and advanced enrichment technology to Iran, and Iran has denied that it was ever interested in such technology.[527]

At the same time, reactor sales to Iran present serious risks. Reactor grade uranium and plutonium can be processed for weapons use, and Iran could reject IAEA safeguards once the reactor or reactors are complete. Iran could then use such reactors to enrich its own uranium. The transfer of large scale nuclear technology to Iran will also give it a nuclear technology base that many experts believe will allow it to build covert reactor facilities, centrifuge facilities, and/or chemical separation facilities, even if it does comply with IAEA regulations and inspection agreements in operating its reactors.

Iranian Nuclear Weapons Facilities

The location of declared Iranian nuclear facilities and known nuclear transhipment centers is shown in Map Five. Little credible data is available on the size and nature of Iran's nuclear weapons effort and facilities, or the exact nature of Iran's imports of nuclear weapons related and dual-use technology. There is no way to validate firmly the existence of Iran's nuclear weapons effort, or to describe the current level of that effort and its probable results. Foreign experts also disagree on the issues, although most experts who doubt Iran is seeking nuclear weapons seem to come from exporting countries.

While British, French, German, Israeli, and US experts are convinced that an Iranian nuclear weapons effort exists, nations like China and Russia have effectively rejected this claim. Yevgeny Primakov, Russia's most senior intelligence official, stated on March 23, 1995, "We have not found convincing evidence of the existence in the country of a coherent nuclear program." Lt. General Gennady Yevstafiyev declared on the same day, "We are keeping track of developments. . . . But so far, we see no grounds for sharing the official US position." These Russian statements are very different from ones Russian officials had made a year earlier. They contradict statements made by Russians like Alexei Yablokov, an advisor to Yeltsin, who stated, "Thanks to Russia, Iran will be in a position to get the nuclear bomb in a few years. . . . By signing this contract, Russia is arming Iran." They do, however, illustrate the fact there is no international consensus regarding Iran's activities.[528]

There have been a number of conflicting reports regarding Iran's nuclear facilities. The People's Mujahideen, an anti-regime group of uncertain reliability, has made many detailed claims. The People's Mujahideen has reported that Iran's facilities include a weapons site called Ma'allem Kelayah, near Qazvin on the Caspian. This is said to be an IRGC-run facility established in 1987, which has involved an Iranian investment of $300 million. Supposedly, the site was to house the 10 megawatt reactor Iran tried to buy from India.

The People's Mujahideen has also claimed that the two Soviet reactors were to be installed at a large site at Gorgan on the Caspian, under the direction of Russian physicists. It claimed that the People's Republic of China provided uranium enrichment equipment and technicians for the site at Darkhouin, where Iran once planned to build a French reactor; that a nuclear reactor was being constructed at Karaj; and that another nuclear weapons facility exists in the south central part of Iran near the Iraqi border. The group has also claimed that the ammonia and urea plant that the British firm M. W. Kellog was building at Borujerd in Khorassan province, near the border with Turkistan, might be adapted to produce heavy water.

In addition, the People's Mujahideen has claimed that Amir Kabar Technical University, the Atomic Energy Organization of Iran, Dor Argham Ltd., the Education and Research Institute, GAM Iranian Communications, Ghoods Research Center, Iran Argham Co., Iran Electronic Industries, Iranian Research Organization, Ministry of Sepah, Research and Development Group, Sezemane Sanaye Defa, the Sharif University of Technology, Taradis Iran Computer Company, and Zakaria Al-Razi Chemical Company are all participants in the Iranian nuclear weapons effort.[529]

Another source lists the Atomic Energy Organization of Iran, the Laser Research Center and Ibn-e Heysam Research and Laboratory Complex, the Bonab Atomic Energy Research Center (East Azerbaijan), the Imam Hussein University of the Revolutionary Guards, the Jabit bin al-Hayyan Laboratory, the Khoshomi uranium mine (Yazd), a possible site at Moallem Kalayeh, the Nuclear Research Center at Tehran University, the Nuclear Research Center for Agriculture and Medicine (Karaj), the Nuclear Research Center of Technology (Isfahan), the Saghand uranium mine (Yazd), the Sharif University (Tehran) and its Physics Research Center.[530]

The problem with such lists is that they are virtually a list of all the major research centers in Iran and ignore the fact that much of Iran's effort may take place in facilities that do not have a name relating to nuclear research or consist of purchasing efforts made through Iran's vast network of cutouts and purchasing officers abroad. The German Ministry of Economic, for example, has circulated a wide list of possible Iranian fronts, including the Bonyad e-Mostazafan, the Defense Industries Organization (Sazemane Sanaye Defa), the Pars Garma Company, the Sadadja Industrial Group (Sadadja Sanaye Daryaee), the Defense Industries Organization (Sazemane Sanaye Defa), the Iran Telecommunications Industry (Sanaye Mokhaberet Iran), the Shahid Hemat Industrial Group, the State Purchasing Organization, Education Research Institute (ERI), Iran Aircraft Manufacturing Industries (IAI), Iran Fair Deal Company, Iran Group of Surveyors, Iran Helicopter Support and Renewal Industries (IHI), Iran Navy Technical Supply Center, Iran Tehran Kohakd Daftar Nezarat, Industrial Development Group, and Ministry of Defense (Vezerate Defa).[531]

There is no question that Iran has a large enough research and industrial base to hide a nuclear weapons effort of moderate size, and a highly sophisticated purchasing network. The problem is to determine what organizations and facilities are guilty.

IAEA Inspections and Non-Inspections

There is little direct evidence to confirm such claims regarding given Iranian facilities and sites, and some seem to have been partially discredited by the IAEA. The IAEA has regularly inspected declared

Iranian sites, and has made two special visits to suspect sites. The IAEA conducted a limited pre-arranged visit to six of 10 suspected sites in February, 1992, and found no sign of weapons activity at any of these sites. It found that the uranium mining site at Saghand was at least five years away from production and had no uranium concentration plant. It also found the facility at Ma'allem Kelayah, which was said to be a nuclear weapons research center, to be little more than a motel-sized training and conference center. Further, the People's Republic of China-supplied Calutron at Shiraz was found to be so small that it could only be used to produce isotopes for medical research.[532]

Some sources have charged that the IAEA only conducted a "familiarization tour," and that the IAEA may have been led to a decoy site, when it thought it was investigating a facility called Ma'allem Kelayah. Nevertheless, the IAEA did not find any of the rumored facilities and IAEA spokesman David Kydd vehemently denied reports that it was led to the wrong site.[533]

Iran let a new team from the IAEA visit in October–November, 1993. This team had been given detailed briefings by the US and other Western countries, and was allowed to visit suspected buildings at three main nuclear research complexes near Tehran, Isfahan, and Karaj. Like the previous IAEA mission, however, it was a visit, not a full or special inspection mission. The IAEA was not equipped or organized to find covert Iranian activities or examine all of the activities in the research facilities it was allowed to visit. Further, the IAEA team did not have adequate access to soil and particle samples in the facilities it was allowed to visit.[534]

This debate over the value of IAEA inspections has revealed a broader problem in the Nuclear Non-Proliferation Treaty (NPT). Under the terms of the treaty, nations are entitled to import nuclear reactors and substantial amounts of nuclear technology, as long as they allow IAEA inspection of the reactors in their declared facilities. The IAEA, however, only inspects declared facilities with declared nuclear material. Any visits to other facilities do not involve the kind of intrusive inspection that can differentiate between a legitimate nuclear facility, and one dedicated to a covert weapons program. As a result, IAEA efforts to date can neither confirm nor deny the existence of an Iranian nuclear weapons program. There is also a serious debate among American experts over whether the expansion of IAEA inspection capabilities, made possible by the renewal of the NPT and improvements in IAEA inspection technology following the end of the Gulf War, will give the IAEA the ability to detect well-concealed nuclear weapons facilities. Opinions are deeply divided on this issue.

Iran has never publicly admitted to a nuclear weapons effort, has often denied that such an effort exists. Although Deputy President Ayatollah Mohajerani stated in October, 1991, that Iran should work with other Islamic states to create an "Islamic bomb," the Iranian government has denied seeking nuclear weapons and has made proposals to create a nuclear-free zone in the Middle East.[535] Senior Iranian officials—such as Reza Amrollahi, the head of the Iranian Atomic Energy Organization— have repeatedly denied Iran was seeking a bomb and have claimed Iran is fully complying with all NPT and IAEA requirements. The Iranian official news agency declared on January 8, 1995, "Iran simply does not have the ambition to become a nuclear weapons state. Iran does not, and will not, in light of its own interest, engage in a nuclear weapons program."[536]

Nevertheless, limited IAEA visits and Iranian denials do not mean that Iran does not have a clandestine nuclear program. Iran has demonstrated that it is capable of copying the sheltering and satellite deception techniques used by Iraq before the Gulf War.[537] Many Western experts believe that the fact that Iran has clandestinely sought the material needed for a nuclear weapons effort for more than a decade is more important than the ability to target given facilities. They feel that Iran has repeatedly attempted to avoid Western controls on nuclear weapons technology since 1984, and that Iran made new efforts to buy nuclear weapons related components in 1994. Further, they believe Iran has bought extensive amounts of nuclear centrifuge technology from Germany—although it has denied it doing so—and that an audit trail of Iran's purchases indicate that it has bought a great deal of the specialized gear necessary to design and manufacture nuclear weapons, and simulate nuclear tests.[538]

Possible Dates for Iran's Acquisition of Nuclear Weapons

There is also no way to estimate when Iran will get nuclear weapons. Some sources indicate that Iran may be able to build a weapon relatively quickly. Robert Gates, then Director of Central Intelligence, testified to Congress in February, 1992, that Iran was "building up its special weapons capability as part of a massive . . . effort to develop its military and defense capability."[539] In 1992 press reports by the US Central Intelligence Agency (CIA), National Intelligence Estimates (NIE) on this subject indicated that the CIA estimated Iran could have a nuclear weapon by the year 2000. Reports coming out of Israel in January 1995, also claimed that the US and Israel estimated Iran could have a nuclear weapon in five years.[540]

Other sources believe it may take Iran substantially longer to obtain nuclear weapons. US intelligence sources denied the reports coming out of Israel and estimated that it might take seven to fifteen years for Iran to acquire a nuclear weapon.[541] US Secretary of Defense William Perry stated on January 9, 1995, "We believe that Iran is trying to develop a nuclear program. We believe it will be many, many years until they achieve such a capability. There are some things they might be able to do to short-cut that time."[542]

In referring to "short cuts," Secretary Perry was concerned with the risk that Iran could obtain fissile material and weapons technology from the former Soviet Union or some other nation capable of producing fissile material. This risk creates another serious uncertainty affecting Iran's future nuclear capabilities. Reports during 1992 and 1993 that Iran had hired large numbers of Soviet nuclear scientists have proven to be unreliable.[543] Similarly, far more dramatic reports that Iran had succeeded in buying weapons-grade material from the former Soviet Union, or nuclear armed missiles from Kazakhstan are unsubstantiated.

At present, most experts feel that Iran has all the basic technology to build a bomb, but only keeps a low to moderate level weapons design and development effort.[544] They indicate that no major weapons material and production effort has yet been detected. Iran seems to be at least three to five years away from acquiring the ability to design a nuclear weapon that can be fitted in the warhead of a long range missile system, and may be five to nine years away from acquiring a nuclear device using its own enriched material.

The situation would became very different, however, if Iran could buy fissile material from another nation or source—such as the 500 kilograms of fissile material the US airlifted out of Kazakhstan in 1994.[545] If Iran could obtain weapons grade material, a number of experts believe that it could probably develop a gun or simple implosion nuclear weapon in nine to 36 months.

The risk of such a transfer of fissile material is significant. There is a growing black market in nuclear material. While the radioactive material sold on the black market by the CIS and Central European citizens to date has consisted largely of plutonium 240, low grade enriched uranium, or isotopes of material which has little value in a nuclear weapons program, this is no guarantee for the future. There are also no guarantees that Iran will not be able to purchase major transfers of nuclear weapons components and design technology.

Iran's Nuclear War Fighting Capabilities

It is possible to speculate at vast length on what Iran would do with nuclear weapons. It is almost impossible to determine, however, how aggressively Iran would exploit such a capability in terms of threatening or intimidating its neighbors, or putting pressure on the West. Trying to guess at Iran's war fighting doctrine and actions is equally speculative. It is quite possible that Iran has not yet looked beyond its acquisition efforts to work out detailed plans for possession. There is no way to know if Iran would choose a relatively stable model of deterrence or aggressively exploit its possession politically. It is equally difficult to guess whether Iran would develop an aggressive doctrine for use, consider developing a launch on warning/launch under attack capability, or reserve the use of such a weapon as a last resort.

What is clear is that if Iran acquired a working nuclear device, this would suddenly and radically change perceptions of the military balance in the region. Iran could destroy any hardened target, area target, or city within the range of its delivery systems. Iran's Southern Gulf neighbors are extremely vulnerable to attacks on a few cities, and even one successful nuclear attack might force a fundamental restructuring of their politics and/or economy. They are effectively "one bomb" countries.

Iranian nuclear capabilities would raise major mid-term and long-term challenges to the Southern Gulf states and the West in terms of deterrence, defense, retaliation, and arms control. It would almost certainly accelerate efforts to deploy theater missile defenses although such systems seem more likely to be "confidence builders" than leak proof. It would almost certainly lead the US to consider counter-proliferation strikes on Iran, and to work with its Southern Gulf allies in developing an adequate deterrent. Given the US rejection of biological and chemical weapons, this raises the possibility of creating a major US theater nuclear deterrent, although such a deterrent could be sea and air based and deployed outside the Gulf. If the US failed to provide such a deterrent, it seems likely that the Southern Gulf states would be forced to accommodate Iran or seek weapons of mass destruction of their own. Further, such Iranian possession would almost certainly trigger a major new Iraqi effort to acquire such weapons, and make any efforts at arms control meaningless for some years to come.

Weapons of Mass Destruction and Policy Implications

The complex mix of unclassified evidence and indicators available on Iran's efforts to acquire long range missiles, chemical weapons, biological weapons, and nuclear weapons does not add up to a "smoking gun" that clearly labels Iran as an aggressive power, or "proves" Iran is actively engaged in efforts that will make it a major proliferator. In fact, there is little evidence that Iran is involved in the kind of grandiose effort that Iraq indulged in before the Gulf War.

At the same time, there is little doubt that Iran's search for weapons of mass destruction is the most threatening single aspect of its behavior. The acquisition of highly lethal biological weapons, or nuclear weapons, is the one action Iran could take to threaten the present balance of deterrence in the West, by offsetting the conventional military superiority of US power projection forces and presenting a potential threat to the flow of oil exports out of the Gulf on a long-term basis.

Further, there is little reason to assume that Iran will use weapons of mass destruction to create the relatively stable balance of mutual assured destruction and highly structure deterrence that gave a great deal of stability to the nuclear arms race during the Cold War. Iran may well fail to articulate detailed war plans and employment doctrine beyond the prestige of acquiring such weapons, broad threats, and efforts to intimidate their neighbors and the West.

Like many other developing nations, Iran is unlikely to develop a strategy or doctrine that fits Western norms. Even if it appears to articulate a strategy of deterrence or employment, this strategy may often consist more of words than detailed war fighting capabilities and its crisis behavior may be very different. Iran is also nearly certain to engage in concealment, denial, and compartmentation—and focus more on the acquisition and development of weapons of mass destruction than on planning for their employment. Its targeting plans, test and evaluation methods, and understanding of weapons lethality is likely to be limited, particularly at the leadership level.

Given its past reliance on the Revolutionary Guards, Iran's forces with weapons of mass destruction are likely to be covert and compartmented from other Iranian forces, and under the direct control of ruling elites with little real military experience. They are likely to have separate lines of C^4I/BM, which report directly to the leadership. Iran's actual weapons of mass destruction may also normally be held separately from delivery systems and by special units chosen more for loyalty than capability.

Iran's employment of such weapons is unlikely to be irrational or reckless, but its restraint in attacking civilian targets or mass employment against armed forces may be limited. Iran may make carefully structured threats in a crisis, but any actual Iranian employment of such weapons is likely to be crisis driven. Iran's utilization and escalation with such weapons will be more a product of the attitudes and decisions of a narrow ruling political elite than any part of the military command chain. Its level of risk taking will often be leader-specific and based on perceptions of a crisis shaped more by internal political attitudes than an objective understanding of the military situation. An Iranian regime may also take existential risks in escalating if it feels it is likely to lose power or be defeated.

Iran will pay detailed attention to US counterproliferation and ATBM efforts at the technical level, and the lessons of previous wars. They will seek to steadily improve concealment, denial, and countermeasures. Iran can use unconventional delivery means to deliver weapons of mass destruction, and its use of proxies and unconventional delivery means may well be improvised without warning. There are many possible ways Iran can employ weapons of mass destruction, but no examination of Iranian warfighting capabilities can ignore the following issues relating to unconventional warfare or terrorism:

- Existing and projected detection and control technologies, arms control proposals, and concepts for missile defense assume that the primary threats are organized states and that relatively large weapons efforts must be used.
- Conventional structures of deterrence assume identifiable and limited sets of opponents and similar values in dealing with issues like mutual destruction. Terrorist movements may be willing to take catastrophic risks, as may leaders who identify themselves with the state and/or see martyrdom as a valid alternative to victory.
- War may not be between states or fought for limited strategic objectives. It may be a war of proxies or terrorists. It may be fought to destroy peoples or with minimal regard for collateral damage and risks.
- The target of unconventional uses of weapons of mass destruction may not be military in the normal sense of the term. It may be a peace process, US commitment to the defense of a given region, a peace keeping force, an election or ruling elite, or growing cooperation between formerly hostile groups.
- Terrorist organizations have already attempted to use crude chemical weapons. The development and use of chemical and biological weapons is well within the capability of many extremist and terrorist movements, and states can transfer weapons or aid such movements indirectly or with plausible deniability.
- Covert or unconventional delivery means may be preferable to both states and non-state organizations. Cargo ships, passenger aircraft, commercial vehicles, dhows, or commercial cargo shipments can all be used, and routed through multiple destinations. A well established series of covert transport and smuggling networks exist throughout the region. Biological weapons can be manufactured in situ.
- The Marine Corps Barracks incident has already shown the potential value of "mass terrorism," as the media impact of the Oklahoma City bombing and disruptive effect of far more limited events like the suicide bombings by Hamas and the assassination of Yitzhak Rabin demonstrate.

- Biological and chemical weapons present special problems because they can be used in so many ways. Chemical poisons were once used to contaminate the Israeli fruit crop. Infectious biological agents could be used to mirror image local diseases or with long gestation times. Persistent nerve agents could be used in subways, large buildings, shopping malls/bazaars, etc. to create both immediate casualties and long term risks. Mixes of biological and chemical agents could be used to defeat detection, protection gear or vaccines.

- Arms control efforts assume large state efforts with detectable manufacturing and weaponization programs in peacetime. The development of a capability to suddenly manufacture several hundred biological and chemical weapons with little or no warning is well within the state of the art using nothing but commercial supplies and equipment, and much of the R&D effort could be conducted as civil or defensive research.

- Unconventional and terrorist uses of weapons can involve the use of extremely high risk biological weapons transmitted by human carriers, commercial cargoes, and similar carriers.

- The incentives for the unconventional use of weapons of mass destruction increase in proportion to the lack of parity in conventional weapons, the feelings of hopelessness by alienated or extremist groups, or the prospect of catastrophic defeat.

- Similarly, the incentive for the unconventional use of weapons of mass destruction will increase in direct proportion to the perceived effectiveness of theater missile and other regular military defense systems.

- Rogue operations will be a constant temptation for state intelligence groups, militant wings of extremist groups and revolutionary forces.

Given Iran's current and projected capabilities, its efforts to acquire biological and nuclear weapons virtually forces the Southern Gulf states and the West to focus on capabilities rather than intentions. This is particularly important because Iran has already shown that it regards arms control as an extension of conflict and rivalry by other means and not as a valid security option.

Iran's behavior is also unlikely to be regime-specific as long as other Middle Eastern states continue to proliferate. Iran cannot trust its neighbors, and this means its neighbors cannot trust Iran. Further, even if the character and actions of Iran's future regime could be predicted, and a new regime was extraordinarily moderate, the US and Iran's neighbors could not avoid planning for the risk that Iranian behavior might change suddenly in the course of some coup or revolution, or as the result of a catastrophic miscalculation in the course of a crisis. "Trust" is an oxymoron in dealing with threats of this scale.

This makes an exceptionally strong case for a form of military containment that restricts transfers of weapons and technology as much as possible. While the case for political and military containment may be uncertain, it is difficult to argue that Iran has any serious need for dual use technologies. Instead, Iran has a clear priority to concentrate its resources on economic development and more cost-effective forms of power generation. There is also a significant risk that any nation that profits in the short-run from sales of related weapons and technology will pay far more in the long-run for the resulting disruption of oil exports, new conflicts in the Gulf, and/or the resulting impact on the world's economy.

14

Dealing with the Threats and Non-Threats from Iran

It is easy to generalize about Iran's future and to use strategic rhetoric to support either those who wish to "demonize" Iran, by calling it a major threat to its neighbors and the West, or those who wish to "sanctify" Iran, by claiming that it is evolving into a moderate state. The preceding analysis has shown, however, that there is no way to resolve this debate. Iran has growing capabilities to threaten its neighbors, but it is unclear that it will aggressively use such capabilities or that they will necessarily lead to war. Further, Iran has complex mix of political, economic and weaknesses and strengths.

The Future of Strategic Limitations

Iran faces serious near-term and mid-term limitations on its strategic options and the military forces it can develop. No Iranian regime can quickly overcome these limitations, regardless of its political character and intentions:

- Iran is a divided nation whose revolution has lost most of its luster. It can support Islamic movements in other state, and play a "spoiler" role throughout the region. However, Iran lacks charismatic leadership, has little ability to influence Sunni religious thinking and Shi'ite thinking outside Iran, and is perceived as "Persian" both ethnically and in terms of its strategic ambitions. Like the Soviet Union before it, it represents a powerful destabilizing force, but not a force that can hope to create client states and regimes.
- Iran has structural economic and demographic problems that will take years to correct, even if Iran can adopt far more extensive economic reforms than it has to date. It has failed to demonstrate that it can create a revolutionary economic model for other states, and it

lacks the resources to support a massive military build-up of the kind that took place under the Shah.

- Any Iranian regime is likely to import significant numbers of major weapons and improve Iranian military capabilities in the process. Iran lost some 40 to 50% of its major ground force equipment in 1988, during the final battles of the Iran-Iraq War. Its navy suffered serious losses during the "tanker war." Iran has lacked effective military resupply and modernization for its Western supplied land weapons, aircraft, and ships for more than 15 years, and maintenance standards were low and foreign contractor dependent during the time of the Shah. While Iran was able to make massive imports during the Iran-Iraq War, it not only lost much of this equipment during the fighting, but many of its imports were aging Soviet bloc systems or came from low technology suppliers like China and North Korea.
- Iran faces severe limits on its ability to modernize and expand its forces. Both the Shah and Iran's new religious regime have systematically squandered Iran's development opportunities. Its large population has meant that it is particularly hard hit by the current drop in oil prices, and Iran has only a limited capability to fund new major arms imports and modernize its forces. Regardless of the intentions of Iran's current and future regime, there are severe near-term financial limitations on its ability to fund a massive build-up of conventional capabilities of the kind that occurred under the Shah.
- Iran faces powerful strategic constraints. Its Southern Gulf neighbors are modernizing and expanding their forces at a much faster rate than Iran. In spite of currently programmed force cuts, the US retains the capability to intervene decisively in the Gulf. It can rapidly achieve naval and air supremacy, and while it cannot rapidly deploy land forces against Iran, it can carry out the kind of strategic bombing campaign it carried out against Iraq. Further, in spite of Iraq's defeat in the Gulf War, Iran is still a substantial military power and poses a potential threat to Iran.
- Geography limits Iran's military capabilities in the Gulf. Iran has very limited amphibious capabilities, and little air assault capability. Its only land route to the Southern Gulf is through Iraq, and its aircraft must fly relatively exposed routes over the Gulf to attack targets in the Southern Gulf.
- Future Iranian regimes are likely to have to continue a low level war with opponents of the regime. It is unlikely that anything other than coming to power will end the challenge the People's Mujahideen poses in terms of bombings, assassination, and attacks out of its bases in Iraq. Iran is likely to face low level military chal-

lenges from extremist ethnic movements such as the KDPI, and no regime is likely to suppress entirely internal and external violence over the issue of religion. Regardless of whether it is called terrorism, future Iranian regimes are likely to have to use their intelligence services, and their military forces to deal with opposition movements.

These constraints that make it difficult to distinguish between "aggressive" and "defensive" Iranian actions. They also make it likely that many aspects of Iran's strategic future will look much the same as its present, regardless of the character and intentions of its regime. Most types of an Iranian regime will attempt to modernize many aspects of Iran's military forces because they have no alternative—other than to see Iran's military capabilities decay relative to those of its neighbors.

At the same time, few types of future regimes will be able to transform Iran's current strategic posture and process of military modernization into regional hegemony or a massive military build-up. They will lack the resources to do so unless they can force Iran's population to make massive new economic sacrifices and are willing to further mortgage Iran's economic development opportunities. Even if a regime arises that is willing to sacrifice Iran's people, Iran will not be able to achieve strategic hegemony in the Gulf unless the US mysteriously withdraws from the region. At the same time, Iran will face significant geographic limitations on its ability to attack its neighbors.

Put differently, most types of future Iranian regimes are likely to feel that Iranian conventional military capabilities are marginal for at least the next decade. Instead of being able to create conventional forces that will give Iran hegemony in the Gulf, Iran faces a near term decline in the capability of its surface fleet, and a combination of US, other Western, and Southern Gulf capabilities that can defeat it in a matter of days. Unless Iraq remains under UN sanctions for the next five years, or there is a major change in Iraq's political character, Iran's future leaders are likely to believe that Iran continues to face the prospect of another Iran-Iraq War.

Unless UNSCOM is far more successful than it has been to date, Iran's future leaders will also believe that Iraq will recover many of its chemical and biological warfare capabilities over the next five to seven years, and some of its missile delivery capabilities. These trends may lead a variety of different types of Iranian regimes to continue to seek weapons of mass destruction, and to see nuclear weapons and long range missiles as a potential equalizer in dealing with Iraq and compensating for Iran's conventional weakness.

A Future of Strategic and Military Opportunities

The preceding analysis has also shown that there are important areas where a given Iranian regime can enhance Iran's defensive capabilities and acquire the capability to threaten and intimidate Iran's neighbors and the West:

- Iran can use unconventional warfare to attack its neighbors and the West. Regardless of whether the West chooses to call this "terrorism," Iran can conduct covert unconventional warfare against foreign officials, and use bombings and other unconventional means to attack military and civilian targets. It can also use its large Revolutionary Guards forces, particularly the naval branch of the Guards, to attack offshore oil facilities, plant mines, attack ships, or attack critical facilities like oil and gas loading ports and desalinization plants. Iran has already used such tactics during the "tanker war" of 1987–1988, and in its war against the People's Mujahideen. It may have used them—at least in proxy form— against Israel.

- Iran can use proxies to achieve its strategic objectives. It can use the training and funding of extremist or terrorist groups to attack given targets indirectly. It can also support Shi'ite movements in Bahrain and Saudi Arabia. In addition, Iran can encourage the Hezbollah in Lebanon, cooperate with the Sudan in supporting given movements, provide funds for the "Afghani" training camps and movements, and support groups like the Hamas and Islamic Jihad.

- Iran can conduct "wars" of threats and intimidation. It can use the threat of military action to influence the behavior of neighboring and Western states without escalating the issue to overt military action. It may employ these threats in an attempt to force compromises or changes in the actions of other states. Iran has already acquired many such capabilities. It has built up large unconventional warfare forces, moved anti-ship missile sites to the Straits of Hormuz, deployed submarines, and purchased smart and deep water mines. It is building a port on the Gulf of Oman, and has conducted large scale amphibious exercises. It has also strengthened its naval guards bases in the Gulf, and built up its military capabilities on Abu Musa.

- Iran can tailor its military capabilities to attack the vulnerable oil traffic through the Gulf. Rather than attempt to win a direct battle with the US Navy, Iran can develop a wide mix of capabilities for threatening or attacking tanker traffic through the Gulf—the most vulnerable link between the Gulf's economy and Western strategic interests. Once again, Iran has many such capabilities already. These include the unconventional warfare forces, anti-ship missile sites, submarines, smart and deep water mines, and naval guards bases in the Gulf described earlier.

- Iran can acquire and threaten to use, or actually use, weapons of mass destruction. Iran already has chemical weapons and used them in limited amounts during the final phases of the Iran-Iraq War. It has conducted extensive research into biological agents, and is developing nuclear capabilities. Further, Iran has Scud and Scud C missiles, and is expected to acquire a longer range system like the No Dong during the next three to five years. These weapons can partially offset Iran's limited conventional warfare capabilities—particularly if Iran can acquire and weaponize biological and nuclear weapons. They will enhance Iran's capabilities for intimidation, deterrence, and war fighting—although they can also sharply raise the level of conflict and threshold of damage to Iran.

- Iran can seek an alliance with Iraq, or attempt to divide the Southern Gulf. The military balance in the Gulf would change radically if Iran and Iraq could agree on an alliance, or if Iran could exploit religious divisions in a state like Bahrain and acquire a "base" in the Southern Gulf. There seems to be only a limited probability Iran would, or could, reach an alliance with Iraq or divide the Southern Gulf, but it is at least a strategic possibility and one Iran could explore at relatively little cost.

- Iran can attempt to exploit US vulnerabilities by trying to attack a key US facility, with the intent of inflicting high casualties—similar to the attack on the Marine Corps barracks in Beirut. It can also attempt to engage the US in costly deployments and politically complex conflicts where the US may choose not to pay the cost of prolonged engagement.

- Iran can pursue counterbalancing strategic relationships. Potential relationships could include economic and military relationships with Russia, which could ease many of the problems in Iran's military build-up and give Iran a potential counterweight to the US. Further, Iran could expand its relationship with the new Asiatic republics to the north, or make a major shift in its present policy and create stronger economic and military relations with Turkey. It could also create a strong relationship with an Asian state to acquire weapons of mass destruction, such as China, North Korea, or Pakistan.

- Iran can seek counterbalancing economic relationships. It seems doubtful that Iran will have any near or mid-term incentive to pursue common oil and economic policies with its Southern Gulf neighbors. Any probable effort to maximize Iran's oil exports and export earnings is likely to be at least partially dependent on limiting the exports of its Southern neighbors. Iran can, however, attempt to develop strong economic relations with key trading partners like Germany and Japan. Such relations would not enhance Iran's military strength, but they could undercut any international efforts aimed at containing Iran.

Few of these "opportunities" or options are mutually exclusive. Iran can exploit several of these options at the same time. It is also important to point out that none of these options require a radical change in Iran's regime. A truly radical religious regime might be isolated from options that require cooperation with other states, and counterbalancing strategic relationships, but the Rafsanjani government has already shown that a pragmatic religious regime would encounter few problems in dealing with Turkey and Russia, and might well be able to compromise with Iraq. Accordingly, either a secular or religious Iranian regime could pursue most of the strategic opportunities open to Iran.

It is again difficult to label the pursuit of some of these "opportunities" as "aggressive" or "defensive." A future Iranian regime might well see pursuing such "opportunities" as a necessary defensive measure to compensate for Iran's military problems and weakness; as a means of deterring or defending against Iraq; or as a defensive reaction to US strength in the Gulf and the build-up of Southern Gulf military forces.

Any future Iranian regime that actively pursued a wide range of such options, or which pursued any option that directly challenged another state, would obviously be more threatening than a regime that did not. At the same time, it seems doubtful that any future Iranian regime will fail to pursue at least some of these "opportunities" in the future. Further, such a regime might pursue these "opportunities" even while it attempted to establish a rapprochement with the US, Europe, and its Southern Gulf neighbors.

In fact, a somewhat more moderate Iranian regime might actually find it easier to develop Iran's military capabilities. The moment Iran ceases to attempt to export its revolution aggressively, it will be able to re-establish many of its past economic ties to Europe and Asia. It would take comparatively little political and economic change to encourage foreign investment. Recent Russian arms and nuclear reactor sales have already shown that it would take relatively little additional political change to persuade Russia to fully assist Iranian efforts to build-up its military capabilities. In many ways, Iran's current strategic problems are a self-inflicted wound. They are the legacy of Khomeini's extremism, and an erratic mix of post-Khomeini actions.

The Continuing Need for Military Containment

There is no easy way to deal with the present Iranian regime, or with the political uncertainties affecting Iran. There is no easy way transform Iran's mix of strategic strengths and weaknesses into firm conclusions about policy.

While some of Iran's actions and rhetoric have moderated since the death of Khomeini, the preceding analysis has shown that many of its actions and rhetoric remain disturbing and there is no clear political trend toward pragmatism and moderation. Iran has not been openly aggressive, but it has taken actions which threaten its Southern Gulf neighbors. Further, Iran has taken a hard-line rejectionist effort that denies Israel's right to exist, and has provided at least indirect support for Islamic extremists in the civil war in the Sudan, Algeria, and Egypt. Therefore, neither the West nor southern Gulf states have any reason to build-up Iran's forces as a counterbalance to Iraq. Regardless of the Arab proverb, the enemy of our enemy is rarely a friend.

As a result, there seems to be a clear need to maintain current efforts at military containment. Regardless of how given Western and Southern Gulf states may feel about Iranian "pragmatism," they cannot count on such "pragmatism" or "moderation." In fact, Iran's future willingness to risk intimidation and military action are likely to be heavily dependent on whether the West maintains strong power projection forces, whether the southern Gulf builds up its military capabilities and cooperation with the West, and whether continuing efforts are made to limit the more threatening aspects of Iran's military build-up.

There seems to be good reason to discourage destabilizing arms transfers to Iran, particularly modern armor, long-range attack aircraft, advanced anti-ship and surface-to-surface missiles, submarines, and amphibious ships. There are also good reasons to control "dual-use" technology transfers to Iran. Regardless of any safeguards short of constant inspection, all dual-use technology may be put to military use whenever this is to Iran's advantage. This guarantees that virtually every item of nuclear, chemical, biological, and aerospace technology that Iran can use in advancing its acquisition of weapons of mass destruction will be put to that use.

The West and the southern Gulf need to recognize that improved economic ties, arms control, and controls on technology transfer are not a substitute for power projection and war fighting capabilities. Such measures cannot prevent Iran from building up its conventional forces, or improving its capabilities to use weapons of mass destruction. Iran already has chemical weapons and will probably succeed in weaponizing highly lethal biological weapons. It may succeed in acquiring a nuclear device. The West and southern Gulf should do what they can to keep Iran's policies pragmatic and encourage the development of a moderate Iran. But, they must also be ready to use conventional military force, improve their defenses against weapons of mass destruction, and develop their capabilities to preempt and retaliate.

At the same time, such military containment requires the US to do far more to establish its credibility in describing the Iranian threat. It has failed to provide the kind of detailed unclassified discussion of Iran's military modernization, actions, and efforts to acquire weapons of mass destruction that made US claims regarding the Soviet and Warsaw Pact build-up convincing. It has often used rhetoric as a substitute for substance, and it has been careless and vague it discussing Iran's role in terrorism and the support of extremist movements and the role of Iran's top leadership in such efforts.

Discussions with Gulf, European, and Russian officials also indicate that even classified US briefing tend to use sweeping rhetoric, fail to provide suitable back up data, and fail to convince their audience. Containment cannot succeed without credibility and the US is the only nation with the intelligence and analytic resources to make the case for military containment in a detailed and objective form. Providing an annual white paper, similar to the document "Soviet Military Power," might be one such solution to this problem.

"Dual Containment" Versus "Constructive Engagement"

At the same time, military containment is very different from the present US policy of dual containment, and the threat from Iran must be kept in careful perspective. Military capabilities are only threats to the extent states use them in a hostile manner. Iran still has a hostile ideology and regional ambitions, but this does not mean Iran will always act on its ideology and ambitions or use force to do so. Further, Iran does have legitimate defense needs in its attempt to deal with threats like Iran, and every new military development in Iran cannot be seen as threatening to the Southern Gulf states, moderate Arab states, Israel, and the West.

It is dangerous to transform a clear strategic interest in the military containment of Iran into a rigid and much more dubious effort to isolate Iran, cut off political and cultural dialogue, and halt all outside economic ties and investment. The fact that Iran is a potential threat does not justify "demonization." Iran has neither exploited every opportunity to take aggressive action nor maintained constant pressure on its neighbors and the West. Iran is not a strong or wealthy power. It has serious military weaknesses as well as serious limited access to advanced weapons and military technologies. Iran faces a serious economic crisis, and has serious internal divisions and popular unrest. Iran may become a worse threat over time, but Iranian regimes and ruling elites may also find it in their interest to act in more pragmatic ways.

There are other reasons to question whether it is prudent for the US or its allies to attempt to politically and economically isolate Iran.

- First, it is far from clear that such a strategy of isolation is practical. There is little reason to assume that most states in the region, the West, and Asia will support such US policies. If anything, such policies may isolate the US or divide it from the rest of the West and the Arab world—particularly if the US tries to enforce its policies through trade legislation and sanctions on nations and companies that trade or invest in Iran. An extreme approach to containment may discredit US warnings about the military threat from Iran, and prevent the US from obtaining international support for the military containment which should be a lasting aspect of Western and regional policy.
- Second, such a strategy of isolation seems more likely to lock Iran into a pattern of hostility than to moderate its conduct. At best, the political and economic isolation of Iran may threaten its economic development and ability to act as a major oil and gas producer. At worst, it is highly unlikely to change the character and conduct of the Iranian regime. US attempts to isolate Iran politically and economically may end in alienating Iran's people in ways that breed a kind of resentment and revanchism which outlives its current ruling elite or driving it into some kind of limited alliance with Iraq.
- Third, it leaves the US with no clear way to respond to any signals from the Iranian leadership. Rafsanjani responded to the Clinton Administration's new sanctions by stating, "The embargo has deprived Americans of the benefits that cooperation could bring (which) have been good to other countries. . . . Relations with the US have worsened; I do not see any bright horizon in our relations."[546] It may be that Iran never sought better relations, but only the technology and investment necessary to increase oil and gas production and ease its economic crisis. At the same time, denying the possibility of dialogue and better relations tends to be a self-fulfilling prophecy.

A strategy of constructive political and economic engagement—that emphasizes the search for dialogue without concessions—seems more likely to enhance regional stability than the present US interpretation of "dual containment." Such a "constructive engagement" strategy would offer a greater chance of consensus between the US and its allies while allowing for the fact that Europe and the Gulf states already have adopted many aspects of this policy. It would focus on a step by step improvement in political relations, and increased international acceptance, in return for less hostile Iranian behavior, an end to terrorism and support of violent extremist movements, acceptance of the Arab-Israeli peace process, better protection of internal human rights and ethnic groups, and meaningful arms control agreements.

Such a strategy would not mean abandoning efforts at military containment, but it would mean adopting economic policies that recognize Iran's strategic importance as an oil exporter. It would recognize that denying Iran the resources it needs to expand its mid and long term export capability will encourage Iranian extremism and limit the contribution it can make to the rising world demand for oil exports.

Constructive engagement would combined "carrots" with "sticks" in ways which focused on limiting Iran's military building and ability to deploy weapons of mass destruction, rather than attempt to punish the Iranian people with unfocused sanctions. Like the normalization of relations, however, any economic "carrots" that the US and its allies would provide would not include concessions. Instead, they would trade step by step increases in opportunities for trade, investment, and loans for clearly defined improvements in Iran's behavior.

The Limits of "Constructive Engagement"

There are, however, significant caveats that must be applied to the adoption of a strategy of "constructive engagement." Such a strategy must be founded on the understanding that Iran poses very real threats, and that support of "military containment" is an essential aspect of such a strategy. There must be a similar understanding that "constructive engagement" does not mean that Iran should be treated as a "moderate state," and that the US should tie every improvement in political and economic relations to clearly defined changes in Iran's policies and actions.

Nothing about Iran indicates that it is "misunderstood," or that the problems its poses can be overcome simply by tolerance or concessions. Most important, a strategy of "constructive engagement" may fail or take years to be effective. Such a strategy will only be as successful as Iran will allow it to be. Its success depends on the conduct of the Iranian regime at a time when Iran is in the midst of internal political changes that are only partially subject to outside influence. No policy adopted by outside states can offer a firm assurance that it will shape Iran's future actions.

The key reason for pursuing "constructive engagement" is that policy must have an endgame. Hostile regimes not only need to be contained, they need to be encouraged to change. "Dual containment" has no endgame other than a blind hope that the US can persuade its allies to join it in a policy of isolating Iran, and that this will lead to political upheavals that will somehow produce a moderate regime. The US and the West never attempted such a strategy of isolation in dealing with the Soviet Union and Warsaw Pact—even during the height of the Cold War. Instead, the West mixed military containment with efforts at engagement and détente.

Further, if the US aggressively and publicly sought "constructive engagement," and clearly defined its conditions for improving relations with Iran, it would strengthen any forces for pragmatism and moderation in Iran, defuse much of the foreign criticism of US policy, and place the burden for change solidly on the Iranian government. Even if the US effort did not succeed, it would have a more beneficial policy impact than pushing dual containment to extremes.

The Other Key Elements of
an Effective Policy Towards Iran

There are three other important conclusions for policy making that emerge from this analysis of security developments in Iran:

- *Arms control:* There is little near term prospect that Iran will abide by arms control agreements, rather than attempt to exploit the weaknesses in these agreements, effectively bypassing them, or simply cheat. This does not mean that arms control should not be pursued, or that arrangements affecting suppliers will not be effective. It does mean that arms control agreements with gaps and without provisions for constant intrusive challenge inspections are likely to be ineffective, or be treated as little more than scraps of paper.
- *Collective security:* The Southern Gulf states, and other states in the region, need to do everything possible to enhance collective security, and need Western support in achieving these goals. Particular emphasis needs to be placed on collective air defense, wide areas theater missile defense, maritime and coastal surveillance and defense, anti-infiltration and anti-terrorist defense, mine warfare defense, and defense of tankers, oil facilities, pipelines, desalinization plants, power plants, and other critical facilities.
- *Western power projection:* The West, and particularly the United States, must keep a strong deterrent military presence in the region. The United States and its allies must be able to project power rapidly

to win decisive sea control and air supremacy in the face of an Iranian attack on any Southern Gulf state or maritime traffic in the Gulf, and develop the prepositioning and rapid deployment capability to defeat any Iraqi attack on Kuwait and Saudi Arabia and Iranian heliborne or amphibious threat. The West must also develop a mid term capability to assist the Southern Gulf states in missile and CBW defense, to fight in a chemical and biological warfare environment, to carry out counter-proliferation attacks, and to deter any Iranian and Iraqi effort to exploit the acquisition of nuclear weapons with the threat of Western conventional and nuclear retaliation.

All of these conclusions are reinforced by the fact that Iraq poses a threat to the Gulf as well as Iran, and by the need to develop a strategy that deals with the threat from both states. It is important to note that while the US may have exaggerated the scope of "dual containment," the need to contain both Iran and Iraq is very real. So is the need for collective action and realism in dealing with the regimes of both nations. In this sense, the "sanctification" of such ruling elites is likely to prove even more dangerous than their "demonization."

Notes

Chapter 1

1. Anthony Lake, "Confronting Backlash States," *Foreign Affairs*, March/April, 1994, computer version.

2. Anthony Lake, "Confronting Backlash States," *Foreign Affairs*, March/April, 1994, computer version.

3. Anthony Lake, "Confronting Backlash States," *Foreign Affairs*, March/April, 1994, computer version.

4. White House Internet data base, December 22, 1995; *Washington Times*, December 21, 1995, p. A-15.

5. *Washington Post*, December 22, 1995, p. A-21, Reuters, January 4, 1996, 0801; *New York Times*, January 26, 1996; *Washington Times*, December 27, 1995, p. A-10.

6. Anthony Lake, "Confronting Backlash States," *Foreign Affairs*, March/April, 1994, computer version.

7. For a detailed chronology of events, see Kenneth Katzman, "Iran and Iraq: US National Security Problems Since the Gulf War—A Chronology: July 1993–July 1994," Congressional Research Service 94-561F, July 12, 1994.

8. Robert H. Pelletreau, Assistant Secretary for Near Eastern Affairs, Department of State, testimony before the Senate Foreign Relations Committee Subcommittee on Near Eastern and South Asian Affairs, March 2, 1995.

9. Secretary William J. Perry, "Working With Gulf Allies to Contain Iraq and Iran," *Defense Issues*, Volume 10, No. 61.

10. *Washington Post*, May 1, 1995, p. A-1, May 2, 1995, p. A-14; June 9, 1995, p. A-18; *Washington Times*, May 4, 1995, p. A-19; *New York Times*, May 1, 1995, p. A-1, May 2, 1995, p. D-5

11. *Wall Street Journal*, December 12, 1995, p. A-16; *New York Times*, December 11, 1995, p. D-1, Associated Press, December 21, 1701; *Washington Post*, December 13, 1995, p. A-34, December 22, 1995, p. A-21.

12. *New York Times*, December 11, 1995, p. D-1, December 13, 1995, p. D-1, Associated Press, December 21, 1995, 1701; *Washington Post*, December 13, 1995, p. A-34.

13. Reuters, December 28, 1995, 0838, January 4, 1996, 0801; *New York Times*, January 26, 1996, p. A-8; *Washington Times*, December 27, 1995, p. A-10; Reuters, November 11, 1995, 0518.

14. *Reuters*, August 5, 1996.

15. Vahe Petrosian, "Europe, US lock horns over Iran and Libya," *Middle East Economic Digest*, August 9, 1996, p. 9.

16. *The Guardian*, August 24, 1996, p. 16.

17. *The Guardian,* August 24, 1996, p. 16; *Middle East Economic Digest,* August 9, 1996, p. 9.

18. Quoted in *The Guardian,* August 24, 1996, p. 16.

19. On the significance of Erbakan's visit to Tehran see *Financial Times,* August 9, 1996, p. 4.

20. *Reuters,* August 12, 1996.

21. *The Guardian,* August 24, 1996, p. 16.

22. Reuters, February 17, 1996, 1105, March 5, 1996, 1224, March 7, 1996, 1231.

23. *New York Times,* February 23, 1995, p. 8.

24. *Washington Times,* February 23, 1995, p. 3.

25. James Moore, *The Middle East and North Africa: Review of the Regional Security Environment 1994–1995,* Ottawa: Department of National Defence: Directorate of Strategic Analysis, Research Note No. 95/11, p. 16.

26. *Foreign Broadcasting Information Service, Central Eurasia* (henceforth *FBIS-SOV*), September 28, 1994, p. 14.

27. *Washington Post,* March 24, 1995, p. 28.

28. *FBIS-SOV,* February 15, 1995, pp. 8–9.

29. *FBIS-SOV,* June 29, 1995, p. 6.

30. *FBIS-SOV,* April 17, 1995, p. 8.

31. James Moore, *The Middle East and North Africa,* p. 16.

32. *The Reuters European Business Report,* May 8, 1994.

33. *Near East Report,* vol. XL, no. 5, February 26, 1996, p. 1, 19.

34. *Jane's Defence Weekly,* May 20, 1995, p. 6.

35. "EU's critical dialogue hits rocky path," *Iran Focus,* April, 1996, pp. 13–14.

36. Quoted in *FBIS-NES,* November 17, 1995, p. 49.

37. Marjane Saidi, "Elles sont venues, elles sont toutes la . . . " *Arabies,* February 1996, p. 40.

38. IMF Report SM/95/240, *Islamic Republic of Iran—Recent Economic Developments,* September, 19, 1995, Appendix V, Table 55.

39. *Le Monde,* December 31, 1995–January 1, 1996, p. 2.

40. Marjane Saidi, "Elles sont venues, elles sont toutes la . . ." p. 40.

41. *Reuters,* July 27, 1995.

42. Joseph Schechla, "Minding Their Own Business: Germany's Policy toward Iran," *US-Iran Review,* vol. 2, no. 1, January 1994, p. 6.

43. IMF Report SM/95/240, *Islamic Republic of Iran—Recent Economic Developments,* September, 19, 1995, Appendix V, Table 55.

44. FBIS-NES-95-062, March 31, 1995, pp. 53–57; *New York Times,* March 8, 1996, p. A-8, March 23, 1996, p. A-5; Associated Press, March 16, 1996.

45. *Christian Science Monitor,* March 16, 1995, p. 7.

46. *Financial Times,* March 8, 1996, p. 4.

47. "EU's critical dialogue hits rocky patch," p. 13.

48. IMF Report SM/95/240, *Islamic Republic of Iran—Recent Economic Developments,* September, 19, 1995, Appendix V, Table 55.

49. *New York Times,* May 2, 1995, p. D5.

50. Ryoji Tateyama, "Japan, Iran and the United States: A Delicate Triangular Relationship in the 90s," *US-Iran Review,* vol. 2, no. 1, January 1994, pp. 1–5.

51. *Chicago Tribune*, Masy 19, 1996, p. I-4.

52. *FBIS-NES*, January 19, 1996, p. 61.

53. *FBIS-NES*, January 19, 1996, p. 61.

Chapter 2

54. Reuters, August 2, 1995, 1452.

55. Quoted in *Financial Times*, March 6, 1990, p.4.

56. For an excellent analysis of the manipulation of the election of the Majlis see David Menashri, "The Domestic Power Struggle in the Fourth Iranian Majlis Elections," *Orient*, Vol. 33, No. 3. 1992, pp. 387–408. For related reporting on the role of senior leaders see *New York Times*, March 24, 1992, p. A-8, May 10, 1992, p. A-15; *Washington Post*, April 14, 1992, p. A-16, April 18, 1992, pp. A-14 & A-20; *Washington Times*, April 15, 1992, p. A-1, May 18, 1992, p. E-4; *Wall Street Journal*, April 16, 1992, p. A-18; Dr. Anoushiravan Ehteshami, "The Armed Forces of the Islamic Republic of Iran," *Jane's Intelligence Review*, February, 1993, pp. 76–79; *US News and World Report*, November 23, 1993, pp. 51–53; *Washington Post*, February 12, 1993, p. A-29; *The Middle East*, March, 1993, pp. 13–15.

57. IMF, *Financial Statistics*, IEA, *Middle East Oil and Gas*, p. 241.

58. For details see Ahmed Hashim, *The Crisis of the Iranian State: Domestic, Security, and Foreign Policies in post-Khomeini Iran*, Adelphi Paper No. 296, IISS, London, Oxford University press, 1995, pp. 10–21.

59. See International Energy Agency (IEA) *Middle East Oil and Gas*, Paris, 1995, pp. 241–242, and OECD, *Financing and External Debt of Developing Countries*, (debt and debt service data).

60. *Wall Street Journal*, June 7, 1993, p. A-10; *Christian Science Monitor*, August 12, 1993, p. 9; CIA, *World Factbook, 1994* "Iran"; CIA, *World Factbook, 1995*, "Iran."

61. CIA, *World Factbook, 1995*, "Iran."

62. This, however, only amounts to about 1,362 cubic meters per person, less than half the total for a citizen of the US, *Los Angeles Times*, January 28, 1992, p. C-1.

63. Eliahu Kanovsky, *The Economy of Iran: Past, Present, and Future*, System Planning Corporation, Arlington Virginia, Final Report SPC 1415, April 1992, p. 28.

64. Kaveh Ehsani, "Tilt but don't spill": Iran's Development and Reconstruction Dilemma," *Middle East Report*, November-December 1994, p. 19.

65. *Middle East Economic Digest*, November 5, 1993.

66. Petroleum Economist, Petroleum Finance Company, and Congressional Quarterly, *The Middle East, 7th Edition*, Washington, Congressional Quarterly, 1990, p. 195.

67. Much of this discussion of Iran's current politics and economics is based on discussions, working papers, and interviews during the American Academy for the Advancement of Science's conference on developments in the Middle East, held in Barcelona during October 27-November 1, 1993. Also see *Wall Street Journal*, November 25, 1992, p. A-1, and Paul Stevens, *Oil and Politics: The Post-War Gulf*, London, Royal Institute of International Affairs, 1992; *Christian Science Monitor*, June 22, 1993, p. 18.

68. *Wall Street Journal*, June 7, 1993, p. 10.

69. *Wall Street Journal*, June 7, 1993, p. A-10; *Christian Science Monitor*, August 12, 1993, p. 9.

70. As defined by Felix Rohatyn, 'World Capital: The Need and the Risks,' *The New York Review of Books*, July 14, 1994, p. 49.

71. See Margie Lindsay, "Iran: Reasons to Reform," *World Link*, May-June 1995, pp. 56–57.

72. See *Gulf States Newsletter*, no. 414, 1 July 1991, p. 9.

73. *Middle East Economic Digest*, January 26, 1996, pp. 2–3, January 19, 1996, pp. 21–22, February 16, 1996, p. 22.

74. *Middle East Economic Digest*, January 26, 1996, pp. 2–3, January 19, 1996, pp. 21–22, February 16, 1996, p. 22.

75. *Middle East Economic Digest*, August 12, 1995, February 16, 1996, p. 22.

76. *Middle East Economic Digest*, January 26, 1996, pp. 2–3, January 19, 1996, pp. 21–22, February 16, 1996, p. 22.

77. *Middle East Economic Digest*, May 3, 1996, p. 20.

78. *Middle East Economic Digest*, January 26, 1996, p. 3.

79. Some estimates put Iran's 1991 oil revenues at about $15 billion and its domestic spending needs at $15 billion. Economist Intelligence Unit, *Country Report on Iran, 1993*; *New York Times*, February 11, 1992, p. A-11; *Defense News*, March 2, 1992, p. 3 and 29; *Washington Post*, September 10, 1991, p. A-21, February 2, 1992, p. A-1; *Wall Street Journal*, September 16, 1991, p. A-1; *Washington Times*, April 29, 1989, p. A-9; *Jane's Defense Weekly*, June 17, 1989, pp. 1254–1255; *Los Angeles Times*, January 13, 1992, p. A9.

80. See *British Broadcasting Corporation, Summary of World Broadcasts*, MEW/0330, 26 April 1994, WME/2–WME/6.

81. *British Broadcasting Corporation, Summary of World Broadcasts*, August 27, 1994, ME/2085 S1/11.

82. See *Middle East Economic Digest*, 30 September 1994, p. 12.

83. *The Echo of Iran*, no. 69, November 1993, p. 13.

84. *Middle East Economic Digest*, December 22, 1995, January 26, 1996, February 2, 1996, p. 20.

85. *New York Times*, November 7, 1992, p. A-1; Colin Barrclough, "The Mullah's Money Machine," *Institutional Investor*, March, 1995, pp. 70–73.

86. *Philadelphia Inquirer*, June 28, 1991, p. 8.

87. Michel Malinsky, "L'Iran et ses defis: les poids de l'economie et du social," *Defense Nationale*, January 1995, p. 95.

88. *Washington Times*, August 31, 1993, p. A-7; *New York Times*, May 28, 1993, p. A-8, June 11, 1993, p. A-3; June 14, 1993, p. A-8, August 30, 1993, p. A-3; *Christian Science Monitor*, June 11, 1993, p. 8; *Washington Post*, June 14, 1993, p. A-30; *Defense and Foreign Affairs*, June 1993, p. 20.

89. *New York Times*, August 17, 1993, P. A-8; *Washington Times*, August 11, 1993, p. A-7.

90. Economist Intelligence Unit, *Country Report for Iran, 3rd Quarter 1994*, pp. 7–8.

91. US State Department, *Country Reports on Human Rights Practices, 1994*, online Internet edition, June 24, 1995.

92. *Middle East International,* September 9, 1994, p. 14.

93. *The Economist,* August 27, 1994, p. 44.

94. *Al Majallah,* April 16–22, 1995, pp. 6–7.

95. Cited in *Middle East International,* June 23, 1995, pp. 12–13.

96. Executive News Service, September 29, 1995, 0503; *Jane's Intelligence Review,* October, 1995, pp. 446–453.

97. *Jane's Intelligence Review,* October, 1995, pp. 446–453.

98. US imported rose by $223 million, or 77%, over the previous 6 months as importers rushed to acquire US goods before the sanctions became effective. *Middle East Economic Digest,* September 29, 1995, p. 18.

99. For succinct analyses of the origins of and problems posed by Ayatollah Khomeini's theory of government, see in particular, Shireen Hunter, *Iran After Khomeini,* pp. 14–28; Shaul Bakhash, 'Iran: The Crisis of Legitimacy.

100. For more details on the powers of the Supreme Leader see Anoushiravan Ehteshami, *After Khomeini: The Iranian Second Republic,* London: Routledge, 1995, pp. 48–51; and J. Behrouz, "Imam Khomeini's predictions on post-Khomeini Iran," *The Echo of Iran,* September 1989, pp. 14–18; Silvia Tellenbach, "Zur Anderung der Verfassung der Islamischen Republik Iran vom 28. Juli 1989," *Orient,* vol. 31, no. 1, 1990, pp. 47–54.

101. See "The economic role of the Bonyad Mostazafan," *Iran Focus,* July-August 1995, pp. 8–9.

102. The most detailed analysis of the constitutional reforms of 1989 is to be found in Ralph Kauz, *Die Verfassungsanderung in Iran: Eine chance fur Stabilitat,* Ebenhausen: Stiftung Wissenschaft und Politik, Forshungsinstitut fur Internationale Politik und Sicherheit, November 1990.

103. Amir Taheri, 'Téhéran: Le Thermidor avorté,' *Politique Internationale,* no. 64, Summer 1994, p. 147.

104. See *BBC, Summary of World Broadcasts,* ME/1898, 18 January 1994, p. MED/11.

105. 'Iran: La faction radicale aux commandes,' *Arabies,* no. 87, March 1994, p. 7.

106. *Middle East Monitor,* February 1994, p. 11.

107. Cited in *The Echo of Iran,* August-September 1990, p. 8.

108. For more extensive data see "Iranians polled on the woes of their country," *Iran Focus,* January 1996, p. 9.

109. *New York Times,* February 12, 1995, p. 14.

110. BBC, *Summary of World Broadcasts,* ME/1643, 22 March 1993, p. A-1.

111. "Political factions within the clergy," *Iran Focus,* February 1996, p. 9.

112. *Financial Times,* February 28, 1996, p. 4.

113. *Middle East Economic Digest,* February 2, 1996, p. 20; Reuters, January 10, 1996, 1316; United Press January 30, 1996, 1442.

114. Rainer Hermann, "Von der Wirtschaft-zur Legitimationskrise: Die Ara Khamenei/Rafsanjani in der Islamischen Republik Iran," *Orient,* no. 4, vol. 35, 1994, p. 549.

115. *FBIS-NES,* July 12, 1995, p. 69.

116. "Political factions in the clergy," *Iran Focus,* February 1996, pp. 9–11.

117. *Associated Press,* March 5, 1996.

118. They were contesting the elections as individuals. *The Financial Times*, March 4, 1996, p. 6.

119. "Results prove a blow to the right wing," *Iran Focus*, April 1996, p. 8.

120. *Washington Times*, May 20, 1996, p. A-1.

121. *Iran Focus*, May 1996, p. 8.

122. *Iran Focus*, May 1996, p. 8.

123. *Iran Times*, April 26, 1996, p. 1.

124. *Iran Focus*, May 1996, p. 8.

125. *Baltimore Sun*, May 2, 1996, p. 22.

126. *Gulf Times*, June 2, 1996.

127. See the interview with Ata'ollah Mohajerani in *Al Majallah*, 6 November 1994, p. 30.

128. For more extensive details on this wide-ranging political debate within Iranian intellectual, clerical, and official circles as well as the emerging changes in political thought, see *Christian Science Monitor*, March 17, 1995, p. 1, 7; April 5, 1995, p. 1, 7; April 12, 1995, p. 6; April 20, 1995, p. 6; Fariba Adelkhah, "L'offensive des intellectuels en Iran," *Le Monde Diplomatique*, January 1995, p. 20; Ali Banuazizi, "Iran's Revolutionary Impasse: Political Factionalism and Societal Resistance," *Middle East Report*, November-December 1994, pp. 2–8; "Secular movements gain ground," *Iran Focus*, May 1995, p. 8; 'Rafsanjani stresses need for political parties," *Iran Focus*, December 1995, p. 9; *New York Times*, May 30, 1995, p. A1; *Los Angeles Times*, December 31, 1995, p. M2.

129. For extensive analyses of these issues see Lamis Andoni, "Winds of Change in Iran," *Middle East International*, May 12, 1995, pp. 20–21; Eric Rouleau, "La Republique islamique d'Iran confrontee a la societe civile," *Le Monde Diplomatique*, June 1995, p. 12; Shaul Bakhash, "Prisoners of the Ayatollah," *The New York Review of Books*, August 11, 1994, pp. 42–45.

130. See "Iran: An economy in disarray," *The Middle East*, December 1994, pp. 28–29.

131. See *Iran, Economist Intelligence Unit*, 2nd Quarter, 1995, pp. 5–6.

132. On the powerful role of the bazaar in Iranian politics and commerce see Marjane Saidi, "Iran: Bazar . . . Vous avez dit bazar?" *Arabies*, nos. 103–104, July-August 1995, pp. 38–47.

133. See Homa Omid (pseud.), *Islam and the Post-Revolutionary State in Iran*, New York: St. Martin's Press, 1994, pp. 98–99

Chapter 3

134. *Wall Street Journal*, December 7, 1994, p. 10; *Los Angeles Times*, December 13, 1994, pp. C1, C5; *New York Times*, November 28, 1994, p. A-5.

135. *New York Times*, December 11, 1994

136. *Wall Street Journal*, December 7, 1994, p. 10.

137. *Philadelphia Inquirer*, January 11, 1995, p. A-6.

138. Amnesty International, *Report, 1994*, New York, Amnesty International, 1994, pp. 163–166; US State Department, *Country Reports on Human Rights Practices for 1994*, Internet Edition, June 24, 1995.

139. Excerpted from US State Department, *Country Reports on Human Rights Practices for 1994*, Internet Edition, June 24, 1995.

140. *Washington Times*, May 18, 1996, p. B-8.

141. *Chicago Tribune*, May 19, 1996, p. I-4.

142. This description of the Iranian court system and legal procedures is adapted from the description in the US State Department, *Country Reports on Human Rights Practices for 1994*, Internet Edition, June 24, 1995, and Amnesty International, *Report, 1994*, New York, Amnesty International, 1994, pp. 163–166.

143. This description is adapted from the text in the US State Department, *Country Reports on Human Rights Practices for 1994*, Internet Edition, June 24, 1995.

144. This description is adapted from the text in the US State Department, *Country Reports on Human Rights Practices for 1994*, Internet Edition, June 24, 1995.

145. This description is adapted from the text in the US State Department, *Country Reports on Human Rights Practices for 1994*, Internet Edition, June 24, 1995.

146. This description is adapted from the text in the US State Department, *Country Reports on Human Rights Practices for 1994*, Internet Edition, June 24, 1995.

147. This description is adapted from the text in the US State Department, *Country Reports on Human Rights Practices for 1994*, Internet Edition, June 24, 1995.

148. This description of the Iranian court system and legal procedures is adapted from the description in the US State Department, *Country Reports on Human Rights Practices for 1994*, Internet Edition, June 24, 1995, and Amnesty International, *Report, 1994*, New York, Amnesty International, 1994, pp. 163–166.

149. This description is adapted from the text in the US State Department, *Country Reports on Human Rights Practices for 1994*, Internet Edition, June 24, 1995.

Chapter 4

150. *Al Majallah*, November 6, 1994, pp. 26–28; IISS, *Military Balance, 1994–1995*, pp. 127–129; CIA, *World Factbook, 1995*, "Iran."

151. International Energy Agency (IEA) *Middle East Oil and Gas*, Paris, 1995, pp. 227–228, IMF, *International Financial Statistics*, and OECD, *Main Economic Indicators*.

152. ACDA, *World Military Expenditures and Arms Transfers, 1993–1994*, Washington, ACDA, 1995 and material provided by the CIA

153. *Los Angeles Times*, December 2, 1994, p. A-1.

154. Assad Homayoun, "Assessing the Islamic Republic," *Global Affairs*, vol. 8, Spring 1993, pp. 71–82.

155. See *Jane's Intelligence Review, Pointer, June*, 1996, p. 7.

156. *Middle East Economic Digest*, July 28, 1995, p. 11; *CIA World Factbook*, 1995, "Iran."

157. *Middle East Economic Digest*, July 28, 1995, p. 11; *CIA World Factbook*, 1995, "Iran."

158. World Bank, *World Population Projections, 1994–1995*, Washington, World Bank, 1994; *Middle East Economic Digest*, July 28, 1995, p. 11; *CIA World Factbook*, 1995, "Iran."

159. Based on CIA estimates. Sources disagree sharply on the exact percentages involved.

Chapter 5

160. International Energy Agency, *Middle East Oil and Gas*, Paris, IEA/OECD, 1995, pp. 117–118.

161. The high US estimate is by James Placke, Cambridge Associates, October 29, 1993; other estimates indicate that Iran has only 63 billion barrels of proven reserves and 52 billion barrels of probable reserves. See Joseph P. Riva, Jr. of the Congressional Research Service, writing in the *Oil and Gas Journal*, September 23, 1991, p. 62; *Wall Street Journal*, November 25, 1992, p. A-1; Paul Stevens, *Oil and Politics: The Post-War Gulf*, London, Royal Institute of International Affairs, 1992; *Christian Science Monitor*, June 22, 1993, p. 18.

162. Adapted from the material in the DOE/EIA Internet data base, analysis section, country chapters, as accessed on July 15, 1995, and *Middle East Economic Digest*, July 21, 1995, pp. 26–32.

163. International Energy Agency (IEA) *Middle East Oil and Gas*, Paris, 1995, pp. 117–122, 232–236

164. International Energy Agency (IEA) *Middle East Oil and Gas*, Paris, 1995, pp. 117–122, 232–236.

165. Energy Information Agency, *International Energy Outlook, 1995*, Washington, Department of Energy DOE/EIA-0484(95), June, 1995, pp. 29 and EIA Internet on-line data base, analysis section, accessed July 28, 1995.

166. International Energy Agency (IEA) *Middle East Oil and Gas*, Paris, EIA/OECD, 1995, pp. 232–236.

167. International Energy Agency (IEA) *Middle East Oil and Gas*, Paris, EIA/OECD, 1995, pp. 232–236.

168. International Energy Agency (IEA) *Middle East Oil and Gas*, Paris, EIA/OECD, 1995, p. 128.

169. International Energy Agency (IEA) *Middle East Oil and Gas*, Paris, EIA/OECD, 1995, pp. 232–237, and OPEC, *Annual Statistical Bulletin*, OECD, *Main Economic Indicators*, IMF, *International Financial Statistics*.

170. *Middle East Economic Digest*, July 21, 1995, pp. 26–32; International Energy Agency (IEA) *Middle East Oil and Gas*, Paris, EIA/OECD, 1995, pp. 120–121.

171. Adapted from the material in the DOE/EIA Internet data base, analysis section, country chapters, as accessed on July 15, 1995; and the discussion in *Middle East Economic Digest*, July 21, 1995, pp. 26–32.

172. International Energy Agency (IEA) *Middle East Oil and Gas*, Paris, EIA/OECD, 1995, pp. 121–123.

173. Adapted from the material in the DOE/EIA Internet data base, analysis section, country chapters, as accessed on July 15, 1995.

174. Reuters, July 20, 1995, 1412; *Middle East Economic Digest*, July 21, 1995, pp. 26–32.

175. International Energy Agency (IEA) *Middle East Oil and Gas*, Paris, EIA/OECD, 1995, pp. 128.

176. Energy Information Agency, *Monthly Energy Review*, December, 1995, p. 48.

177. Adapted from the material in the DOE/EIA Internet data base, analysis section, country chapters, as accessed on July 15, 1995.

178. East-West Center, *Energy Advisory*, Number 143, February 28, 1995; *New York Times*, June 21, 1995, p. A-6; Reuters, July 10, 1995, 0355, July 25, 1995, 0502.

179. Based on working data provided by the IEA, *Jane's Intelligence Review*, January, 1996, p. 8; *Jane's Defense Weekly*, January 3, 1996, p. 4.

180. Based on conversations with IEA experts and the discussions in *Middle East Economic Digest*, July 21, 1995, pp. 26–32, January 19, 1996, pp. 9–10, and January 26, 1996, pp. 2–3.

181. Reporting by Bank Markazi; *Middle East Economic Digest*, January 19, 1996, p. 21.

182. Adapted from the material in the DOE/EIA Internet data base, analysis section, country chapters, as accessed on July 15, 1995; and the discussion in *Middle East Economic Digest*, July 21, 1995, pp. 26–32

183. Adapted from the material in the DOE/EIA Internet data base, analysis section, country chapters, as accessed on July 15, 1995.

184. Adapted from the material in the DOE/EIA Internet data base, analysis section, country chapters, as accessed on July 15, 1995; and the discussion in *Middle East Economic Digest*, July 21, 1995, pp. 26–32.

185. Adapted from the material in the DOE/EIA Internet data base, analysis section, country chapters, as accessed on July 15, 1995.

186. Adapted from the material in the DOE/EIA Internet data base, analysis section, country chapters, as accessed on July 15, 1995.

187. Adapted from the material in the DOE/EIA Internet data base, analysis section, country chapters, as accessed on July 15, 1995 and March 14, 1996.

188. Adapted from the material in the DOE/EIA Internet data base, analysis section, country chapters, as accessed on July 15, 1995; and the discussion in *Middle East Economic Digest*, July 21, 1995, pp. 26–32.

189. US protests had no effect. Reuters, July 14, 1995, 1452.

190. Reuters, July 13, 1995, 1414; *Wall Street Journal*, July 14, 1994, p. A-8.

191. Reuters, July 17, 1995, 0632, November 7, 1995, 0749; *Middle East Economic Digest*, January 26, 1996, pp. 2–3, February 16, 1996.

192. Reuters, August 3, 1995, 0853.

193. EIA, Oil Market Simulation Model Spreadsheet, 1994, data provided by the EIA Energy Markets and Contingency Information Division, and EIA, *International Energy Outlook, 1994*, pp. 11–20; and Energy Information Agency, *International Energy Outlook, 1995*, Washington, Department of Energy DOE/EIA-0484(95), June, 1995, p. 29.

194. Adapted from the material in the DOE/EIA Internet data base, analysis section, country chapters, as accessed on July 15, 1995; Reuters, July 12, 1995, 0904.

195. Some experts make the argument that Iran can still save money because Russia and China are sharply underpricing reactor sales. This thesis seems extremely doubtful. Burning gas and oil fuel is inherently much more thermally efficient in heating and many industrial processes than electric

power, and the reactors are site in areas which create major power distribution costs.

196. *Middle East Economic Digest*, January 26, 1996, pp. 2–3.

197. *Oil and Gas Journal*, December 19, 1994; International Energy Agency (IEA) *Middle East Oil and Gas*, Paris, EIA/OECD, 1995, pp. 125–126.

198. Adapted from the material in the DOE/EIA Internet data base, analysis section, country chapters, as accessed on July 15, 1995; and the discussion in *Middle East Economic Digest*, July 21, 1995, pp. 26–32.

199. Adapted from the material in the DOE/EIA Internet data base, analysis section, country chapters, as accessed on July 15, 1995 and March 14, 1996.

200. International Energy Agency (IEA) *Middle East Oil and Gas*, Paris, EIA/OECD, 1995, pp. 125–126.

201. Adapted from the material in the DOE/EIA Internet data base, analysis section, country chapters, as accessed on July 15, 1995 and March 14, 1996.

202. International Energy Agency (IEA) *Middle East Oil and Gas*, Paris, EIA/OECD, 1995, pp. 129–133; DOE/EIA, *International Energy Outlook*, Washington, DOE/EIA-0485(95), June, 1995, p. 37.

203. International Energy Agency (IEA) *Middle East Oil and Gas*, Paris, EIA/OECD, 1995, pp. 129–133; DOE/EIA, *International Energy Outlook*, Washington, DOE/EIA-0485(95), June, 1995, p. 37.

204. Adapted from the material in the DOE/EIA Internet data base, analysis section, country chapters, as accessed on July 15, 1995 and March 14, 1996.

205. Adapted from the material in the DOE/EIA Internet data base, analysis section, country chapters, as accessed on July 15, 1995 and March 14, 1996.

206. International Energy Agency (IEA) *Middle East Oil and Gas*, Paris, EIA/OECD, 1995, pp. 125–126. DOE/EIA Internet data base, analysis section, country chapters, as accessed on July 15, 1995.

207. International Energy Agency (IEA) *Middle East Oil and Gas*, Paris, EIA/OECD, 1995, pp. 125–126. DOE/EIA Internet data base, analysis section, country chapters, as accessed on July 15, 1995.

208. Adapted from the material in the DOE/EIA Internet data base, analysis section, country chapters, as accessed on July 15, 1995.

209. International Energy Agency (IEA) *Middle East Oil and Gas*, Paris, EIA/OECD, 1995, pp. 125–126. DOE/EIA Internet data base, analysis section, country chapters, as accessed on July 15, 1995.

210. Adapted from the material in the DOE/EIA Internet data base, analysis section, country chapters, as accessed on July 15, 1995 and March 14, 1996.

211. *Christian Science Monitor*, March 20, 1996, p. 8; *Energy Compass*, March 15, 1995, p. 1.

212. *Washington Post*, March 22, 1996, p. A-31; *Washington Times*, March 22, 1996, p. A-17; *Wall Street Journal*, March 8, 1996, p. A-3; *Christian Science Monitor*, March 20, 1996, p. 8; *Energy Compass*, March 15, 1995, p. 1.

213. *Washington Post*, November 10, 1995, p. A-37, March 22, 1996, p. A-31; *Washington Times*, March 22, 1996, p. A-17; *Wall Street Journal*, May 2, 1995, p. A-4, March 8, 1996, p. A-3, December 13, 1995, p. A-6; *Christian Science Monitor*, March 20, 1996, p. 8; *Energy Compass*, March 15, 1995, p. 1; *Journal of Commerce*,

October 12, 1995, p. 3A, December 15, 1995, p. 34, December 18, 1995, p. 8A; *New York Times*, May 2, 1995, p. D-5, May 3, 1995, p. A-7, December 13, 1995, p. D-1.

Chapter 6

214. E.g. in April 1990 then Vice-President Ata'ollah Mohajerani wrote an article advocating the establishment of relations with the USA, causing an outcry on the part of the Supreme Leader and radicals.

215. Cited in *The Independent*, June 10, 1994, p. 5.

216. Xinhua News Agency, June 9, 1994.

217. Office of the Assistant Secretary of Defense for International Security Affairs (Middle East and African Affairs), "United States Security Strategy for the Middle East," Washington, Department of Defense, May, 1995, pp. 16–17.

218. Testimony before the Senate Foreign Relations Committee Subcommittee on Near Eastern and South Asian Affairs, March 2, 1995.

219. CIA, *World Factbook, 1994*, pp. 189–190.

220. Reuters, November 4, 1995, 1235.

221. *Washington Post*, May 15, 1995, p. A-16; *The Estimate*, May 10, 1996, p. 4.

222. *Washington Times*, December 27, 1995, p. A-10.

223. The Strait of Hormuz is about 180 kilometer long (112 miles) and 39 kilometer (24 miles) wide at it is narrowest point. Its minimum depth is 45 meters (148 feet).

224. See J. B. Kelly, *Arabia, the Gulf, and the West*, New York, Basic Books, 1980, p. 96.

225. A development that did Emir Khalid of Sharjah little good. The British had deposed his predecessor, Saqr ibn Sultan of the Bani Sultan branch of the royal family, six years earlier for hostile political activity. In January, 1972, Saqr ibn Sultan returned covertly by dhow and led a coup financed with Iraqi money. He attacked Khalid for giving up Abu Musa, stormed the palace with his supporters, and killed Khalid and several others. Saqr ibn Sultan, in turn, was arrested by the Trucial Oman Scouts and Abu Dhabi Defense Forces and was imprisoned in Abu Dhabi. Another member of the royal family, Sultan ibn Muhammed then became Emir.

226. The Shah had, however, discussed his actions with the British government, and had made a massive 100 million pound purchase of Chieftains in May, 1971.

227. *Washington Post*, April 17, 1992, p. A-18, September 25, 1992, p. 31, September 29, 1992, p. A-15; *New York Times*, April 16, 1992, September 17, 1992, p. A-12; *Armed Forces Journal*, July, 1992, p. 23.

228. EIU Country Report, *United Arab Emirates*, 1st Quarter, 1995, p. 5; *Armed Forces Journal*, May, 1995, p. 30; *Jane's Defense Weekly*, March 11, 1995, p. 2, April 1, 1995, p. 3, March 27, 1996, p. 14; *Washington Times*, March 27, 1995, p. A-1.

229. *Jane's Defense Weekly*, March 11, 1995, p. 2, and March 18, 1995, p. 5, March 27, 1996, p. 14, May 29, 1996, p. 15; *Defense News*, February 6, 1995, p. 1.

230. *Washington Times*, December 27,v 1995, p. A-10.

231. J. B. Kelley, *Arabia, the Gulf and the West*, New York, Basic Books, pp. 54–56, 87, 179–180.

232. This description is excerpted in part from Anthony H. Cordesman, *The Gulf and the West*, Boulder, Westview, 1984, pp. 587–589.

233. The author was briefed on these incidents several times during visits to Bahrain in the 1980s. Also see Emile Nakhleh, "Democracy in the Gulf," *Middle East*, August, 1980, pp. 32–35; *Washington Post*, November 25, 1982, *8 Days*, May 23, 1981.

234. *Wall Street Journal*, June 12, 1995, p. 1; *Los Angeles Times*, May 3, 1995, p. A-2, June 26, 1995, p. A-2.

235. *Washington Times*, February 2, 1996, p. A-16.

236. *Defense News*, April 10, 1995, p. 4; *Wall Street Journal*, June 12, 1995, p. 1; *Los Angeles Times*, May 3, 1995, p. A-2, June 26, 1995, p. A-2.

237. *Gulf Times*, June 3, 1996, p. 2; *Khaleej Times*, June 3, 1996, p. 1.

238. This survey relies heavily on the following works for the background to the development of Irano-Syrian relationship: Patrick Seale, *Asad: The Struggle for the Middle East*, Berkeley: University of California Press, 1988, pp. 349–363; Moshe Ma'oz, *Asad: The Sphinx of Damascus*, New York: Grove Weidenfeld, 1988, pp. 191–193.

239. Patrick Seale, *Asad*, pp. 304–307.

240. For the definitive study of Syrian-Iraqi rivalry over the past thirty years, see Eberhard Kienle, *Ba'th versus Ba'th: The Conflict between Syria and Iraq 1968–1989*, London: I.B Tauris, 1990.

241. Quoted in Seale, *Asad*, p. 353.

242. United Press, October 28, 1995, 1144; February 21, 1996, 1413.

243. *Defense News*, March 2, 1992, p. 3 and 29; *Washington Post*, March 2, 1991, p. A-17, May 20, 1992, p. A-25, May 27, 1992, p. A-19; *Washington Times*, February 28, 1992, p. F-1, September 24, 1994, p. A-8; *New York Times*, February 22, 1992, p. A-4; *Wall Street Journal*, May 16, 1995, p. A-15; *Financial Times*, December 13, 1994, p. 6; Reuters, January 4, 1995, July 18, 1995, 1015; *Los Angeles Times*, January 4, 1995, p. 2.

244. *Washington Post*, August 20, 1993, p. A-26; *Washington Times*, April 12, 1993, p. A-7; September 3, 1993, p. 2; *Baltimore Sun*, August 15, 1993, p. 6-A; *New York Times*, April 13, 1993, p. A-5

245. *Jane's Intelligence Review and Sentinel, Pointer*, June 1996, p. 7.

246. *New York Times*, March 9, 1995, p. A-10.

247. *Patterns of Global Terrorism, 1994*, Washington, US Department of State, April, 1995, p. 23.

248. Reuters, September 29, 1995, March 5, 1996; *Washington Times*, September 30, 1995, p. A-7; *Jane's Military Exercise & Training Monitor*, January-March 1996, p. 13.

249. Reuters, September 29, 1995, March 5, 1996; *Washington Times*, September 30, 1995, p. A-7; *Jane's Military Exercise & Training Monitor*, January-March 1996, p. 13.

250. Reuters, November 8, 1995, 1239; November 11, 1995, 1352.

251. *Christian Science Monitor*, April 18, 1996, p. 1.

Chapter 7

252. *Los Angeles Times*, May 9, 1995, p. 1.

253. See US State Department, annual reports on terrorism, and *Policywatch*, March 11, 1996.

254. James Moore, *The Middle East and North Africa*, p. 19.

255. Based on interviews and a wide range of press sources. For typical reports, see *Time*, March 21, 1994, pp. 50–54. Also see *Washington Post*, August 22, 1994, p. A-17; October 28, 1994, p. A-17, November 27, 1994, p. A-30; *Los Angeles Times*, November 3, 1994, pp. A-1, A-12; Reuters, August 3, 1995, 1247; *Le Monde*, December 31-January 1, 1996, p. 2; Reuters April 1, 1996, 1212; *New York Times*, March 8, 1996, p. A-8, March 23, 1996, p. A-5. Associated Press, March 16, 1996, Reuters, March 17, 1996; Report of the German office for the Protection of the Constitution excerpted in FBIS-NES-95-062, March 31, 1995.

256. The author has questioned the amount of direct involvement by the Iranian leadership in such incidents and actions in the past. Extensive interviews indicate, however, that many US and European intelligence experts now feel there is no apparent split between the Iranian leadership in supporting many of these actions and that they do receive the direction and support of the Iranian leadership. For a good European discussion of the issue, see the Report of the German office for the Protection of the Constitution excertped in FBIS-NES-95-062, March 31, 1995. For typical press reporting, see James P. Wootten, "Terrorism: US Policy Options, Congressional Research Service, IB92074, October 6, 1994, pp. 6–7; Kenneth Katzman, Iran: Current Developments and US Policy, Congressional Research Service, IB93033, September 9, 1994, pp. 5–7; *Christian Science Monitor*, March 22, 1994, p. 6, June 28, 1994, p. A-1; *Time*, March 21, 1994, pp. 50–54; *Washington Times*, December 19, 1993, p. A-3, February 19, 1994, p. A-8, March 9, 1994, June 22, 1994, p. A-14, June 24, 1994, p. A-1, June 27, 1994, p. A-22; *Washington Post*, January 1, 1994, p. A-15, February 4, 1994,p. A-14; *New York Times*, December 24, 1994, p. A-5. For fuller details, see the author's *Iran and Iraq: The Threat from the Northern Gulf*, Boulder, Westview, 1994.

257. *BBC, SWB*, ME/1708, June 7, 1993, pp. A/1-A/3.

258. See James P. Wootten, "Terrorism: US Policy Options, Congressional Research Service, IB92074, October 6, 1994, pp. 6–7; Kenneth Katzman, Iran: Current Developments and US Policy, Congressional Research Service, IB93033, September 9, 1994, pp. 5–7; *Christian Science Monitor*, March 22, 1994, p. 6, June 28, 1994, p. A-1; *Time*, March 21, 1994, pp. 50–54; *Washington Times*, December 19, 1993, p. A-3, February 19, 1994, p. A-8, March 9, 1994, June 22, 1994, p. A-14, June 24, 1994, p. A-1, June 27, 1994, p. A-22; *Washington Post*, January 1, 1994, p. A-15, February 4, 1994,p. A-14; *New York Times*, December 24, 1994, p. A-5. For fuller details, see the author's *Iran and Iraq: The Threat from the Northern Gulf*, Boulder, Westview, 1994.

259. *Patterns of Global Terrorism, 1994*, Washington, US Department of State, April, 1995, p. 21.

260. *Wall Street Journal*, October 4, 1994, p. 1; *Washington Post*, October 28, 1994, p. A-27; Reuters, December 31, 1994, Level 1, 47; *Los Angeles Times*, November 3, 1994, pp. A1, A12; *Washington Times*, May 3, 1995, p. A-11.

261. For typical reporting see *Jane's Intelligence Review*, "Pointers," March 1996, 3; *Washington Times*, March 7, 1996, p. A-1, April 9, 1996, p. A-1; *Los Angeles Times*, April 18, 1996, p. A-2; *Washington Post*, March 7, 1996, p. A-19; Reuters, February 17, 1996, 0532, April 23, 1996, 1055.

262. *Washington Times*, September 4, 1994, p. A-1; November 5, 1994, p. A-6; May 18, 1995, p. A-3; *Washington Post*, April 14, 1995, p. A-1; Reuters, February 22, 1996, 0955; Associated Press, February 22, 1996, 1650.

263. *New York Times*, December 24, 1994, p. A-5.

264. *Patterns of Global Terrorism, 1994*, Washington, US Department of State, April, 1995, p. 23.

265. *New York Times*, December 31, 1991, p. A-7, December 24, 1994, p. A-5; *Washington Post*, March 2, 1991, p. A-17; *Washington Times*, February 28, 1992, p. F-1, April 17, 1995, p. A-13; *Philadelphia Inquirer*, January 16, 1992; *Newsweek*, February 24, 1992, p. 32.

266. *Washington Times*, September 14, 1994, p. A-14.

267. *Washington Post*, July 1, 1993, p. A-18.

268. US State Department, *Country Reports on Human Rights Practices, 1994*, on-line Internet edition, June 24, 1995.

269. *Jane's Defense Weekly*, September 4, 1993, p. 27.

270. *Washington Times*, October 26, 1994, p. A-12, November 7, 1994, p. A-16; *New York Times*, November 7, 1994, p. A-6.

271. *New York Times*, February 21, 1995, p. A-9; *Washington Times*, February 22, 1995, p. A-14, May 26, 1995, p. A-18, June 11, 1995, p. A7, June 12, 1995, p. A-13, June 14, 1995, p. A-19.

272. UP, July 18, 1995, 0807; *Washington Times*, July 11, 1995, p. A-15.

273. Reuters, July 31, 1995, 0914.

274. Reuters, August 8, 1995, 0730; *Jane's Military Exercise & Training Monitor*, January-March 1996, p. 3.

275. *Jane's Defense Weekly*, November 18, 1995, p. 16; Reuters, March 27, 1996, 1405.

276. Iranian military intelligence was directed by Mohammed Ali Nazaran until he was killed in a road accident on October 22, 1994. Najaf was appointed on October 22, 1994. The importance of this appointment is indicated by the fact that Najaf had previously be commander of Iran's regular army. *Jane's Intelligence Review*.

277. US State Department, *Country Reports on Human Rights Practices, 1994*, on-line Internet edition, June 24, 1995.

278. *Patterns of Global Terrorism, 1995*, Washington, US Department of State, April, 1996, pp. 24–25.

279. *Patterns of Global Terrorism, 1994*, Washington, US Department of State, April, 1995, pp. 20–21.

280. *New York Times*, November 7, 1994, p. A-6; *Washington Times*, November 1, 1994, p. A-13; State Department Report, October 31, 1994; *Wall Street Journal*, October 14, 1994, p. 1; Reuters, March 27, 1996, 1405.

281. US State Department, *Terrorist Group Profiles*, Washington, GPO, 1991; US State Department, *Patterns of Global Terrorism*, Washington, GPO, 1993, p. 22; *Washington Post*, November 21, 1993, p. A-1 and A-35.

282. *Wall Street Journal*, October 4, 1994, p. 1; *Washington Post*, October 28, 1994, p. A-27; Reuters, December 31, 1994, Level 1, 47; *Los Angeles Times*, November 3, 1994, pp. A1, A12; *Washington Times*, May 3, 1995, p. A-11.

283. Washington Times, July 11, 1995, p. A-15; US State Department, *Country Reports on Human Rights Practices, 1994*, on-line Internet edition, June 24, 1995.

284. US State Department, *Country Reports on Human Rights Practices, 1994*, on-line Internet edition, June 24, 1995.

285. US State Department, *Country Reports on Human Rights Practices, 1994*, on-line Internet edition, June 24, 1995.

286. The details of this involvement are uncertain, and a great deal of the literature involved adds charges that cannot be confirmed. For a good press summary of the evidence, see *Time*, March 21, 1994, pp. 50–54. Also see *Washington Post*, August 22, 1994, p. A-17; October 28, 1994, p. A-17, November 27, 1994, p. A-30; *Los Angeles Times*, November 3, 1994, pp. A-1, A-12; Reuters, August 3, 1995, 1247.

287. *Wall Street Journal*, October 4, 1994, p. 1; 1994, Reuters, December 31, 1994, Level 1, 47; *Los Angeles Times*, November 3, 1994, pp. A1, A12; *Minneapolis Star Tribune*, August 14, 1993, p. B-1; *Washington Post*, March 17, 1993, p. A-26, May 14, 1993, p. 31, May 16, 1993, p. A-21, October 28, 1994, p. A-27; *New York Times*, April 11, 1993, p. A-28, April 18, 1993, p. A-8, July 28, 1993, p. A-6, March 18, 1993, p. A-8; August 22, 1993, p. D-1, June 17, 1995, p. A-5, June 25, 1995, p. A-12; *Washington Times*, March 17, 1993, p. A-7, May 3, 1995, p. A-11; *Time*, May 31, 1993, pp. 46–51; US State Department, *Terrorist Group Profiles*, Washington, GPO, 1991; US State Department, *Patterns of Global Terrorism*, Washington, GPO, 1993, p. 22; *Washington Post*, November 21, 1993, p. A-1 and A-35.

288. Washington Post, June 23, 1995, p. A-30; Washington Times, June 11, 1995, p. A-6, June 13, 1995, p. A-17.

289. *Washington Post*, ; *New York Times*, May 26, 1993, p. A-8, June 24, 1992, p. A-3, July 17, 1993, p. A-14, Agence France Presse, April 12, 1993, May 15, 1993, July 19, 1993, BBC ME/1664/A, April 16, 1993, ME/1721/A, June 22, 1993 ; *Armed Forces Journal*, July, 1992, p. 23; *Christian Science Monitor*, ; *Financial Times*, May 26, 12993, p. 6 ; *Washington Times*, April 12, 1993, p. A-2, Baltimore Sun, May 24 ,1993, p. 5-A.

290. For typical recent reporting on such events see Reuters, December 31, 1994, BC cycle.

291. For further details, see "Patterns of Global Terrorism, 1992,," Washington, US Department of State, April 1993, pp. 21–22; Yedidya Atlas, "Iran, An Islamic Threat," *Midstream*, October, 1992, pp. 2–7; Anoushiravan Ehteshami, "The Armed Forces of the Islamic Republic of Iran, *Jane's Intelligence Review*, February 1993, pp. 76–80; Paul Wilkinson, "Terrorism, Iran, and the Gulf Region," *Jane's Intelligence Review*, May, 1992, pp. 222–226, pp. 76–80, and "Terrorist Trends in the Middle East," *Jane's Intelligence Review*, February, 1993, pp. 222–226, pp. 73–75; *Los Angeles Times*, October 30, 1992, p. A-3.

292. *Boston Globe*, February 11, 1995, p. 6.

293. US State Department, *Patterns of Global Terrorism, 1995*, Washington, GPO, April 1996, pp. 24–25; *Foreign Report*, April 25, 1996, pp. 1–3; *New York Times*, March 15, 1996, p. A-1; *Los Angeles Times*, May 24, 1996, p. A-2; *Washington Times*, May 14, 1995, p. A-9, May 17, 1996, p. A-19.

294. *New York Times*, March 15, 1996, p. A-1.

295. *British Broadcasting Corporation, Summary of World Broadcasts*, ME/1708, June 7, 1993, p. A/2.

296. *Tehran Times,* July 10, 1995, p. 15.

297. *FBIS-NES,* January 18, 1996, p. 69.

298. *United Press International,* February 16, 1996.

299. Reuters, December 29, 1994, Level 1BC. 68.

300. *Washington Post,* May 8, 1995, p. A-4.

301. *Washington Post,* March 2, 1991, p. A-17; *Washington Times,* February 28, 1992, p. F-1, May 8, 1992, p. 9; *Security Intelligence Report,* November 4, 1991, p. 4; *Economist,* November 16, 1991, p. 51; UPI, January 14, 1992; Professor Paul Wilkinson, "Terrorism, Iran, and the Gulf Region ," *Jane's Intelligence Review,* May 1992, pp. 222–224.

302. *Patterns of Global Terrorism, 1994,* Washington, US Department of State, April, 1995, p. 21; US State Department, *Patterns of Global Terrorism, 1995,* Washington, GPO, April 1996, pp. 24–25.

303. Secretary of State Warren Christopher, Testimony to the House Foreign Relations Committee, January 26, 1995; *Washington Times,* May 3, 1995, p. A-13; *Washington Post,* August 22, 1994, p. A-17; *Los Angeles Times,* November 3, 1994, pp. A1, A12; US State Department, *Patterns of Global Terrorism, 1995,* Washington, GPO, April 1996, pp. 24–25.

304. *Jane's Defense Weekly,* January 31, 1996, p. 4.

305. *Washington Times,* November 9, 1995, p. A-33.

306. *Jerusalem Post,* December 29, 1994, p. 2.

307. *Washington Times,* December 8, 1995, p. A-17; Reuters, December 6, 1995, 1857, January 21, 1996, 1153.

308. *Washington Post,* October 28, 1994, p. A-27; Reuters, December 31, 1994, Level 1, 47; Reuters, August 3, 1995, 1247.; *Los Angeles Times,* November 3, 1994, pp. A1, A12.

Chapter 8

309. *Jane's Defense Weekly,* June 30, 1990, pp. 1301–1302

310. *Washington Post,* August 20, 1989, p. A-1.

311. Much of this analysis is based on work by Kenneth Katzman in *The Warriors of Islam: Iran's Revolutionary Guard,* Boulder, Westview, 1993.

312. There purges continued in March and April of 1989, *Washington Times,* April 20, 1989, p. A-2.

313. Teheran domestic radio, English service, September 12, 1988.

314. *New York Times,* September 3, 1989, p. A-4; *Washington Post,* September 3, 1989, p. A-25.

315. Iran domestic radio service, May 11, 1986, November 15, 1987, and March 2, 1988.

316. Afshar was Deputy Chief of Staff at the armed forces headquarters when Rafsanjani had command over the military.

317. FBIS, July 25, 1990, pp. 60–62.

318. *Jane's Defense Weekly,* June 30, 1990, pp. 1301–1302; March 18, 1989, p. 428; *Baltimore Sun,* February 28, 1989, p. 2A; *Washington Times,* March 23, 1989, p. A-7, April 20, 1989, p. A-2, *Jane's Intelligence Monthly,* July, 1993, pp. 311–312.

319. *Jane's Defense Weekly*, March 18, 1989, p. 428; *Baltimore Sun*, February 28, 1989, p. 2A; *Washington Times*, March 23, 1989, p. A-7, May 26, 1992, p. A-2, June 9, 1992, p. A-2, June 16, 1992, p. A-2, July 8, 1992, p. A-7; *The Estimate*, October 13–16, 1989, p. 1; *Washington Post*, April 28, 1992, p. A-1, July 16, 1992, p. A-18; *Wall Street Journal*, May 5, 1992, p. A-1.

320. *Jane's Defense Weekly*, May 20 1995, p.3

321. Office of the Assistant Secretary of Defense for International Security Affairs (Middle East and African Affairs), "United States Security Strategy for the Middle East," Washington, Department of Defense, May, 1995, pp. 16–17.

322. Testimony before the Senate Foreign Relations Committee Subcommittee on Near Eastern and South Asian Affairs, March 2, 1995.

323. There are major uncertainties in these data. An alternative set of estimates is shown below:

Arms Sales to Iran by Year (in Millions of Current Dollars)

	Deliveries		Agreements	
Year	Dollar Value	Rank in Third World	Dollar Value	Rank in Third World
1989	—	—	1,290	5
1990	2,860	3	1,400	4
1991	1,900	4	1,500	3
1992	300	10	—	—

Notes: *France, UK, Germany, and Italy.
**Out of top ten buyers. Not shown if rank is more than tenth.
Source: Data in Sections A & B are adapted from Richard F Grimmett, *Conventional Arms Transfers to the Third World, 1986–1993*, Congressional Research Service, 94-612F, pp. 57. The annual data in part C are taken from various editions of Grimmett's work.

324. British sources quoted in *Jane's Defense Weekly*, February 1, 1992, p. 158. *The Egyptian Gazette* projected expenditures of $5 billion per year in 1992, 1993, and 1994 in its January 29, 1992, issue. The Jaffee Center estimated expenditures of $8.5 billion in 189 and $8.6 billion in 1990. Andrew Duncan of the IISS estimated expenditures of $10 billion annually in 1992, 1993, and 1994 in *Defense News*, January 27, 1992. The CIA estimate is taken from CIA, *World Factbook, 1992*, "Iran;" CIA, *World Factbook, 1993*, "Iran;" CIA, *World Factbook, 1994*, "Iran;" and CIA, *World Factbook, 1995*, "Iran." It is extremely difficult to relate any Iranian statistics to dollar figures because Iran uses multiple exchange rates, and often reports inaccurate statistics. See Patrick Clawson, *Iran's Challenge to the West, How, When, and Why*, Washington, The Washington Institute Policy Papers, Number Thirty Three, 1993. p. 58.

325. IISS, *Military Balance*, 1990–1991 and 1991–1992 editions. The IISS has since quoted Iranian official government statistics.

326. Author's guesstimate. Iran claimed on February 1992 that it was spending only 1.3% of its GNP on defense. *Washington Times*, February 20, 1992, p. A-9.

327. Table One, ACDA, *World Military Expenditures and Arms Transfers, 1993–1994*, Washington, GPO, 1995.

328. *New York Times*, November 2, 1992, p. A-4.

329. Richard F. Grimmett, *Conventional Arms Transfers to the Third World, 1986–1993*, Washington, Congressional Research Service, CRS-94-612F, July 29, 1994, p. 57, and Richard F. Grimmett, *Conventional Arms Transfers to the Third World, 1987–1995*, Washington, Congressional Research Service, CRS-95-862F, August 4, 1995, pp. 57–58, 67–69.

330. Richard F. Grimmett, *Conventional Arms Transfers to the Third World, 1986–1993*, Washington, Congressional Research Service, CRS-94-612F, July 29, 1994, p. 57, and Richard F. Grimmett, *Conventional Arms Transfers to the Third World, 1987–1995*, Washington, Congressional Research Service, CRS-95-862F, August 4, 1995, pp. 57–58, 67–69.

331. Richard F. Grimmett, *Conventional Arms Transfers to the Third World, 1987–1995*, Washington, Congressional Research Service, CRS-95-862F, August 4, 1995, pp. 57–58, 67–69.

332. Richard F. Grimmett, *Conventional Arms Transfers to the Third World, 1986–1993*, Washington, Congressional Research Service, CRS-94-612F, July 29, 1994, p. 57, and Richard F. Grimmett, *Conventional Arms Transfers to the Third World, 1987–1995*, Washington, Congressional Research Service, CRS-95-862F, August 4, 1995, pp. 57–58, 67–69.

333. ACDA, *World Military Expenditures and Arms Transfers, 1994–1995*, Washington, GPO, 1996, draft version.

334. Richard F. Grimmett, *Conventional Arms Transfers to the Third World, 1986–1993*, Washington, Congressional Research Service, CRS-94-612F, July 29, 1994, p. 57, and Richard F. Grimmett, *Conventional Arms Transfers to the Third World, 1987–1995*, Washington, Congressional Research Service, CRS-95-862F, August 4, 1995, pp. 57–58, 67–69.

335. Office of the Secretary of Defense, *World-Wide Conventional Arms Trade (1994–2000): A Foprcecast and Analysis*, Washington, Department of Defense, December, 1994.

336. Richard F. Grimmett, *Conventional Arms Transfers to the Third World, 1987–1995*, Washington, Congressional Research Service, CRS-95-862F, August 4, 1995, pp. 57–58, 67–69.

337. Richard F. Grimmett, *Conventional Arms Transfers to the Third World, 1987–1995*, Washington, Congressional Research Service, CRS-95-862F, August 4, 1995, pp. 57–58, 67–69.

338. Richard F. Grimmett, *Conventional Arms Transfers to the Third World, 1987–1995*, Washington, Congressional Research Service, CRS-95-862F, August 4, 1995, pp. 57–58, 67–69.

339. *Jane's Defense Weekly*, November 4, 1995, p. 4, February 7, 1996, p. 15, March 27, 1996, p. 14; Reuters, October 17, 1995, 0617, February 14, 1996, 1054; *Defense News*, January 29, 1996, pp. 1, 29.

340. *Jane's Defense Weekly*, November 4, 1995, p. 4, February 7, 1996, p. 15; Reuters, October 17, 1995, 0617, February 14, 1996, 1054; *Defense News*, January 29, 1996, pp. 1, 29.

341. *Jane's Defense Weekly*, May 20, 1995, p. 6, November 4, 1995, p. 4, February 7, 1996, p. 15; *Washington Times*, June 21, 1995, p. A-17, July 15, 1995, p. A-8; Reuters, July 14, 1995, 0940; Executive News Service, August 6, 1995, 1342; Reuters, October 17, 1995, 0617, February 14, 1996, 1054; *Defense News*, January 29, 1996, pp. 1, 29.

342. *Washington Post*, November 10, 1992, pp. A-1 and A-30, May 23, 1993, p. A-26, June 10, 1993, p. A-27; *New York Times*, November 18, 1992, p. A-5; *Defense News*, March 8, 1993, p. 4; *Business Week*, June 14, 1993, p. 31; *Los Angeles Times*, June 10, 1993, p. A-3; *Washington Times*, June 10, 1993, p. A-1, June 21, 1995, p. A-17, July 15, 1995, p. A-8; *Philadelphia Inquirer*, November 21, 1993, p. A-2.

343. *Jane's Defense Weekly*, June 30, 1989, pp. 1299–1301.

344. Iran has long been making light arms and ammunition. The Shah set up the Import Substitute Industrialization (ISI) program in 1970 with the goal of making Iran self-sufficient in arms.

345. *International Defense Review*, 4/1994, pp. 72–73.

346. *Jane's Defense Weekly*, June 5, 1996, p. 15.

347. *International Defense Review*, 4/1994, pp. 72–73.

348. BBC, Middle East, ME/2191/MED, January 3, 1995.

349. Executive News Service, September 9, 1995, 0902.

350. See *Middle East Defense News*, March 1, 1993, and *JINSA Security Affairs*, June/July 1993, p. 7; Anoushiravan Ehteshami, "Iran Boosts Domestic Arms Industry," *International Defense Review*, 4/1994, pp. 72–73.

351. *Washington Post* May 8, 1992, p. A-17; CIA, *World Factbook, 1995*, "Iran."

352. IISS, *Military Balance, 1995–1996*, "Iran."

353. IISS, *Military Balance, 1995–1996*, "Iran."

Chapter 9

354. In addition to the general sources on Iranian force strength referenced at the beginning of this section, this analysis draws on the *Washington Times*, May 2, 1989, p. A-9, June 23, 1989, p. A-9; March 1, 1992, p. B-3, March 22, 1989, p. A-8, January 17, 1992, p. A-1, February 20, 1992, p. 9; *Armed Forces Journal*, March 1992, pp. 26–27; *Defense Electronics*, March, 1992, p. 16; *Inside the Air Force*, February 28, 1992, p. 1; *Jane's Defense Weekly*, November 19, 1988, pp. 1252–1253, June 3, 1988, p. 1057, February 11, 1989, p. 219, June 30, 1990, pp. 1299–1302, February 11, 1992, p. 158–159; Dr. Andrew Rathmell, "Iran's Rearmament: How Great a Threat?" *Jane's Intelligence Review*, July, 1994, pp. 317–322; *Armed Forces (UK)*, May, 1989, pp. 206–209; *Washington Post*, June 23, 1989, p. A-1; August 18, 1989, p. A-25; August 20, 1989, p. A-1, September 3, 1989, p. A-25, February 1, 1992, p. A-1 February 2, 1992, p. A-1, February 5, 1992, p. A-19; *New York Times*, September 3, 1989, p. A-4; *The Estimate*, October 13–26, 1989, p. 1; *Christian Science Monitor*, February 6, 1992, p. 19; *Philadelphia Inquirer*, February 6, 1992, p. A-6; *Los Angeles Times*, January 7, 1992, p. A-1; *Baltimore Sun*, January 25, 1992, p.

4A; *Defense News,* January 27, 1922, p. 45, February 17, 1992, p. 1; *Chicago Tribune,* January 19, 1992, p. 1.

355. The author visited this display in August after a substantial amount of the equipment had been moved to Jordan and to other areas. Even then, there were immense stocks of heavy weapons, almost all of which had been abandoned without any combat damage. It should be noted, however, that Iraq made claims about capturing tanks that seem to have included all light tanks and BMP-1s.

356. The identification of unit size and title is a major problem for all Middle Eastern Armies. Most do not have standard tables of organization and equipment, and unit titles may have little to do with the actual total manpower and equipment mix.

357. Dr. Anoushiravan Ehteshami, "The Armed Forces of the Islamic Republic of Iran," *Jane's Intelligence Review,* February, 1993, pp. 76–79.

358. *New York Times,* May 17, 1995, p. A-3; *Los Angeles Times,* May 18, 1995, p. 8; IISS, *Military Balance, 1995–1996,* "Iran."

359. *Jane's Defense Weekly,* January 7, 1995, p. 4; February 25, 1995, p. 4, November 25, 1995, January 31, 1996, p. 18.

360. Based on estimates by Israeli and US civilian experts, and the IISS, *The Military Balance, 1993–1994,* IISS, London, 1993, pp. 115–117, *The Military Balance, 1994–1995,* pp. 127–129, and IISS, *Military Balance, 1995–1996,* "Iran."

361. *Jane's Defense Weekly,* January 7, 1995, p. 4; February 25, 1995, p. 4.

362. These counts are very uncertain and mix interview and IISS data.

363. Iran publicly displayed the Oghab at a military show in Libreville in 1989. It is 230 mm in diameter, 4,820 mm long, and weighs 320 kilograms, with a 70 kilogram warhead. Iran also displayed another rocket called the Nazeat, which is 355 mm in diameter, 5,900 mm long, weighs 950 kilograms and has a 180 kilogram warhead. *Jane's Defense Weekly,* February 11, 1989, p. 219; Lora Lumpe, Lisbeth Gronlund, and David C. Wright, "Third World Missiles Fall Short," *The Bulletin of the Atomic Scientists,* March, 1992, pp. 30–36.

364. *Jane's Defense Weekly,* June 20, 1987, p. 1289; Lora Lumpe, Lisbeth Gronlund, and David C. Wright, "Third World Missiles Fall Short," *The Bulletin of the Atomic Scientists,* March, 1992, pp. 30–36.

365. Some estimates indicate a range of up to 200 kilometers. For background on the system, see *Financial Times,* June 8, 1988, p. 20, and *The Middle East,* April 1988, pp. 1 and 18.

366. In addition to the general sources on Iranian force strength referenced at the beginning of this section, this analysis draws on the *Washington Times,* May 2, 1989, p. A-9, June 23, 1989, p. A-9; March 1, 1992, p. B-3, March 22, 1989, p. A-8, January 17, 1992, p. A-1, February 20, 1992, p. 9; *Armed Forces Journal,* March 1992, pp. 26–27; *Defense Electronics,* March, 1992, p. 16; *Inside the Air Force,* February 28, 1992, p. 1; *Jane's Defense Weekly,* November 19, 1988, pp. 1252–1253, June 3, 1988, p. 1057, February 11, 1989, p. 219, June 30, 1990, pp. 1299–1302, February 11, 1992, p. 158–159; Dr. Andrew Rathmell, "Iran's Rearmament: How Great a Threat?," *Jane's Intelligence Review,* July, 1994, pp. 317–322; *Armed Forces (UK),* May, 1989, pp. 206–209; *Washington Post,* June 23, 1989, p. A-1; August 18, 1989, p. A-25; August

20, 1989, p. A-1, September 3, 1989, p. A-25, February 1, 1992, p. A-1 February 2, 1992, p. A-1, February 5, 1992, p. A-19; *New York Times*, September 3, 1989, p. A-4; *The Estimate*, October 13–26, 1989, p. 1; *Christian Science Monitor*, February 6, 1992, p. 19; *Philadelphia Inquirer*, February 6, 1992, p. A-6; *Los Angeles Times*, January 7, 1992, p. A-1; *Baltimore Sun*, January 25, 1992, p. 4A; *Defense News*, January 27, 1922, p. 45, February 17, 1992, p. 1; *Chicago Tribune*, January 19, 1992, p. 1.

367. Division, brigade, regiment, and battalion are Western terms applied to Iranian and Iraqi formations. Actual unit strengths and organization often have nothing to do with the titles applied in Western reporting.

368. Dr. Andrew Rathmell, "Iran's Rearmament: How Great a Threat?," *Jane's Intelligence Review*, July, 1994, pp. 317–322; *Defense and Foreign Affairs*, No. 1, 1994, pp. 4–7; *Jane's Defense Weekly*, January 31, 1996, p. 18.

369. Adapted from interviews with US, British, and Israeli experts, Iranian exiles, Anthony H. Cordesman, *Iran and Iraq: The Threat from the Northern Gulf*, Boulder, Westview, 1994, John W. R. Taylor and Kenneth Munson, "Gallery of Middle East Air Power," *Air Force*, October, 1994, pp. 59–70; the IISS, *The Military Balance, 1993–1994*, IISS, London, 1993, pp. 115–117, and *The Military Balance, 1994–1995*, pp. 127–129; USNI Data Base. Military Technology, *World Defense Almanac: The Balance of Military Power*, Vol. XVII, Issue 1-1993, ISSN 0722-3226, pp. 139–142; Anoushiravan Ehteshami, "Iran's National Strategy," *International Defense Review*, 4/1994, pp. 29–37; and working data from the Jaffee Center for Strategic Studies and the *Washington Times*, January 16, 1992, p. G-4; *Washington Post*, February 1, 1992, p. A1, February 2, 1992, pp. A1 and A25, February 5, p. A-19; *Financial Times*, February 6, 1992, p. 4; *Christian Science Monitor*, February 6, 1992, p. 19; *Defense News*, February 17, 1992, p. 1.

370. *Jane's Defense Weekly*, June 24, 1995, p. 5.

371. Based on various interviews. strength data are taken from IISS, *The Military Balance, 1993–1994*, IISS, London, 1993, pp. 115–117, *The Military Balance, 1994–1995*, pp. 127–129, and IISS, *Military Balance, 1995–1996*, "Iran"; USNI Data Base. Military Technology, *World Defense Almanac: The Balance of Military Power*, Vol. XVII, Issue 1-1993, ISSN 0722-3226, pp. 139–142; and working data from the Jaffee Center for Strategic Studies.

372. Amnesty International, *Report, 1994*, New York, Amnesty International, 1994, pp. 163–166.

373. The details of this involvement are uncertain, and a great deal of the literature involved adds charges that cannot be confirmed. For a good press summary of the evidence, see *Time*, March 21, 1994, pp. 50–54. Also see *Washington Post*, August 22, 1994, p. A-17; October 28, 1994, p. A-17, November 27, 1994, p. A-30; *Los Angeles Times*, November 3, 1994, pp. A-1, A-12.

374. *Jane's Defense Weekly*, June 5, 1996, p. 15.

375. *Defense and Foreign Affairs*, No. 1, 1994, pp. 4-7.

376. *Defense and Foreign Affairs*, No. 1, 1994, pp. 4-7.

377. See James P. Wootten, "Terrorism: US Policy Options, Congressional Research Service, IB92074, October 6, 1994, pp. 6-7; Kenneth Katzman, Iran: Current Developments and US Policy, Congressional Research Service, IB93033, September 9, 1994, pp. 5-7; *Christian Science Monitor*, March 22, 1994, p. 6, June 28,

1994, p. A-1; Time, March 21, 1994, pp. 50–54; *Washington Times*, December 19, 1993, p. A-3, February 19, 1994, p. A-8, March 9, 1994, June 22, 1994, p. A-14, June 24, 1994, p. A-1, June 27, 1994, p. A-22; *Washington Post*, January 1, 1994, p. A-15, February 4, 1994, p. A-14.

Chapter 10

378. In addition to the general sources on Iranian force strength referenced in this section, this analysis draws on the *Washington Times*, March 1, 1992, p. B-3, March 22, 1989, p. A-8, January 17, 1992, p. A-1, February 20, 1992, p. 9; *Armed Forces Journal*, March 1992, pp. 26–27; *Defense Electronics*, March, 1992, p. 16; *Inside the Air Force*, February 28, 1992, p. 1; Dr. Andrew Rathmell, "Iran's Rearmament: How Great a Threat?," *Jane's Intelligence Review*, July, 1994, pp. 317–322; *Jane's Intelligence Review*, Special Report No. 6, May, 1995; *Jane's Defense Weekly*, February 11, 1992, p. 158–159, ; *Armed Forces (UK)*, May, 1989, pp. 206–209; *Washington Post*, February 1, 1992, p. A-1 February 2, 1992, p. A-1, February 5, 1992, p. A-19; *The Estimate*, ; *Christian Science Monitor*, February 6, 1992, p. 19; *Philadelphia Inquirer*, February 6, 1992, p. A-6; *Los Angeles Times*, January 7, 1992, p. A-1; *Baltimore Sun*, January 25, 1992, p. 4A; *Defense News*, January 27, 1922, p. 45, February 17, 1992, p. 1; *Chicago Tribune*, January 19, 1992, p. 1.

379. *Wall Street Journal*, February 10, 1995, p. 19; *Washington Times*, February 10, 1995, p. A-19.

380. Based on interviews with British, Israeli, and US experts, and Anthony H. Cordesman, *Iran and Iraq: The Threat from the Northern Gulf*, Boulder, Westview, 1994; IISS, *The Military Balance, 1993–1994*, IISS, London, 1993, pp. 115–117, *The Military Balance, 1994–1995*, pp. 127–129, and IISS, *Military Balance, 1995–1996*, "Iran."; USNI Data Base. Military Technology, *World Defense Almanac: The Balance of Military Power*, Vol. XVII, Issue 1-1993, ISSN 0722-3226, pp. 139–142; Anoushiravan Ehteshami, "Iran's National Strategy," *International Defense Review*, 4/1994, pp. 29–37; and working data from the Jaffee Center for Strategic Studies. US and Israeli experts do not confirm reports that Iran has ordered and taken delivery on 12 TU-22M Backfire bombers. There are some indications that it may have discussed such orders with the USSR.

381. Dr. Anoushiravan Ehteshami, "The Armed Forces of the Islamic Republic of Iran," *Jane's Intelligence Review*, February, 1993, pp. 76–79.

382. *Philadelphia Inquirer*, February 5, 1994, p. A-18.

383. Office of Naval Intelligence, *Worldwide Challenges to Naval Strike Warfare*, Washington, Department of the Navy, Jnuary, 1996, p. 31.

384. Based on interviews with British, Israeli, and US experts. *Washington Times*, January 16, 1992, p. G-4; *Washington Post*, February 1, 1992, p. A1, February 2, 1992, pp. A1 and A25, February 5, p. A-19; *Financial Times*, February 6, 1992, p. 4; *Christian Science Monitor*, February 6, 1992, p. 19; *Defense News*, February 17, 1992, p. 1; Flight International, February 17–23, 1992, p. 4.

385. See *London Financial Times*, February 8, 1993, p. 4. Northrop helped Iran set up an Iran Aircraft Industries in 1970, but this operation virtually ceased operation in 1979.

386. One source indicates that Iran is modifying its F-7M fighters to use Western avionics at old Iranian Aircraft Industries facility, but such modification efforts have had little value in other countries.

387. *Defense News*, March 28, 1994, p. 38.

388. *Jane's Intelligence Review*, Special Report No. 6, May, 1995, p. 23; *Washington Times*, January 16, 1992, p. G-4; *Washington Post*, February 1, 1992, p. A1, February 2, 1992, pp. A1 and A25, February 5, p. A-19; *Financial Times*, February 6, 1992, p. 4; *Christian Science Monitor*, February 6, 1992, p. 19; *Defense News*, February 17, 1992, p. 1; Jane's Defense weekly, February 1, 1992, p. 159.

389. Executive News Service, August 8, 1995, 0826; Associated Press, August 8, 1995, 1456.

390. Dick Pawloski, *Changes in Threat Air Combat Doctrine and Force Structure, 24th Edition*, General Dynamics DWIC-91, Fort Worth Division, February, 1992, pp. I-85 to 1-117.

391. Rostislav Belyakov and Nikolai Buntin, "The MiG 29M Light Multirole Fighter," Military Technology, 8/94, pp. 41–44; Dick Pawloski, *Changes in Threat Air Combat Doctrine and Force Structure, 24th Edition*, General Dynamics DWIC-91, Fort Worth Division, February, 1992, pp. I-85 to 1-117.

392. Dick Pawloski, *Changes in Threat Air Combat Doctrine and Force Structure, 24th Edition*, General Dynamics DWIC-91, Fort Worth Division, February, 1992, pp. I-85 to 1-117.

393. *Aviation Week and Space Technology*, April 10, 1989, pp. 19–20; *New York Times*, April 5, 1989, September 7, 1989; *Washington Times*, January 16, 1989; *FBIS/NES*, April 10, 1989.

394. The Su-24 has a wing area of 575 square feet, an empty weight of 41,845 pounds, carries 3,385 gallons or 22,000 pounds of fuel, has a take off weight of 87,150 pounds with bombs and two external fuel tanks, carries 2,800 gallons or 18,200 pounds of external fuel, has a combat thrust to weight ratio of 1.02, a combat wing loading of 96 pounds per square foot, and a maximum load factor of 7.5G. *Jane's Soviet Intelligence Review*, July, 1990, pp. 298–300; *Jane's Defense Weekly*, June 25, 1985, pp. 1226–1227; and Dick Pawloski, *Changes in Threat Air Combat Doctrine and Force Structure, 24th Edition*, General Dynamics DWIC-91, Fort Worth Division, February, 1992, pp. I-65 and I-110 to 1-117.

395. Based on interviews with British, Israeli, and US experts, and Anthony H. Cordesman, *Iran and Iraq: The Threat from the Northern Gulf*, Boulder, Westview, 1994; IISS, *The Military Balance, 1993–1994*, IISS, London, 1993, pp. 115–117, and *The Military Balance, 1994–1995*, pp. 127–129; USNI Data Base. Military Technology, *World Defense Almanac: The Balance of Military Power*, Vol. XVII, Issue 1-1993, ISSN 0722-3226, pp. 139–142; and working data from the Jaffee Center for Strategic Studies; *Jane's Defense Weekly*, November 18, 1995, p. 16.

396. *Jane's Defense Weekly*, November 18, 1995, p. 16.

397. *Jane's Intelligence Review*, Special Report No. 6, May, 1995, p. 23.

398. Source: USAF briefing, September, 1981. One B-727 and 2 B-767ERs are unaccounted for.

399. In addition to the general sources on Iranian force strength referenced at the beginning of this section, this analysis draws on the *Washington Times*, May 2,

1989, p. A-9, June 23, 1989, p. A-9; March 1, 1992, p. B-3, March 22, 1989, p. A-8, January 17, 1992, p. A-1, February 20, 1992, p. 9; *Armed Forces Journal*, March 1992, pp. 26–27; *Defense Electronics*, March, 1992, p. 16; Dr. Andrew Rathmell, "Iran's Rearmament: How Great a Threat?," *Jane's Intelligence Review*, July, 1994, pp. 317–322; *Inside the Air Force*, February 28, 1992, p. 1; *Jane's Defense Weekly*, November 19, 1988, pp. 1252–1253, June 3, 1988, p. 1057, February 11, 1989, p. 219, June 30, 1990, pp. 1299–1302, February 11, 1992, p. 158–159, ; *Armed Forces (UK)*, May, 1989, pp. 206–209; *Washington Post*, June 23, 1989, p. A-1; August 18, 1989, p. A-25; August 20, 1989, p. A-1, September 3, 1989, p. A-25, February 1, 1992, p. A-1 February 2, 1992, p. A-1, February 5, 1992, p. A-19; *New York Times*, September 3, 1989, p. A-4; *The Estimate*, October 13–26, 1989, p. 1; *Christian Science Monitor*, February 6, 1992, p. 19; *Philadelphia Inquirer*, February 6, 1992, p. A-6; *Los Angeles Times*, January 7, 1992, p. A-1; *Baltimore Sun*, January 25, 1992, p. 4A; *Defense News*, January 27, 1922, p. 45, February 17, 1992, p. 1; *Chicago Tribune*, January 19, 1992, p. 1.

400. Based on interviews with British, Israeli, and US experts, and Anthony H. Cordesman, *Iran and Iraq: The Threat from the Northern Gulf*, Boulder, Westview, 1994; IISS, *The Military Balance, 1993–1994*, IISS, London, 1993, pp. 115-117, *The Military Balance, 1994–1995*, pp. 127–129, and IISS, *Military Balance, 1995–1996*, "Iran"; USNI Data Base; Anoushiravan Ehteshami, "Iran's National Strategy," *International Defense Review*, 4/1994, pp. 29–37; Military Technology, *World Defense Almanac: The Balance of Military Power*, Vol. XVII, Issue 1-1993, ISSN 0722-3226, pp. 139–142; and working data from the Jaffee Center for Strategic Studies; Dr. Andrew Rathmell, "Iran's Rearmament: How Great a Threat?" *Jane's Intelligence Review*, July, 1994, pp. 317–322.

401. *Jane's Defense Weekly*, February 7, 1996, p. 14, March 27, 1996, p. 14.

402. Based on interviews with British, Israeli, and US experts. Reports of MiG-31s do not seem to be correct. Adapted from the IISS, Annapolis, and JCSS data bases, and the Washington *Times*, January 16, 1992, p. G-4; *Washington Post*, February 1, 1992, p. A1, February 2, 1992, pp. A1 and A25, February 5, p. A-19; *Financial Times*, February 6, 1992, p. 4; *Christian Science Monitor*, February 6, 1992, p. 19; *Defense News*, February 17, 1992, p. 1

403. Adapted from the IISS, Annapolis, and JCSS data bases, and the Washington *Times*, January 16, 1992, p. G-4; *Washington Post*, February 1, 1992, p. A1, February 2, 1992, pp. A1 and A25, February 5, p. A-19; *Financial Times*, February 6, 1992, p. 4; *Christian Science Monitor*, February 6, 1992, p. 19; *Defense News*, February 17, 1992, p. 1

404. *Defense and Foreign Affairs*, No. 1, 1994, pp. 4–7. There have also been reports from Czechoslovakia that it might sell Iran an advanced mobile air surveillance system called Tamara. The manufacturer of this system—Tesla Pardubice—has claimed it is capable of tracking stealth aircraft. Tamara, however, seems to be a signals intelligence system with some air defense applications, and its claims to special advantages in detecting "stealth" aircraft seem to be nothing more than sales propaganda. *Defense News*, July 12, 193, p. 1; *New York Times*, December 27, 1993, p. A-17.

405. *Jane's Defense Weekly*, October 28, 1995, p. 19.

406. *Flight International*, August 24, 1993, p. 12.

407. Based on interviews with British, US, and Israel experts. *Washington Times*, January 16, 1992, p. G-4; *Washington Post*, February 1, 1992, p. A1, February 2, 1992, pp. A1 and A25, February 5, p. A-19; *Financial Times*, February 6, 1992, p. 4; *Christian Science Monitor*, February 6, 1992, p. 19; *Defense News*, February 17, 1992, p. 1.

Chapter 11

408. In addition to the general sources on Iranian force strength referenced at the beginning of Chapter III, this analysis draws on Anthony H. Cordesman, *Iran and Iraq: The Threat from the Northern Gulf*, Boulder, Westview, 1994; Dr. Andrew Rathmell, "Iran's Rearmament: How Great a Threat?," *Jane's Intelligence Review*, July, 1994, pp. 317–322; US Naval Institute, *The Naval Institute Guide to the Combat Fleets of the World, 1993: Their Ships, Aircraft, and Armament*, Annapolis, Naval Institute, 1993; John Jordan, "The Iranian Navy," *Jane's Intelligence Review*, May 1992, pp. 213–216; Anoushiravan Ehteshami, "Iran's National Strategy," *International Defense Review*, 4/1994, pp. 29–37; *Washington Times*, May 2, 1989, p. A-9, June 23, 1989, p. A-9; March 1, 1992, p. B-3, March 22, 1989, p. A-8, January 17, 1992, p. A-1, February 20, 1992, p. 9; *Armed Forces Journal*, March 1992, pp. 26–27; *Defense Electronics*, March, 1992, p. 16; *Inside the Air Force*, February 28, 1992, p. 1; *Jane's Defense Weekly*, November 19, 1988, pp. 1252–1253, June 3, 1988, p. 1057, February 11, 1989, p. 219, June 30, 1990, pp. 1299–1302, February 11, 1992, p. 158–159, ; *Armed Forces (UK)*, May, 1989, pp. 206–209; *Washington Post*, June 23, 1989, p. A-1; August 18, 1989, p. A-25; August 20, 1989, p. A-1, September 3, 1989, p. A-25, February 1, 1992, p. A-1 February 2, 1992, p. A-1, February 5, 1992, p. A-19; *New York Times*, September 3, 1989, p. A-4; *The Estimate*, October 13–26, 1989, p. 1; *Christian Science Monitor*, February 6, 1992, p. 19; *Philadelphia Inquirer*, February 6, 1992, p. A-6; *Los Angeles Times*, January 7, 1992, p. A-1; *Baltimore Sun*, January 25, 1992, p. 4A; *Defense News*, January 27, 1922, p. 45, February 17, 1992, p. 1; *Chicago Tribune*, January 19, 1992, p. 1.

409. FBIS-NES-89-144, July 28, 1989, p. 51; FBIS-NES-89-191, October 4, 1989, p. 66, FBIS-NES-89-206, October 26, 1989, p. 66, FBIS-NES-89-214, November 7, 1989, p. 73; *International Defense Review*, June 1990, pp. 51–52.

410. *Defense and Foreign Affairs*, No. 1, 1994, pp. 4–7; *Navy News and Undersea Technology*, April 11, 1994, p. 4; *Defense News*, January 17, 1994, p. 1.

411. This analysis draws heavily on US Naval Institute, *The Naval Institute Guide to the Combat Fleets of the World, 1993, Their Ships, Aircraft, and Armament*, Annapolis, Naval Institute, 1993; Anthony H. Cordesman, *Iran and Iraq: The Threat from the Northern Gulf*, Boulder, Westview, 1994; Anoushiravan Ehteshami, "Iran's National Strategy," *International Defense Review*, 4/1994, pp. 29–37; *Jane's Fighting Ships, 1992–1993* and *1994–1995*; IISS, *The Military Balance, 1993–1994*, IISS, London, 1993, pp. 115–117, *The Military Balance, 1994–1995*, pp. 127–129, and IISS, *Military Balance, 1995–1996*, "Iran"; USNI Data Base. Military Technology, *World Defense Almanac: The Balance of Military Power*, Vol. XVII, Issue 1-1993, ISSN 0722-3226, pp. 139–142. USNI Data Base; *Washington Times*, January 16, 1992, p. G-4; *Washington Post*, February 1, 1992,

p. A1, February 2, 1992, pp. A1 and A25, February 5, p. A-19; *Financial Times,* February 6, 1992, p. 4; *Christian Science Monitor,* February 6, 1992, p. 19; *Defense News,* February 17, 1992, p. 1, and working data from the Jaffee Center for Strategic Studies.

412. Adapted from the IISS, Annapolis, and JCSS data bases, and the *Washington Times,* January 16, 1992, p. G-4; *Washington Post,* February 1, 1992, p. A1, February 2, 1992, pp. A1 and A25, February 5, p. A-19; *Financial Times,* February 6, 1992, p. 4; *Christian Science Monitor,* February 6, 1992, p. 19; *Defense News,* February 17, 1992, p. 1.

413. *Jane's Fighting Ships, 1992–1993* and *1995–1996.*

414. *Jane's Fighting Ships, 1992–1993* and *1995–1996.*

415. *Jane's Fighting Ships, 1992–1993* and *1995–1996.*

416. *Jane's Fighting Ships, 1992–1993* and *1995–1996.*

417. *Washington Times,* March 27, 1996, p. A-1.

418. *Jane's Defense Weekly,* October 1, 1994, p. 6, March 11, 1995, p. 2, March 18, 1995, p. 5; *Sea Power,* November, 1994, p. 21; *Jane's Armor and Artillery, 1995–1996,* pp. 759–762.

419. *Washington Times,* March 27, 1996, p. A-1.

420. *Defense News,* January 17, 1994, pp. 1, 29.

421. *Jane's Defense Weekly,* October 7, 1995, p. 22.

422. Anthony H. Cordesman, *Iran and Iraq: The Threat from the Northern Gulf,* Boulder, Westview, 1994; IISS, *The Military Balance, 1993–1994,* IISS, London, 1993, pp. 115–117, *The Military Balance, 1994–1995,* pp. 127–129, and IISS, *Military Balance, 1995–1996,* "Iran"; USNI Data Base. Military Technology, *World Defense Almanac: The Balance of Military Power,* Vol. XVII, Issue 1-1993, ISSN 0722-3226, pp. 139–142; and working data from the Jaffee Center for Strategic Studies.

423. *Inside the Navy,* January 8, 1994, p. 1; *Defense and Foreign Affairs,* No. 1, 1994, pp. 4–7; *Navy News and Undersea Technology,* April 11, 1994, p. 4; *Defense News,* January 17, 1994, p. 1.

424. Estimates that the HY-2 has a range of 95–100 kilometer range and a 513 kilogram warhead seem to slightly exaggerate the capability of this system, but could be correct.

425. *Jane's Defense Weekly,* June 6, 1987, p. 1113; Dick Palowski, *Changes in Threat Air Combat Doctrine and Force Structure, 24th Edition,* Fort Worth, General Dynamics DWIC-01, February, 1992, pp. 11–275 to 11–275.

426. *Jane's Defense Weekly,* May 1, 1996, p. 20.

427. *Jane's Defense Weekly,* December 9, 1995, p. 3, February 7, 1996, p. 14.

428. *World Missiles Briefing,* Teal Group Corporation.

429. *Jane's Defense Weekly,* December 9, 1995, p. 3, February 7, 1996, p. 14, March 27, 1996, p. 14; *Washington Times,* March 27, 1996, p. A-1., *New York Times,* January 31, 1996, p. A-5; *Washington Post,* January 31, p. A-10; *The Estimate,* February 2, 1996, p. 4; Reuters, November 11, 1995, 0954, February 2, 1996, 0345.

430. Dr. Anoushiravan Ehteshami, "The Armed Forces of the Islamic Republic of Iran," *Jane's Intelligence Review,* February, 1993, pp. 76–79; Gordon Jacobs and Tim McCarthy, "China Missile Sales—Few Changes for the Future," *Jane's Intelligence Review,* December, 1992, pp. 559–563.

431. *Naval Forces*, Vol. 15, No. 3, 1994, p. 62; *World Missiles Briefing*, Teal Group Corporation; *Defense and Foreign Affairs*, No. 1, 1994, pp. 4–7; *Defense News*, January 17, 1994, pp. 1, 29; *Inside the Navy*, January 10, 1994, p. 1; *Navy News and Undersea Technology*, April 1, 1994, p. 4; *Washington Times*, March 9, 1989, p. A-1, May 11, 1993, p. A-7; *Los Angeles Times*, February 14, 1989, p. 5; *Inside the Navy*, January 8, 1994, p. 1; *Defense and Foreign Affairs*, No. 1, 1994, pp. 4–7; *Navy News and Undersea Technology*, April 11, 1994, p. 4; *Defense News*, January 17, 1994, p. 1, *Jane's Defense Weekly*, May 1, 1996, p. 20.

432. *Jane's Intelligence Review*, November, 1992, pp. 512–513; *Time*, April 25, 1994, p. 39.

433. *Jane's Defense Review*, May 22, 1996, p. 17.

434. The submarines are based on World War II designs. They can lay mines, have a five man crew, have a maximum range of 1,200 miles, and have a speed of 6 knots. Iran claims to have made one of the submarines. The first underwent trials in 1987. The second was delivered in 1988. These ships are difficult to use in mine laying and often require frogmen to place the mines. It is not surprising if Iran abandoned them as lacking effectiveness once the Iran-Iraq War was over. Jane's, *Fighting Ships, 1992–1993*, London, Jane's Publishing; Naval Institute data base.

435. Reuters, November 11, 1995, 0954, February 2, 1996, 0345; *Jane's Defense Weekly*, October 28, 1995, p. 19.

436. *Washington Times*, January 16, 1992, p. G-4; *Washington Post*, February 1, 1992, p. A-1, February 2, 1992, pp. A-1 and A-25, February 5, p. A-19, September 26, 1992, p. A-15, October 2, 1992, p. A-40, October 30, 1992, p. A-1, November 5, 1992, p. A-3; *Financial Times*, February 6, 1992, p. 4; *Christian Science Monitor*, February 6, 1992, p. 19; *Defense News*, February 17, 1992, p. 1; *Defense News*, February 17, 1992, p. 1, March 1, 1993, p. 1; *Time*, December 7, 1992, p. 26; *The Wall Street Journal*, November 16, 1992, p. A-4; *Jane's Defense Weekly*, October 3, 1992, p. 12, November 21, 1992, p. 9, February 27, 1992, p. 9; *London Times*, October 5, 1992, p. 9.

437. *Washington Post*, August 4, 1993, p. A-12; *Washington Times*, June 120, 1993, p. A-2.

438. Only two torpedo tubes can fire wire guided torpedoes. *Defense News*, January 17, 1994, pp. 1, 29.

439. *Defense News*, December 6, 1993, p. 1.

440. *Jane's Defense Weekly*, October 8, 1994, p. 4, March 11, 1995, p. 2, March 18, 1995, p. 5; *The Estimate*, May 5, 1994, p. 4; *International Defense Review*, 12/1994, p. 9; *Washington Times*, January 17, 1995, p. A-11, March 8, 1995, p. A-10; *Sea Power*, November, 1994, p. 21.

441. See David Miller, "Submarines in the Gulf," *Military Technology*, 6/93, pp. 42–45.

442. There have been unconfirmed reports that Iran is seeking to modify the Silkworm to extend its range and use it to deliver weapons of mass destruction.

443. There have been unconfirmed reports that Iran is seeking to modify the Silkworm to extend its range and use it to deliver weapons of mass destruction.

444. In addition to the sources listed at the start of this section, these assessments are based on various interviews, prior editions of the IISS *Military Balance*;

the *Jaffee Center Middle East Military Balance,* and *Jane's Defense Weekly,* July 11, 1987, p. 15.

445. Counts of these vessels differ sharply. Some estimates of the number of operational PBI types exceed 60. There are some reports that Iran is building its own version of the Boghammer.

446. Jane's Defense Weekly, October 7, 1995, p. 22, October 28, 1995, p. 19; Reuters, October 17, 1995, 1331, February 1, 1996, 0345.

Chapter 13

447. Office of the Assistant Secretary of Defense for International Security Affairs (Middle East and African Affairs), "United States Security Strategy for the Middle East," Washington, Department of Defense, May, 1995, pp. 16–17.

448. Testimony before the Senate Foreign Relations Committee Subcommittee on Near Eastern and South Asian Affairs, March 2, 1995.

449. *Jane's Defense Weekly,* May 13, 1995, p. 5.

450. *Jane's Defense Weekly,* May 6, 1995, p. 15.

451. *Washington Post,* April 6, 1995, p. 1.

452. Office of the Secretary of Defense, *Proliferation: Threat and Response,* Washington, Department of Defense, April, 1996, pp. 12–16;W. Seth Carus and Joseph S. Bermudez, "Iran's Growing Missile Forces," *Jane's Defense Weekly,* July 23, 1988, pp. 126–131.

453. For additional details, see Anthony H. Cordesman, *Iran and Iraq: The Threat from the Northern Gulf,* Boulder, Westview, 1994; Office of the Secretary of Defense, *Proliferation: Threat and Response,* Washington, Department of Defense, April, 1996, pp. 12–16; and Roger C. Herdman, Director, *Technologies Underlying Weapons of Mass Destruction,* Office of Technology Assessment, US Congress, OTA-BP-ISC-115, December, 1993 (Washington, GPO), pp. 197–255.

454. *Jane's Defense Weekly,* May 1, 1996, p. 3, May 8, 1996, p. 4.

455. *Christian Science Monitor,* December 27, 12993, p. 4; *Washington Times,* February 25, 1994, p. A-15, June 16, 1994, p. A-13. The reader should be aware that all such performance data are nominal, and that various source report significant differences in given performance characteristics.

456. Office of the Secretary of Defense, *Proliferation: Threat and Response,* Washington, Department of Defense, April, 1996, pp. 12–16; CRS Report for Congress, *Missile Proliferation: Survey of Emerging Missile Forces,* Congressional Research Service, Report 88-642F, February 9, 1989, pp. 52–53.

457. Edward L. Korb Editor, *The World's Missile Systems, Seventh Edition,* General Dynamics, Pomona Division, April, 1982, pp. 223–226; Office of the Secretary of Defense, *Proliferation: Threat and Response,* Washington, Department of Defense, April, 1996, pp. 12–16;.

458. The following details of the Iranian missile program are taken from Office of the Secretary of Defense, *Proliferation: Threat and Response,* Washington, Department of Defense, April, 1996, pp. 12–16; W. Seth Carus and Joseph S. Bermudez, "Iran's Growing Missile Forces," *Jane's Defense Weekly,* July 23, 1988, pp. 126–131; Dr. Anoushiravan Ehteshami, "The Armed Forces of the Islamic Republic of

Iran," *Jane's Intelligence Review*, February, 1993, pp. 76–79; Gordon Jacobs and Tim McCarthy, "China Missile Sales—Few Changes for the Future," *Jane's Intelligence Review*, December, 1992, pp. 559–563; *Jane's Intelligence Review*, Vol. 4, No. 5, pp. 218–222; *Jane's Intelligence Review*, Vol. 4, No. 4, p. 149.

459. *New York Times*, June 22, 1995, *Baltimore Sun*, June 23, 1995, p. 9-A; *Defense News*, June 19, 1995, p. 1; *Insight*, February 27, 1995, p. 13; *Jane's Intelligence Review*, Special Report, No. 6, May, 1995, pp. 16–18.

460. US State Department press release, "Joint US-PRC Statement on Missile Proliferation," Washington, DC, October 4, 1994; Office of the Secretary of Defense, *Proliferation: Threat and Response*, Washington, Department of Defense, April, 1996, pp. 12–16; Robert Shuey and Shirley A. Kan, *Chinese Nuclear and Missile Proliferation*, Congressional Research Service, IB92056, October 4, 1994; *Jane's Intelligence Review*, Special Report, No. 6, May, 1995, pp. 16–18.

461. See "Iran's Ballistic Missile Program," *Middle East Defense News*, Mednews, December 21, 1992, Vol. 6, No. 6; Office of the Secretary of Defense, *Proliferation: Threat and Response*, Washington, Department of Defense, April, 1996, pp. 12–16; Gordon Jacobs and Tim McCarthy, "China Missile Sales—Few Changes for the Future," *Jane's Intelligence Review*, December, 1992, pp. 559–563; James Wyllie, "Iran—Quest for Security and Influence," *Jane's Intelligence Review*, July 1993, pp. 311–312; and material in Patrick Clawson, *Iran's Challenge to the West, How, When, and Why*, Washington, The Washington Institute Policy Papers, Number Thirty Three, 1993; Dr. Anoushiravan Ehteshmi, "The Armed Forces of the Islamic Republic of Iran," *Jane's Intelligence Review*, February 1993, pp. 76–80; *New York Times*, June 22, 1995, p. A-1; *Washington Post*, June 17, 1995, p. A-14; *Jane's Defense Weekly*, July 1, 1995, p. 3.

462. *Insight*, February 27, 1995, p. 13; Agence France Presse, January 4, 1995 05:22.

463. *Jane's Intelligence Review*, Special Report, No. 6, May, 1995, pp. 16–18.

464. *Jane's Defense Weekly*, March 4, 1995, p. 18.

465. Iran allowed a Northern Korean freighter, the Dae Hung Ho, to dock at Bandar Abbas and transshipped to missiles by air. Syria is reported to have allowed Iran to deliver arms to the Hezbollah and Party of God in Lebanon in return. *Defense News*, October 16, 1989, p.60, January 17, 1994, p. A-1; Office of the Secretary of Defense, *Proliferation: Threat and Response*, Washington, Department of Defense, April, 1996, pp. 12–16; *Washington Times*, June 18, 1990, p. A1, March 10, 1992, p. A-3; Lora Lumpe, Lisbeth Gronlund, and David C. Wright, "Third World Missiles Fall Short," *The Bulletin of the Atomic Scientists*, March, 1992, pp. 30–36; *Mednews*, Vol. 5,16, May 18, 1992, pp. 1–5; *Newsweek*, June 22, 1992, pp. 42–44; *Washington Times*, May 24, 1991, p. 5, October 23, 1993, p. A-6, February 24, 1994, p. A-15, June 16, 1994, p. A-13; Gordon Jacobs and Tim McCarthy, "China Missile Sales—Few Changes for the Future," *Jane's Intelligence Review*, December, 1992, pp. 559–563; Wall Street Journal, July 19, 1993, p. A-6; New York Times, April 8, 1993, p. A-9; *Jane's Defense Weekly*, July 24, 1993, p. 7, January 15, 1994, p. 4, May 7, 1994, p. 1; *Aviation Week*, July 5, 1993, p. 17; Agence France Press, January 4, 1995; *Christian Science Monitor*, December 27, 1993, p. 4.

466. Dr. Robert A, Nagler, *Ballistic Missile Proliferation: An Emerging Threat*; Systems Planning Corporation, Arlington, 1992.

467. *Defense and Foreign Affairs*, No. 1, 1994, pp. 4–7; *Baltimore Sun*, March 9, 1989; *New York Times*, March 12, 1992, p. A-12, March 18, 1992, p. A-12; *Washington Post*, February 2, 1992, p. A-1; Lora Lumpe, Lisabeth Gronlund, and David C. Wright, "Third World Missiles Fall Short," *The Bulletin of the Atomic Scientists*, March 1992, p. 30–36; "North Korea Corners ME Missile Market," *Mednews*, Vol. 5,16, May 18, 1992, pp. 1–5; *Newsweek*, June 22, 1992, pp. 42–44; Gordon Jacobs and Tim McCarthy, "China Missile Sales—Few Changes for the Future," *Jane's Intelligence Review*, December, 1992, pp. 559–563; *Jerusalem Post*, November 6, 1993, p. 24; Office of the Secretary of Defense, *Proliferation: Threat and Response*, Washington, Department of Defense, April, 1996, pp. 12–16.

468. Some US experts believe Iran has less than 100 missiles. *Jane's Defense Weekly*, May 13, 1995, p. 5.

469. *Jane's Intelligence Review*, Special Report, No. 6, May, 1995, pp. 16–18.

470. *Jane's Intelligence Review*, Special Report, No. 6, May, 1995, pp. 16–18; *Washington Times*, October 23, 1993, p. A-6, February 24, 1994, p. A-15, June 16, 1994, p. A-13; Gordon Jacobs and Tim McCarthy, "China Missile Sales—Few Changes for the Future," *Jane's Intelligence Review*, December, 1992, pp. 559–563; *Wall Street Journal*, July 19, 1993, p. A-6; New York Times, April 8, 1993, p. A-9; *Jane's Defense Weekly*, July 24, 1993, p. 7, January 15, 1994, p. 4, May 7, 1994, p. 1; *Aviation Week*, July 5, 1993, p. 17; Agence France Press, January 4, 1995; *Christian Science Monitor*, December 27, 1993, p. 4, December 27, 1993, p. 4.

471. *Jane's Defense Weekly*, March 19, 1994, May 7, 1994, p. 1; January 15, 1994, p. 4, November 11, 1995, p. 16; *Washington Times*, February 25, 1994, p. A-15; *Jane's Intelligence Review*, Special Report, No. 6, May, 1995, pp. 16–18.

472. *Jane's Defense Weekly*, May 1, 1996, pp. 19–21.

473. *Jane's Intelligence Review*, Special Report, No. 6, May, 1995, pp. 16–18; *Jane's Defense Weekly*, 30 January 1993, pp. 20–21; *Defense Electronics and Computing*, IDR press, September 1992, pp. 115–120, *International Defense Review*, May, 1992, pp. 413–415; *Jane's Remotely Piloted Vehicles, 1991–1992*; Keith Munson, *World Unmanned Aircraft*, London, Jane's 1988; *Air Force Magazine*, March, 1992, pp. 94–99, May, 1992, p. 155; Alan George, "Iran: Cut-price cruise missiles," , March, 1993, pp. 15–16.

474. The technical content of this discussion is adapted in part from the author's discussion of the technical aspects of such weapons in *After the Storm: The Changing Military Balance in the Middle East*, Boulder, Westview, 1993 and *Iran and Iraq: The Threat from the Northern Gulf*, Boulder, Westview, 1994; working material on biological weapons prepared for the United Nations, and from Office of the Secretary of Defense, *Proliferation: Threat and Response*, Washington, Department of Defense, April, 1996, pp. 12–16; Office of Technology Assessment, *Proliferation of Weapons of Mass Destruction: Assessing the Risks*, United States Congress OTA-ISC-559, Washington, D.C., August, 1993; Kenneth R. Timmerman, *Weapons of Mass Destruction: The Cases of Iran, Syria, and Libya*, Simon Wiesenthal Center, Los Angeles, August, 1992; Dr. Robert A, Nagler, *Ballistic Missile Proliferation: An Emerging Threat*; Systems Planning Corporation, Arlington, 1992; and translations

of unclassified documents on proliferation by the Russian Foreign Intelligence Bureau provide to the author by the staff of the Government Operations Committee of the US Senate.

475. For additional details, see Anthony H. Cordesman, *Iran and Iraq: The Threat from the Northern Gulf*, Boulder, Westview, 1994; Office of the Secretary of Defense, *Proliferation: Threat and Response*, Washington, Department of Defense, April, 1996, pp. 12–16; Roger C. Herdman, Director, *Technologies Underlying Weapons of Mass Destruction*, Office of Technology Assessment, US Congress, OTA-BP-ISC-115, December, 1993 (Washington, GPO), pp. 15–70; and *Jane's Intelligence Review*, Special Report, No. 6, May, 1995, pp. 16–18.

476. General references for this section include "Chemical and Biological Warfare," Hearing Before the Committee on Foreign Relations, US Senate, 91st Congress, April 30, 1969;[nbs]Department of Political and Security Council Affairs, *Chemical and Bacteriological (Biological) Weapons and the Effects of Their Possible Use*, Report of the Secretary General, United Nations, New York, 1969; Office of the Secretary of Defense, *Proliferation: Threat and Response*, Washington, Department of Defense, April, 1996, pp. 12–16; unpublished testimony of W. Seth Carus before the Committee on Governmental Affairs, US Senate, February 9, 1989; W. Seth Carus, "Chemical Weapons in the Middle East," *Policy Focus*, Number Nine, Washington Institute for Near East Policy, December, 1988; unpublished testimony of Mr. David Goldberg, Foreign Science and Technology Center, US Army Intelligence Agency, before the Committee on Governmental Affairs, US Senate, February 9, 1989; unpublished testimony of Dr. Barry J. Erlick, Senior Biological Warfare Analyst, US Army, before the Committee on Governmental Affairs, US Senate, February 9, 1989; unpublished testimony of Dr. Robert Mullen Cook-Deegan, Physicians for Human Rights, before the Committee on Governmental Affairs, US Senate, February 9, 1989; Elisa D. Harris, "Chemical Weapons Proliferation in the Developing World," RUSI and Brassey's Defense Yearbook, 1989, London, 1988, pp. 67–88; and "Winds of Death: Iraq's Use of Poison Gas Against Its Kurdish Population," Report of a Medical Mission to Turkish Kurdistan by Physicians for Human Rights, February, 1989.

477. IRNA (English) October 19, 1988, as reported in FBIS, *Near East and South Asia*, October 19, 1988, pp. 55–56.

478. Unpublished "Statement of the Honorable William H. Webster, Director, Central Intelligence Agency, Before the Committee on Governmental Affairs, Hearings on Global Spread of Chemical and Biological Weapons, February 9, 1989; Office of the Secretary of Defense, *Proliferation: Threat and Response*, Washington, Department of Defense, April, 1996, p. 15.

479. Unpublished "Statement of the Honorable William H. Webster, Director, Central Intelligence Agency, Before the Committee on Governmental Affairs, Hearings on Global Spread of Chemical and Biological Weapons, February 9, 1989; Office of the Secretary of Defense, *Proliferation: Threat and Response*, Washington, Department of Defense, April, 1996, p. 15.

480. *Journal of Commerce*, January 6, 1993, p. 5A; *Washington Post*, January 6, 1992, p. A-22, September 3, 1993, p. A-33; *Washington Times*, August 14, 1993, p. A-2; *New York Times*, August 9, 1993, p. A-6; *Defense News*, September 27, 1993, p. 23.

481. *Washington Post*, March 8, 1996, p. A-26.

482. Based on discussions with various experts, the sources listed earlier, Office of the Secretary of Defense, *Proliferation: Threat and Response*, Washington, Department of Defense, April, 1996, pp. 12–16, and working papers by Leonard Spector; *Observer*, June 12, 1988; *US News and World Report*, February 12, 1990; *FBIS-NES*, March 23, 1990, p. 57; *Defense and Foreign Affairs*, November 20, 1989, p. 2; *New York Times*, July 1, 1989, May 9, 1989, June 27, 1989; *Financial Times*, February 6, 1992, p. 3, *Washington Times*, January 8, 1995, p. A-9.

483. *Insight*, February 27, 1995, p. 13; Agence France Presse, January 4, 1995 05:22.

484. *Jane's Intelligence Review*, Special Report, No. 6, May, 1995, pp. 16–18; *Insight*, February 27, 1995, p. 13; Agence France Presse, January 4, 1995 05:22.

485. For additional details, see Anthony H. Cordesman, *Iran and Iraq: The Threat from the Northern Gulf*, Boulder, Westview, 1994; Office of the Secretary of Defense, *Proliferation: Threat and Response*, Washington, Department of Defense, April, 1996, pp. 12–16; and Roger C. Herdman, Director, *Technologies Underlying Weapons of Mass Destruction*, Office of Technology Assessment, US Congress, OTA-BP-ISC-115, December, 1993 (Washington, GPO), pp. 71–118.

486. Such reports begin in the SIPRI Yearbooks in 1982, and occur sporadically through the 1988 edition.

487. *New York Times*, August 13, 1989, p. 11; *Jane's Intelligence Review*, Special Report, No. 6, May, 1995, pp. 16–18.

488. The technical content of this discussion is adapted in part from the author's discussion of the technical aspects of such weapons in *After the Storm: The Changing Military Balance in the Middle East*, Boulder, Westview, 1993 and *Iran and Iraq: The Threat from the Northern Gulf*, Boulder, Westview, 1994; working material on biological weapons prepared for the United Nations, and from Office of the Secretary of Defense, *Proliferation: Threat and Response*, Washington, Department of Defense, April, 1996, pp. 12–16; Office of Technology Assessment, *Proliferation of Weapons of Mass Destruction: Assessing the Risks*, United States Congress OTA-ISC-559, Washington, D.C., August, 1993; Kenneth R. Timmerman, *Weapons of Mass Destruction: The Cases of Iran, Syria, and Libya*, Simon Wiesenthal Center, Los Angeles, August, 1992; Dr. Robert A, Nagler, *Ballistic Missile Proliferation: An Emerging Threat*; Systems Planning Corporation, Arlington, 1992; and translations of unclassified documents on proliferation by the Russian Foreign Intelligence Bureau provide to the author by the staff of the Government Operations Committee of the US Senate.

489. Office of Technology Assessment, *Proliferation of Weapons of Mass Destruction*, Washington D.C., GPO, August, 1993, especially p. 53.

490. For additional details, see Anthony H. Cordesman, *Iran and Iraq: The Threat from the Northern Gulf*, Boulder, Westview, 1994; Office of the Secretary of Defense, *Proliferation: Threat and Response*, Washington, Department of Defense, April, 1996, pp. 12–16; and Roger C. Herdman, Director, *Technologies Underlying Weapons of Mass Destruction*, Office of Technology Assessment, US Congress, OTA-BP-ISC-115, December, 1993 (Washington, GPO), pp. 119–196.

491. *Washington Post*, April 17, 1995, p. A-12; *New York Times*, May 2, 1995, p. A-6.

492. *Washington Post*, April 17, 1995, p. A-12; *New York Times*, May 2, 1995, p. A-6.

493. According to one report by Zalmay Khalizad in *Survival*, Pakistan was deeply involved in this $10 billion effort, as was China. US experts do not confirm these reports. *Washington Post*, May 17, 1995, p. A-23.

494. *Jane's Intelligence Review*, Special Report No. 6, May, 1995, p. 14.

495. The agreement made under the Shah was have given Iran about 250–300 metric tons of Uranium enriched to 3%. During 1980–1990, Iran refused to accept the material or pay for it. When Iran did ask for the material in 1991, France used the fact that Iran's option to obtain enriched material for its investment had expired to deny Iran shipment of the material guaranteed under the original terms of the Iranian investment. *Washington Times*, November 15, 1991, p. F-4; David Albright and Mark Hibbs, "Spotlight Shifts to Iran," *Bulletin of the Atomic Scientists*, March, 1992, pp. 9–12.

496. *Washington Post*, April 12, 1987, p. D-1; James Bruce, "Iraq and Iran: Running the Nuclear Technology Race," *Jane's Defense Weekly*, December 5, 1988, p. 1307; working papers by Leonard Spector; JPRS-TND, October 6, 1989, p. 19.

497. *El Independent*, Madrid, February 5 and 6, 1990; *FBIS-Middle East*, December 1, 1988; *Jane's Intelligence Review*, Special Report No. 6, May, 1995, p. 14.

498. *Jane's Intelligence Review*, Special Report No. 6, May, 1995, p. 14.

499. *El Independent*, Madrid, February 5 and 6, 1990; *FBIS-Middle East*, December 1, 1988.

500. *El Independent*, Madrid, February 5 and 6, 1990; *FBIS-Middle East*, December 1, 1988.

501. Working papers by Leonard Spector; *Observer*, June 12, 1988; Office of the Secretary of Defense, *Proliferation: Threat and Response*, Washington, Department of Defense, April, 1996, pp. 12–16; *US News and World Report*, February 12, 1990; *FBIS-NES*, March 23, 1990, p. 57; *FBIS-EAS*, December 9, 1989, December 11, 1989; *Defense and Foreign Affairs*, November 20, 1989, p. 2; *New York Times*, May 8, 1989, June 27, 1989.

502. *Nucleonics Week*, May 2, 1991; Robert Shuey and Shirley A Kan, *Chinese Missile and Nuclear Proliferation*, Congressional Research Service, IB92056, October 4, 1994, pp. 6–7; *Jane's Intelligence Review*, Special Report No. 6, May, 1995, p. 14.

503. Robert Shuey and Shirley A. Kan, *Chinese Nuclear and Missile Proliferation*, Congressional Research Service, IB92056, October 4, 1994; *Washington Times*, October 16, 1991, November 6, 1991, p. F-4, November 1, 1991, p. 7; *Los Angeles Times*, October 31, 1991, p. B-4, March 17, 1992, p. 1; David Albright and Mark Hibbs, "Spotlight Shifts to Iran," *Bulletin of the Atomic Scientists*, March, 1992, pp. 9–12; *Washington Post*, October 31, 1991, p. 1, January 12, 1992, p. C-7, February 2, 1992, p. A-1, September 12, 1992, p. A-13, June 26, 1991, October 30, 1991; "Iran's Nuclear Weapons Program," *Mednews*, Vol. 5,17/18, June 8, 1992, pp. 1–7; *New York Times*, September 11, 1992, p. A-6, May 27, 1993; *Nucleonics Week*, May 2, 1991, September 24, 1992, October 1, 1992; *Los Angeles Times*, January 18, 1993, p. A-1, March 17, 1992, p. A-1; *Jane's Intelligence Review*, Special Report No. 6, May, 1995, p. 14.

504. Robert Shuey and Shirley A Kan, *Chinese Missile and Nuclear Proliferation*, Congressional Research Service, IB92056, October 4, 1994, pp. 6–7; *Washington Post*, April 17, 1995, p. A-1, April 18, 1995, p. A-13.

505. *New York Times*, May 16, 1995, p. A-1; Leonard S. Spector, Mark G. McDonough, and Evan S. Medeiros, *Tracking Nuclear Proliferation*, Washington, Carnegie Endowment, 1995, pp. 119–123; *Washington Times*, May 17, 1995, p. A-15.

506. Office of the Secretary of Defense, *Proliferation: Threat and Response*, Washington, Department of Defense, April, 1996, pp. 12–16; Leonard S. Spector, Mark G. McDonough, and Evan S. Medeiros, *Tracking Nuclear Proliferation*, Washington, Carnegie Endowment, 1995, pp. 119–123; *Washington Times*, May 17, 1995, p. A-15.

507. *Jane's Intelligence Review*, Special Report No. 6, May, 1995, p. 14.

508. *Washington Post*, November 17, 1992, p. A-1, April 18, 1995, p. A-13; *Wall Street Journal*, May 11. 1993, p. 14; Robert Shuey and Shirley A Kan, *Chinese Missile and Nuclear Proliferation*, Congressional Research Service, IB92056, October 4, 1994, pp. 6–7; *Nucleonics Week*, September 24, 1992, October 1, 1992; *New York Times*, May 27, 1993; *The Middle East*, July/August, 1994, pp. 9–10.

509. *Washington Post*, November 17, 1992, p. A-1, April 18, 1995, p. A-13; *Wall Street Journal*, May 11. 1993, p. 14; Robert Shuey and Shirley A Kan, *Chinese Missile and Nuclear Proliferation*, Congressional Research Service, IB92056, October 4, 1994, pp. 6–7; *Nucleonics Week*, September 24, 1992, October 1, 1992; *New York Times*, May 27, 1993; *The Middle East*, July/August, 1994, pp. 9–10.

510. *New York Times*, February 23, 1995, May 16, 1995, p. A-1, May 18, 1995, p. A-11; *Washington Post*, April 18, 1995, p. A-13, May 8, 1995, p. A-22, May 18, 1995, p. A-22; *Nucleonics Week*, February 13, 1992, p. 12, October 14, 1993, p. 9, December 16, 1993, p. 11, September 22, 1994, p. 1, October 6, 1994, p. 11; *Washington Post*, February 14, 1992, February 12, 1995; *Nuclear Fuel*, March 14, 1994, p. 9, March 28, 1994, p. 10; *Nuclear Engineering*, April 1992, p. 67, November, 1994, pp. 4, 10, UPI, November 21, 1994, Reuters, November 20, 1994.

511. *Washington Times*, April 18, 1996, p. A-7.

512. *New York Times*, February 23, 1995, May 18, 1995, p. A-11; *Washington Post*, April 18, 1995, p. A-13, May 8, 1995, p. A-22, May 18, 1995, p. A-22; *Nucleonics Week*, February 13, 1992, p. 12, October 14, 1993, p. 9, December 16, 1993, p. 11, September 22, 1994, p. 1, October 6, 1994, p. 11; *Washington Post*, February 14, 1992, February 12, 1995; *Nuclear Fuel*, March 14, 1994, p. 9, March 28, 1994, p. 10; *Nuclear Engineering*, April 1992, p. 67, November, 1994, pp. 4, 10, UPI, November 21, 1994, Reuters, November 20, 1994.

513. Executive News Service, September 23, 1993, 1730, September 28, 1995, 1647; *Washington Times*, September 25, 1995, p. A-1; *Washington Post*, September 28, 1995, p. A-22; *New York Times*, September 30, 1995, p. A-4.

514. *Khaleej Times*, January 11, 1995, p. 1; *New York Times*, January 5, 1995, p. A-10.

515. *New York Times*, January 8, 1995, p. A-8, February 23, 1995, p. A-8; *Washington Post*, January 7, 1995, p. A-17, February 11, 1995, p. A-11, March 3, 1995, p. A-32, April 17, 1995, p. A-13; *Washington Times*, February 21, 1995, p. A-13; *Jane's Intelligence Review*, "Iran's Weapons of Mass Destruction," Special Report Number 6, May, 1995, pp., 4–14; Gerald White, *The Risk Report*, Volume 1, Number 7, September, 1995; *Jane's Intelligence Review*, October, 1995, p. 452.

516. *New York Times*, February 23, 1995, May 18, 1995, p. A-11; *Washington Post*, May 8, 1995, p. A-22; *Nucleonics Week*, February 13, 1992, p. 12, October 14, 1993, p. 9, December 16, 1993, p. 11, September 22, 1994, p. 1, October 6, 1994, p. 11;

Washington Post, February 14, 1992, February 12, 1995; *Nuclear Fuel,* March 14, 1994, p. 9, March 28, 1994, p. 10; *Nuclear Engineering,* April 1992, p. 67, November, 1994, pp. 4, 10, UPI, November 21, 1994, Reuters, November 20, 1994; *Los Angeles Times,* March 10, 1995, p. A-3 *Jane's Intelligence Review,* "Iran's Weapons of Mass Destruction," Special Report Number 6, May, 1995, pp., 4–14; Gerald White, *The Risk Report,* Volume 1, Number 7, September, 1995; *Jane's Intelligence Review,* October, 1995, p. 452.

517. Leonard S. Spector, Mark G. McDonough, and Evan S. Medeiros, *Tracking Nuclear Proliferation,* Washington, Carnegie Endowment, 1995, pp. 119–123; *Washington Post,* March 3, 1995, p. A-32.

518. *New York Times,* February 23, 1995, May 18, 1995, p. A-11; *Washington Post,* May 8, 1995, p. A-22; *Nucleonics Week,* February 13, 1992, p. 12, October 14, 1993, p. 9, December 16, 1993, p. 11, September 22, 1994, p. 1, October 6, 1994, p. 11; *Washington Post,* February 14, 1992, February 12, 1995; *Nuclear Fuel,* March 14, 1994, p. 9, March 28, 1994, p. 10; *Nuclear Engineering,* April 1992, p. 67, November, 1994, pp. 4, 10, UPI, November 21, 1994, Reuters, November 20, 1994; *Los Angeles Times,* March 10, 1995, p. A-3.

519. FBIS-SOV, July 21, 1995, p. 1.

520. *FBIS-SOV,* June 29, 1995, pp. 5–7.

521. *Washington Post,* April 17, 1995, p. A-12, May 17, 1995, p. A-23; *New York Times,* May 19, 1995, p. A-1, May 22, 1995, p. A-1; Leonard S. Spector, Mark G. McDonough, and Evan S. Medeiros, *Tracking Nuclear Proliferation,* Washington, Carnegie Endowment, 1995, pp. 119–123.

522. *New York Times,* February 23, 1995, May 18, 1995, p. A-11; *Washington Post,* May 8, 1995, p. A-22; *Nucleonics Week,* February 13, 1992, p. 12, October 14, 1993, p. 9, December 16, 1993, p. 11, September 22, 1994, p. 1, October 6, 1994, p. 11; *Washington Post,* February 14, 1992, February 12, 1995; *Nuclear Fuel,* March 14, 1994, p. 9, March 28, 1994, p. 10; *Nuclear Engineering,* April 1992, p. 67, November, 1994, pp. 4, 10, UPI, November 21, 1994, Reuters, November 20, 1994; *Los Angeles Times,* March 10, 1995, p. A-3.

523. *Khaleej Times,* January 11, 1995, p. 1; *New York Times,* January 5, 1995, p. A-10.

524. AP, June 2, 1996.

525. Leonard S. Spector, Mark G. McDonough, and Evan S. Medeiros, *Tracking Nuclear Proliferation,* Washington, Carnegie Endowment, 1995, pp. 119–123; *Washington Post,* March 3, 1995, p. A-32, April 4, 1995, p. A-19, May 4, 1995, p. A-17, May 5, 1995, p. A-29; *Washington Times,* February 21, 1995, p. A-13, August 8, 1995, p. A-9; *Iran Business Monitor,* Volume IV, Number 6, June, 1995, p. 1; *Newsweek,* May 15, 1995, p. 36; *New York Times,* May 5, 1995, p. A- 8; Executive News Service, October 6, 1995, 1640; October 10, 1995, 1522, October 12, 1995, 1045.

526. Leonard S. Spector, Mark G. McDonough, and Evan S. Medeiros, *Tracking Nuclear Proliferation,* Washington, Carnegie Endowment, 1995, pp. 119–123; Office of the Secretary of Defense, *Proliferation: Threat and Response,* Washington, Department of Defense, April, 1996, pp. 12–16; *Washington Post,* March 3, 1995, p. A-32, April 4, 1995, p. A-19, May 4, 1995, p. A-17, May 5, 1995, p. A-29; *Washington Times,* February 21, 1995, p. A-13, August 8, 1995, p. A-9; *Iran Business Monitor,*

Volume IV, Number 6, June, 1995, p. 1; *Newsweek*, May 15, 1995, p. 36; *New York Times*, May 5, 1995, p. A- 8; Executive News Service, October 6, 1995, 1640; October 10, 1995, 1522, October 12, 1995, 1045.

527. Leonard S. Spector, Mark G. McDonough, and Evan S. Medeiros, *Tracking Nuclear Proliferation*, Washington, Carnegie Endowment, 1995, pp. 119–123; *Washington Post*, March 3, 1995, p. A-32, April 4, 1995, p. A-19, May 4, 1995, p. A-17, May 5, 1995, p. A-29; *Washington Times*, February 21, 1995, p. A-13; *Iran Business Monitor*, Volume IV, Number 6, June, 1995, p. 1; *Newsweek*, May 15, 1995, p. 36; *New York Times*, May 5, 1995, p. 8; *Jane's Intelligence Review*, "Iran's Weapons of Mass Destruction," Special Report Number 6, May, 1995, pp., 4–14; Gerald White, *The Risk Report*, Volume 1, Number 7, September, 1995; *Jane's Intelligence Review*, October, 1995, p. 452.

528. Office of the Secretary of Defense, *Proliferation: Threat and Response*, Washington, Department of Defense, April, 1996, pp. 12–16; *Washington Post*, March 24, 1995, p. A-28, April 29, 1995, p. A-8, May 5, 1995, p. A-29; *New York Times*, April 3, 1995, p. A-1, April 29, 1995, p. A-6; *Philadelphia Inquirer*, May 3, 1995, p. A-3; , February 27, 1995, p. 27; *Jane's Intelligence Review*, "Iran's Weapons of Mass Destruction," Special Report Number 6, May, 1995, pp., 4–14; Gerald White, *The Risk Report*, Volume 1, Number 7, September, 1995; *Jane's Intelligence Review*, October, 1995, p. 452.

529. *Washington Times*, November 15, 1991, p. F-4; *Washington Post*, February 7, 1992, p. A-18, February 15, 1992, p. A-29; AP PM Cycle, February 6, 1992; "Iran's Nuclear Weapons Program," *Mednews*, Vol. 5,17/18, June 8, 1992, pp. 1–7.

530. Gerald White, *The Risk Report*, Volume 1, Number 7, September, 1995.

531. Gerald White, *The Risk Report*, Volume 1, Number 7, September, 1995.

532. Robert Shuey and Shirley A Kan, *Chinese Missile and Nuclear Proliferation*, Congressional Research Service, IB92056, October 4, 1994, pp. 6–7; *Jane's Intelligence Review*, "Iran's Weapons of Mass Destruction," Special Report Number 6, May, 1995, pp., 4–14; Gerald White, *The Risk Report*, Volume 1, Number 7, September, 1995; *Jane's Intelligence Review*, October, 1995, p. 452.

533. Patrick Clawson, *Iran's Challenge to the West, How, When, and Why*, Washington, The Washington Institute Policy Papers, Number Thirty Three, 1993, pp. 60–61; *Financial Times*, February 6, 1992; *Washington Post*, February 15, 1992, pp. A-29-A-30, November 17, 1992, p. A-30; *Los Angeles Times*, March 17, 1992, p. 1; AP, AM Cycle, February 12, 1992; Agence France Presse, February 12, 1992. *Christian Science Monitor*, February 18, 1993, p. 7; *Wall Street Journal*, May 11, 1993, p. A-14; *Middle East Economic Digest*, March 17, 1995, p. 7.

534. The major uncertainty in such matters is whether Iran not has a significant centrifuge effort in a secret or underground locations. A few experts feel there is some risk that Iran might also have a secret reactor to produce Plutonium, but this seems unlikely. *Washington Post*, November 20, 1993, p. A-13.

535. Congressional Research Service, Issue Briefs 92076, 92056, and 93033; *Washington Times*, December 19, 1994, p. A-18.

536. *Khaleej Times*, January 9, 1995, p. 6; *New York Times*, January 5, 1995, p. A-10, January 8, 1995, p. A-8, January 10, 199, p. A-3; *Washington Times*, December

19, 1994, p. A-18, January 6, 1995, p. A-15; *Washington Post*, January 7, 1995, p. A-17.

537. Leonard S. Spector, Mark G. McDonough, and Evan S. Medeiros, *Tracking Nuclear Proliferation*, Washington, Carnegie Endowment, 1995, pp. 119–123; *New York Times*, April 3, 1995, p. A-1.

538. For more background, see the author's *Weapons of Mass Destruction in the Middle East*, Brassey's, London, 1992 and *Iran and Iraq: The Threat From the Northern Gulf*, Boulder, Westview, 1994. Also see Office of the Secretary of Defense, *Proliferation: Threat and Response*, Washington, Department of Defense, April, 1996, pp. 12–16; *US News*, November 14, 1994, pp. 87–88; and *New York Times*, December 27, 1994, p. A-17.

539. *Los Angeles Times*, March 17, 1992, p. 1.

540. *New York Times*, November 30, 1992, pp. A-1 and A-6, January 5, 1995, p. A-10; *Washington Times*, January 6, 1995, p. A-15.

541. *New York Times*, January 10, 1995, p. A-3; *Jane's Intelligence Review*, "Iran's Weapons of Mass Destruction," Special Report Number 6, May, 1995, pp., 4–14; Gerald White, *The Risk Report*, Volume 1, Number 7, September, 1995; *Jane's Intelligence Review*, October, 1995, p. 452.

542. *Khaleej Times*, January 10, 1995, p. 31; *Washington Times*, January 19, 1995, p. A-18.

543. Although the possibility is a real one. *Financial Times*, January 30, 1992, p. 4; Agence France Presse, January 26, 1992; *Sunday Times*, January 26, 1992; *Der Spiegel*, July 20, 1992, p. 117; Patrick Clawson, *Iran's Challenge to the West, How, When, and Why*, Washington, The Washington Institute Policy Papers, Number Thirty Three, 1993, pp. 63–65; *United States News and World Report*, November 14, 1994, p. 88; *Jane's Intelligence Review*, "Iran's Weapons of Mass Destruction," Special Report Number 6, May, 1995, pp., 4–14; Gerald White, *The Risk Report*, Volume 1, Number 7, September, 1995; *Jane's Intelligence Review*, October, 1995, p. 452.

544. *Washington Times*, May 17, 1995, p. A-15; Office of the Secretary of Defense, *Proliferation: Threat and Response*, Washington, Department of Defense, April, 1996, pp. 12–16.

545. *New York Times*, May 14, 1995.

Chapter 14

546. Tehran News Service, October 12, 1995.

Sources and Methods

This volume is part of a series of volumes on each of the Gulf states which has been developed by the Center for Strategic and International Studies as part of a dynamic net assessment of the Middle East. This project has had the sponsorship of each of the Southern Gulf states as well as US sponsors of the CSIS, and each text has been widely distributed for comment to experts and officials in each Southern Gulf country, to US experts and officials, to several international agencies and institutions, and various private experts.

Sources

The authors have drawn heavily on the inputs of such reviewers throughout the text. It was agreed with each reviewer, however, that no individual or agency should be attributed at any point in the text except by specific request, and that all data used be attributed to sources that are openly available to the public. The reader should be aware of this in reviewing the footnotes. Only open sources are normally referred to in the text, although the data contained in the analysis has often been extensively modified to reflect expert comment.

There are other aspects of the sources used of which the reader should be aware. It was possible to visit each Southern Gulf states at various times during the preparation of this book and to talk to local officials experts. Some provided detailed comments on the text. Interviews also took place with experts in the United States, United Kingdom, France, Switzerland and Germany. Portions of the manuscript were circulated for informal review by European officials and diplomats in some cases. Once again, no details regarding such visits or comments are referenced in the text.

Data from open sources are deliberately drawn from a wide range of sources. Virtually all of these sources are at least in partial conflict. There is no consensus over demographic data, budget data, military expenditures and arms transfers, force numbers, unit designations, or weapons types.

While the use of computer data bases allowed some cross-correlation and checking of such sources, the reporting on factors like force strengths, unit types and identities and tactics often could not be reconciled. Citing multiple sources for each case is not possible and involves many detailed judgments by the authors in reconciling different reports and data.

The Internet and several on-line services were also used extensively. Since such data bases are dynamic, and change or are deleted over time, there is no clear way to footnote much of this material. Recent press sources are generally cited, but are often only part of the material consulted.

Methods

A broad effort has been made to standardize the analysis of each country, but it became clear early in the project that adopting a standard format did not suit the differences that emerged between countries. The emphasis throughout this phase of the CSIS net assessment has been on analyzing the detailed trends within individual states and this aspect of the analysis has been given priority over country-to-country consistency.

In many cases, the authors adjusted the figures and data use in the analysis on a "best guess" basis, drawing on some thirty years of experience in the field. In some other cases, the original data provided by a given source were used without adjustment to ensure comparability, even though this leads to some conflicts in dates, place names, force strengths, etc. within the material presented—particularly between summary tables surveying a number of countries and the best estimates for a specific country in the text. In such cases, it seemed best to provide contradictory estimates to give the reader some idea of the range of uncertainty involved.

Extensive use is made of graphics to allow the reader to easily interpret complex statistical tables and see long-term trends. The graphic program used was deliberately standardized, and kept relatively simple, to allow the material portrayed to be as comparable as possible. Such graphics have the drawback, however, that they often disguise differences in scale and exaggerate or minimize key trends. The reader should carefully examine the scale used in the left-hand axis of each graphs.

Most of the value judgments regarding military effectiveness were made by Anthony H. Cordesman on the basis of American military experience and standards. Although the author has lived in the Middle East, and worked as a US advisor to several Middle Eastern governments, he feels that any attempt to create some Middle Eastern standard of reference is likely to be far more arbitrary than basing such judgments on his own military background.

Mapping and location names presented a major problem. The authors used US Army and US Air Force detailed maps, commercial maps, and in some cases commercial satellite photos. In many cases, however, the place names and terrain descriptions used in the combat reporting by both sides, and by independent observers, presented major contradictions that could not be resolved from available maps. No standardization emerged as to the spelling of place names. Sharp differences emerged in the geographic data published by various governments, and in the conflicting methods of transliterating Arabic and Farsi place names into English.

The same problem applied in reconciling the names of organizations and individuals—particularly those being transliterated from Arabic and Farsi. It again became painfully obvious that no progress is being made in reconciling the conflicting methods of transliterating such names into English. A limited effort has been made to standardize the spellings used in this text, but many different spellings are tied to the relational data bases used in preparing the analysis and the preservation of the original spelling is necessary to identify the source and tie it to the transcript of related interviews.

About the Book and Author

This volume provides a detailed analysis of Iran's politics, economics, energy exports, security and military forces, as well as an examination of current Western policy toward Iran and its regional activities and support of Islamic extremists. The impact of sanctions and the U.S. policy of "dual containment" are examined in detail along with different strategies for dealing with Iran and Iran's efforts to acquire weapons of mass destruction.

Anthony H. Cordesman has served in senior positions in the office for the secretary of defense, NATO, and the U.S. Senate. He is currently a senior fellow and Co-Director of the Middle East Program at the Center for Strategic and International Studies, an adjunct professor of national security studies at Georgetown University, and a special consultant in military affairs for ABC News. He lives in Washington, D.C. **Ahmed S. Hashim** is a fellow in Political-Military Affairs and the Middle East Program at the Center for Strategic and International Studies in Washington, D.C., where he specializes in strategic issues. Previously, he was a research associate at the International Institute for Strategic Studies in London. He lives in Virginia.